This book considering the role of Public Accounts Committees and national audit offices provides a timely and original contribution to the literature. Its significance lies in its focus on matters of governance and accountability at the government level, an area that has not been well studied in the accounting domain. This particular text significantly extends our understanding by providing consideration of these institutions in regions across the globe and in continents that are, despite their importance to the global economy, very much under-researched. To add to the richness of the material, practitioners as well as academics have contributed to the book. This should be a "must read" for researchers, students and practitioners working in the area.

Jane Broadbent, *Professor, Royal Holloway, University of London, UK*

This research monograph is an excellent analysis of the importance of public accounts committee and audit offices in making governments accountable in contemporary times. The selection of papers by leading international authors provides a contemporary perspective that is geared to comprehend the current and future challenges and provides sign-posts for students, academics and public sector actors to strategically act on these challenges.

James Guthrie, *Professor, Macquarie University, Australia and University of Bologna, Italy*

This book gives a unique insight into the way in which public sector accounts committees and national audit offices contribute to accountability in the public sector. Its uniqueness particularly stems from the types of contributions, from both practitioners and academics, and covers practices in developed countries, such as the UK, Australia and Denmark as well as developing countries, like India, Bangladesh and Kenya.

Jan van Helden, *Emeritus Professor, University of Groningen, the Netherlands*

Democratic accountability for the authorisation and use of public monies is one of the bedrocks of our various systems of modern government. This book has produced an excellent collection of studies of these systems, covering some 14 countries/regions across the globe and even including Sweden which operates without a public accounts committee. Their expert analyses reveal the investigative roles of public accounts committees, how well they work with other accountability agents, their effectiveness and the benefits overall to good governance. With an informative introduction, this volume offers a definitive contribution which will be of interest to scholars of various disciplines, parliamentary practitioners, accountability actors, interest groups and the media, as well as the general reader interested in how modern-day accountabilities are exercised.

John Wanna, *Professor, Australian National University, Australia*

Making Governments Accountable

Over the past two decades, there has been a paradigm shift in public administration and public sector accounting around the world, with increasing emphasis on good governance and accountability processes for government entities. This is all driven both by economic rationalism, and by changing expectations of what governments can and should do. An important aspect of this accountability and governance process is the establishment and effective functioning of a Public Accounts Committee (PAC), a key component of democratic accountability.

With contributions from renowned scholars and practitioners, and using case studies from around the world, this research-based collection examines the rationales for current roles of the PACs and explores the links between PACs and National Audit Offices. It also compares PAC practices from developing and developed countries such as Africa, Asia, Pacific Islands and Europe with both Westminster and non-Westminster models of government.

This will be valuable reading for academics, researchers and advanced students in public management, public accounting and public sector governance.

Zahirul Hoque is Professor and Head of the Department of Accounting at La Trobe Business School, La Trobe University, Australia and the founding Editor-in-Chief of the *Journal of Accounting & Organizational Change* (Emerald).

Routledge critical studies in public management
Edited by Stephen Osborne

The study and practice of public management has undergone profound changes across the world. Over the last quarter century, we have seen:

- increasing criticism of public administration as the over-arching framework for the provision of public services;
- the rise (and critical appraisal) of the 'New Public Management' as an emergent paradigm for the provision of public services;
- the transformation of the 'public sector' into the cross-sectoral provision of public services; and
- the growth of the governance of inter-organizational relationships as an essential element in the provision of public services.

In reality these trends have not so much replaced each other as elided or co-existed together – the public policy process has not gone away as a legitimate topic of study, intra-organizational management continues to be essential to the efficient provision of public services, whist the governance of inter-organizational and inter-sectoral relationships is now essential to the effective provision of these services.

Further, whilst the study of public management has been enriched by contribution of a range of insights from the 'mainstream' management literature it has also contributed to this literature in such areas as networks and inter-organizational collaboration, innovation and stakeholder theory.

This series is dedicated to presenting and critiquing this important body of theory and empirical study. It will publish books that both explore and evaluate the emergent and developing nature of public administration, management and governance (in theory and practice) and examine the relationship with and contribution to the over-arching disciplines of management and organizational sociology.

Books in the series will be of interest to academics and researchers in this field, students undertaking advanced studies of it as part of their undergraduate or postgraduate degree and reflective policy makers and practitioners.

Making Governments Accountable

The role of public accounts committees and national audit offices

Edited by Zahirul Hoque

Routledge
Taylor & Francis Group

LONDON AND NEW YORK

First published 2015 by Routledge

2 Park Square, Milton Park, Abingdon, Oxon, OX14 4RN
605 Third Avenue, New York, NY 10017

Routledge is an imprint of the Taylor & Francis Group, an informa business

First issued in paperback 2020

British Library Cataloguing in Publication Data
A catalogue record for this book is available from the British Library

Library of Congress Cataloging-in-Publication Data
Making governments accountable : the role of public accounts committees
and national audit offices / edited by Zahirul Hoque. – 1 Edition.
    pages cm. – (Routledge critical studies in public management)
    Includes bibliographical references and index.
    1. Finance, Public–Accounting–Case studies. I. Hoque, Zahirul.
    HJ9733.M45 2015
    352.4'3–dc23   2014046596

ISBN: 978-1-138-78358-4 (hbk)
ISBN: 978-0-367-73832-7 (pbk)

Typeset in Times New Roman
by Wearset Ltd, Boldon, Tyne and Wear

I dedicate this book to my primary school teacher, *Mr Fazlur Rahman*, who had touched my life in so many ways as a teacher, mentor and friend. Thank you *Sir* for guiding me, inspiring me and making me what I am today! The dedication is also to my elder brother, *Mr Shah Alam*, for his support when I needed it. Special dedication to my wife, *Shirin*, for her endless love, support and encouragement in producing this book.

Contents

Figures

Tables

Contributors

Ethugalage Anura Gotabaya Ananda is an Assistant Auditor-General in the Auditor-General's Department of Sri Lanka. He has been working in the Department for the last 35 years. Ananda obtained his undergraduate degree and postgraduate diploma from the University of Sri Jayawardenapura, Sri Lanka. He also obtained the Master of Commerce by Research degree from La Trobe University, Melbourne under the supervision of Professor Zahirul Hoque. He is responsible for conducting environmental and performance audits. His present position covers overall supervision and finalized audit reports of 52 public institutions and assisting the Parliamentary Oversight Committees in the examination of the Auditor-General's Reports.

Louise Bringselius PhD is Associate Professor of Strategic Management at the School of Economics and Management at Lund University, Sweden. Her research focuses on the public sector in general, and state audit in particular.

Alistair Brown is a former Chutian Scholar of Zhongnan University of Economics and Law in Hubei Province, People's Republic of China. He is now a member of the Public Sector Accountability and Disclosure Research Cluster (PSAD), Curtin University, Australia.

Bikram Chatterjee PhD, CPA is a lecturer in Accounting at Deakin University. He has held academic positions at Charles Sturt University, Australia, Curtin University, Australia and Massey University, New Zealand. His research interests include International Financial Reporting Standards, reporting in emerging economies, public sector reporting and private sector reporting.

Mark Christensen is Associate Professor of Accounting at Southern Cross University, Australia. His research interests are broadly focused on accounting as a social construction and include accounting for non-accountants; behavioral aspects of management accounting; reforms of public sector accounting; management consultants in accounting change and Japanese management.

Kylie Coulson is an Adjunct Professor at the Curtin University School of Accounting, Western Australia. Her professional experience has focused on public financial management and policy in Australian state and federal government.

David Gilchrist is Professor of Accounting at Curtin Business School, Curtin University. He is a historian and accountant. He has held a number of senior roles in the not-for-profit and public sectors and, most recently, was Assistant Auditor-General for Western Australia. He researches in the areas of government and not-for-profit performance, regulation, governance, accounting and economic history.

Haslida Abu Hasan PhD is a Senior Lecturer in Accounting at the Faculty of Business and Accountancy of the University of Malaya, Malaysia. Her research interests lie in the area of public sector performance measurement.

Zahirul Hoque PhD, FCPA, FCMA is Professor and Head of the Department of Accounting at La Trobe University, Melbourne, Australia. He has held positions at Deakin University, Charles Darwin University, Griffith University, Victoria University of Wellington, and Dhaka University in Bangladesh. He is the Founding Editor-in-Chief of the *Journal of Accounting & Organizational Change*. His research interests include management accounting, public sector management, accounting in developing economies, NGOs and non-profits accounting.

Sajjad H. Khan PhD is currently a sessional lecturer in accounting for a number of universities in Melbourne. Prior to this, he was a lecturer in accounting at the Faculty of Business of Charles Sturt University, Albury-Wodonga Campus, Australia.

Danielle Morin PhD, MBA is a professor of auditing at HEC Montréal. Her research interests are government auditing, legislative auditors, performance audit and public sector governance.

Bosire Nyamori teaches tax law at The University of Nairobi. He has previously taught taxation at Jomo Kenyatta University of Agriculture and Technology and Massey University in New Zealand. His principal research interest is taxation, but he has a continuing interest in related areas of budget policy and law, public governance and the interaction between law and accounting.

Robert Ochoki Nyamori PhD taught public sector accounting and management accounting at La Trobe University and management and financial accounting at Massey and Qatar Universities. Robert's research interests include accounting and accountability in the public sector, strategic management accounting, corporate governance and accounting and subjectivity.

Jonathan O'Dea holds two Bachelor degrees (Arts and Law) and two Masters degrees (Law and MBA). He has also provided honorary service on other not-for-profit boards. Jonathan was elected as the Member for Davidson, New South Wales, was soon appointed to the Committee on the Independent Commission Against Corruption and later served as Opposition Waste Watch Coordinator. He now serves as Chair of the Public Accounts Committee.

Des Pearson was Auditor-General of Victoria from 2006 to 2012. He was previously Auditor-General of Western Australia (1991–2006). He has been a

Convenor of the Australasian Council of Auditor-General from 1997 to 1999, a member of the Auditing and Assurance Standards Board from 1997 to 2000, and a member of the Australian Accounting Standard Board from 2005 to 2008. He is a Life Member and Fellow of CPA Australia, Life Member and Fellow of the Australian Institute of Management, Western Australia, and a National and Victorian Fellow of the Institute of Public Administration.

Chandra Ery Prasetyo is on the audit and assurance staff of the JSG Division of Deloitte Touche Tohmatsu Indonesia. He joined the accounting firm after graduating from the accounting study program of the Faculty of Business of the Sampoerna University, Jakarta, Indonesia.

Supot Saikaew PhD works as the Vice-President of Valaya Alongkorn Rajabhat University under The Royal Patronage, Thailand. He is also a lecturer and a member of Public Administration curriculum boards for the Master and PhD degrees at the College of Innovative Management, Valaya Alongkorn Rajabhat University.

Zakiah Saleh PhD is an Associate Professor of Accounting and Deputy Dean (Higher Degree) at the Faculty of Business and Accountancy, University of Malaya, Malaysia. She is one of the associate editors of the *Asian Journal of Business and Accounting*. She specializes in public sector accounting and reporting.

Bambang Setiono is the Vice Dean of Administration in the Faculty of Business of the Sampoerna University in Jakarta, Indonesia. He has spent more than twenty years in promoting better governance in public financial management in Indonesia. In the last ten years, he has focused on reducing irregularities in financial management of government revenues in the forestry sector including the introduction of anti-money laundering instruments for curtailing illegal logging. He is the initiator of the Indonesian Public Accountability (IPA), a center for promoting a culture of accountability in Indonesia and other parts of the world.

Peter Skærbæk holds a current position as Professor of accounting at the Copenhagen Business School. He holds a PhD in public sector accounting and his research interests include management accounting, cost management, behavioral aspects of accounting and budgeting, accounting as social and institutional practice, information politics, performance auditing, new public management, accounting and strategy, expertise, risk management and economic models performing outsourcing. He has held positions as Strategic Research Advisor, Newcastle University Business School and Professor at Trondheim Business School.

Anthony Staddon is a lecturer in British and European Union Politics at the Department of Politics and International Relations, University of Westminster, UK. His main research interests concern parliamentary development and he has led a number of parliamentary support programs across the Commonwealth. Anthony worked in the private office of former British Prime

Minister, Sir Edward Heath before joining the Commonwealth Parliamentary Association. He is currently a consultant on legislative affairs for the World Bank.

Prapaipim Sutheewasinnon is currently a lecturer at the Department of General Business, Faculty of Management Science, Silpakorn University, Thailand. She holds a PhD in Accounting from La Trobe University, Australia. Her thesis investigates the performance measurement system in Thailand's public sector.

Thiru Thiagarajah holds a Master's degree in Accounting from Monash University and is a member of the Chartered Institute of Management Accountants (UK) and a Certified and Practising Accountant in Australia. She is a sessional lecturer in accounting at both undergraduate and postgraduate level, has taught Strategic Management Accounting at Central Queensland University, Charles Sturt University, Kaplan Business School and Monash University, and presents courses for CPA students. She is currently a senior research assistant with La Trobe University and has a research interest in performance measurement for equity and access under new public management.

Victoria Wise PhD is MBA Director and Associate Professor of Accounting in the Deakin Graduate School of Business, Deakin University, Australia. She was also Professor at the University of Tasmania and Associate Editor for The International Journal of Doctoral Studies. Her research interests include social responsibility reporting and disclosure and doctoral studies.

Foreword

A well-accepted role of parliaments around the world, whether elected by the people or established through other means, is to hold the executive government to account. A leading means by which the Parliament does this is through the establishment of a public accounts committee, or equivalent, that generally has a focus on government expenditure and matters of public administration. Public account committees also commonly have a formal relationship with Auditors-General to reinforce the special relationship between the Auditor-General and the parliament, and as a means of reviewing the reports of the Auditor-General.

Public accounts committees have a very long history, with their origins having been traced back to the nineteenth century in both the British and Canadian parliaments. In recognition of the importance of the role of public accounts committees, the 2011 Commonwealth Heads of Government Meeting reaffirmed that strong and independent parliamentary oversight plays an important role in preserving the trust of citizens in the integrity of government, through public accounts committees that are effective, independent and transparent.

A particular characteristic of public accounts committees is that the membership is generally drawn from representatives of the main political parties represented in their respective parliaments. As such, when a committee speaks with one voice, it sends a powerful message to government that the views expressed represent a cross-party position. Governments are much more likely to respond positively to a committee's views and recommendations in these circumstances.

At the federal level in Australia, reports of the public accounts committee of the Australian parliament have, over many years, been a rich source of information on many aspects of public administration as well as issues of the day that have involved spending by the executive government and contemporary issues of public administration. In recent times, the committee has played a key role in scrutinising key public sector reforms and reforms to the mandates of the Auditor-General. Given the standing of the committee, the parliament as a whole has been guided by their views in considering the legislative proposals involved.

Over many years, the federal public accounts committee has had a key role to play in relation to the budget and work program of the Australian National Audit Office (ANAO) and has a positive influence in strengthening the mandate of the ANAO, particularly to the broadening of its performance audit mandate that, in certain circumstances, allows the ANAO to assess the performance of the recipients of Commonwealth funding and contractors engaged by the Commonwealth – commonly referred to as follow-the-money powers.

Against this background, this volume provides a very useful and informative collection of views and commentaries into the operations of a number of public accounts committees and national audit offices around the world, covering both developed and developing countries. It draws out the strengths of current practices but also points to some concerns. Most importantly though, it builds on the body of knowledge of the activities of public accounts committees, and highlights issues for further research that, over time, will assist committees, audit institutions and other stakeholders to better appreciate the factors than can contribute to effective committees, including their interaction with audit institutions.

Ian McPhee
Auditor-General for Australia
November 19, 2014

Preface

An important aspect of government accountability and governance process is the establishment and effective functioning of the Public Accounts Committee (PAC). The PAC is a part of the parliamentary infrastructure of a democratic government that helps to ensure that governments account for their operating policies and actions, and their management and use of public resources. Over the recent decade, the public sector of most countries has undergone substantial reforms centred on the emergence of New Public Management (NPM) ideals, improvement of accountability and governance, efficiency and effectiveness. Our understanding of how the PACs on government entities function to strengthen public accountability, financial scrutiny and good governance world-wide is limited. The idea of this book is to establish a dialogue – a bridge of ideas – between public sector accounting and development studies academics, researchers, parliamentarians, parliamentary oversight bodies and public sector practitioners and consultants.

This research monograph focuses on both conventional and contemporary issues facing PACs around the world and the role of national audit offices therein. The overall aim is to provide an international overview, comparison and commentary on the role of public accounts committees and national audit offices in public accountability.

This book incorporates PAC practices in both developed and developing democratic nations in a single volume investigating how various internal and external institutional agents may shape the development and working of a PAC. In addressing the above issues the book provides not only a comparative set of insights but allows the development of themes that are now emergent.

The chapters in this volume will be useful to academic researchers in public administration and development studies fields as they will help researchers grasp the potential external and internal forces that are likely to influence PAC structures and practices. The insights offered by a country-specific PAC will also be useful to parliamentary bodies and governments in other countries implementing similar PAC structures and practices and facing similar socio-political environments. This book will also help in gaining an understanding of the issues of government accountability from a management point of view as well as from a socio-political point of view.

Structure of the book

As shown in the table of Contents, this monograph comprises of 17 chapters organized in five thematic sections.

The first part is essentially introductory in character, seeking to explore the roles of public accounts committees and national audit offices in making governments accountable.

The introductory chapter by Hoque and Thiagarajah reviews the literature available on the contemporary approach adopted by the State Audit Institution (also known as the Auditor-General's Office) in making a valuable contribution to the Public Accounts Committee in its legislative oversight function. It contributes to the existing literature by critically evaluating the legislative oversight function and how the public accounts committee and the state audit institutions address the key challenges in effectively carrying out this function.

In Chapter 2, Des Pearson, the former Auditor-General for the states of Victoria and Western Australia, provides a personal reflections overview of the contributions the Auditor-General can make in facilitating and assisting with improving the functioning of the Public Accounts Committee based on his experience across the two jurisdictions.

Chapter 3 by Hoque and Ananda reports on an empirical study that examines the extent to which parliamentary financial oversight committees and the Auditor-General's Office in Sri Lanka play vital roles in monitoring public sector enterprises and government performance. Their findings indicate that the institutional structure of the public accounts committees is in disarray and inadequate in making the executive members of government accountable.

From 2001 to 2011, the Auditor-General of Canada, Sheila Fraser, emphasised the "accountability" dimension of her role by ceaselessly reminding the federal Administration of its obligation to render accounts to Parliament. Through performance audits, the AG highlighted repeatedly the need for rules of sound management, transparency and accountability that the governments must obey in their management of public funds entrusted to them by the Canadian people. The content of the fourth chapter, produced during her ten-year mandate, in terms of both findings and subjects covered, illustrates an unshakeable will to fully assume her duties as Officer of Parliament.

The fifth chapter, by Skærbæk and Christensen, reviews the relationship between the National Audit Office of Denmark (NAOD) and the Danish Public Accounts Committee (DPAC) for performance audits. That relationship is shown to be one between a powerful PAC and a compliant SAI. The tango of DPAC–NAOD relations reveals a deficiency of independent decision-making on what is audited, how it is audited and what is included in an audit report.

Taken together, these five chapters bring out the generic PAC–NAO relationships and lay a solid foundation for the rest of the book, which has a global focus, covering PACs of a number of developed and developing nations, namely the UK, Sweden, Australia, the Pacific Islands, Bangladesh, Malaysia, Indonesia, India, Thailand, Kenya and the Caribbean nations.

In this regard, the second part covers the PAC of the British Isles in Chapter 6, and Chapter 7 discusses Sweden, which is not a Commonwealth country. Chapter 6 evaluates the PAC of the House of Commons in light of recent changes to public audit and broader changes across United Kingdom governance. Structural and organizational features are analysed, as are working practices and relationships.

Sweden is one of the countries which does *not* have a PAC. Since the Swedish National Audit Office was formed in 2003, two non-PAC models for the channelling of audits to Parliament have been tested. Chapter 7 discusses the Swedish experience from these two non-PAC models and suggests that one reason why Sweden has avoided forming a PAC is the wish to preserve a political culture focused on collaboration and pragmatic improvement, rather than confrontation and accountability debates.

The subsequent parts cover country-specific PACs' operations in a total of ten chapters.

In Chapter 8 the authors examine the Westminster Model as it applies to PACs in Australia. In particular they are interested in the extent to which the precepts of the Westminster Model are represented in Australian PACs and the extent to which their modern-day operations are reflective of the operations of the Parliament at Westminster or of the pragmatic political realities of government in Australia. Chapter 9 examines seven major factors that crucially influence the success of a PAC in encouraging the efficiency and effectiveness of the government and acting as a safety mechanism or check on executive power. In doing so, it makes observations particularly relevant to experience in New South Wales (NSW), the leading state in Australia.

In 2001, the Public Expenditure and Financial Accountability (PEFA) Framework was established to develop a commonly accepted and internationally consistent method of assessing the maturity of a country's public financial management systems and processes. Chapter 10 examines key performance indicators contained in the PEFA assessment reports relating to external scrutiny and audit, in order to identify those factors that make PACs effective and, thereby, to use the PEFA to assess their likely effectiveness. The jurisdictions under investigation are the Cook Islands, Samoa, the Solomon Islands, Tonga and Vanuatu. This sample of countries includes different cultures (Melanesian and Polynesian), different political and constitutional structures (a kingdom, constitutional monarchies and a self-governing state) and different relationships with multinational and bilateral donors.

The fourth part covers the PACs of some Asian nations, namely Bangladesh (Chapter 11), Malaysia (Chapter 12), India (Chapter 13), Indonesia (Chapter 14) and Thailand (Chapter 15).

Chapter 11 describes the development of the PAC of Bangladesh. The findings revealed significant changes in the internal governance modes, operational policies and processes of the PAC. The findings also revealed a range of factors influencing and impacting on the functioning of the PAC.

The twelfth chapter provides an overview of the institutional framework of Malaysia's federal Public Accounts Committee (PAC), and the Committee's role in enhancing public sector accountability. The development of the PAC and its relationship to the government structure in Malaysia are discussed alongside other institutions within the administrative framework of accountability. These include the Accountant General's Department and the National Audit Department. A description of the PAC's powers, responsibilities, membership and working practices precedes a discussion on its effectiveness in supporting the enhancement of accountability.

The aim of Chapter 13 is to analyse responses by ministries and government departments to reports by the PAC of India. The chapter suggests that while the Indian PAC has been successful in scrutinising government accounts and making recommendations, suggestions and comments that promote good governance, it has had limited success in promoting the integrity of data, the assigning of responsibilities to individuals, and general operational efficiency.

In Chapter 14, the authors reviewed past efforts of the Indonesian parliament, Dewan Perwakilan Rakyat (DPR), to improve the accountability of the public sector management by creating Indonesia's PAC, Badan Akuntabilitas Keuangan Negara (BAKN). The authors found BAKN was an ideal committee to improve public sector management in Indonesia. They argue that, given the current Indonesian political environment, this could be one of the reasons for BAKN's dissolution in July 2014.

The Thai parliament is authorized to control the budget in two ways: first, controlling before spending (pre-control), which involves an ad hoc committee appointed by Parliament; and second, controlling after spending (post-Control), which necessitates a permanent committee called the Public Accounts Committee (PAC) to monitor such spending. Chapter 15 seeks to address the role of the PAC in Thailand, the problems it encounters and suggestions for the future.

The final part covers the PACs of an African and two Caribbean nations: the Kenyan PAC (Chapter 16) and the PACs of Jamaica and Trinidad and Tobago (Chapter 17). Chapter 16 examines the formation and evolution of the Kenyan PAC from colonialism to independence, from one-party dictatorship to multi-party democracy and from the old to the new constitution. The chapter also analyses how effective the PAC has become following these developments. It concludes that the strengthening of the PAC should be accompanied by reforms to their institutions of government in order to tame the excesses of executive power.

Recent efforts to strengthen the oversight capacity of the parliaments of Jamaica and Trinidad and Tobago have paid particular attention to the public accounts committee. Chapter 17 provides an analysis of the PACs in these two Caribbean nations. The committees have some similar features in terms of mandate and composition, but both have struggled to be effective, partly because of the difficulties in developing functioning committees in small jurisdictions and partly because of an unhelpful external context.

Acknowledgments

The contributors and I (the editor) have been equal partners in the compilation of this volume. I am grateful to the contributors whose chapters are presented here. I would also like to thank Terry Clague (Publisher, Routledge: Business, Management and Accounting), Jacqueline Curthoys (Commissioning Editor for Routledge Research) and Sinead Waldron (Editorial Assistant, Routledge, Taylor & Francis (UK): Business, Management and Accounting) for their support. Thanks are also due to Professor Peter Loney and Dr Bill Stent for their support during the initial stage of this project. I also thank Mrs Shirin Hoque, Thiru Thiagarajah and Celina McEwen for their editorial assistance in producing this book.

Part I

Public Accounts Committees and National Audit Offices

An introduction

1 Public accountability

The role of the Auditor-General in legislative oversight

Zahirul Hoque and Thiru Thiagarajah

Introduction

This chapter reviews the literature available on the contemporary approach adopted by the Supreme Audit Institution (SAI) – also known as the Auditor-General's Office – in making a valuable contribution to the Public Accounts Committee (PAC) in its legislative oversight function. Public Accounts Committees provide a vital legislative oversight function in scrutinising public expenditure in the Westminster parliamentary system. Although the first public expenditure committees were formally recognised in the nineteenth century, the function of scrutiny dates back to the time of Aristotle, in ancient Greece, before the formation of the first official parliament in Europe. As ancient as it is, the accountability function of the committee has remained consistent with the principles on which Aristotle based the need for a state's accountability. He emphasised the need to protect public monies from embezzlement and reveal to the citizens the details of financial activity by publicly displaying copies of expenses. The PACs are parliamentary committees set up to scrutinise governments and make them accountable (Friedberg and Hazan, 2012).

The notion of legislative oversight was developed further under the British monarchical system, where approval from the representatives of the upper class was required by a monarch to raise additional tax revenues (Friedberg and Hazan, 2012). In the nineteenth century, the great British philosopher, John Stuart Mill (1861: 104 as cited in Friedberg and Hazan, 2012) contributed to distinguishing the role of the government and the legislative branch by defining the role of the legislative branch as one of overseeing the government:

> The proper office of a representative assembly is to watch and control the government: to throw the light of publicity on its acts; to compel a full exposition and justification of all of them which anyone considers questionable; to censure them if found condemnable, and, if the men [sic] who compose the government abuse their trust, or fulfil it in a manner which conflicts with the deliberate sense of the nation, to expel them from office and either expressly or virtually appoint their successors.

This brief history confirms that the notion of accountability for public funds was in existence even before the first PAC was established. Notwithstanding, the emergence of select committees occurred in the nineteenth century. As early as 1840 in Canada, when the provinces of Upper and Lower Canada were united, select committees were appointed to annually investigate the government's income and expenditure. This later developed into a committee of public accounts and, after that, in 1852–3, into a standing committee on public accounts (Balls, 1963: 21–2 as cited in Jones and Jacobs, 2006).

In the UK, Sir Francis Baring, who chaired the select committee on Public Moneys, made a series of reforms that enabled the establishment of the Select Committee of Public Accounts in 1861 by William Gladstone – who had become Chancellor of the Exchequer in 1859. A Standing Order was issued in 1862 under which the committee would operate:

> [T]here shall be a Standing Committee of Public Accounts; for the examina-tion of the Accounts showing the appropriation of sums granted by Parlia-ment to meet the Public Expenditure, to consist of nine members, who shall be nominated at the commencement of every Session, and of whom five shall be a quorum.
>
> (Jones, 1987 as cited in Jones and Jacobs, 2006: 69)

This chapter presents an overview of the significance and the functionality of the PAC and the SAI in making governments accountable. It contributes to the exist-ing literature by critically evaluating the legislative oversight function and how the PAC and the SAI address key challenges in effectively carrying out this function. It is evident from the research carried out that the SAIs have zealously contributed to holding governments accountable, predominantly through enhanc-ing their strategic and operational capability. There is some evidence, however, that also shows that this increased stature of accountability has unintentionally caused an imbalance in access and equity.

The remainder of the chapter is organised in the following manner. The next section discusses the research method used. The third section discusses the dif-ferent dimensions of oversight. A comparison is made between the Westminster parliamentary system and the US Congressional system, and between potential and effective oversight. In the fourth section, we look at the functionality of the PAC and the relationship between the Auditor-General (AG) and PACs. The fifth section gives an overview of the changing nature of accountability from one of equity, access, service appropriateness and client empowerment to economy and efficiency, fuelled by the introduction of Corporate Governance principles and New Public Management (NPM). The sixth section outlines the four key challenges: the lack of responsiveness of governments; the variability in the quality of audit reporting; the evolving nature of audit content; and the increased institutional complexity of the government faced by the PAC and the AG in addressing the accountability paradigm. We illustrate this point with examples from four Commonwealth nations: Australia, Canada, New Zealand and the UK.

The seventh section gives a summary of case studies and argues that the government's accountability was enhanced by the role of the SAI in providing legislative oversight function and making governments accountable. Finally, we conclude with recommendations to help strengthen the role of the AG as well as suggestions for future research.

Research method

This research was based on archival evidence. The articles researched for this chapter were retrieved using Google Scholar and other online databases, namely EBSCOhost, JSTOR and ProQuest. The keywords used to retrieve the articles were Public Accounts Committee, PAC, Auditor-General (AG), and National Audit Office. After a preliminary search on the background and role of the PAC/ AG worldwide, we gathered further evidence to highlight the importance of the legislative function. While researching the current status of PACs, we discovered that the role of the PAC has evolved over time. We then pursued our research to determine the challenges faced by PACs as highlighted by previous research. We continued our research by analysing the content of AGs' websites to draw inferences on how these challenges were addressed in the four jurisdictions studied. Finally, we draw upon four real case studies to highlight the AGs' roles before concluding and making recommendations.

Dimensions of parliamentary oversight

There are two primary elements of legislative oversight: the mechanisms of oversight and the effectiveness of oversight. While researching the literature on legislative oversight, an interesting theme emerged in relation to the mechanisms and effectiveness of oversight. Friedberg and Hazan (2012) found in their study comparing the Westminster parliamentary system with the presidential system prevalent in the USA that the separation of powers in the USA presidential regime has 'strong' political oversight whereas the parliamentary democracy under the Westminster system exhibits a 'weak' administrative oversight. This is due to the fact that parliamentary oversight is influenced by the relationship between the legislative and the executive branches, while, in a presidential democracy, oversight is based on strict separation of powers, which means that the legislature draws its authority directly from the public and is usually independent and strong. Mezey's (1979) research demonstrates that presidential democracies, based on separation of powers, are able to effectively oversee the executive branch, especially through their committees, whereas parliamentary democracies have limited oversight capabilities, because the government and its leader, who act through a disciplined majority party (or coalition), control the legislature (for details, see Friedberg and Hazan, 2012). Further, Lees (1977) shows that one of the most significant factors that affect legislative oversight is legislators' motivation (Friedberg and Hazan, 2012). When legislators have a relatively high degree of freedom to act, when their progress is not dependent on party leaders and they are not bound by party discipline, they have greater aspirations to oversee the Executive more effectively. This is more so in the case in a presidential regime with non-cohesive political parties, a system where there is a clear separation of powers, such as in the USA.

Pelizzo and Stapenhurst (2006) further scrutinised the different levels of legislative oversight. They differentiated between 'oversight potential' and 'effective oversight'. 'Effective oversight' is when legislatures actually oversee governments' actions and activities and has an impact on the political system, and, more specifically, on governments' behaviour. 'Oversight potential' is when legislatures have a set of formal powers and instruments to oversee governments' activities regardless of whether these powers and instruments are actually used. Pelizzo and Stapenhurst (2006) argue that the real test of whether a government is truly democratic depends not only on the ability to perform oversight function, but also the level of scrutiny and control subjected to a government's actions. The legislative control is implemented through several tools that oversee the actions of the executives, committees' hearings, hearings in the plenary assembly, the creation of inquiry committees, parliamentary questions, question time, the interpellations and the ombudsman (Maffio, 2002; Pennings, 2000; cited in Pelizzo and Stapenhurst, 2006).

Functionality of the Public Accounts Committee and the State Audit Institution

Public Accounts Committees scrutinise governments' accounts and make the Executive answerable for their public spending. McGee (2002) showed in his study that, though PACs are considered an effective oversight tool, they have many problems associated with oversight (Pelizzo and Stapenhurst, 2006). First, parliamentarians do not engage in serious oversight of governments' accounts. Second, scrutinising public accounts provides very little advantage in the re-election of Members of Parliament (MPs). Thirdly, government party MPs (or coalitions) are apprehensive about scrutinising governments' accounts as they risk being eschewed by their party. As a result, some regimes only have PACs because their presence is considered necessary, but this does not mean that they provide an effective legislative oversight. Pelizzo and Stapenhurst (2006: 17) conclude that 'Parliaments must have not only the tools but also the political will to oversee the government.' This applies to the PAC and is a necessary condition for effective oversight of governments' accounts.

Joachim Wehner's (2003) research highlights several key challenges inherent to public spending, resulting in the PACs' need to find innovative responses to safeguard and maximise their contribution to financial scrutiny. He states that the PAC takes on an *ex post* perspective to public spending where it carries out an assurance process to confirm that the monies have been spent in accordance with the intent, economically, efficiently and effectively. The *ex ante* process of budget setting and allocations of monies are based on political decisions. This is in stark contrast to the congressional system in the United States, where the appropriation committees fulfil the budget-writing function. Congress demonstrates a powerful role in allocating monies and aggregate spending levels. However, in the congressional system, *ex post* scrutiny is not as strong as in the Westminster system, where PACs focus on assessing public spending.

The SAI complements the PAC in making governments accountable. Malloy (2004: 165) argues that 'the best Committees are able to complement and enhance the role of legislative auditors, primarily by providing an important public forum for the further exploration of issues identified by auditors via the Public Accounts Committee'.

Friedberg and Hazan (2012) suggest that strengthening the relationship between the SAI and the PAC will enhance the knowledge of the executives of the supervised government departments and will effectively fulfil the role of legislative oversight. They support this view with a report that was published on the relations between top SAI and their legislatures in 14 European countries. The report shows that the legislature was most effective in its oversight role when it used the work of the SAI as foundation. When the legislature provides a platform to the SAI to submit its findings and stimulate public discourse, the audit proves to be more effective (Friedberg and Hazan, 2012; Galea and Miroslaw, 2001).

The changing nature of accountabiliity

Prior to discussing the key challenges faced by PACs and the SAI, it is imperative to note the changing nature of accountability. Degeling *et al.* (1996) suggest that the modern dimensions of service provision by the PAC are economic, financial and managerial, which displaces accountability to make place for other considerations, such as equity and access (Degeling *et al.*, 1996; Guthrie, 1993; Pollitt, 1986, 1994). The PACs endorse the financial accountability of the Executive to the Parliament. In performing this function, the committee, first, makes certain that the Parliament exercises financial control over the Executive. Second, it maintains the legitimacy of a representative system of government (Bland, 1946; Day and Klein, 1987; Normanton, 1966 as cited in Degeling *et al.*, 1996). Finally, according to Stewart (1984 as cited in Degeling *et al.*, 1996), a PAC's effectiveness arises from its capacity to specify what is to be incorporated in the financial accounts prepared by government departments and instrumentalities as well as its capacity to complete the circle of control *ex post*, which is a financial review of public expenditure by the Treasury, the AG and the Parliament. Accordingly, PACs have a legislative endorsement that extends beyond accounting and economic discourses into administrative and professional domains. This has created a platform where economy and efficiency have displaced concern for other values, such as equity, access, service appropriateness and client empowerment (Degeling *et al.*, 1996).

Another dimension to PACs' accountability mechanisms is the overarching view of corporate governance principles. Scholars have attempted to incorporate the phenomenon of 'governing the government' (Jacobs and Jones, 2006) into the study of PACs. In 1980, 'corporate governance' was not known in professional circles, and was, therefore, not the subject of serious academic study (Tricker, 1993; Hodges *et al.*, 1996). Corporate governance in parliamentary accountability is now well researched and forms a growing body of scholarly literature. The early adoption of corporate governance principles, such as openness, integrity and accountability, in the public sector is embedded in the Cadbury report (Cadbury Committee 1992 as cited in Hodges *et al.*, 1996). The principles of corporate governance were of much interest to the public with the introduction of the NPM, resulting in structural changes to the public sector. Examples of such changes include

> [The] desegregation of separable functions into contractual or quasi-market forms, opening up provider roles to competition through compulsory competitive tendering, decentralising provider roles to agencies and creating a network of contracts which link incentives to performance.
>
> (Hodges *et al.* 1996: 8)

Implementing the NPM in the Westminster parliamentary system has gained popularity, because of the shared parliamentary system, which makes it easier for government to implement major reforms. A strong party discipline – a two-party system with minor parties playing a minor role – and a strong executive are necessary conditions for firm government actions (Jones and Jacobs, 2006). New Public Management had its origins in Margaret Thatcher's 1980s radical reforms to the British public sector (Aucoin, 1995; Jones and Jacobs, 2009) and in New Zealand's 1986 reforms, commencing with the State Owned Enterprise Act, followed by other legislations affecting the public service and financial management (Boston *et al.*, 1996; Constitutional Arrangements Committee, 2005; Jones and Jacobs, 2009). When public service institutions are governed based on the principles of private enterprises, the scale is tilted towards managerial accountability, away from political accountability (Fowles, 1993; Gray and Jenkins, 1993 cited in Jones and Jacobs, 2006). The PAC deals not with policy but with policy implementation and the Executive are held responsible for economical, effective and efficient disbursement of public monies in accordance with policy prerogative.

Addressing key challenges

What then are the key challenges faced by PACs? How does the SAI enhance the accountability and assist the PAC in addressing these challenges? Joachim Wehner (2003) claims that, apart from internal structures and the workings of PACs, they (PACs) operate in a much larger environment, which influences the effectiveness of the financial scrutiny. He identified four key challenges faced by PACs in the modern era: the lack of responsiveness of governments; the variability in the quality of audit reporting – a traditional challenge; the evolving nature of audit content; and the increased institutional complexity of the government, which arises from structural changes, discussed previously under the changing nature of accountability. A brief look at these challenges is necessary prior to examining further the oversight function of PACs.

First, governments' defiance and lack of responsiveness, characterised by the dominance of the Executive in the parliamentary context, deter the PAC from adding value derived from the adoption of recommendations pertaining to issues raised in the report to the PAC. Second, the quality of audit reports determines the effectiveness of scrutiny; this will very much depend on the availability of qualified staff and other resources to the SAI. The third and fourth challenges are dominated by structural changes that have taken place in the past 20 years with the public sector adopting the NPM approach, discussed earlier in this chapter. With the invention of the NPM principles, the evolving nature of audit content is an issue for many SAIs. It leads to questioning policy choices in relation to effectiveness and increased volume of audit reports, which reduces the time-frame to review reports. Some PACs have adopted new types of audits, such as the adoption of 'value for money' audit by the Canadian AG in 1977. Increased institutional complexity has brought on its own problems. As public monies are channelled through different sources, a host of different agencies and other bodies are funded with public monies (Schick, 2002 as cited in Wehner, 2003). This is in contrast to the framework of the first PAC implemented by William Gladstone in Britain, where, essentially, there was only one central government body responsible for spending public monies (Wehner, 2003).

Governments' responsiveness to PAC recommendations

Governments' responsiveness to PACs' recommendations is an important feature in the effective functioning of the PAC, which also infers the PAC's legitimacy. The lack of responsiveness can be a common issue facing PACs in some juris-dictions. In the Australasian jurisdiction, this challenge is addressed by the short response times available to the government to respond to the PAC's recom-mendations. In Australia, the time required to respond to the PAC is between three and six months, except in two of the eight states and territories – Tasmania and Northern Territory – where there is no formal requirement for the govern-ment to respond. In New Zealand, the response time is three months. This requirement is imperative for the PAC to achieve its aim of accountability (KPMG, 2006 as cited in Jacobs *et al.*, 2007). In some cases, governments responding to the PAC's recommendations may require extensive co-ordination by several departments or agencies. In some jurisdictions, a partisan approach to the PAC membership may result in the government not responding effectively to recommendations made by the PAC.

In the UK, a member of the opposition chairs the PAC and the acceptance rate of recommendations is as high as 90 per cent (McGee, 2002). However, in Australia and New Zealand, it is considered beneficial to have a government member as chair. Indeed, 80 per cent of the Australian and New Zealand PACs have chairs that are members of the government – only the Australian Capital Territory (ACT) has a Chair who is a member of the opposition while Tasmania has an independent chair – and 70 per cent have a government majority – the exceptions are New Zealand, Tasmania and the ACT. The reason for having government members as chairs is because it is thought that when they advocate for the PAC's recommendations, they can persuade reluctant ministers to act. This perspective assumes that a government member can work more collaboratively with government ministers than an opposition member could, as they might not have the confidence of the ministers (McGee, 2002). Apart from government's responsiveness, the AG plays a crucial monitoring role in adopting PACs' recommendations. In Canada, for instance, the AG's role is to follow up on recommendations within a period of up to two years and oversee the initiation of changes announced by the government in response to PACs' recommendations (McGee, 2002). However, McGee (2002) also notes that having a government member as the chair could be an impediment to the independence of the PAC and, therefore, might lead to a lack of effectiveness of the legislative oversight function. He also points out that the 'lack of response reflects the perennial problem of finding time on the floor of the House to debate every matter that might be considered worthy of attention' (McGee, 2002: 80). He further reveals that, in Canada, it is a rare occurrence for a debate of this nature to be held and, in the UK, an annual debate is held on up to six PAC reports.

From this discussion, it is clear that the stipulated response time, composition of the PAC and the AG's role in monitoring recommendations are all critical to the extent to which governments are responsive to PAC recommendations. Even in jurisdictions where challenges arise due to the power of the Executive being dominant, it is still possible to enhance the legitimacy of the PAC through internal processes and channel the power of the Executive to effectively implement PAC recommendations.

The quality of audit reporting

It might be useful to refer to the origins of the term audit to establish what might be meant by a quality audit report. 'Audit' comes from the Latin word *audire*, which means 'to hear'. In ancient Rome, the term *audire* referred to the 'hearing of accounts', a process in which officials compared their records with each other (Treasury Board of Canada Secretariat 2004, as cited in Ramkumar and Krafchick, 2005). As many people interested in the audit findings were illiterate, audits were presented orally. In modern times, auditing was recognised as a technical discipline practised by professional auditors. However, audit opinions are still based on the principles of one performing an oversight function over another's annual financial statements to attest their compliance against a list of criteria. The role of the AG is one of carrying out financial, compliance and performance audits in order to submit reports to the PAC that support its legislative oversight function. Financial audits assess the accuracy and fairness of both the accounting procedures and the financial statements reported by the agency. Compliance audits assess whether allocated funds were utilised for the purposes for which they were appropriated, in compliance with relevant laws and regulations.

Performance audits analyse cost-effectiveness (economy), operational efficiency and the overall effectiveness of government programmes in meeting their object- ives (Transparency International, 2004 as cited in Ramkumar and Krafchick, 2005).

Next, we explore the notion of quality of an audit report from the perspective of the auditor's independence and the availability of resources to carry out state's audit effectively. McGee (2002) argues that the auditor's independence is defined by the extent of his/her independence from the entity being audited, which in this context is the government. He also states that

> independence does not mean insulation from the suggestions and persua- sions of others. Auditors General must be sensitive to political and public concerns, and it is perfectly legitimate, indeed essential, that those concerns should be important influences on how Auditors General distribute their audit resources.
>
> (McGee, 2002: 21)

It should be noted too that PACs can help maintain this independence.

In the four commonwealth jurisdictions central to this study, the SAI (or Supreme Audit Institutions) are known by different names. In Australia, it is known as the Australian National Audit Office (ANAO) and its chief as the Auditor-General (AG). In Canada, it is known as the Office of the Auditor- General of Canada headed by the Auditor-General of Canada. In New Zealand, the SAI is known as the Office of the Auditor-General with the Controller and Auditor-General as its chief. In the UK, it is known as the National Audit Office (NOA) and its chief as the Comptroller and Auditor-General (C&AG).

In Australia, new legislation was passed to protect and maintain the AG's independence. In Australia, Canada, New Zealand and the UK, the AG is an officer of the Parliament. The ANAO views the Australian Parliament as their primary client. Its purpose is to provide Parliament with an independent assess- ment of selected areas of public administration and assurance about public sector financial reporting, administration and accountability. Further, the ANAO views the Executive and public sector entities as important clients. The organisation states that it provides an objective assessment of areas where improvements can be made in public administration and service delivery. The ANAO aims to do this in a constructive and consultative manner (Australian National Audit Office, 2014a).

In Canada, the AG is independent from the government and reports directly to their Parliament. The duties of the AG relate to legislative auditing and, in certain cases, to the monitoring of federal departments and agencies, Crown cor- porations, territorial governments and other entities (Office of the Auditor- General of Canada, 2013).

In New Zealand, the Controller and Auditor-General is independent of the executive government and the Parliament in discharging the functions of the statutory office, but is answerable to the Parliament for their stewardship of the public resources with which they are entrusted. In New Zealand, the Auditor-General's Department is not a government department. The Parliament seeks independent assurance that public sector organisations are operating, and accounting for their performance, in accordance with the parliament's intentions. As an Officer of Parliament, the Controller and Auditor-General provides his independent assurance to both the Parliament and the public (Controller and Auditor-General New Zealand, 2014a).

In the UK, the C&AG is independent of the Executive and the Judiciary. The C&AG has no relationship with investigating agencies. A key principal is the independence of external audit from the Executive. The National Audit Office (NAO) has financial independence and is established by Act of Parliament, or by a legislative body. The C&AG is vested with all statutory powers and rights governing the audit of central government finances. The NAO has no independent corporate status; NAO staff are employees of the C&AG and the C&AG himself is part of the NAO. The C&AG is appointed in consultation with the Chairman of the PAC by HM The Queen, on an address from the House of Commons moved by the Prime Minister. The C&AG can only be removed from office by HM The Queen on an address from both Houses of Parliament (INTOSAI, 2014).

From the excerpts above, it is evident that, although the AG is an Officer of Parliament, under the four jurisdictions reviewed here, he/she maintains an independent status from the Executive. This bestows power upon the AG to carry out his/her audit independent of the legislature, which is an important ingredient for determining the quality of the audit. He/she is also responsible for making recommendations in view of the government audit, which then becomes the responsibility of the Parliament to implement. In some jurisdictions, he/she may participate in the capacity of an overseer with regard to implementing recommendations.

The resources available to the AG influence the quality of the audit. The SAI must be allocated sufficient resources, in staff, information technology and training and education to carry out high-quality work. They also state that staff should be adequately qualified and skilled in their area of expertise as well as well remunerated to be able to add value to the audit. This holds true across all jurisdictions. At present, though, there is general consensus that the Supreme Audit Institutions in the developed world are better resourced than their counterparts in the developing world. Further, the sharing of ideas, knowledge and experience among Supreme Audit Institutions harmonises standards and promotes best practice, and working closely with law enforcement officers assists in uncovering corruption (Stapenhurst and Titsworth, 2001).

McGee (2002: 43) highlights that

> [c]ritical to the effective performance of the Auditor General's functions are the budget and resources provided for the office. The increasing complexity of the modern audit function demands multi-disciplinary audit teams with the need for a range of expertise: legal, economic, environmental and so on.

The days when only accountants were employed on public sector audit work are gone. Autonomy of operation depends heavily on sufficiency of resources.

He also states that simply having robust procedures does not ensure the delivery of high-quality services. Instead, having the AG's involvement in pre-budget resource allocation processes ensures the PAC or the Parliament can finalise the AG's budget allocations without alteration. In Australia, when funding is recommended, it has the added protection of being legally guaranteed.

Having sufficient resources does not only equate to having sufficient financial resources; it also means having sufficient human and technological resources. As stated in ANAO's strategic statement, some of their priorities are to invest in leadership, mentoring and coaching of their staff and commit to technical excellence and knowledge sharing, while creating alliances and partnerships nationally and internationally (ANAO, 2014b).

In the UK, the PAC is a non-parliamentary body, chaired by a PAC member, and performs the function of allocating resources. The NAO's strategy implies that it is an organisation with access to a unique level of resourcing in terms of accounting and professional skills, with the ability to look across the full breadth of government activities and focus on the use of resources across government that drive value for money (UK National Audit Office, 2014c).

In Canada, the AG submits his/her expenditure estimates to Parliament and maintains a credible balance between resources and service delivery. In the February 2001 report of the Auditor-General of Canada (Office of the Auditor General Canada, 'Section VIII', para. 275) it is stated that:

> Although the Audit Office has faced a lengthy period of government restraint, the productivity of the Office has remained high. Several new initiatives have stretched the accumulated human and physical capital of the organization. New audit methods, technology and training are required and it is necessary improve the audit staff's knowledge of government and the outside world. It is imperative to review the human resource management and ensure that staff in key positions enhance their skill base as the 'baby boom' employees retire in the next few years.

In New Zealand, the practice of funding the Audit Office takes on a different dimension. The AG is funded by the Crown through vote audit for outputs provided to the Parliament, and by audit fees paid by public entities for annual audits. The AG appoints Audit New Zealand, a not-for-profit organisation, and other private sector accounting firms to audit public entities. A significant part of the AG's role is to monitor the work of these contracted firms. This approach requires extensive monitoring of audit independence (Controller and Auditor-General of New Zealand, 2014c: 20–1). Further, in the strategic intent of the AG, it is mentioned that their key priority is to keep abreast of developments in auditing and accountability by contributing to the international auditing community and sharing skills, knowledge and expertise with other audit bodies throughout the world, in general, and with the Pacific region in particular (Controller and Auditor-General New Zealand, 2014b: 16).

This discussion about quality reinforces McGee's claims that the quality of audit is a factor of adequacy of resources, availability of advanced technology, skilled staff to carry out the audits and knowledge sharing. From the above, we can state that the four jurisdictions under consideration here adequately meet the criteria for enhancing the quality of audits.

Another factor that is deemed to improve the quality of audits is the relationship between the AG, the PAC and the Executive. While maintaining their independence, this relationship needs to be cordial. Although this area is under-explored, Campbell (1961: 30) states:

> the audit of public finance at its highest level rests on close co-operation by the auditor with the executive and the administration, rather than on reporting disharmony. Under such a co-operative relationship critical reporting should not be necessary for the correction of an abuse or irregularity and other than in exceptional cases. The public interest may be best served should audit rest on the rectification of a matter rather than that it be allowed to make news.

He argues that there is an obligation to value the AG's findings and take remedial actions if required. However, in cases where the AG promulgates administrative inefficiency, there will be a tendency for the administration to be intolerant towards the auditor.

It is worth noting that in studies comparing the operations of the SAI in the United States and the United Kingdom, there is an interesting theme emerging within the context of NPM. Norton and Smith (2008) found that the Government Accountability Office (GAO) in the US is more effective than its NAO counterpart in the UK. This is because the GAO derives its power and legitimacy from written constitution, in contrast to the NAO, which has no equivalent document. Consequently, the power, duties and perceptions of the NAO are significantly weaker than those of the GAO. This argument about audit quality proposes a different perspective on this issue and is a new contribution to the body of literature on government accountability.

The evolving nature of audit content and the increased institutional complexity

The evolving nature of audit content and increased institutional complexity of the government arise from structural changes and have posed their own challenges to the role of the AG. Many jurisdictions have been subject to structural changes since the NPM approach was adopted two decades ago. The NPM has its origins in Osborne and Gaebler's (1992) book *Reinventing Government*, which sparked a debate on government and public management in many countries. In Australia, the beginnings of NPM were embedded in the reforms of Prime Minister Hawke's Labour Government in the 1980s and 1990s. It was further entrenched in government practices by the election of the Liberal National Party Coalition Government led by John Howard in 1996 (Jones and Jacobs, 2009).

Glor (2001: 122) states that in Canada:

> while managerialism began federally in the Clark and Trudeau governments of 1979–84, the Mulroney government elected in 1984 took up NPM, especially, following the adoption of free trade with the USA in 1989. Although the Mulroney government cut back federal programmes and transfers, the largest cuts occurred under the Liberal government elected in 1993.

The implementation of NPM has had many consequences, among which is, most notably, the effect on the role of the AG. McGee (2002) notes that structural changes resulted in extensive privatisation of enterprises and changes to public service delivery. In the case of privatisation, the AG's responsibility is terminated in relation to the audit of the organisation. He/she, however, takes on the role of reporting on the process affecting the privatisation and on whether it conforms to the values of economy, efficiency and effectiveness. This leads the AG into government policy arena, which is outside of his/her mandate. This overlapping of audit mandate with government policy objectives may be immaterial, especially as the audit of the privatisation process will yield more than superficial benefits. McGee (2002) states that auditing the privatisation process will reveal inefficient choices of the privatisation methods and ensure public assets are sold through a fair value mechanism.

However, June Pallot's (2003) examination of the New Zealand Audit Office challenges their adoption of NPM. She argues that the NPM model, which was advocated for by the Treasury, is deep rooted in an ideology of making the public sector more private, not just in terms of the management styles and techniques, but because it effectively shields the sector from public scrutiny and discussion. This creates a favourable atmosphere to contracting out services or even selling institutions to the private sector, who stand to benefit from such sales.

Further, a point of concern is the diminishing role of the AG in auditing contractual arrangements for the delivery of public services by agencies in receipt of government funding. In this context, a claim may be made that the AG's role is restricted to examining the effectiveness of the service delivery contract rather than the service delivery itself. Pat Barrett (2001: 17), AM, AG for Australia comments:

> Over recent years, reflecting the greater involvement of the private sector in providing a wide range of public services, there has been considerable focus through the audits of the ANAO on the necessity of having in place the 'right' contract, as well as appropriate contract management arrangements, to assist in meeting organisational objectives and strategies. A common theme of these audit reports has been the deficiencies in the project management skills of

agency decision makers. This is of concern given that some of these projects involve substantial resources and complexity. As well, reports have flagged a need for care in assessing value for money and negotiating, preparing, administering and amending major contracts.

McGee (2002) identifies the problem of potential reduction in the AG's mandate when there are outsourcing arrangements. He further states that the PAC does not deal with legislation restricting or removing the AG's role, but claims that the PAC can be more supportive and warrants greater involvement by the AG under such circumstances.

The introduction of NPM has focused increasingly on efficiency and effectiveness of government operations, which, in turn, has increased the number of performance audits in the past decade. In research undertaken by Gendron *et al.* (2001) in the Canadian province of Alberta, they found that the performance audit carried out by the SAI compromises, to a certain extent, the independence of the State Auditor. This is so when the State Auditor audits systems implemented according to his/her own best practice recommendations as a result of his/her prior audit. The authors compare it to the relationship of a private consultant introducing systems in places where they are carrying out audits. Performance audits go well beyond issues of compliance, assessing the extent to which policy objectives are realised and how resources have been used to secure economy, efficiency and effectiveness. In fact, these audits address matters that extend beyond the traditional concerns of the PAC (Aucoin, 1998).

Interestingly, the former AG of New South Wales in Australia, Tony Harris (2000: 2) also commented that 'there was strong opposition from the bureaucracy to performance audits'. This opposition to performance audits was due to the fact that they would lead AGs to question the policies of ministers, rather than the policies' objectives.

More issues about NPM's 'performance focus' were raised by the New Zealand Audit Office. Pallot (2003: 145) suggests that

> of these issues, perhaps the one impacting most directly on the work of the Office itself was non-financial performance measurement. The rapid development of reporting on performance in the public sector, such as the requirement to publish statements of corporate intent, statements of service performance and other non-financial information, had created an entirely new set of challenges for the scope of audits and their evidential requirements. The main concern for the New Zealand Audit Office was that reliability of measures had been emphasised at the possible expense of their usefulness and purpose.

She goes on to say the Audit Office facilitated New Zealand's public sector reforms, and can be seen as legitimising the effort especially in the form of performance reporting.

Accountability and the Auditor-General's role

In this section, we explore four cases, within the four jurisdictions studied. They illustrate the ways in which SAIs were instrumental in bringing to light irregularities in public expenditure. The first case study is from Australia as described by the then AG, Pat Barrett (2001). The case is based on private financing in the area of public sector infrastructure. The Melbourne City Link project was one of the largest infrastructure projects ever undertaken in Australia with an estimated total cost of around $2 billion. It involved approximately 22 kilometres of road, tunnel and bridge works linking three of Melbourne's largest freeways. Though it is difficult to scrutinise privately financed projects due to the obstacles faced by parliaments in accessing contract documents, this high-profile project was subjected to external scrutiny. This raised concerns about the exact distribution of risk and financial benefits between the public and private sectors. A report by the State AG found that, while users of the City Link would, in essence, be the financiers of the project via toll payments, the private sector had accepted substantial obligations associated with the delivery and operation of the City Link, including traffic and revenue risks. However, the auditors found that the decision to establish the City Link as a toll road was not supported by an initial financial model, which compared project costing on the basis of private sector financing versus government borrowings. This then raised the question about whether private financing was the most efficient approach for this project. Barrett (2001) states that these risk transfer and accountability issues will, increasingly, become a focus of AGs. He argues that such scrutiny can assist in optimising outcomes and providing assurance to the public and parliaments, and points to the example of the UK's NAO in providing a solid direction to auditors on how to examine value for money of privately financed deals.

The next case study is based on the Canadian Auditor-General's experience (Office of the Auditor General of Canada, 2014). Correctional Service Canada (CSC) is responsible for the safe and secure custody of offenders sentenced by the courts to terms of imprisonment of two years or more. In the 2012/13 fiscal year, CSC spent about $2 billion – 82 per cent of its operating expenses – on the custody of offenders and on programmes for their rehabilitation. In March 2013, CSC held 15,224 offenders in 57 federal penitentiaries across Canada. The Office of the AG's responsibility was to conduct an independent examination of correctional services. It was considered a performance audit and the objective was to determine whether CSC increased the capacity of Canada's correctional facilities in a manner that met its needs and was cost-effective. The AG found that CSC was adding over 2,700 cells to 37 facilities. It was conducting the expansion in a rapidly changing environment and successfully closed older institutions in a timely fashion, as directed by the government. However, the AG concluded that CSC did not plan the expansions to its penitentiaries in a manner that took into account its accommodation needs in the long term; it had not considered the condition of many of its facilities before determining which ones to expand. It did not have up-to-date guidelines for some of its space requirements, including those for providing health care and correctional programmes. As well, CSC did not assess the extent to which further investments were needed for the expansions and to upgrade the ageing infrastructure within its penitentiaries.

In August 2003, the New Zealand public was shocked to learn that the Ministry of Social Development had been defrauded of about $1.9 million, or $1.1 million in US dollars (Bishop and Burrowes, 2003). The fraud occurred over 28 months. The Ministry of Social Development conducted a ministry-wide audit across the national office and commissioned an independent investigation by Deloitte Touche Tohmatsu. The focus of the investigation was to determine if this particular fraud could have been prevented or detected earlier. The Ministry of Social Development had begun four similar outsourced investigations since 2001. Previously, it was revealed in the AG's reports of 1997–8 to 1999–2000, 136 employee frauds had been identified in 22 government departments. Further, the AG's investigation showed that only 16 of the 43 government departments had formal policies and procedures for managing employee fraud, and six departments explicitly said that employee fraud was neither a risk nor worth considering. The AG concluded that the Ministry of Social Development did not see the fraud detection controls as imperative for public accountability. It was found that the control mechanism lacking in this instance was the segregation of duties between services received and authorisation of payment. Having fraud detection policies alone is not sufficient, but the department must ensure they are implemented in order for fraud to be reduced.

In the UK, one of the functions of the Home Office is to provide accommodation to asylum seekers and their families while their cases are being processed. The cost of providing this accommodation in 2011–12 was £150 million. In March 2012, the department decided to contract out the provision of these services, collectively called Commercial and Operating Managers Procuring Asylum Support (COMPASS), to six organisations that would implement a new delivery model involving fewer bigger housing providers than the previous contracts signed in 2011–12 (UK National Audit Office, 2014b). The Home Office aimed to save around £140 million over seven years through the introduction of the new contractual arrangements. In 2012–13, it achieved a saving of £8 million. Contracts were awarded to G4S, Serco and Clearel. Of these three providers, only Clearel had previous experience in the asylum housing sector. Following a brief transition period, contracts were to be fully operational in all areas by January 2013.

During 2012 and 2013, the NAO received correspondence from individuals and Ministers of Parliament concerned about the contractors' operations. The NAO conducted an investigation and found that, although these organisations had been operating for almost one year, there remained unresolved issues in the delivery of the COMPASS contracts. In particular, the new providers struggled to establish their supply chains, resulting in poor performance, delays and additional costs to the Home Office. Providers were failing to meet some of their key performance indicators, especially around property standards, and some users (asylum seekers) of these facilities were having negative experiences. At the time of writing this chapter, commercial negotiations were still under way over whether the contracts needed to be changed, what additional costs might be incurred by the Home Office and what service credits should be applied. Until these issues are resolved it will be difficult for the Home Office, the providers and local authorities to develop the mature relationship needed to deliver the intended savings and an effective service regime. The NAO has made many recommendations, including that the Home Office work with providers to resolve outstanding issues over contract delivery and conclude commercial negotiations to move the contract forward (UK National Audit Office, 2014a).

Conclusion

Malloy (2004) stated that Public Accounts Committees are an important adjunct to the work of legislative auditors and generally act independently but in close relationship. Committees provide a valuable and unique public forum for further discussion and investigation of the work of legislative auditors and are an important aspect of the system of accountability in Canadian governments.

This is true given the intricate role the AG performs bringing forth accountability to the government by assisting in the legislative oversight function of the PAC. At this point we highlight the following recommendations made by the Department of Economic and Social Affairs of the United Nations (2007) in their report on *Auditing for Social Change: A Strategy for Citizen Engagement in Public Sector Accountability*. First, participation of civil societies in the auditing process can enhance accountability and align public services to citizens' needs. Second, participation of SAI in the budgeting and planning processes can proactively strengthen the accountability process, and third, media can help engage citizens directly with the auditing process and improve transparency and compliance guarding against issues such as corruption, misappropriation of public resources and mismanagement. Fourth, by strengthening the legislative oversight, audit can enable parliamentarians to play a more pro-active role in public sector expenditure. Finally, protecting the role of the AG is imperative; therefore, we draw upon recommendations made by Stapenhurst *et al.* (2005) that the AGs and their staff are given appropriate legal protection to enable them to carry out their duties, such as the guarantee that an AG can only be removed from office on limited grounds that are specified in advance by law.

Although SAIs take centre stage in ensuring governments' accountability, this chapter has demonstrated that there is a shift in focus towards performance accountability. It is imperative the concepts of equity and access are not omitted from the notion of accountability. Future research in this direction will help consolidate the relationship between accountability and equity, access, service appropriateness and client empowerment in the provision of public services.

References

Aucoin, P. (1998) *Auditing for Accountability: The role of the Auditor General*, Ottawa: Institute on Governance.

Aucoin, P. (1995). *The New Public Management: Canada in Comparative Perspective*, Montreal, Canada: Institute for Research on Public Policy.

Auditor-General's Office Victoria (1999) *Report on Ministerial Portfolios*, May, pp. 123–4.

Australian National Audit Office (2014a), 'About US', www.anao.gov.au/About-Us (accessed 25 September 2014).

Australian National Audit Office (2014b), 'Strategic Statement', www.anao.gov.au/About-Us/~/media/Files/General/2014/ANAO_Strategic_Statement.pdf (accessed 25 September 2014).

Balls, H. R. (1963) 'The Public Accounts Committee', *Canadian Journal of Public Administration*, 6(1): 15–34.

Barrett, P. (2001) 'Corporate governance in the public sector context', address to seminar on public services in the new millennium, Australian National Audit Commission, Canberra.

Bishop, H. and Burrowes, A. (2003) 'Fraud in New Zealand Government – Despite Auditor General's Warning', *Journal Of Government Financial Management*, 52: 42–7.

Boston, J., Martin, J., Pallot, J. and Walsh, P. (1996) *Public Management: The New Zealand Model*, Auckland: Oxford University Press.

Bland, F. A. (1946) *Budget Control*, 4th edn, Sydney: Angus and Robertson.

Cadbury Committee (1992) *Report of the Committee on the Financial Aspects of Corporate Governance*, London: Professional) Publishing.

Campbell, W. (1961) 'The Role of the Auditor-General in public administration', *Australian Journal of Public Administration*, 20: 23–32.

Constitutional Arrangements Committee (2005) 'Inquiry to Review New Zealand's Existing Constitutional Arrangements', Report of the Constitutional Arrangements Committee, House of Representatives, Forty-seventh Parliament, August, www.converge.org.nz/pma/cacrep05.pdf (accessed 26 January 2015).

Controller and Auditor-General New Zealand (2014a) 'The role of the Controller and Auditor-General', www.oag.govt.nz/about-us/cag-role (accessed 25 September 2014).

Controller and Auditor-General New Zealand (2014b) *The Auditor-General's Strategic Intentions 2014/15 to 2017/18*, www.oag.govt.nz/2014/strategic-intentions/docs/strategic-intentions.pdf (accessed 25 September 2014).

Controller and Auditor-General New Zealand (2014c) *MPs' guide to the Auditor-General*, www.oag.govt.nz/2012/mps-guide-to-the-auditor-general/docs/mps-guide-to-the-auditor-general.pdf (accessed 25 September 2014).

Day, P. and Klein, R. (1987) *Accountabilities: Five Public Services*, London: Tavistock.

Degeling, P., Anderson, J. and Guthrie, J. (1996) 'Accounting for public accounts committees', *Accounting, Auditing & Accountability Journal*, 9, 30–49.

Fowles, A. J. (1993) 'Changing notions of accountability: a social policy view', *Accounting, Auditing and Accountability Journal*, 6(13): 97–108.

Friedberg, C. and Hazan, R. Y. (2012) 'Legislative Oversight', Comparative Assessments of Parliament (CAP) Note, Center for International Development, Rockefeller College University at Albany, State University of New York.

Galea, J. G. and Miroslaw, S. (2001) *Report on Relations Between Supreme Audit Institutions and Parliamentary Committees*, Malta: National Audit Office.

Gendron, Y., Cooper, D. J. and Townley, B. (2001) 'In the name of accountability: state auditing, independence and new public management', *Accounting, Auditing & Accountability Journal*, 14: 278–310.

Glor, E. D. (2001) 'Has Canada adopted the new public management?', *Public Management Review*, 3: 121–30.

Gray, A, and Jenkins, B. (1993) 'Codes of accountability in the new public sector', *Accounting, Auditing & Accountability Journal*, 6(3): 52–67.

Guthrie, J. (1993) 'Australian public sector accounting: transformations and managerialism', *Accounting Research Journal*, Spring: 15–25.

Harris, T. (2000) *Auditors-General: Policies and Politics*, Canberra: Department of the Senate.

Hodges, R., Wright, M. and Keasey, K. (1996) 'Corporate governance in the public services: concepts and issues', *Public Money & Management*, 16, 7–13.

INTOSAI (2014) ' Comptroller and Auditor General and National Audit Office', www.intosaiitaudit.org/mandate_brief_lists/89 (accessed 22 November 2014).

Jacobs, K., Jones, K. and Smith, D. (2007) 'Public Accounts Committees in Australasia: The state of play', *Australasian Parliamentary Review*, 22: 28–43.

Jones, C. (1987) 'The Origins of the Victorian Parliamentary Public Accounts Committee', MA theses, University of Melbourne.

Jones, K. and Jacobs, K. (2006) 'Governing the government: the paradoxical place of the Public Accounts Committee', *Australasian Parliamentary Review*, 21(1): 63–79.

Jones, K. and Jacobs, K. (2009) Public Accounts Committees, New Public Management, and Institutionalism: A Case Study', *Politics & Policy*, 37: 1023–46.

KPMG (2006) *The Parliamentary Public Accounts Committee: An Australian and New Zealand Perspective*, Canberra: KPMG.

Lees, J. D. (1977) 'Legislatures and Oversight: A Review Article on a Neglected Area of Research'," *Legislative Studies Quarterly*, 2(2): 193–208.

McGee, D. G. (2002) *The Overseers: Public Accounts Committees and Public Spending*, London, Commonwealth Parliamentary Association, with Pluto Press.

Maffio, R. (2002) 'Quis custodiet ipsos custodes? Il controllo parlamentare dell'attivita' di governo in prospettiva comparata', *Quaderni di Scienza Politica*, 9(2): 333–83.

Malloy, J. (2004) 'An auditor's best friend? Standing committees on public accounts', *Canadian Public Administration*, 47, 165–83.

Mezey, M. L. (1979) *Comparative Legislatures*, Durham, NC: Duke University Press.

Mill, J. S. (1861) *Considerations on Representative Government*, London: Parker, Son and Bourn.

Normanton, E. L. (1966) *The Accountability and Audit of Governments*, Manchester: Manchester University Press.

Norton, S. D. and Smith, L. M. (2008) 'Contrast and Foundation of the Public Oversight Roles of the US Government Accountability Office and the UK National Audit Office', *Public Administration Review*, 68, 921–31.

Office of the Auditor General of Canada (2001), 'Section VIII: The Evolving Role of Legislative Audit and the Office of the Auditor General, New Demands create pressure on the office', *2001 February Report of the Auditor General of Canada*, p. 275, www.oag-bvg.gc.ca/internet/English/parl_otp_200102_e_11649.html (accessed 25 September 2014).

Office of the Auditor General of Canada (2013) *Quarterly Financial Report, for the quarter ended 30 September 2013*, www.oag-bvg.gc.ca/internet/docs/acc_rpt_e_38853.pdf (accessed 25 September 2014).

Office of the Auditor General of Canada (2014), *2014 Spring Report, Chapter 4, Expanding the Capacity of Penitentiaries – Correctional Service Canada*, www.oag-bvg.gc.ca/internet/English/parl_oag_201405_e_39319.html (accessed 21 November 2014).

Osborne, D. and Gaebler, T. (1992) *Reinventing Government: How the entrepreneurial spirit is transforming government*, Reading, MA: Addison Wesley.

Osborne, D. (1993) 'Reinventing government', *Public Productivity & Management Review*, 16(4): 349–56.

Pallot, J. (2003) 'A Wider Accountability? The Audit Office and New Zealand's Bureaucratic Revolution', *Critical Perspectives on Accounting*, 14: 133–55.

Pelizzo, R. and Stapenhurst, R. (2006) 'Democracy and Oversight', Research Collection School of Social Sciences, Singapore Management University, http://ink.library.smu.edu.sg/soss_research/130/ (accessed 22 November 2014).

Pennings, P (2000) 'Parliamentary Control of the Executive in 47 Democracies', paper prepared for the workshop on Parliamentary Control of the Executive, ECPR Joint Sessions of Workshops, Copenhagen, 14–19 April.

Pollitt, C. (1986) 'Beyond the managerial model: the case for broadening performance assessment in government and the public services', *Financial Accountability and Management*, 2(3): 155–70.

Pollitt, C. (1994) *Managerialism and the Public Sector*, 2nd edn, Oxford: Blackwell.

Ramkumar, V. and Krafchik W. (2005) 'The Role of Civil Society Organizations in Auditing and Public Finance Management', in United Nations (2007), *Auditing for Social Change: A Strategy for Citizen Engagement in Public Sector Accountability*, Department of Economic and Social Affairs, New York, pp. 21–48.

Schick, A. (2002) 'Can national legislatures regain an effective voice in budget policy', *OECD Journal on Budgeting*, 1(3): 15–42.

Stapenhurst, R. and Titsworth, J. (2001) *Features and Functions of Supreme Audit Institutions*, Washington, DC: World Bank, https://openknowledge.worldbank.org/handle/10986/11363 (accessed 22 November 2014).

Stapenhurst, R., Sahgal, V., Woodley, W. and Pelizzo, R. (2005) *Scrutinizing Public Expenditures: Assessing the Performance of Public Accounts Committees*, Washington DC: World Bank Publications.

Stewart, J. D. (1984) 'The role of information in public accountability', in A. Hopwood and C. Tomkins (eds), *Issues in Public Sector Accounting*, London: Philip Allen, pp. 15–34.

Transparency International (2004) *Anti-Corruption Handbook*, Berlin: Transparency International.

Treasury Board of Canada Secretariat (2004) 'History of Internal Audit in the Federal Government', updated 26 May 2004, www.tbs-sct.gc.ca/ia-vi/abu-ans/history-histoire-eng.asp (accessed 10 February 2015).

Tricker, R. (1993) 'Corporate governance: the new focus of interest', *Corporate Governance*, 1(1): 1–4.

UK National Audit Office (2014a) 'COMPASS contracts for the provision of accommodation for asylum seekers', press release, www.nao.org.uk/press-releases/compass-contracts-provision-accomodation-asylum-seekers (accessed 1 October 2014).

UK National Audit Office (2014b) *COMPASS contracts for the provision of accommodation for asylum seekers*, report by the Comptroller and Auditor General, www.nao.org.uk/wp-content/uploads/2014/01/10287-001-accommodation-for-asylum-seekers-Book.pdf (accessed 22 November 2014).

UK National Audit Office (2014c) *National Audit Office Strategy*, www.nao.org.uk/

search/keyword/Strategic+Intent/type/report/%202010-11/2012-13 (accessed 25 September 2014).

United Nations (2007) *Auditing for Social Change: A Strategy for Citizen Engagement in Public Sector Accountability*, Department of Economic and Social Affairs, New York, pp xi–xv.

Wehner, J. (2003) 'Principles and patterns of financial scrutiny: Public Accounts Committees in the Commonwealth', *Commonwealth and Comparative Politics*, 41: 21–36.

2 Partnering with the Auditor-General's Office to improve the effectiveness of a Public Accounts Committee

An Auditor-General's perspective

Des Pearson AO

Introduction

The traditional, complementary role of the 'Public Accounts Committee' (PAC), which is to follow up on reports of the Auditor-General, is a core and crucially important role of a Public Accounts Committee.

More broadly recognising the Public Accounts Committee as the 'audit committee' of the Parliament, however, means there is a strong common objective for the Auditor-General and the Public Accounts Committee. This provides a strong incentive to work in a complementary manner to 'assist Parliament to hold the government to account for its use of public funds and resources'.[1]

At the same time in Australia the Public Accounts Committee is generally the vehicle the Parliament uses for 'oversight' of the Auditor-General, a situation that has the potential for conflict and which needs to be sensitively and carefully managed.

Nevertheless, the core role for audit of conducting relevant audits and of the committee following up reports of the Auditor-General is central. This also presents the Public Accounts Committee with the means of both 'holding the Executive to account' and also overseeing the effectiveness of the audit function.

When considering the effectiveness of a Public Accounts Committee in the context of 'partnering' with the Auditor-General's Office, the core areas of audit planning, audit reporting and PAC follow-up of reports are the obvious areas of focus. There are, however, other complementary initiatives by the Auditor-General that can also facilitate and assist with improving the effectiveness in operation of the Public Accounts Committee.

It is in this context that the current chapter sets out the experiences and approaches that have been used to address issues and challenges experienced operationally as an Auditor-General and to advance strategic objectives of the Office at particular points of time. Undoubtedly further refinements and variations in approach will be adopted over time as circumstances and priorities change.

Before addressing these focus areas and approaches, however, it is important to first explain my perception of the nature of public sector operations on one hand and the nature of the relationship between the PAC and the Auditor-General as it is experienced on the other hand.

The public sector context

Turning first to the nature and context of public sector operations it should be recognised that, in a democracy, public sector resources are 'extracted' from the community via taxes and charges. These resources are then intended to be applied by the elected government, which is accountable to the Parliament, and in turn to the community at large, via programmes designed to meet the 'common good' and serve 'the public interest'.

Effectively these resources should therefore be considered as akin to being 'held in trust' from the point of collection through to the delivery of the intended outcome, for the benefit of the community as a whole and citizens individually. It is therefore important not only that these resources should be prudently applied. Importantly they need to be seen by the community to have been prudently applied.

This, however, can be a challenging remit as invariably the role of government is to ration limited resources against excess demand, not the easiest context in which to please all the people all the time or to readily demonstrate equitable programme delivery.

Compounding this challenge are today's tighter economic circumstances, where we are beginning to respond to harder times after more than two decades of extraordinary prosperity.[2] There is a growing expectation that the Auditor-General's role will extend beyond assurance. Increasingly there is an expectation that audits will be a catalyst for improving the efficiency and effectiveness of public sector programmes.

The adage that Parliament's auditor is the Auditor-General, NOT the Consultant-General, increasingly warrants consideration. The primary responsibility for the efficient and effective delivery of programme objectives and outcomes rests with the Executive. While the auditor will endeavour to assist, the Executive cannot become reliant on the auditor to relieve itself of accountability for programme delivery.

There remains a real challenge of reliably and demonstrably measuring programme performance in the public sector. Programme outcomes are invariably subjective. Programme objectives are invariably longer term in nature, generally extending well beyond the conventional financial year financial reporting convention.

This is all the more significant 'because results are not measured in dollars alone, and it is difficult to secure agreement on how best to determine the effectiveness of government programmes'.[3] Australia's Westminster-based parliamentary system with 'government' and 'opposition', and the robust politics involved, means that there will always be vigorous public debate and a diversity of views as to the appropriateness of programmes and the extent to which object-ives and outcomes are being achieved.

The audit mandate

Independent and objective opinions and reports by the Auditor-General con-sequently assume a particularly important role in informing this debate and pro-viding a more objective basis for the prioritisation of issues.

In Australia the Auditor-General is therefore typically given the mandate to undertake both a financial audit – the attest audit of the annual financial reports of government entities[4] – and a performance audit, undertaken on an 'as sees fit basis' to

> determine whether an authority is achieving its objectives effectively and doing so economically and efficiently and in compliance with all relevant Acts or whether the operations or activities of the whole or part of the ... public sector ... are being performed effectively, economically and effi-ciently in compliance with all relevant Acts.[5]

In undertaking audits and making recommendations for improvements in the accountability and performance of the public sector, the Auditor-General has no executive authority. The only sanction available is to report 'opinions' directly to Parliament as 'he or she thinks desirable', setting 'out the reasons for opinions expressed' and including 'any recommendations arising out of the audit that he or she thinks fit to make'.[6]

The role of Public Accounts Committees

Australian and New Zealand Public Accounts Committees have a mandate to review public accounts and Auditor-General reports and the power to investi-gate any items or matters in connection with those accounts or reports.[7] This is a broad mandate and open to significant variation in interpretation and application. A range of factors can influence this. Contextually they range from the size of the committee, resources available to the committee and the capability and willingness of the Auditor-General's Office to engage and support.

Elements of a co-operative and supportive relationship

A range of approaches to the relationship generally emerge. These tend to be rel-atively informal and differ from jurisdiction to jurisdiction.

One structured approach, although now somewhat dated, is useful in distilling the elements of a sound relationship.

In Western Australia the 'commonality that has developed'[8] between' the respective objectives of the Auditor-General and the Public Accounts Committee

was recognised and a Statement of Understanding was developed which identified four major components:[9]

1   Support for the true independence of the Auditor-General;
2   Sharing of information and referral of matters that will assist in both parties
    meeting their objectives;
3   Follow-up of Auditor-General's Reports; and
4   Each party respecting the independent rights and obligations of the other.

In practice this provided a sound basis for a particularly constructive, very supportive and mutually respectful relationship to enhance the accountability mechanisms of the Parliament, ensuring that public moneys have been spent lawfully,
effectively and efficiently.

Support for the independence of the Auditor-General

Independence is a term commonly used in relation to audit and the role of the
Auditor-General. It is nevertheless a multi-faceted concept both in theory and in
application. A useful reference is the declaration by the International Organisation of Supreme Audit Institutions (INTOSAI) which sets out eight core independence principles considered essential for effective public sector auditing:[10]

1   An effective statutory legal framework.
2   Independence and security of tenure for the head of the audit institution.
3   Full discretion to exercise a broad audit mandate.
4   Unrestricted access to information.
5   A right and obligation to report on audit work.
6   Freedom to decide the content and timing of audit reports and to publish
    them.
7   Appropriate mechanisms to follow up on audit recommendations.
8   Financial, managerial and administrative autonomy and availability of
    appropriate resources.

Against these principles establishing the independence of the Auditor-General is
a prerequisite for an effective audit function. Fortunately in Australia these principles are generally well respected.

   In practice, however, the independence of the Auditor-General has also been
addressed in recent times by recognising the Auditor-General as an 'Independent
Officer of the Parliament ... having complete discretion in the performance or
exercise of his or her functions or powers and, in particular, is not subject to direction from anyone in relation to –

•   whether or not a particular audit is to be conducted;
•   the way in which a particular audit is to be conducted;
•   the priority to be given to any particular matter.'[11]

Appointment of Auditor-General

Generally in Australia the Public Accounts Committee is now involved in the appointment of the Auditor-General, either directly, as in Victoria where the Auditor-General is to be appointed by the Governor in Council on the recommendation of the Parliamentary Committee,[12] or as in other jurisdictions where the appointment is undertaken by the Executive; however, it is subject to consultation, and in some cases veto by the Public Accounts Committee.[13]

Annual plan

The better practice of the Auditor-General tabling an annual plan of audits for the ensuing year is being progressively recognised and practised across Australia, with the National, Victorian and Queensland Auditors-General now required to table an annual plan. The Victorian situation statutorily requires[14] that the plan be prepared in consultation with the Public Accounts and Estimates Committee.

This process better assures that the proposed audits address the priorities of the Parliament and leads to a better mutual understanding between the Auditor-General and the Public Accounts Committee as to the accountability and performance issues and priorities facing the sector.

In Victoria the approach taken in recent years has been to adopt a three-staged approach over a period of around six months leading up to the tabling of the Annual Plan in the Parliament.

This built on the Auditor-General's Office's ongoing environmental scanning undertaken both as part of individual audits and via engagement with the Parliament, the community via peak and other representative bodies and the entities subject to audit.

The first significant event was a preliminary briefing of the Public Accounts and Estimates Committee. This briefing essentially provided a high-level acquittal of the previous year's Annual Plan covering both financial statement and performance audits. This provided the Office's initial thinking in relation to the challenges and risks facing the sector and the proposed audits under consideration. This had the advantage of opening a dialogue between the Committee and the Office and providing a level of assurance that respective views are reasonably aligned or, alternatively, identification of areas of difference of view for further consideration.

Following this briefing the Office proceeded over a period of around three months to refine its thinking and produced a preliminary draft of the Annual Plan for a more structured briefing of the Committee. At this point the Office had refined its thinking and was principally seeking assurance from the Committee that it had understood the views previously provided by the Committee and ascertained that there were not further issues which needed to be considered.

Over approximately another month the preliminary draft Annual Plan was developed into a consultation draft which was then referred formally to the Committee for consideration and advice of any comment on the plan.[15]

The Act requires the Auditor-General to indicate in the Annual Plan the nature of any changes suggested by the Committee that have not been adopted. In practice, however, comments offered are normally supportive. Nevertheless an acquittal response is included in the Annual Plan tabled in the Parliament each year.

Four-year rolling plan

A further initiative adopted was to develop the Annual Plan into a four-year rolling plan. This went beyond the one-year legislative requirement, but served both strategic and operational purposes. It provided more comprehensive information to the Parliament regarding audit priorities and also served to facilitate earlier engagement with audit clients.

Recognising that performance audits generally involve an elapsed time approaching 12 months and represent a significant investment of resources, taking a more structured and holistic approach to selecting audit topics was considered to be warranted. This enabled a more strategic approach and improved focus in the extensive consultation process undertaken in developing each year's annual plan.

For the 2007–8 Annual Plan, a decision was taken to adopt a four-year outlook. The ensuing year plus three 'out years' proposed audit programme mirrors the approach to budgeting in Australia with each annual budget also including three years' forward estimates in addition to the actual budget year estimates.

In the audit context this provides significant forewarning to agencies of audits proposed and provides those entities with the opportunity to prepare for audits. Also, by publishing planned audits over such a period a more structured transparent and strategic approach was demonstrated.

Having this 'four-year rolling plan' also enabled the development of a more focused dialogue with audit clients where audits proposed in the immediate future were almost certain to be undertaken, although the scope would still be informed by agency advice and evidence of initiatives taken. Audits proposed for the out years were, however, more likely to be varied in scope or actually substituted, depending on agency initiatives or changes in broader contexts.

This 'rolling programme' also provided added comfort for the Auditor-General regarding the relevance and appropriateness of the proposed audits, recognising that selection of audit topics is subjective and that the number of audits possible given available resources will always be restricted. The absence of challenges to the merits of proposed audits provides negative assurance at least that the planned audit topics are the more relevant and are consistent with a prioritised and risk-based approach to selecting audit topics. Alternatively, challenges to the selection of certain topics provides a more objective basis for review of the topic's selection.

Further, by aligning the Audit Plan with the elected government of the day's stated strategic objectives, as outlined in the Governor's address at the opening of each new session of Parliament, a more objective and analytical basis for selecting audit topics was possible.

This initiative provided greater assurance of the relevance and appropriateness of the planned audits, particularly in the context of applying limited audit resources to areas promising the greatest audit contribution, i.e. by providing assurance as to the integrity of approach to programme delivery, providing assurance regarding the extent to which programme objectives are being met and drawing to attention areas warranting remedial action.

Reporting approach

Core to the auditor's role is reporting. As the approach to reporting is for the Auditor-General to determine there is a valuable opportunity to represent in the best light the audit work undertaken and to leverage this work to assist the Public Accounts Committee and the Parliament in holding the Executive to account.

Over time a range of initiatives were taken to make reports more user-friendly and relevant. A well-received initiative that has been progressively adopted across Australia has been to use plain English while at the same time aiming to report as concisely as possible. This has seen a trend to shorter and more focused reports to Parliament.

In the case of Victoria a general objective for performance audit reports adopted was to try to report within 25 to 30 pages. Clearly some topics require a longer report; however, on review it is notable how effective this objective has been in reducing the 'bulk' of reports without compromising analysis and the expression of conclusions and recommendations.

Another related initiative was to structure reports so they are inviting rather than confronting to read, as well as to adopt a facilitative structure to assist the busy, time-poor parliamentarians. In addition to the use of plain English, formatting reports to provide a clear three-to-five-page 'audit summary' at the front of the report, followed by an 'at a glance' summary page for each chapter to distil the Background, Findings and Recommendations was a very favourably received initiative.

A further 'user-friendly' reporting initiative in the context of reporting on the annual financial attest audit of entities was the adoption of reporting by sector. This replaced the traditional reporting on financial statement audits, primarily based on balance date.

By breaking the content out into a number of discrete sector-based reports, such as portfolio departments and related entities, local government entities, water entities, hospitals and health services entities and education entities, it was possible to report more contextually to the particular circumstances of the sector.

This approach was well received because, although now far more voluminous, it has provided a more relevant context and enabled the Auditor-General to also inform Parliament of sector-wide issues. Each sector report now provides a comprehensive overview of the accountability and financial performance of the respective sectors as well as of the individual entities.

Typically these sector-based reports currently comprise 50 to 100 pages each and now cover issues such as financial sustainability of entities and the effectiveness of internal controls in operation. This has led to the accrual accounting information being used as a management tool, and action to better manage balance sheets and sector-wide approaches to enhancing internal controls.

This has been a notable catalyst for improvement in the accountability and performance of the public sector. For example, the local government sector has addressed the financial sustainability issues that were reported. Also these sector-based reports tend to be used as a form of league table, which in turn brings about continuous improvement initiatives.

In addition this approach has improved the operational effectiveness of the Auditor-General's Office itself. Greater clarity regarding operational management responsibility within the Office was achieved. Staff are now more focused on their respective sector and there is a notable level of cross-fertilisation of ideas and initiatives, both in the way audits are undertaken and in the way audit results are reported.

Briefing on audit reports

A well-received initiative that has been acknowledged as improving the effectiveness of Public Accounts Committees is the provision of a briefing to parliamentarians on the day of tabling. Members of the Public Accounts Committee have been regular attendees at these briefings.

This involved providing a succinct overview of each report via an overview presentation to parliamentarians. Presentations were generally of 15 to 20 minutes' duration with the opportunity for discussion to assist parliamentarians to quickly get across the matters of significance being raised in the report. In this way parliamentarians are better able to recognise reports they need to study more fully from those of which a general overview is sufficient.

These briefings assist members of the Public Accounts Committee as they provide an early indication of reports warranting PAC attention. They also provide a convenient opportunity for early discussion of matters related to the report in question as well as providing members with the opportunity to raise broader issues that otherwise would likely not be discussed in a timely fashion, if at all.

Follow-up of audit reports

Public Accounts Committee follow up and Inquiries are central to holding accountable officers and authorities to account.

Although audit reports are taken seriously and the overwhelming majority of recommendations are accepted, in practice competing priorities and emerging issues can lead to delays in remedial action. Public Accounts Committee follow-up of audit reports is therefore an important contributor to encouraging timely action and to providing assurance regarding the effectiveness of the implementation of audit recommendations.

While an Auditor-General can follow up on earlier reports to Parliament, Public Accounts Committee follow-up is considered far preferable. The Committee brings an informed scrutiny to the matters being raised. Committee feedback also provides useful intelligence to the Auditor-General as to the nature of the Committee's interest and concerns. This can usefully inform future audit focus.

Audit office briefing of the Public Accounts Committee can assist with expediting the identification of the reports, and elements within them, most warranting follow-up by correspondence or Inquiry. Because audit staff are attuned to the workings of the public sector and interact with entities on a regular basis they are generally aware of the rate of progress with responses to audit recommendations and other developments. Providing the Public Accounts Committee with insights of this nature generally in informal meetings and discussions, as well as via submissions in response to Committee invitations, provides Committees with objective information and advice to consider in selecting audit reports for further Committee attention. Audit office advice can also assist the Committee in deciding which reports to follow up by correspondence and which to progress to formal Inquiry.

Audit staff can assist with PAC consideration of entity responses to Committee correspondence. Similarly where Committee undertakes an Inquiry there can be opportunity for Audit staff to assist the Committee Inquiry. In my experience this has been done with mutual benefits both with the Public Accounts Committee and with other Committees of the Parliament. There are benefits to the Committee from using audit expertise. There are also professional development benefits to audit staff from working with Committees and better understanding how they work.

Case study

The following case study provides an overview illustration of the process and the benefits of an Inquiry into issues raised in an audit report. Of particular note is the resolution of an issue of contention between the views of the auditor and the programme manager.

Auditor-General's Report on Preparedness to Respond to Terrorism Incidents: Essential Services and Critical Infrastructure[16]

The Auditor-General's Report was tabled in January 2009. In 2011 the Committee sought information from the subject departments, Premier and Cabinet, Justice, including Victoria Police, and the Office of the Emergency Services Commissioner as well as additional comments from the Auditor-General.

The Committee expressed in its report disappointment with the position taken by the Department of Premier and Cabinet in regard to its critical infrastructure protection oversight and governance responsibilities.

The Committee noted the Auditor-General's concerns about 'oversight deficit' by agencies responsible for policy development but not directly involved with the implementation of policy.

The Committee recorded that the Department of Premier and Cabinet viewed their role in managing the protection of critical infrastructure as strictly one of strategic leadership on policy and legislative advice, while responsibility and accountability for the effectiveness of the arrangements is devolved to relevant Ministers and their departments, with the Department's involvement in monitoring, and oversight is largely based on its chairing of the Security and Continuity Network-Coordination Group and the Central Government Response Committee.

The Inquiry took evidence from the Department of Premier and Cabinet, Department of Justice, Victoria Police, the Office of the Emergency Services Commissioner and the Victorian Auditor-General's Office.

In this respect the Committee recommended that,

> as a matter of good governance and due and proper accountability and assurance, the Department of Premier and Cabinet take a greater lead in providing guidance and monitoring compliance as part of their strategic responsibilities for the oversight of critical infrastructure protection arrangements in Victoria.

The Committee went on to also recommend:

> the critical infrastructure protection management structure ... should clearly show the Department of Premier and Cabinet as the agency ultimately responsible for overseeing management arrangements across the whole of government ... and their responsibility to the Premier as the 'Minister' accountable to the Parliament for these arrangements.

This case study provides an overview of the typical mutually beneficial effect of the auditor and the PAC working in a complementary fashion with the auditor drawing to notice a matter of significance and the PAC reviewing the facts and circumstances and expressing further views and recommendations. Without the Committee follow-up it is doubtful the Executive response would have been as timely, nor that the difference of view would have been addressed so effectively.

Conclusion

There is an inherent alliance in the respective roles of Auditors-General and Public Accounts Committees. As summarised by Vincent Smith, Chairperson of the African Association of Public Accounts Committees in the foreword to a best practice handbook, 'An environment where accountability is an integral way of life, contributes to raising the levels of confidence that all society, the electorate, organised labour, business and donors, has in our system of democracy'.[17]

The better the alliance between the Auditor-General and the Public Accounts Committee the more it serves to optimise the Parliament's ability to hold to account the government of the day. Further, the more cohesive the actions of the auditor and the committee, the more effective the outcome. Accordingly there is much to be gained from developing and maintaining a mutually respectful and trusting relationship.

The Auditor-General is in a particularly privileged position to contribute to facilitating and assist with improving the effectiveness of the Public Accounts Committee. Committees, as with effectively all areas of the public sector, will always be limited by the resources available to them. Aligning with the Auditor-General is an obvious and mutually advantageous opportunity to leverage limited resources for overall advantage. The more aligned the activities the more likely the objective of achieving improved levels of accountability and performance in the public sector will be achieved.

A range of initiatives that contributed to building on and enhancing the Auditor-General/Public Accounts Committee relationship have been explored in this chapter. They are not the only ones available, rather they represent the more notable initiatives that have in my experience served to improve the relationship between the Public Accounts Committee and the Auditor-General and enable more cost-effective achievement of their respective goals.

More importantly, these initiatives show that there are real benefits in the Auditor-General taking legislative and other formal requirements as minimum requirements and building on them with a focus on the needs and circumstance of the Parliament and the community. The Public Accounts Committee is a core stakeholder within the Parliament, and serving the interests and needs of that Committee was always a primary focus during my tenure as Auditor-General.

Notes

1 The Parliamentary Public Accounts Committee: an Australian and New Zealand Perspective, KPMG, November 2006, VIC 10522RAS, P 1.
2 Ross Garnaut, *Dog Days: Australia after the Boom*, Collingwood: Redback, 2013, p. 2.
3 *Monitoring and Reporting Financial and Non-financial Performance of Australian Government Organisations*, Issues Paper Series No. 5, February 2008, Australian National Audit Office/CPA Australia, University of Canberra Corporate Governance ARC Project, p. 1.
4 Audit Act 1994, Parliament of Victoria, section 8.
5 Ibid., section 15.
6 Ibid., section 16.
7 The Parliamentary Public Accounts Committee: an Australian and New Zealand Perspective, op. cit., p. 5.
8 *Report on Statement of Understanding Between The Auditor-General and the Public Accounts and Expenditure Review Committee*, Report No 32, 24 October 1996, Legislative Assembly, Western Australia.
9 Ibid., p. 1.
10 *ISSAI 10 – The Mexico Declaration on SAI Independence*, www.intosai.org/issai-executive-summaries/view/article/issai-10-the-mexico-declaration-on-sai-independence-eger.html (accessed 8 February 2014).
11 Constitution Act 1975, Parliament of Victoria, section 94B.
12 Ibid., section 94A.

13 Public Finance and Audit Act 1983, Parliament of New South Wales, sections 57A and 28A.
14 Audit Act 1994, Parliament of Victoria, section 7A.
15 Ibid.
16 Public Accounts and Estimates Committee, *Review of the Auditor-General's Report on Preparedness to Respond to Terrorism Incidents: Essential Services and Critical Infrastructure*, December 2011, 105th Report to Parliament, Parliament of Victoria.
17 Vincent Smith, *Effective Public Accounts Committees: A best practice handbook for Public Accounts Committees in South Africa*, Cape Town: APAC, 2003, Foreword.

3 Government accountability in Sri Lanka

The roles of Parliamentary Oversight Committees and the Auditor-General's Office

Zahirul Hoque and
Ethugalage Anura Gotabaya Ananda

Introduction

Like many developing countries in the past two decades, significant public sector reforms have taken place in Sri Lanka. In the late 1980s, the Sri Lankan government started privatising public entities and decentralising public administration (Kelegama, 1998; Balasooriya *et al.*, 2008; Samaratunga and Bennington, 2002). A range of parliamentary committees provides the control framework required to carry out the oversight functions of the government and the public sector. There are four types of committees: Select Committees, Consultative Committees, Standing Committees and Committees for Special Purposes. In view of the large number of statutory corporations and other government bodies engaged in profit-making activities, another body called the Committee on Public Enterprises (COPE) was established on 21 June 1979 to control public finance and review the performance of public corporations and other semi-government bodies. It is important to note that the COPE is unique to Sri Lanka; in other Commonwealth countries only the Public Accounts Committee (PAC) examines both government institutions and public enterprises. The Committee on Public Accounts (COPA) and the COPE come under the Committee for Special Purposes. These committees are required to report to the Parliament on their activities. At the commencement of every session of Parliament, a Committee of Selection is appointed to nominate members to serve on various committees, including the COPA and the COPE. On average, each Member of Parliament (MP) is a member of about five parliamentary committees. The committees also reflect the political party composition in the House, and each committee has members from each party represented in Parliament.

The role of the PACs in monitoring the performance and accountability of government entities is crucial for the country's sustainability and economic growth. Several empirical studies have demonstrated that organisations tend to incorporate external constituents' perceptions of appropriate accountability systems into their performance measurement systems to acquire legitimacy (Modell, 2001). An alternative view is that organisations also implement a particular accountability system as part of their quest for internal economic efficiency (Hood, 1995). While considerable research depicts both sets of behaviour predominantly in developed nations, the literature has so far remained largely silent on this issue in developing nations. Our research sought to address this apparent gap by empirically examining the rationales of current PAC practices in Sri Lanka.

Many elements of public sector organisations, such as organisation structure, management policies and procedures and accounting, exist as a result of widespread societal and institutional expectations around what constitutes acceptable practices and behaviours (DiMaggio and Powell, 1983; Meyer and Rowan, 1977). A closer examination in the initial stages of our research showed that major functions of the PAC might lie, in part, elsewhere in the socio-political arena.

Institutional theorists posit that rationalised ideas or modes of organising are socially constructed and confer legitimacy to organisations that make steps towards adopting them, leading to various forms of isomorphism within an organisational field (DiMaggio and Powell, 1983; Meyer and Rowan, 1977). Institutional theory is based on the belief that organisational structures and management processes are shaped by their social environment, and, vice versa, that environments shape organisations. According to this theory, for the PAC to function effectively and achieve external legitimacy, it needs to conform to political norms of acceptable behaviour. Drawing on the notion of mimic isomorphism (DiMaggio and Powell, 1983), uncertainty about organisational goals and social and political expectations often leads to organisations imitating best practices within their given institutional field. In such a context, the Sri Lankan government might tend to copy models of PACs from other countries that are considered successful in promoting good governance and financial oversight.

While considerable research depicts both sets of behaviour outlined above predominantly in developed nations, the literature has so far remained largely ignorant on this issue in developing nations. It is recognised in the literature that developing nations differ in their socio-cultural and political settings from their counterpart developed countries. Seen in such a context, we examine whether the current PAC systems in Sri Lanka meet internal and external expectations of relevant stakeholders using the two related notions of rationality: economic rationality and institutional rationality.

The remainder of this chapter is structured in the following manner. The next section outlines the research method used for this study. The following section presents and discusses the study's findings. Finally, we provide a detailed discussion of the practical implications of the study as well as directions for future research.

Research method

This study used several sources of data collection, namely government archival records, internal organisational documents, and semi-structured face-to-face interviews with 30 key personnel. Table 3.1 presents the profile of interviewees.

Table 3.1 Group of interviewees

Group	Category	Number of interviewees	Details
1	Parliamentarians- (COPA/COPE members)	5	3 Cabinet Ministers
		9	1 Non-Cabinet Minister
	Ruling Opposition		1 Deputy Minister
			4 Main Opposition
			4 Other Parties
			1 Independent
2	Secretaries to the Ministries	2	Cabinet Ministries
3	Head of the Departments	3	'A' Grade Departments
4	Deputy Heads of the Departments	4	1 Dept. State Accounts
			2 AG's Dept
			1 AG's Dept (Ex-Officer)
5	Government Consultants	1	Ministry of Finance
6	Parliamentary Officers	1	Deputy Director
7	Parliamentary Consultants	2	1 Ex-Govt Officer
			1 Senior Govt Officer
8	Chairmen of the Corporations	3	1 'A' Grade Corporation
			2 Ex-Chairmen
	Total	30	

Interviewees were asked to talk about their practical knowledge and experiences. Although interviews were broadly non-directive, the interviewer wanted to ensure he gathered interviewees' views about PAC and government accountability related issues. Therefore, when interviewees failed to address particular issues, to elicit further information, the interviewer posed questions that had not originally been identified at the onset, but arose from the interview. Interviews were recorded and transcribed verbatim by the principal researcher. Field study notes were also recorded in notebooks. Interviews conducted in Sinhala (the official language) were translated into English. Interviews were conducted in an ethical manner. Interviewees were assured beforehand that their interview would be taped for research purposes only. All interviewees were treated with equal importance and were assured that their responses would be treaty with great confidentiality.

Data from interview transcripts were systematically arranged, grouped and coded around major themes to determine patterns or common elements of responses and evidence. More specifically, data were thematically grouped by colour coding the appropriate sections of each transcript, while documentary evidence was arranged by cutting and pasting the relevant parts of transcripts into separate documents. Coding was used to make visible patterns or sequences of details, issues or perceptions and to highlight consistencies or inconsistencies within the data (Miles and Huberman, 1994). In the next sections, we present the findings.

Committee on Public Accounts (COPA)

The COPA was established in response to a motion by a Legislative Councillor on 26 October 1921:

> Since the council has no means of ascertaining that the grants of the Council for each financial year, including supplementary grants have been applied to the objects with the Legislative Council prescribed and also in view of the fact that any balances that have been left unexpended at the year are not made available to meet the following year's expenditure. I move that 'a Standing Committee of Public Accounts' be appointed for the ensuring financial year, viz. 1921–1922.
>
> (Ceylon Sessional Papers, 1924)

The Committee of Public Accounts was appointed on 5 September 1923 and its first meeting was held on 17 October 1923. During their first meeting, members present dealt with the Colonial Auditor's report for the year 1921/22 (Ceylon Sessional Papers, 1924; Soysa, 1966). The COPA summoned and interrogated several witnesses, including the Colonial Auditor. In order to make their interrogation effective, the Colonial Auditor was requested to group his observations under separate headings in respect of various votes so that they could pay due attention to them. This showed that at the initial phase certain lines of investigation were established (Warnapala, 2004).

Certain development of the COPA took place between 1931 and 1946 under the Donughmore Constitution (Warnapala, 2004; Soysa, 1966). It was during this period that the issue of the COPA came to be raised as a necessity for the proper functioning of the State Council. The traditional method of preparing minutes on the basis of the observations made by the COPA was continued, and the relevant matters referred to the Executive Committee, which discussed and suggested corrective action (Warnapala, 2004). The establishment of a fully fledged parliamentary system of government under the Soulbury Constitution in 1947 brought into existence a PAC as a vital part of parliamentary control of finance.

Under Standing Order 125 of the Parliament, the COPA examines the appropriation of the sums granted by the Parliament to meet the public expenditure and such other accounts laid before the Parliament along with the report of the Auditor-General (AG). The AG's reports are referred to the COPA for examination as it is the only channel through which Parliament can directly examine the government's institutions about their management of public funds. The committee reports on the accounts examined, the finances, financial procedures and the performance and management of all government ministries, departments and local authorities (Wijesekera, 2002). The committee's examination of the accounts usually involves calling before it various officials of the departments questioned in regard to specific items contained in the AG's report. Figure 3.1 diagrammatically demonstrates the roles of the COPA and the COPE.

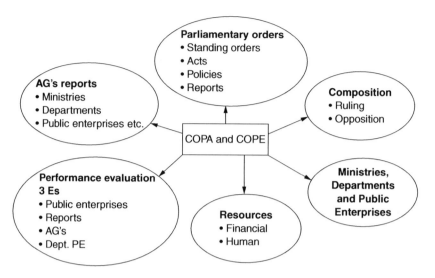

Figure 3.1 Roles of the COPA and the COPE.

Notes:
AG = Auditor-General; COPA = Committee on Public Accounts; COPE = Committee on Public Enterprises; PE = Public Enterprises; Dept = Departments.

The COPA originally consisted of four members (Ceylon Sessional Papers 4, 1924). In 1937 its membership increased to seven, then to ten members in 1979, to 12 in 1993, and in 2001 this number was increased to 15, to 19 in 2004, and finally to 31 members in 2006. The present committee includes a chairperson, needs a quorum of four members to meet and is composed of representatives from all parties, with senior MPs forming a majority from the government party. At the time of this study, nearly all government party members were Cabinet/ Non-Cabinet or Deputy Ministers. Though the COPA consists of members from the government and the opposition, it has to function entirely on a non-partisan basis. A member of the committee is formally appointed as chair (Warnapala, 2004; Wijesekera, 2002).

Initially, an opposition member was appointed as chairperson of the COPA, a legacy inherited from the House of Commons. This tradition was maintained for three decades and the appointment of a government party member, Deputy Minister or Minister as chairperson began post-1977. This tradition changed in 2001 when a member of the opposition was appointed as the Chairperson of COPA. In 2008, a member of the government benches, who was also a Cabinet Minister, was appointed as chair.

Matters assessed by the COPA generally relate to the propriety, efficiency and economy of the ministries and the government departments. Monies over-spent by each ministry and department must be examined and reported to Parliament. As a result the COPA is a powerful instrument for the exposure of waste, inefficiency and all forms of financial maladministration (Kandasamy, 2003; Warnapala, 2004; Wijesuriya, 1979; AG's Department of Sri Lanka, 1980).

The COPA examination process begins by following up on actions taken in response to previous COPA recommendations and seeking clarifications on questions raised by the AG or his/her representative. The representatives from the Department of Public Finance or Department of State Accounts also attend these meetings to assist the COPA. At the request of the chair, COPA members or the AG raise questions. It is the responsibility of the Chief Accounting Officer (CAO) to give satisfactory responses in keeping with the written explanations already submitted. The CAO has to give reasons for any deficiencies mentioned in audit reports and answer any questions raised.

The COPA may appoint sub-committees that have the power to summon any person, to question and examine any files and records as well as to access stores and properties. Failure to attend COPA meetings is treated as Contempt of Parliament (Kandasamy, 2003; Wijesuriya, 1979). Hearings of the COPA are not open to the public or the media. Proceedings of the COPA are recorded on tape as well as with typed shorthand notes and then archived.

The COPA is required to submit reports that include recommendations to Parliament on the accounts examined, finances, financial procedures, performance and management generally of any department, local authority, project and statutory funds. In general, the COPA's reports are not discussed in the House. However, the recommendations in the report need to be considered as directions from the House to be followed by the relevant institutions in the future. The final step in the financial control cycle consists of the periodic reports made to the parliament by the COPA (Kandasamy, 2003; AG's Department of Sri Lanka, 1980; Wijesekera, 2002). Once the COPA's reports have been submitted, the Treasury is expected to follow up and report back to the Parliament on actions taken in response to the COPA's recommendations.

Committee on Public Enterprises (COPE)

The establishment of the COPE represented another landmark in the sphere of parliamentary control of public finance in public corporations and other semi-government bodies, in which the government has a financial stake. Monies needed for these public enterprises are provided from the government's consolidated fund. The duty of the COPE is to examine the accounts, the budgets, annual estimates, financial procedures, the performance and management of public corporations and of any business or other undertaking vested by the government under any written law in these entities, along with the reports of the AG, and report back to Parliament (Parliament of Sri Lanka, 2007; Wijesekera, 2002).

The COPE was established in 1979. At the time, it consisted of ten members nominated by the Committee of Selection. In 2010, the COPE was composed of 31 members, including a chairperson. Formerly, the chair was appointed through internal elections. Often, respective parties would unofficially designate the member of the COPE whom they thought should be appointed. From the COPE's inception, a government party member, Deputy Minister or Minister was appointed chair.

Members of the COPE are required to examine the accounts of public enterprises along with the report of the AG laid before the Parliament. Under the terms of Article 154(6) of the Constitution, the AG's reports on the accounts of each public enterprise are to be presented to Parliament and published as a part of the *Parliamentary Series*.

According to these current procedures, the Chair of the COPE performs the major role of examination. However, the AG and representatives of the Treasury assist him/her in their work. Under instruction from the chair, the COPE's Secretary issues letters summoning public entities' CAO, chair, board of directors, general manager and/or any other senior management member and official of the Treasury to appear before them at a specified date and time in the COPE's room in Parliament to review the evidence. As in the case of the COPA, failure to appear before the COPE without a valid excuse is treated as Contempt of Parliament.

The examination begins by following up on the actions recommended during previous COPE meetings. The chair and other members of the COPE also raise matters of public interest. The CAO, the chair, board of directors and other officials of the public enterprises are required to provide satisfactory responses. The AG's report is then referred to the chair or general manager and other officials of the public enterprises and examined in detail. Public enterprises are generally requested to submit written explanations about their current position on each matter under review, addressing each of the paragraphs contained in the AG's reports, along with the remedial actions they are planning to take. The COPE is required to submit a report to the Parliament based on the accounts examined, the budgets, finances, financial procedures, performance, and management in general, and on other matters, as needed (Kandasamy, 2003; AG's Department of Sri Lanka, 1980; Wijesekera, 2002).

When deemed necessary, the COPE may establish sub-committees composed of its own members, with the power to summon any person and examine any paper, book or records and to access stores and properties (Kandasamy, 2003; AG's Department of Sri Lanka, 1980; Wijesekera, 2002). The recording and the reporting process of the COPE is the same as the COPA's (AG's Department of Sri Lanka, 1980; Wijesekera, 2002).

Mandate of the COPA and COPE

Under the terms of Article 154(1) of the Sri Lankan Constitution, the AG has the power to audit the accounts of government departments, local authorities and public corporations and businesses or other government-related undertakings. Further, the Constitution empowers the AG to carry out any other duties supported by the laws of Parliament. However, 98 state-owned companies do not come under the mandate of the AG and the purview of the COPE.

Powers given to the Parliament and its committees should enable them to exercise full oversight functions over such companies. The need for the COPE to review and the AG to audit these companies was mentioned by almost all interviewees as the following quotes illustrate:

> As these public institutions handle public funds, they need to be audited by the Auditor-General. Although the Auditor-General is not expected to audit state-owned companies established under the Companies Act, according to the Article 154(3) of the Constitution, the Parliament has power to assign any duties to the Auditor-General. Therefore, the opportunity is there.
>
> (Interviewee 25, a senior ex-public officer)

> It is my opinion that these state companies should be under COPE examination and be brought under parliamentary control.
>
> (Interviewee 3, a ruling party member)

> I have a general opinion that all institutions owned by the government should be audited by the AG. It is very important when we consider public finance.
>
> (Interviewee 9, an opposition party member)

Standing Orders 125 and 126 of the Parliament and the directions issued by the Speaker under the Standing Orders regulate the mandate and the scope, composition, functions, terms of office, quorum and procedures in conducting examinations by the COPA and the COPE. These Standing Orders took effect on 1 May 1979. Under Standing Order 126, the COPE's functions are to examine the accounts of public corporations and of any businesses or other undertakings vested under any written law along with the report of the AG. However, after establishment of the state-owned companies in 1987, no amendments were made to this Standing Order to allow the COPE to examine state-owned companies. Failure to bring those institutions under the purview of the COPE has resulted in an erosion of public accountability, as most interviewees remarked.

The Finance Act No. 38 of 1971 of the Parliament of Ceylon outlines the monitoring process of the affairs of public corporations. Following a privatisation drive in the country, many public corporations reformed into state-owned companies in the mid-1980s. Although the functions and responsibilities of state-owned companies were revised in order to cater for the needs of the private sector, the Finance Act (1971) was not amended to enable the AG to audit these companies. A former Director General of the Treasury (Interviewee 3) commented that:

> Although attempts have been made to amend the Finance Act No. 38 of 1971, which deals with control of public corporations, this has not been successful.

The majority of interviewees commented that it is necessary to make constitutional and other statutory arrangements to provide a mandate to the AG and amend Standing Orders to provide power to the COPA and the COPE to suit the current situation.

At present, the chairs of both the COPA the COPE are members of the government benches as well as Cabinet Ministers. The majority of interviewees stated that knowledge, experience, capability and honesty are the most important factors, above party loyalty, that need to be considered when appointing a chairperson. Interviewee 3, a ruling party member of the committee, offered this interpretation:

> My position is … it depends on the person. It is not a matter whether the person is coming from the ruling or the opposition party. But the chairperson should be a knowledgeable person and have some kind of background of accounting, project planning and project management etc.

Supporting the above comment, Interviewee 13, an opposition party committee member, remarked:

> If we separate party politics from the committee, the Chairmanship can be … any member. If the person thinks that he is responsible to the Parliament it is not a problem although he is member of the ruling party.

A considerable number of interviewees disagreed with appointing a chairperson from the governing party and they strongly believed that the chair should be appointed from the opposition party. Half of these interviewees were opposition party members. They argued that a chairperson from the ruling party cannot be impartial. However, some of the government officers also shared similar views. The quote from Interviewee 8, a senior government officer, highlights this point:

> I totally disagree with the present system prevailing in Sri Lanka, having a ruling party member chairing the COPE. We know in the past we too had an opposition party member heading the COPA. I certainly feel that it is better to have an independent opposition party member heading the COPA.

Interviewees referred to Australia as an example where committees are usually led by ministers and agreed that the appointment of the chairperson should be based on merit.

The COPE and the COPA have 31 committee members, the majority of which are government members. This is a significant number compared with other Commonwealth countries. Some of the interviewees commented that the reason for increasing the number of members on committees was to maintain a quorum. The following comments by Interviewee 25 illustrates this point:

> Although the number was increased to 31 to maintain a quorum we still find the minimum number is a problem…. Increasing the number is not the solution to maintain the required minimum. There are some other facts which

need to be addressed. The government party committee members are not attending these committees unless their presence is highly needed by the government. That means … in some cases they were instructed to come and participate [in] the meetings to voice down the opposition.

Currently there are too many parliamentary committees. The COPA and the COPE suffer from poor attendance and struggle to maintain a quorum to carry out their duties. Out of 31 members, there are often only ten members attending committee meetings. That is because members are also often members of between ten and 17 other committees. Five people are members of both the COPA and the COPE. Meetings are often postponed due to lack of a quorum. Therefore, it has been suggested by most interviewees that committee members should be selected based on their interests and expertise rather than on their position within the government or political parties. It would appear that the increase in Cabinet size after the 2000 parliamentary elections was politically driven by the new coalition government.

When the oversight committees of the legislation are comprised of the majority of the executive members of government (ministers), there is a risk that the executive arm might take over the legislative oversight functions. This is inappropriate because this often results in ministers overseeing their own work, but also because, since Cabinet Ministers are allowed to serve on the COPA and the COPE, there is a risk they might try to slow down or mislead the committees' investigations to protect the Cabinet in which they also serve. Interviewee 1, a senior government officer, offered a solution to this problem:

> There is a conflict when ministers themselves, on a committee, examine the institutions and agencies coming under their purview. This could be overcome by disclosing the interest, not participating [in the] examination of such institutions. Currently it is difficult to identify the government members who are not ministers to serve [on] these committees, because all of the government party members are ministers.

The roles and functions of the COPA and COPE

In Standing Orders 125(2), it is unclear whether the COPA's examinations should be done along with the AG's reports. As for the COPE, Standing Order 126(2) clearly states that examinations must be carried out along with the reports of the AG. But it is not a mandatory requirement to examine each and every report of the AG tabled in the Parliament. In addition to this, the COPA and the COPE are able to initiate their own inquiries. Interviewees remarked that in Sri Lanka the AG's report is the main base of investigation.

A ruling party member commented that in order to have all the reports tabled in the Parliament, the government would need to strengthen the committees and their Secretariat. It would also need to include a research unit in the Parliament. Almost all interviewees agreed that the COPA and the COPE primarily worked with the AG's reports.

In general, almost all interviewees (20 out of the 30 interviewees) agreed that sufficient attendance and preparation by committee members and the witnesses would enhance the outcome of the COPA and the COPE's deliberations. Members attend meetings without proper examination of the documents tabled, therefore leaving the responsibility to the chairs and the AG to undertake the bulk of the work. Weak attendance and cancellation of committee sittings diminishes the morale of the public officers. In Sri Lanka, if members attended regularly they would improve self-learning and then improve their contribution during deliberations. Then public officers would take care in preparation of the materials for the committees and give evidence. Interviewee 24, an ex-chair of the COPA, described his experience as follows:

> Both [committee members and officers] must study the files and attend the meetings well prepared. If not we have to call them another day. Very rarely they attend with preparation.

A senior Cabinet Minister argued that members of the committees did not have sufficient time to prepare or attend meetings regularly, because committees sat on parliament days. However, Interviewee 12, another opposition party member of the COPA, commented:

> We meet only on parliamentary sittings dates. If we can meet on non-sitting days I think we can expect good results. Due to Ministers as members, we are facing a problem to allocate time for hearings. That is the reason we ask for [the appointment of] MPs for the committee.

Interviewee 25, a senior ex-government officer, also mentioned the lack of preparation time:

> Institutions which are summoned before the committee should get sufficient time to prepare for the deliberations. In some cases two weeks' notice is given and they do not know what areas of the AG's reports and other areas are going to be discussed.

The follow-up actions on committee deliberations are poorly tracked or not tracked at all. Knowing this is the case, officials appearing before these committees do not take examinations seriously. There is no generally accepted questioning time in parliamentary oversight committees in Sri Lanka. Current practice is for the committees' secretariat to develop a set of questions, gather some information and distribute this among committee members. Individual members are given an opportunity to pose their own questions to the witness as well. There is no time limit and members use time differently. The majority of interviewees thought that the questioning time was sufficient; as an opposition party members commented, 'Questioning time is fairly acceptable.' However, another opposition party member of the COPA (Interviewee 12), said, 'Time is not sufficient,' and Interviewee 25, a senior ex-government officer, further commented:

> Here it is not like other countries. No separate questioning and answering time. It's a mixture. Therefore, right now there are no time allocations for questioning and answering. It is going simultaneously. Before answering the first question, the second question is asked. In some cases the same question is repeated. Therefore, time management [is] essential.

Due to time constraints, some institutions are not examined at all or not examined for very lengthily periods of time. This shows that the time allocated for committee discussions pertaining to public enterprises is not sufficient. An opposition party member of the committee, Interviewee 18, remarked:

> There are over 300 to 400 institutions. By sitting like that we can't cover even one-fourth of the institutions. When the majority of the members are ministers, they can't spend desirable time for sitting as the members of the committee.

When the committee examines an institution, it is opportune to address all other major issues relating to the institution in addition to the items reported by the AG. Further, as a senior government officer explained, committee hearing' time is dependent on the subject matters of the enquiries. All depends on the level of depth required to discuss the matters and agenda items of the meeting.

When asked whether the COPA and the COPE can request that the AG conduct special investigations or that the AG provide advice or comment on specific issues under consideration, the majority of interviewees said that the committees had no right to give instructions to the AG. However, as the AG fulfils the requirements of the committees, the COPA and the COPE can require additional information to continue the examination and they can suggest new areas to be discussed. A senior ex-deputy head of department stated:

> Yes, committees can [make] requests [to the AG]. It is not mandatory, but COPE asked [the AG] several times to do investigations. According to the Standing Orders, committees cannot do so.

At present, the AG reports to the Parliament, not to the committees. Interviewee 6, a Treasury official, commented:

> It is a very rare instance that the committee asks the AG to do special examinations. They appoint sub-committees to do the special examinations. Sometimes committees ask the secretary to furnish reports to the committee with [a] copy to the AG.

Further, Interviewee 25, another government officer, noted that it happens in:

a very informal manner when a request [is] made by [a] committee or the members. If it is appropriate the AG will comply, but [the AG] is not bound to carry out audits members require. Some members individually request the AG to look at some areas which are not reported to the Parliament.

Interviewees were also asked what kinds of resources are presently available to the committees' secretariat and whether these are sufficient for the smooth functioning of the committees. The majority of interviewees highlighted the committee secretariats' lack of resources. They also stated that this was a crucial factor affecting the quality of committee deliberations. The committees' secretariat consists of five officers headed by an Assistant Director. His/her educational background and experience is not on par with the specialised knowledge required for committee activities. Indeed, Interviewee 1, a senior Treasury official, explained the situation as follows:

> The committee secretariat does not have the required resources in terms of professional skilled human resources and even modern communications equipment, Internet multimedia facilities.

Further, there is neither a research unit in the secretariat, nor professionally qualified and sufficiently trained staff who can interpret audit reports, annual reports and the corporate plans and briefings given to the members, so as to enable the members to engage in meaningful discussions. With no internal research staff and capability, the committees depend on the work of the AG and the research efforts of individual members. An opposition party committee member commented:

> We don't have a single qualified person. When we have to submit the report to the Parliament, it is taking more than one year.

Though committee structure and human resources are important prerequisites to the oversight function, they do not guarantee that the function will be carried out, or that it will be systematic, comprehensive or responsible. An interviewee (Interviewee number 3) thought that the committee secretariat urgently needed more qualified people with new competencies, such as interpersonal and communication skills and IT knowledge, to operate efficiently. Interviewee 16, an opposition party committee member, commented:

> Professional qualified officers are needed. There are no knowledgeable officers at the committee secretariat. They have to review the report and should furnish summary reports to us. They work within their capacity, but it is not sufficient compared with the number of government institutions.

The resources available to the administration of the secretariat are important because they determine the efficiency of the committees and the outcome of their activities. Even oversight committees in third world countries would benefit from computer assisted information technologies. According to Interviewee 12, at present, the committees do not have access to an institutional database and there is no separate intranet as in other countries. Interviewee 2, an opposition party member of the COPA committee, explained:

Staff, facilities and capacity building, all of them are insufficient. I must say that the committees do a super job with their little staff. I would say that best way is to make it modernised with peak technologies. Now verbatim reports take months of time to come back. In Australia, they have trans-lations electronically.

In terms of infrastructure, the committees only have dedicated access to two small committee rooms. These rooms cannot accommodate the presence of the media or the public during meetings. A considerable number of interviewees believe that these facilities need to be improved for several reasons. Interviewee 18, an ex-Chair of the COPE, provided this opinion:

The relationship between the AG and the COPE/COPE is very cordial but there is no specific system or proper infrastructure facilities to maintain that cooperation and to maintain the link.

Opposing these views about the lack of resources, an opposition party member of the committee argued that the there was no need to focus on relationship building because that was more of a guiding factor, rather than a factor that assisted with the investigations. Thus, even though members only cooperate during committee sessions – not pre or post meetings – rather than this the issue is seen as pertaining to access only. Moreover, Interviewee 27, a former Chair of the COPA, stated that as the AG had paid due attention to all material and fundamental issues with ade-quate quality, volume and timeliness in relation to committees' examinations, he found the AG's resourcing of the committees to be sufficient.

As mentioned earlier, the COPA and the COPE are highly dependent on the AG's reports and the AG or his representative attending the sittings of the com-mittees to accomplish their work. A majority of interviewees thought that, in Sri Lanka, although the AG lacked competent staff, there was a good level of com-munication between the COPA, the COPE and the AG. An ex-Chair of the COPA, Interviewee 27 commented:

Communication between the AG and the committees [is] excellent. Always the AG plays a very independent role in the committees, giving sufficient material to the members and also to the staff and sometimes interviewing when necessary. So the AG's role is commendable.

Interviewees were also asked whether there were substantial financial incentives, such as extra pay or other in-kind benefits, provided to members to attend meetings and to compensate for their effort and contribution. A substantial portion of interviewees stated that financial incentives, including training, were not sufficient. Interviewee 3, a senior minister, commented:

> I think that is not sufficient. They are devoting their valuable time. It is useful to exchange experiences with other countries where PACs are practising. We can get administrative reforms experience (New Public Management) from countries like New Zealand.

This point was supported by a formal government official, Interviewee 25, who remarked: .

> Right now there are no such payments. But if the meetings are held [on] non-sitting days, members are entitled [to] a day's allowance. Some small amount is paid to the members. But on parliamentary sitting days they are not paid. Other incentives such as foreign trips and foreign training are not widely used. If they are given ... training that will be [an] effective ... encouragement.

Interviewee 23, an ex-Chair of the COPA, expressed the same view: 'I think financial incentives like a sitting allowance can be recommended.' However, a senior government officer, Interviewee 4, totally opposed the payment of financial incentives: 'the members are responsible. It is part of their work; therefore, it is not necessary to pay extra.' A number of interviewees suggested the importance of formal training as expressed by Interviewee 2, a member of the opposition party: 'there was no recognition of varying levels of expertise among members. It is assumed that all members have to be given necessary training and knowledge.'

The need for transparency in the COPA's proceedings and the capacity to hold effective committee deliberations are fundamental to improve public financial accountability. However, no provision has been made for this openness in Sri Lanka. Media coverage and public involvement are important for the success of financial scrutiny of the PAC. Filming proceedings enhances the quality of debates and discussion. Interviewee 13, an opposition party committee member, commented:

> Definitely hearings should be open to media. To allow the media, it can stop 50 per cent of frauds and corruption. That hearings are going to be open to media is message enough. Committee members have a responsibility to attend the meetings, [and] be well prepared.

Another opposition party committee member, Interviewee 2, commented: 'I feel that it is necessary to open [to] the media. They [Committees] have to prevent the character assassination of people. If a person is guilty never mind. But an innocent person comes to detriment.' In the absence of an audience and public pressure, there may not be any motivation for committee members to adequately prepare and engage fully with issues of government expenditure. A great number of interviewees also stated that the COPA and the COPE's hearings should be open to the media. A former government department Deputy Head, Interviewee 15, remarked:

> The inherent reasons are poor attendance of members, poor contribution of members. [So] poor performance of governmental activities will be exposed to the public. It is my view [that] parliamentary privileges for the Members of Parliament, as far as their performance and contribution at committee meetings and in the Parliament, should be removed.

Some of the interviewees believed that considering the socio-political culture prevailing in Sri Lanka, committee sessions should not be opened to the media and public, because senior government officials were only accountable to the committees, but also because some CAOs and audit officers (AOs) faced difficult questions from members. Further, some members were afraid that the media would not objectively report on committee deliberations. They believed that the media might publish reports seeking to embarrass officials and/or the government. Interviewee 23, a senior ruling party member of the COPA, stated:

> It shouldn't be open to the media. Sri Lanka has very destructive press and they want to sensationalise issues which are sensitive. Therefore, the bureaucracy will find [it] difficult to survive thereafter because [the] whole country will think that the bureaucracy consists of robbers. Our press is irresponsible, [they will] televise only the things where people have been [at] crosswords, attacking each other.

Some interviewees believed that committee sessions should be opened under certain conditions. Interviewee 27, a spokesperson of the opposition party, said:

> We must adopt the British system, but you must allow the chairman to control question time or otherwise appropriate time should be decided by the chairman and then media can come. I am not totally opposed, but with this limit of course we can start it.

The roles and functions of the AG

According to Article 153, His Excellency the President has sole power to appoint the Auditor-General. This statutory provision covers the appointment, dismissal and payment of the AG. The AG's mandate is to assist the Parliament in ensuring that there is proper use of public resources by auditing government and public enterprises. The AG provides the COPA and the COPE with evidence on issues where he/she has relevant audit experience. The AG meets with the committees to provide private briefings on the audit issues ahead of a public inquiry, as well as provides evidence to the committee during the course of an inquiry. This close working relationship between the AG and the COPA and the COPE enhances the public's confidence that government resources are used with due regard to the efficient and effective running of the economy.

Therefore, the work of the AG acts to reinforce accountability by independently assessing agencies being audited. Independence will always be of primary importance to audit effectiveness. According to the majority of interviewees the AG in Sri Lanka is not independent financially and administratively. He is subject to control by the General Treasury and the Ministry of Finance for finance and human resources.

The majority of interviewees identified the mandate, sufficient financial resources, adequate competent staff and the training of staff as major problems, limitations and challenges faced by the AG in the functioning of the COPA and the COPE in Sri Lanka. A considerable number of interviewees also suggested that the AG's mandate had to be broadened. Interviewee 17 commented that 'the AG should be given more power, more freedom and more resources'.

Notwithstanding, a majority of interviewees agreed or strongly agreed that the AG submitted reports to Parliament on time and containing adequate information and documentary evidence to carry out committee hearings smoothly. An ex-Chair of the COPE, Interviewee 10 commented that:

> to my knowledge [the] AG always submits his reports on time, but institutions fail to furnish their reports on time according to the stipulated period in accordance with the Treasury Circular.

In the hearing process of oversight committees, the AG is sitting next to the chairperson on the committee. The main justification for this is that the AG is mainly responsible for his report and subsequent questioning process. A summary report is prepared and submitted before the committee hearing by the AG with explanations given by the organisation under scrutiny for the AG's report.

The AG's close relationship with the COPA and the COPE should be used as means of maintaining the AG's independence. It is the COPA and the COPE, however, who have primary responsibility to safeguard the AG's independence. The effectiveness of the Office of the AG is based on the special relationship between the AG and the Parliament rather than based on the AG being an 'independent officer' of the Parliament. An ex-Chair of the COPE, Interviewee 18 remarked:

> He [AG] has not been given specific powers. The Constitution clearly said that there should be an Auditor-General. Powers are not defined. And that is why I have suggested there should be an independent audit commission. That is number one. Number two is he should not be controlled by anybody else. [He] should be attached to the Parliament. Number three his responsibility [is] directly to the Parliament.

The degree to which the AG's independence can be gauged is largely by looking at methods of appointment, tenure, career expectations, method of removal, funding and legal immunities. In Sri Lanka the AG is not an independent officer of the Parliament. The role of the AG is not based in the legislative branch of government, and therefore, is not responsible and accountable to Parliament. This should be changed as Interviewee 19, a senior parliamentary officer, stated: 'Like other countries he [AG] should be directly under Parliament.'

The importance of the issue of independence for the office of the AG is made all the more evident in the manner in which the AG is allocated resources for his office. Executive control over the financial and the human resource levels of the AG's office has meant that the AG has only a conditional form of independence. An opposition party committee member, Interviewee 2 commented: 'He is not provided sufficient funds sufficient people. I suggest that the AGs budget should [be] reviewed by the committee.' The AG is not allowed to determine the number and composition of human resources required to assist him in auditing. A former Chair of the COPA, Interviewee 24 stated that: '[the AG's] budget is not sufficient. [The] AG has to depend on the Secretary to the Ministry of Finance for his budget. So, [the] AG is not independent. We have to correct those things.' According to the interviewees there are only a few qualified accountants in the department. They do not, however, remain long because of low salaries and the appeal of better opportunities in the private sector. Interviewee 15, an ex-government officer, explained the situation as follows:

[The] AG needs qualified, experienced and competent staff … in a large number of institutions … [to] perform his task efficiently, but there are only two or three fully qualified accountants in the AG's staff. Apart from inadequate academic qualified competent staff there are no competent staff to work in three or two languages [Sinhala, Tamil and English]. The limitation is the AG cannot decide [on his] own composition of staff and their salaries. He has to get approval from Ministry of Finance … [to] improve the quality of the AG's report [he] needs competent staff.

It is the government's responsibility to keep competent staff in the department. A former COPA chair, Interviewee 23 commented that 'Due to [a] lack of staff and resources, today public sector auditing is not up to the international standard…. Performance auditing, environmental auditing … areas need to be developed.' Interviewees were asked whether the AG should take into account the views of the COPA and the COPE in framing his/her work in ensuring: (1) financial scrutiny; (2) public accountability; and (3) good governance. A majority of interviewees agreed. A senior member said that the AG should plan his work in such a manner to satisfy the needs of the oversight committees. Further Interviewee15, a senior officer, expressed the view that:

[The] AG must take on the views of the COPA/COPE, other institutions, and professional bodies for framing his overall audit plan, so that he can concentrate on the areas [he] needs to pay attention [to] in [any] particular year. This is more appropriate in the case of value for money auditing. In the selection of VFM [value for money] auditing such advice, suggestions made by the various parties [are] more relevant and appropriate.

In contrast, other interviewees thought that the AG should not take the views of the committee into consideration when framing his/her work programme. Several interviewees said that the AG should have liberty when preparing his annual programme. They argued that if the committee recommended the AG's budget estimate, then the AG should take into account the views of the COPA and the COPE in framing his work programmes. One of the opposition party committee members, Interviewee 12 stated: 'If the annual budget of the AG is approved by the committee or Parliament then he has to furnish his annual plan to the committee. This is the case in other countries but it does not happen in Sri Lanka.'

In the countries of the Commonwealth, the AG performs his/her role in the PAC as a witness and/or advisor. There was again a high degree of consensus among interviewees around the fact that they saw the AG as performing the role of witness and as an advisor within the COPA and the COPE. Interviewee 27, an ex-Chair of the COPA, commented: 'I have seen myself that he forms his opinions.... Most of the time members agree with the AG and there is a very cordial relationship.' The Head of the Department of the Treasury confirmed that the AG 'plays in both roles'. He stated that, due to a lack of understanding in accounting and auditing, the AG fills the 'knowledge gap of the committee members'. Moreover, Interviewee 23, another ex-Chair of the COPA, said that the AG had a greater role to play than just as a witness or an advisor. He stated that the 'AG also can question, but in other committees in other parts of the world, the AG can advise only the chairman'. However, Interviewee 13, a young committee member, expressed a differing opinion:

[The] AG reports to the Committee. If he is a witness, he should be given the opportunity to act as a witness, which does not happen now. If he acts as an advisor his advice has to be accepted, which does not happen either.

Based on the comments of the majority of interviewees, it would appear that the AG performs his role as a witness and an advisor. When asked if there is a proper institutional set-up, adequate resources and training facilities available within the AG's department to sustain the relationship between the AG and the COPA and the COPE, most interviewees said that the facilities were inadequate. Among these, some stated that the lack of people and funds were major problems. However, according to interviewees, the relationship between the AG and the COPA and the COPE was balanced, making their roles and independence clear and separate.

Under the terms of Article 14(2) of the Finance Act No. 38 of 1971, the AG submits his/her audit reports on the financial aspects, rather than on the value for money or performance of audit techniques. It is observed that in some countries, the AG submits a report on the financial audit reports and performance audit reports separately. In countries such as Australia, the UK and India, committees discussed performance reports separately.

Conclusion

The World Bank (2004) suggests that the public audit function of Sir Lanka does not currently meet the standards expected of the audit profession. Further, they state that auditing functions in Sri Lanka could be strengthened by making the AG more independent of the Executive and building its capacity to provide more relevant information to Parliament. These findings are broadly consistent with this study's findings.

The study revealed that the COPA and the COPE are mainly dedicated to dealing with the AG's reports documenting his/her examination of governments' institutions, or from time to time outlining certain issues, which members themselves consider important. According to McGee (2002), traditionally the work of most PACs within the Commonwealth has been to scrutinise public accounts based on the AG's reports tabled in Parliament. In Canada, the PAC maintains an arm's-length relationship with the AG and spends at least 95 per cent of the committee's time examining the AG's reports. Although the Canadian PAC's examinations are based on the AG's reports, many PACs have the opportunity to examine questions of economy, efficiency and effectiveness, depending, of course, on the type of information provided by the AG and the attitude of the committees. In Australia, it is a statutory obligation for the PAC to review all the AG's reports tabled in Parliament. There, the PAC expects high-quality audit reports from the AG. Further, the majority of Australian PACs have the ability to initiate their own inquiries (Jacobs *et al.*, 2007a). Our study's findings are consistent with common practices of the Commonwealth countries.

The AG in Sri Lanka is considered a public officer. In most countries, especially Commonwealth countries such as the UK, Canada, Guyana and Australia, the AG is not a public officer. More specifically, the AG is recognised as an independent statutory officer of Parliament (Clark and De Martinis, 2003; Coghill 2004; English and Guthrie, 2000).

Findings from this study suggest that the lack of resources is a major problem for sustaining the relationship between the AG and the COPA and the COPE in Sri Lanka. The close relationship between the Parliament and the AG is a critical part of public sector accountability, and has been noted as one of the guiding principles of the AG's office (Fiedler, 2003).

The AG's reports to Parliament are the final link in the chain of accountability of the executive government to the Parliament. According to the Sri Lanka Constitution and the Finance Act, the AG is bound to submit his reports to the relevant bodies and the Parliament before 31 October each year. The periodic and compulsory submission of audited accounts to Parliament by the institutions must be implemented effectively to stem the current financial irregularities. According to this research, the AG submits his reports to the Parliament on time and the reports contain adequate information and evidence to carry out committee hearings smoothly.

The AG and the COPA and the COPE can collaborate with each another to considerably strengthen their capacity to better perform their constitutional tasks. These committees need to be more vigilant about reviewing the AG's reports, as this may enable them to identify problem areas in the government. The strength of parliamentary oversight is dependent on the power Parliament has to publically call the Executive to account for their actions. Given that the good relationship with the AG is a cornerstone of public sector accountability, it is reasonable to expect that this source of inquiry be the most common for each PAC (Jacobs *et al.*, 2007b).

The study found that the formal institutional structure of the political system in Sri Lanka created a difficult environment to call the government into account. Due to the prevailing political situation, the government does not take any action against parliamentarians and other officials and is unable to control the power and autonomy of executive members of the government. The AG and the COPE and the COPA seem to have insufficient mandate and power to oversee all the state-owned enterprises. As a result, public accountability has been weakened over time.

Although Standing Orders have been amended, mostly to allow for an increased number of political parties, other major amendments, reflecting the legal, political and administrative changes, have not yet occurred. Instituting changes to strengthen the authority of the AG is only one way to enhance the accountability and effectiveness of the government. Strengthening the internal control and internal audit roles in government is at least as important as strengthening the role of the AG. If the government is willing to accept responsibility for public accountability, financial scrutiny and good governance, recommendations can be implemented. According to our study's findings, the amendments should include extending the mandate and the power of both the AG and the COPA and the COPE to enable them to oversee all state-owned enterprises. This would require the government to make necessary changes to its Constitution, Standing Orders, Finance Act and the Public Companies Act to grant sufficient power and a broader mandate to the committees to carry out their duties independently and impartially.

Future research could extend or modify this study along several dimensions. With respect to the AG, COPA and COPE in Sri Lanka, and issues of accountability and accounting, the researchers believe that there are many opportunities for further research. At this stage, there has been little empirical research undertaken into oversight committees, with the majority of prior work being largely normative. This study focuses on the relationship between parliamentary financial oversight committees and the AG in Sri Lanka. Such research is necessary in order to inform better practice with respect to COPA and COPE operations. Research can also be undertaken to establish a basis for making international comparisons of PACs, and doing so would enhance public sector accountability. By undertaking future research on COPA/COPE practices, it may be possible for the knowledge gained to be used to help COPA/COPE address this gap.

Longitudinal studies would enrich our understanding of the nature and form of COPA and COPE practices across national borders. Future research utilising in-depth case studies may also enable a richer understanding of the complex relationships observed in this chapter.

References

Auditor General's Department of Sri Lanka (1980) 'State Audit in Sri Lanka', Colombo: Government Press.

Balasooriya, A. F., Quamrul, A. and Coghill, K. (2008) 'Market-based reforms and privatization in Sri Lanka', *International Journal of Public Sector Management*, 21(1): 58–73.

Ceylon Sessional Papers (1924) 'Report of the Public Accounts Committees', Colombo: Government Printer.

Clark, C. and De Martinis, M. (2003) 'A Framework for Reforming the Independence and Accountability of Statutory Officers of Parliament: A Case Study of Victoria', *Australian Journal of Public Administration*, 62(1): 32–42.

Coghill, K. (2004) 'Auditing the Independence of the Auditor General', Paper presented to the Political Science Program, 11 February, Research School of Social Sciences, Australian National University, Canberra ACT.

DiMaggio, P. J. and Powell, W. W. (1983) 'The iron cage revisited: institutional isomorphism and collective rationally in organisational fields', *American Sociological Review*, 48: 47–160.

English, L. and Guthrie, J. (2000) 'Mandate, Independence and Funding: Resolution of a Protracted Struggle between Parliament and the Executive over the Powers of the Australian Auditor General', *Australian Journal of Public Administration*, 59(1): 98–114.

Fiedler, F. (2003) 'The Independence of Supreme Audit Institution in INTOSAI: 50 years 1953–2003', *A Special Publication of the International Organization of Supreme Audit Institutions*, Vienna, INTOSAI, www.intosai.org (accessed 19 July 2007).

Hood, C. (1995) 'The "new public management" in the 1980s: Variations on a theme', *Accounting, Organizations and Society*, 20(2): 93–109.

Jacobs, K., Jones, K and Smith, D. (2007a) 'An analysis of the Sources of Public Accounts Committee Inquiries: The Australian Experience', paper presented to the AFAANZ Conference, 1–3 July 2007, Queensland, Australia.

Jacobs, K., Jones, K and Smith, D (2007b) 'Public Accounts Committees in Australia: The State of Play', *Australian Parliamentary Review*, 22(1): 28–43.

Kandasamy, V. (2003) 'Powers and Functions of the Committee on Public Accounts and Committee on Public Enterprises', Working Paper, Auditor General's Department of Sri Lanka, Colombo.

Kelegama, S. (1998) 'Economic development in Sri Lanka during the 50 years of independence: what went wrong?', in *Milestones to Independence: People's Bank of Sri Lanka – Golden Jubilee Volume*, Colombo: People's Bank.

McGee, D. G. (2002) *The Overseers: Public Accounts Committees and Public Spending*, London: Pluto Press.

Meyer, J. W. and Rowan, B. (1977) 'Institutionalized organizations: Formal structure as myth and ceremony', *American Journal of Sociology*, 83(2): 340–63.

Miles, M. B. and Huberman, A. M. (1994) *Qualitative Data Analysis: An expanded sourcebook*, 2nd edn, Thousands Oaks: Sage.

Modell, S. (2001) 'Performance measurement and institutional processes: a study of managerial responses of public sector reform', *Management Accounting Research*, 12: 437–64.

Parliament of Sri Lanka (2007) *The Parliament of Sri Lanka*, www.parliament.lk (accessed 2 March 2008).

Samarathunga, R. and Bennington, L. (2002), 'New Public Management: Challenge for Sri Lanka', *Asian Journal of Public Administration*, 24(1): 87–109.

Soysa, B. (1966) 'The role of audit in a developing country', in The Ceylon Branch of the Commonwealth Parliamentary Association, *Proceedings of a Seminar on the Role of Audit in a Developing Country*, Colombo: Government Press.

Warnapala, W. A. (2004) *Parliament and Public Accountability in Sri Lanka*, Colombo: Godage International Publication (pvt) Ltd.

Wijesekera, P. (2002) *Parliamentary Practice in Sri Lanka*, Colombo: Parliament Secretariat.

Wijesuriya, P. M. W. (1979) 'Audit Profile Sri Lanka', *International Journal of Government Auditing*, 4(1): 16–17.

World Bank (2004) *Sri Lanka – Country Financial Accountability Assessment Study – 2003*, South Asia Region Financial Management Unit, World Bank.

4 Parliamentarians' relations with the Auditor-General of Canada during Sheila Fraser's mandate (2001–2011)

Danielle Morin

Introduction

The Sponsorship Program scandal unveiled by then Auditor-General (AG) of Canada Ms. Sheila Fraser, in a report she published in February 2004 (Auditor General of Canada, 2003), had a striking impact on Canadian political life. "How could situations like this occur? Why did it take so long to deal with them?" she asked Parliamentarians (p. 2). The facts the AG brought to light greatly agitated the Canadian political machinery.

The very close results of the referendum on Quebec sovereignty of October 30, 1995 galvanized Prime Minister Jean Chrétien. He resolved to burnish Canada's image among French-speaking Quebecers. In February 1996, the Sponsorship Program took a new turn in the hands of Jean Pelletier, Prime Minister Chrétien's chief of staff, with assistance from the Privy Council Office and, starting in June 1997, the Minister of Public Works and Government Services, Alfonso Gagliano, gradually took over the program supervision from Mr. Pelletier (Gomery, 2005a: 9–10). Ms. Fraser introduced her report by denouncing the disregard with which Jean Chrétien's Liberal Government (in power since October 25, 1993[1]) had managed this program dedicated to promoting Canadian federalism:

1   We found that the federal government ran the Sponsorship Program in a way that showed little regard for Parliament, the *Financial Administration Act*, contracting rules and regulations, transparency, and value for money. These arrangements – involving multiple transactions with multiple companies, artificial invoices and contracts, or no written contracts at all – appear to have been designed to pay commissions to communications agencies while hiding the source of funding and the true substance of the transactions.
2   We found widespread non-compliance with contracting rules in the management of the federal government's Sponsorship Program, at every stage of the process. Rules for selecting communications agencies, managing contracts, and measuring and reporting results were broken or ignored. These violations were neither detected, prevented, nor reported for over four years because of the almost total collapse of oversight mechanisms and essential

controls. During that period, the program consumed $250 million of tax-payers' money, over $100 million of it going to communications agencies as fees and commissions.

3   Public servants also broke the rules in selecting communications agencies for the government's advertising activities. Most agencies were selected in a manner that did not meet the requirements of the government's contracting policy. In some cases, we could find no evidence that a selection process was conducted at all ...

(Auditor General of Canada, 2003: 1)

However, it was Prime Minister Paul Martin who would have to deal with the chaos created by the AG's report. He was appointed on December 12, 2003, after Prime Minister Chrétien stepped down in October of that year. In February 2004, Prime Minister Martin created the Canadian Government's Commission of Inquiry into the Sponsorship Program and Advertising Activities (known as the Gomery Commission),[2] charged with clarifying the facts criticized by the Auditor-General. In its first report produced following hearings that lasted 136 days, from September 2004 to June 2005, during which 172 witnesses were heard (Gomery, 2005a: 3), Commissioner Gomery expressed dismay at the facts brought to his attention:

The Report that follows chronicles a depressing story of multiple failures to plan a government program appropriately and to control waste – a story of greed, venality and misconduct both in government and advertising and communications agencies, all of which contributed to the loss and misuse of huge amounts of money at the expense of Canadian taxpayers. They are out-raged and have valid reasons for their anger.

(Gomery, 2005b: xix)

"Where were the Parliamentarians?"

In his 2006 final report, Commissioner Gomery noted that in the Sponsorship Program affair, Parliamentarians had lost all control over the Executive:

It was a fair question [*Where were the parliamentarians?*], one that identi-fied a key failure in the management of the Sponsorship Program: the failure of Parliament to fulfill its traditional and historic role as watchdog of spend-ing by the executive branch of the Government. The failure was due to two factors: the invisibility, for all practical purposes, of the Sponsorship Program from the usual procedure for advance parliamentary approval of spending; and the imbalance that has developed between the power of the executive branch of the Government (represented in this case by the Prime Minister's Office) and parliamentary institutions such as the Public Accounts Committee, which should be holding the executive to account for its administration of the public purse.

(Gomery, 2006: 3)

Canada inherited its Westminster-style legislative tradition from the United Kingdom. The Standing Committee on Public Accounts (PACP), which has been in existence since Confederation in 1867, has carried out an accounting and auditing role to ensure that Parliament's authorizations regarding government expenditures have been fulfilled. In 1878, the Auditor-General position was established "to control the issue of public monies and audit expenditures" and to report to the Public Accounts Committee. In 1931, the function of the control of issue was attributed to a new position, the Comptroller of the Treasury, and the ex post audit of government expenditures was reserved exclusively for the Auditor-General. Since 1977, the Auditor-General has been authorized to conduct performance audits "that examine government management practices, controls, and reporting systems in order to assess whether the government has given due regard for economy and efficiency, and has procedures to measure and report on effectiveness."[3]

For nearly four decades, Auditors-General have played a predominant role in the accountability of the Canadian Federal Public Administration by reporting to Parliament not only on the regularity of government expenditures but also on the quality of government management:

> The Auditor General of Canada is an Officer of Parliament who audits federal government departments and agencies, most Crown corporations, and many other federal organizations, and reports publicly to the House of Commons on matters that the Auditor General believes should be brought to its attention …
>
> The Office of the Auditor General of Canada audits federal government operations and provides Parliament with independent information, advice, and assurance regarding the federal government's stewardship of public funds. While the Office may comment on policy implementation in an audit, it does not comment on the merits of the policy itself …[4]

The objective of this chapter is to examine the contribution of the Auditor-General (AG) and of the Standing Committee on Public Accounts (PACP) to the accountability process through the AG's performance audit reports submitted periodically to the House of Commons. Auditor-General of Canada, Ms. Sheila Fraser, ended her non-renewable ten-year mandate on May 31, 2011. Ms. Fraser's tenure as Auditor-General of Canada was evaluated through the lens of her relationship with Parliamentarians. Specifically, the accomplishments that have marked the Fraser decade related to performance audits done in the federal Administration along with her contribution to Parliamentarians' debates were examined. To do so, the level of "attention" given by Public Accounts Committee to the AG's reports was measured.

Methodology

For this study, a database including all the value for money audit reports (performance audits) produced by Ms. Fraser during her ten-year mandate was created.[5] The Standing Committee on Public Accounts' debates were included in this database and linked to the chapters the AG produced during her mandate. The PACP, as parliamentary interlocutor of the Auditor-General, is in charge of following up the recommendations at Administrations.

A total of 342 meetings[6] held by the PACP, with Auditor-General's reports on the agenda, were counted between the first session of the 37th Parliament (starting from meeting 23) and the third session of the 40th Parliament (until meeting 51) that ended on March 26, 2011, namely two months before the end of AG Fraser's mandate. Although most of the PACP hearings are public, some are held "in camera." Consequently, the evidence of these meetings, which are closed to the public, is not easily available. For this study, PACP debates were coded according to number of minutes spent discussing chapters produced by the AG in her reports following performance audits.

The coding of the database information thus permitted qualitative and quantitative analyses of the data. In addition to the PACP's debates, the findings and recommendations contained in the Auditor-General's reports were also coded in terms of substance, for example whether they pertained to the economy, efficiency or effectiveness or accountability of the Administration.

This chapter is organized as follows: First, the Auditor-General (AG) and the Standing Committee on Public Accounts (PACP) are contextualized by establishing their role in the democratic accountability process of the Canadian federal Administration. AG Fraser's achievements in terms of performance audits done between 2001 and 2011 and their impact on the PACP debates are then presented and analyzed. Events that marked the end of AG Fraser's mandate are noted, and the chapter concludes with an analysis of the common thread that unifies the actions of the Auditor-General during her ten-year mandate.

Auditor-General and the Standing Committee on public accounts as actors in the democratic accountability process of the Canadian Federal Administration

On the PACP website, the importance of Auditor-General Sheila Fraser's reports for this committee in recent years is quite evident. Of the seven reports to the House of Commons that the PACP portrays as being among the most important that it produced (notable reports), six were prepared based on AG Fraser's reports.[7] The reports by Legislative Auditors are theoretically a source of preferred information for Parliamentarians in their duty to control the Executive. The mandate of the Canadian (federal) Standing Committee on Public Accounts is to review and report on:

* the *Public Accounts of Canada*;
* all reports of the Auditor-General of Canada;
* the Office of the Auditor-General's reports on plans and priorities and departmental performance reports; and
* any other matter that the House of Commons shall, from time to time, refer to the Committee.[8]

Like the Auditor-General, the Public Accounts Committee is not authorized to question the policies implemented by the government, yet the Committee has full latitude (as does the AG) to evaluate the government's management of "the economy and efficiency of program delivery as well as the adherence to government policies, directives and standards."[9] Together, the AG and the PACP contribute to the accountability process of the Canadian federal Administration regarding its management of public funds. They therefore have a role of guardian that is best assumed if both actors work in concert. So concludes Malloy (2004) in his study of Canadian PACP: Parliamentarians set their work agenda based on reports produced by the AG and in return promote the diffusion of important findings reached by the AG by discussing them in the House of Commons. This visibility granted to AGs fosters the realization of the accountability process, both because the gaps revealed by the AG are known to the population and because public pressure is ultimately exerted on the Administration to bring about the desired changes.

A Canadian study found that the AG's impact on the management of Administrations through performance audits is greater when Parliamentarians become more involved in follow-up with Administrations (Morin, 2008). The same advantages were reported in the United Kingdom, where the PAC maintained the interest of the administration in the findings reached by the National Audit Office (Roberts and Pollitt, 1994; Brown, 2007). Auditors-General of Canada do not have the power to oblige administrations to follow the recommendations formulated in their reports. Consequently, AGs depend heavily on Parliamentarians, who, through Public Accounts Committees, may demand that administrations take action following the AGs' recommendations. In addition to the limits formerly imposed by its Act (Auditor General Act R.S.C., 1985, c. A-17), AGs must remain within their zone of legitimacy when they rule on public affairs management:

> The Auditor General, however, cannot enforce the legal boundaries which shape public service action – its only remedial authority is a reporting requirement to Parliament (which itself can be potentially manipulated by the timing of parliamentary sittings). Further, while an Auditor General, as in the case of the review of the Sponsorship Program, may uncover incidents of rules being broken or procedures being ignored, the Auditor General's mandate does not extend to exploring the root causes of such problems.
>
> (Sossin, 2006: 50)

Therefore, the strength of the AG lies in that person's capacity to publicly disclose the gaps noted in public affairs management. Malloy (2006: 65) asserts that the Auditor-General, especially after having brought scandals to light, ultimately overshadows Parliamentarians, which may result in PAC members' finding "little political visibility or reward in their roles."

The credibility of AGs flows in particular from their independence. The Auditor-General of Canada is appointed by resolution of the Senate and House of Commons for a non-renewable ten-year mandate. These measures shelter AGs from political pressure that the government or opposition may be tempted to exert on them if their reports deal with politically sensitive topics.[10] In the case of the Standing Committees on Public Accounts, the "Chair shall be a Member of the Official Opposition, the first Vice-Chair shall be a Member of the government party and the second Vice-Chair shall be a Member of an opposition party other than the Official Opposition."[11] Franks (2006) maintains that it is the obligation that the PAC be chaired by a member of the Official Opposition that stripped Canadian PACs of their "passivity" and their inability to truly assume control over the Executive:

> The contention that the Canadian Public Accounts Committee has not usually acted in a non-partisan way over the years is correct. In fact, for much of Canada's history, the Committee did not act at all. It was inert. It did not meet. Ministerial control over contracts, grants, appointments and other aspects of administration were the instruments through which Governments won and rewarded supporters. The Government did not want a parliamentary committee to look too closely at its use of funds. The Committee sometimes roused itself when there was a change of government, and it could attack the excesses and improprieties of the previous administration. But, most of the time, with the Government having a majority on the Committee, and the Chair from the Government side as well, the Committee was passive. Only after Prime Minister Diefenbaker in 1958 for the first time appointed an Opposition member as chair did the Canadian Public Accounts Committee begin to become a consistently functioning part of the parliamentary scene.
>
> (Franks, 2006: 194)

Although Canadian AGs are portrayed as independent guardians, the way their works are used by Parliamentarians inevitably involves them in political debates. Sheila Fraser's mandate was marked by some of these episodes in which the AG found herself (undoubtedly unwillingly) at the heart of political debates that followed the publication of her reports.

AG Fraser's achievements and their repercussions on the PACP's debates

Since 1994, the Auditor General Act has allowed the AG to produce a maximum of three reports per year in addition to the Annual Report.[12] These reports generally comprise several chapters that present the AG's findings and recommendations following performance audits. During her mandate, AG Fraser produced roughly 208 chapters distributed in 33 reports.[13] Of these 208 chapters, 106 were more formally debated by the Standing Committee on Public Accounts (PACP), leaving about 102 chapters that did not have supplementary resonance after the reports were submitted to Parliament. After submitting a report to Parliament, the AG appears before the PACP, which holds a meeting to discuss the chapters contained in the report submitted. The chapters which were not subsequently formally debated by the committee could have been discussed by the members of the PACP with the AG during these meetings that account for about 30 hours of discussion time by the PACP during the AG's ten-year mandate. Reports produced periodically by the PACP have allowed the tracing of the debates that preceded their production. This facilitated the identification of chapters discussed by the PACP and meetings during which these chapters were debated, if applicable.

Chapters that attracted the most attention of the Public Accounts Committee

Parliamentarians in the PACP spent roughly 610 hours debating 106 chapters of reports submitted by AG Fraser during her ten-year mandate. Fourteen chapters alone account for 52 percent (316 hours) of these 610 hours of debate (see Table 4.1). For the 92 remaining chapters discussed by the PACP, 63 chapters were discussed for two to five hours each and 29 chapters were discussed for less than two hours each.

Not surprisingly, it was the "Sponsorship Program scandal," triggered by three chapters produced by AG Fraser in November 2003, that intrigued the PACP Parliamentarians the most.[14] Twenty-seven percent (163 hours) of Parliamentarians' total time spent discussing the AG's reports was occupied by debates and hearings related to this specific scandal. The reports produced by the AG in 2006 (in May and November in particular) undoubtedly contained politically sensitive topics because the Parliamentarians dedicated 136 hours (out of 610 hours, or 22 percent of their time) to discussing chapters published in the reports of 2006 (see Table 4.1). It is hard to say whether Parliamentarians' heightened interest is linked to the election in January 2006 of a minority Conservative government (after the Liberal government's 12-year reign), but it is hard to believe that this would be purely coincidental.

In her May 2006 report entitled "Government Decisions Limited Parliament's Control of Public Spending" (Auditor General of Canada, 2006a), Ms. Fraser denounced the Liberal Government's apparent loss of control over the costs incurred as part of the implementation of the Canadian Firearms Program. The AG had published two chapters on this program, one in December 2002 and another in May 2006. Three months after Commissioner Gomery had reported Parliament's failure to control the (Liberal) government during the Sponsorship Program scandal (Gomery, 2006), Ms. Fraser also decried the (Liberal) government's refusal to submit to control by Parliament regarding supplementary costs incurred during the implementation of the Firearms Program:

64. Not seeking proper authority for supplementary funds where there is a reasonable likelihood that an appropriation will be exceeded could be interpreted as a breach of the Standing Orders of the House of

Table 4.1 Chapters discussed most by PACP (2001–11)

Chapter title	Subjects	Year (publication)	Debate before PACP (hours)	Percentage (of 610 hours)
The Sponsorship Program (chapter 3) Advertising activities (chapter 4) Management of public opinion research (chapter 5) (Sponsorship Program scandal)	Government Purchasing Financial Management and Government Spending Ethics	November 2003	163	27%
Pension and Insurance Administration – Royal Canadian Mounted Police (chapter 9)	Income Security	November 2006	63	10%
Department of Justice – Costs of Implementing the Canadian Firearms Program (chapter 10) Canadian Firearms Program (chapter 4) Government Decisions Limited Parliament's Control of Public Spending	Financial Management and Government Spending Safety and security	December 2002 May 2006 (2 chapters)	32	5%
Acquisition of Leased Office Space (chapter 7)	Government Purchasing Real Property	May 2006	23	4%
Relocating Members of the Canadian Forces, RCMP, and Federal Public Service (chapter 5)	Financial Management and Government Spending Government Purchasing Public Service	November 2006	12	2%
National Defence – Military Recruiting and Retention (chapter 2)	National Defence	May 2006	6	1%
The Public Sector Integrity Commissioner of Canada (chapter 1)	Ethics Public Service	December 2010	7	1%
Passport Office – Passport Services (three chapters)	Foreign Affairs Safety and Security	April 2005 February 2007 March 2009	10	2%
		TOTAL:	316 hours	52%

63 chapters: between two and five hours of discussion

29 chapters: fewer than two hours of discussion

Commons. Failure to fully account to Parliament for expenditures against a Vote could also be viewed as an infringement of the privileges of the House of Commons. However, only the House itself can determine whether such a breach has occurred. The Standing Committee on Public Accounts may wish to pursue this matter further if it considers that to be appropriate.

65. In addition, key meetings held and decisions taken by the government were documented poorly, if at all. This serious lack of documentary evidence is inconsistent with the Treasury Board's *Policy on Management of Government Information.*

(Auditor General of Canada, 2006a: 20)

This public funds mismanagement by the Liberal Government had been initially pointed out by Ms. Fraser in 2002 (Auditor General of Canada, 2002b: 1). Specifically, she accused the government of letting these costs, initially estimated at $2 million (net related revenues), spiral out of control:

10.2 In 1995 the Department told Parliament that the Canadian Firearms Program would cost $119 million to implement, which would be offset by $117 million in fees. We requested the Department provide us with information on Program costs and revenues for the period 1995–1996 to 2001–2002. The information the Department provided states that by 2001–2002 it has spent about $688 million on the Program and collected about $59 million in revenues after refunds. We believe that this information does not fairly present the cost of the Program to the government.

10.3 In 2000, the Department of Justice estimated that by 2004–2005 it would spend at least $1 billion on the Program and collect $140 million in fees after refunds. This amount does not include all financial impacts on the government. The Department also did not report to Parliament on the wider costs of the Program as required by the government's regulatory policy.

In her report of May 2006 (Auditor General of Canada, 2006b: 95), the AG noted that the net cost reported by the government for the program to March 2005 was $946 million. In 2006, discussions by the PACP on the reports produced concerning the Canadian Firearms Program lasted 24 hours (eight hours of discussion in 2002 after the publication of the first report). This overspending, covered extensively by the press in both 2002 and 2006, consumed 5 percent of the total hours PACP members spent discussing the chapters produced by AG Fraser (see Table 4.1).

In November 2006, Chapter 9 of the AG's report, entitled "Pension and Insurance Administration – Royal Canadian Mounted Police" (Auditor General of Canada, 2006c) strongly influenced the PAC's activities in the following year. This report would occupy 63 hours of the PACP's time, or 10 percent of the total time dedicated to debating AG reports during her decade-long mandate (see Table 4.1). The AG justified her audit as follows: "In 2003, allegations of fraud and abuse in the management of the Royal Canadian Mounted Police's pension and insurance plans triggered an internal audit, which was followed by a criminal investigation by the Ottawa Police Service (OPS)." She examined "whether the RCMP has responded adequately to the findings of the internal audit and the criminal investigation" (Auditor General of Canada, 2006c: 1)

One year later, the PACP produced a report entitled "Restoring the Honor of the RCMP: Addressing Problems in the Administration of the RCMP's Pension and Insurance Plans" (Murphy, 2007), in which the committee raised important problems with management of the RCMP, gaps brought to light during the many hearings conducted by the PACP in 2007:

> The Committee's hearings on Chapter 9 of the Auditor General's November 2006 Report, Pension and Insurance Administration – Royal Canadian Mounted Police, led to an unexpected series of meetings. What began as an examination of whether the RCMP had responded adequately to the findings of its internal audit and the investigation by the Ottawa Police Service quickly became an investigation of several issues that even the Office of the Auditor General did not touch on in its report. These issues included:
>
> - the poor treatment of the RCMP members that disclosed wrongdoing;
> - the circumvention of contracting policies and procedures in order to outsource of the pension and insurance plans;
> - the lack of disciplinary measures meted out to those who committed wrongdoing;
> - the failure to process access to information requests in a timely manner;
> - the inability of the civilian oversight body to conduct an independent review; and
> - the culture of fear and mistrust created by senior management of the RCMP.
>
> (Murphy, 2007: 65–6)

Other chapters (see Table 4.1) like "Acquisition of Leased Office Space (Chapter 7 – May 2006)," "Relocating Members of the Canadian Forces, RCMP, and Federal Public Service (Chapter 5 – November 2006)," "National Defence – Military Recruiting and Retention (Chapter 2 – May 2006)", "The Public Sector Integrity Commissioner of Canada (Chapter 1 – December 2010)", and "Passport Office – Passport Services (three chapters: 2005–2007–2009)" were taken up by Parliamentarians, but to a much lesser extent than the chapters described above.

The reports produced by AG Fraser in 2006 definitely resonated more strongly with the PACP than the other reports she wrote during her ten-year mandate, apart from the three chapters published in November 2003 that triggered the Sponsorship Program scandal. In addition, six of the chapters most hotly debated by the PACP (see Table 4.1) resulted in the production of four reports that the PACP put forth as having been among the most important in allowing them to exercise control over the Executive during that period:[15]

> The Public Accounts Committee presents numerous reports to the House each year. Some notable reports include:
>
> [...]
>
> • Report 23 – Chapter 7, Acquisition of Leased Office Space
> • Report 2 – Chapter 9, Pension and Insurance Administration – Royal Canadian Mounted Police
>
> [...]
>
> • Report 9 – Chapter 3, the Sponsorship Program, Chapter 4, Advertising Activities and Chapter 5, Management of Public Opinion Research
> • Report 24 – Chapter 10 (Department of Justice – Costs of Implementing the Canadian Firearms Program).

Subjects covered by the AG in her reports vs. time allotted by the PACP

The chapters of the AG's reports cover various subjects related to management of the federal Administration. Table 4.2a compiles the number of chapters produced and time spent discussing them by the PACP for 30 subjects covered partly or entirely in the chapters.[16] Most of the chapters address more than one subject. Therefore, for the compilation appearing in tables 4.2a and 4.2b, the total hours spent by the PACP cannot be compared to the total of 610 hours calculated according to the chapters, nor to the total of 106 chapters debated by Parliamentarians (see previous section).

To reduce the effect on discussion time of the 14 chapters mentioned above (see Table 4.1), hours of discussion per subject were adjusted by omitting hours that could have given the impression that subjects had been amply discussed whereas the discussions covered only one chapter in particular (or an event like the Sponsorship Program scandal) (in Table 4.2a, the column "Adjusted hours" shows the adjustments made; see note 1 for the subjects affected by these adjustments). Despite its limitations, this compilation is nonetheless instructive in many respects.

Apart from the Sponsorship Program scandal and other losses and wastage noted by the AG, particularly in her reports produced in 2006, one can observe that the Parliamentarians of the PACP gave precedence to the subject of Safety and Security, to which they dedicated 25 hours of discussion time during AG Fraser's ten-year mandate (see Table 4.2a). Ranking second (24 hours) is the subject Public Service, followed by the subject of Financial Management and Government Spending (21 hours, ranking third), and Government Purchasing (20 hours) with National Defence (20 hours), ranking both fourth, and the

Table 4.2a Distribution of PACP debates by subjects covered in chapters

Subjects	Number of chapters (complete or partial)	Number of hours before the PACP	Adjusted hours (1)	PACP ranking (1 14)
Safety and Security	27	67	25	1
Public Service	18	43	24	2
Financial Management and Government Spending	53	65	21	3
Government Purchasing	22	218	20	4
National Defence	17	26	20	4
Health	9	19	19	5
Provinces and Territories	13	18	18	6
Justice and Law Enforcement	12	18	18	6
Employment	8	17	17	7
Public Administration	10	17	17	7
Aboriginal Affairs	15	17	17	7
Information Management	21	16	16	8
Agriculture	5	9	9	9
Economic Development	4	9	9	9
Income Security	9	72	9	9
Taxation	16	9	9	9
Ethics	10	16	9	9
Transportation	5	7	7	10
Science and Technology	14	7	7	10
Housing	2	6	6	11
Foreign Affairs	7	14	4	12
Crown Corporations	6	4	4	12
Human Rights	3	3	3	13
Natural Resources	8	3	3	13
Education and Training	3	3	3	13
Environment	9	3	3	13
Real Property	6	25	2	14
Business and Industry	7	2	2	14
Heritage and Culture	7	2	2	14
Financial Institutions	1	2	2	14

Notes

1 Number of hours has been adjusted by eliminating hours spent discussing the thirteen chapters presented in Table 4.1:

Government Purchasing

218 hours – 163 hours (three chapters on the Sponsorship Program) – 23 hours (Acquisition of Leased Office Space) – 12 hours (Relocating Members of the Canadian Forces, RCMP, and Federal Public Service) = 20 hours

Income Security

72 hours – 63 hours (Pension and Insurance Administration – Royal Canadian Mounted Police) = nine hours

Safety and Security

67 hours – 32 hours (Canadian Firearms Program) – ten hours (Passport Office) = 25 hours

Financial Management and Government Spending

65 hours – 32 hours (Canadian Firearms Program) – 12 hours (Relocating Members of the Canadian Forces, RCMP, and Federal Public Service) = 21 hours

Public Service

43 hours – 12 hours (Relocating Members of the Canadian Forces, RCMP, and Federal Public Service) – seven hours (The Public Sector Integrity Commissioner of Canada) = 24 hours

National Defence

26 hours – six hours (National Defence – Military Recruiting and Retention) = 20 hours

Real Property

25 hours – 23 hours (Acquisition of Leased Office Space) = two hours

Foreign Affairs

14 hours – ten hours (Passport Office) = four hours

Ethics

16 hours – seven hours (The Public Sector Integrity Commissioner of Canada) = nine hours (Sponsorship Program scandal excluded).

subject Health (19 hours, ranking fifth). The subjects Provinces and Territories, Justice and Law Enforcement, Employment, Public Administration, Aboriginal Affairs and Information Management were discussed during 16 to 18 hours each. Of the 30 subjects noted, 18 were addressed by the PACP for fewer than ten hours during the decade (see Table 4.2a).

Concerning subjects covered by the AG in the chapters (see Table 4.2b), the most prominent subject is Financial Management and Government Spending (53 full or partial chapters) and Government Purchasing (22) ranks third; the PACP dedicated 41 hours of discussion to these subjects during the decade. The subject "Safety and Security" ranks second (27) with a discussion time by the PACP of 25 hours. The subject Information Management ranks fourth (21 chapters) followed by Public Service (18). For eight subjects, the AG produced between ten and 17 chapters dealing with each of these subjects. For the remaining 17 subjects, she produced between one and nine chapters. Therefore, none of the 30 subjects inventoried was neglected, so to speak, by the AG during her ten-year mandate (see Table 4.2b).

By comparing the ranking of the AG (namely the number of chapters on a subject) with the ranking of the PACP (number of hours dedicated to said subject) (see Table 4.2b), one can see that the subjects prioritized by the AG and by the PACP are quite similar. The top five subjects (ranks 1 to 5) are the same for the AG as for the PACP, apart from Information Management (rank 4 for AG and 8 for PACP) and Health (rank 13 for AG and 5 for PACP).

Ultimately, it appears that a fairly large portion of the AG's work was not taken up by the Parliamentarians of the PACP. Of the 208 chapters, about 102 were not really debated, apart perhaps from the AG's presentation of the report to the PACP just after she submitted her report to Parliament. As for the 106 remaining chapters, more than one-quarter of Parliamentarians' discussion time was dedicated to the Sponsorship Program scandal. The Parliamentarians' agenda was clearly shaped by high-visibility reports that the AG produced, leaving little room for other reports that made up the very essence of the AG's work, which justify her presence in the control environment of the federal Administration.

Further, Parliamentarians' heightened interest in the AG's work coincided very often with its potential to fuel political debate. Admittedly, the scandals reported by the AG and discussed extensively by Parliamentarians deserved to be publicly criticized, and the government in place had to be compelled to explain its actions. In this sense, the accountability process in which the federal Administration, Parliament and the AG participated was fully realized. However, without interest from the Parliamentarians and without the political pressure exerted on the Administration, it is legitimate to question the fate reserved for the 102 chapters never discussed and the 18 subjects covered in the AG's reports that Parliamentarians discussed for fewer than ten hours in one decade. It is also worth questioning the resonance of these chapters on the Administration, which would have little motivation to act upon the AG's recommendations given that these chapters were virtually ignored by Parliamentarians.

Table 4.2b Distribution of chapters (complete or partial) produced by the AG by subjects covered

Ranking AG (1–21)	Subjects	Number of chapters	Number of hours	Ranking PACP (1–14)
1	Financial Management and Government Spending	53	21	3
2	Safety and Security	27	25	1
3	Government Purchasing	22	20	4
4	Information Management	21	16	8
5	Public Service	18	24	2
6	National Defence	17	20	4
7	Taxation	16	9	9
8	Aboriginal Affairs	15	17	7
9	Science and Technology	14	7	10
10	Provinces and Territories	13	18	6
11	Justice and Law Enforcement	12	18	6
12	Public Administration	10	17	7
12	Ethics	10	9	9
13	Health	9	19	5
13	Income Security	9	9	9
13	Environment	9	9	9
14	Employment	8	3	13
14	Natural Resources	8	17	7
15	Foreign Affairs	7	3	13
15	Business and Industry	7	4	12
15	Heritage and Culture	7	2	14
16	Real Property	6	2	14
16	Crown Corporations	6	2	14
17	Agriculture	5	2	12
17	Transportation	5	9	9
18	Economic Development	4	9	10
19	Human Rights	3	7	9
19	Education and Training	3	9	13
20	Housing	2	6	11
21	Financial Institutions	1	2	14

Mandate ends in controversy

One year after being named Auditor-General, Ms. Fraser served her first warning to the Liberal Government in a chapter entitled "Placing the Public's Money Beyond Parliament's Reach" (Auditor General of Canada, 2002a). She looked at the billions of taxpayers' dollars paid by the federal government to private foundations and other delegated arrangements. Her conclusions about the will of the Liberal government to evade control by Parliament are unequivocal:

> 1.1 ... We found that the essential requirements for accountability to Parliament – credible reporting of results, effective ministerial oversight, and adequate external audit – are not being met.
> 1.2 In the delegated arrangements we examined, reporting to Parliament is not adequate for parliamentary scrutiny. None of the arrangements submit corporate plans for tabling in Parliament. Nor do they all provide annual reports with a credible description of accomplishments.
> (Auditor General of Canada, 2002a: 1)

The first years of Sheila Fraser's mandate as AG of Canada were marked by the Sponsorship Program scandal and to a lesser extent by government's over-spending under the Firearms Program. Whereas the Sponsorship scandal originated from the use of public funds for partisan purposes by the government of Jean Chrétien, the problems with the Firearms Program arose from an apparent loss of control by the same government over the costs of putting in place a program intended to control "acquisition, possession, and ownership of firearms; regulating the availability of specific types of firearms; and deterring the misuse of firearms" (Auditor General of Canada, 2002b: 3).

These events had in common the will of the then reigning Liberal Government to shirk control by Parliament. Commissioner Gomery complained of this ruse regarding the Sponsorship Program scandal, and AG Fraser denounced it repeatedly. At the end of her mandate, the AG faced an odd turnaround: Parliamentarians did not want to welcome her onto their premises.

Federal Parliamentarians refuse to have their expenses audited by the Auditor-General

In May 2010, one year before her mandate ended, AG Fraser was categorically barred by Parliamentarians who were loath to have her audit their expenses. In a letter sent to the chair of the Board of Internal Economy of the House of Commons, Ms. Fraser said she regretted this refusal and refuted the argument that Parliamentarians' expenses were beyond the limits of the AG's area of responsibility. In a letter dated May 14, 2010, she wrote:

> Should the Board, at some future time, change its position on this matter [to conduct a performance audit of the administration of the House of

Commons], we remain available to perform this work. In that regard, I would like to address the issue raised concerning the mandate of the Auditor General. The Auditor General Act does not list the agencies and departments to which our mandate applies; rather Section 5 of the Act provides that "the Auditor General is the auditor of the accounts of Canada...." These accounts include amounts received and expended by the House of Commons. However, given our distinct relationship with the House of Commons, we have adopted the practice of requesting an invitation before commencing an audit.[17]

After nine years of rendering "loyal" services to Parliamentarians, the AG was accused by that same group of exceeding the limits of her mandate by asking to do a performance audit of the management of $500 million in public funds allocated annually to the House of Commons for its operating expenses. This opposition to her auditing the House of Commons transcended nearly all the parties, from the Conservative Party in power, to the New Democratic Party (NDP) and the Liberal Party. Only the Bloc Québécois supported her proposal. The *National Post* newspaper (Murphy, 2010) took umbrage at this denial of the AG by the elected officials of the three parties:

Stonewalling the Auditor-General is the dumbest move in the history of Canadian politics. They're for Transparency and Accountability, but not for them. Michael Ignatieff [Liberal Party], who finds a new way to bewilder the Canadian public every passing day, has offered the perplexing comment that the voters are not interested in the "dinner receipts" of MPs. Well cry me a river of Chateau Lafite Rothschild, maybe, pass the caviar, the public is.

Jack Layton and the NDP's position is if anything more curious. Those who scourge the banks and Bay Street, who howl at the moon over capitalism's every greedy excess surely cannot be arguing against the scrutiny of the Auditor General when it comes to their expenditure of the public coin.

And Stephen Harper [Conservative Party], economist, one-time populist Reformer, surely Stephen Harper, flayer of Liberals during Sponsorship, is not disagreeable to Sheila Fraser looking at his MPs' frugal outlay.

Can they not see how odd, shifty, condescending, privileged, one rule for thee another for me, this makes them look?

Parliamentarians' refusal had strong resonance in light of the role played by the AG when applied to control of their own use of public funds. These Parliamentarians, specifically charged with controlling the Executive, refused to let the AG evaluate the management of House of Commons, despite the fact that for nine years Ms. Fraser had helped them exercise control over government spending. On June 15, 2010, after a month of outcry in the national press denouncing Parliamentarians' refusal to submit to an audit, AG Fraser announced that the Board of Internal Economy had decided to invite her Office to conduct a performance audit of the administration of the House of Commons, an invitation that she immediately accepted.[18] The report was finally published in June 2012 (Auditor General of Canada, 2012) by Ms. Fraser's successor, Mr. John Ferguson, and was received with some indifference by the press given that it did not contain revelations that could shock public opinion.

A leak in the latest Auditor-General's report

On May 2, 2011, a majority Conservative Government led by Stephen Harper took power. In fact, a leak from the latest AG report a month earlier, during the electoral campaign, might have influenced Mr. Harper's chances of forming a majority government. Because the House of Commons had been dissolved prior to the election, the AG could not submit her report. It was only after the election that her report was made public. The AG examined "how the G8 Legacy Infrastructure Fund was established, how it was funded, and how projects were selected" after the "Parry Sound–Muskoka region, host of the June 2010 Group of Eight (G8) Summit, received $50 million in federal funding under the G8 Legacy Infrastructure Fund" (Auditor General of Canada, 2011: 33). Consistent with the media leak, the AG confirmed in her report that Parliament was not duly informed by Mr. Harper's Conservative Government of the public funds foreseen to organize the G8 Summit in June 2010 (Auditor General of Canada, 2011: 33–4):

> In the past, some regions that have hosted international events on Canada's behalf have received federal funds to compensate them. The June 2010 G8 host region received $50 million in funding for projects to enhance the area, provide a lasting legacy, and help ensure a safe and secure summit. Of the 242 project proposals submitted, 32 projects were approved for funding.
> Parliament's approval is needed before funding can be provided and monies spent. When Parliament is asked to approve such funding, it should be provided with clear information on the nature of the request.
> What we found
>
> • The funding request presented to Parliament for the G8 Legacy Infrastructure Fund was included within the Supplementary Estimates for Infrastructure Canada under the Border Infrastructure Fund relating to investments in infrastructure to reduce border congestion. This categorization did not clearly or transparently identify the nature of the approval being sought for G8 infrastructure project expenditures or explain that additional terms and conditions were created to accommodate the G8 Legacy Infrastructure Fund in lieu of those in place under the Border Infrastructure Fund.

[...]

Conclusion

Until the very end of her mandate, Ms. Fraser decried the desire by governments in power to escape parliamentary scrutiny. In spring 2002, she highlighted this problem regarding funds allotted to private foundations by the federal government. Her second chastisement followed in 2003, triggering the Sponsorship Program scandal.[19] She echoed the stance in 2006 with the Canadian Firearms Program. In 2011, she again complained that Parliamentarians were poorly informed of expenses incurred to organize the G8 Summit held in June 2010. When she was barred from the House of Commons in May 2010, she invoked the obligation to account for the use of public funds as an argument to impose her presence on the premises.

An analysis of the findings and conclusions formulated in the chapters produced during her mandate shows that a deficient execution of the accountability process by the federal Administration (specifically failure to account to Parliament or an umbrella organization) was mentioned in 77 of the 208 chapters that she produced. Inadequate transparency of management was cited in 28 chapters, and failure to obtain authorization from Parliament was cited in nine chapters. Deficiencies in the economy and efficiency of management (waste, cost excesses, etc.) and in program implementation (failure to implement policies, lack of program evaluation by government departments, etc.) were noted in 37 and 47 chapters respectively.

Evidently, it was the "accountability" dimension of her function as Officer of Parliament that AG Fraser prioritized during her decade-long mandate. She concentrated on the duty of "controller" to demand accounts from Administration, on which she would report to Parliament. In the 1980s, the practice of performance audit by legislative auditors sparked much debate about the role auditors would assume given their new position as evaluators of public affairs management. Auditors have claimed to want take on two specific roles: that of controller of Administrations emphasizing accountability, and that of catalyst for change and improvement (sometimes called "modernizer" or "consultant"), primarily assisting Administrations in their efforts to improve performance (Power, 1997; Pollitt *et al.*, 1999; Gendron *et al.*, 2001; Morin, 2000, 2003, 2011; Radcliffe, 2008; Skaerbaek, 2009; Lonsdale and Bechberger, 2011).

Ms. Fraser did not embark on the same managerialist path as some Supreme Audit Institutions (SAIs)[20] that added the "helping to improve management" dimension to their mission. Instead, she stuck to her duty dictated by law, that of reporting to Parliament on public funds management done by the Canadian federal Administration. The content of 208 chapters produced, in terms of both findings and subjects covered, illustrates an unshakeable will to assume her duty of Officer of Parliament according to the requirements of the position. Regarding the use of her work by Parliamentarians, several of her reports were clearly instrumentalized for political purposes. The problem is not so much this political instrumentalization as it is the place that these reports, covered extensively by the media, occupied in Parliamentarians' discussions relative to other reports produced, thus greatly reducing or completely eliminating discussion time dedicated to a very large number of the chapters the AG produced. This problem is not attributable to the Auditor-General, or a specific holder of the position, but rather to the political context that dictates the priorities of Parliamentarians when they assume their duty to control the Executive.

Notes

1 Information taken from the website http://archives.radio-canada.ca/politique/premiers_ministres_canadiens/clips/5889/ (consulted on November 14, 2012).

2 This commission of inquiry was established by Order in Council P.C. 2004-110, promulgated on February 19, 2004, pursuant to Part I of the Inquiries Act. Information taken from the website: http://epe.lac-bac.gc.ca/100/206/301/pco-bcp/commissions/sponsorship-ef/06-03-06/www.gomery.ca/en/phase2report/index.asp (official site of the Commission of Inquiry into the Sponsorship Program and Advertising Activities) (consulted on March 3, 2014).

3 Information in this paragraph summarized and citations taken from the website: www.parl.gc.ca/CommitteeBusiness/AboutCommittees.aspx?Cmte=PACP&Language=E&Mode=1&Parl=41&Ses=1&View=CH (consulted on March 21, 2014).

4 Information taken from the website of the Office of the Auditor General of Canada (OAG): www.oag-bvg.gc.ca/internet/English/au_fs_e_371.html (consulted on March 28, 2014).

5 This database was produced by Julien Houde-Roy for his Supervised Project as part of the MSc program (HEC Montréal) in 2010, under my direction. Coding was done under my supervision by my research assistant, Dominique Hamel, graduate (MSc) of the London School of Economics (London). I thank them both for their rigorous work.

6 This total is as accurate an estimate as possible of the number of meetings held by Parliamentarians during which they debated reports produced by the AG during her ten-year mandate. Although the tabulations and coding were done with due rigor, errors may have slipped into the count of meetings held, the total number of minutes, or the attribution of the debates to specific chapters. In addition, during the coding of "in camera" meetings, the risk of errors was greater given that the detailed testimonials were not available, only the minutes of meetings (with no details about the duration of the discussions on the various topics). Nonetheless, with the measures taken during the creation of the database, the coding and control of the quality of the coding and the tabulation done, errors, if any, would be marginal and should not have influenced the conclusions of the study.

7 See PACP website: www.parl.gc.ca/CommitteeBusiness/AboutCommittees.aspx?Cmte=PACP&Language=E&Mode=1&Parl=41&Ses=1&View=CH (consulted on March 21, 2014).

8 Citation taken from the website: www.parl.gc.ca/committeebusiness/AboutCommittees.aspx?Cmte=PACP&Language=E&Mode=1&Parl=41&Ses=2 (consulted on March 28, 2014).

9 Ibid.

10 The appointment procedures of AGs are foreseen in Section 3 of the Auditor General Act: "The Governor in Council shall, by commission under the Great Seal, appoint an Auditor General of Canada after consultation with the leader of every recognized party in the Senate and House of Commons and approval of the appointment by resolution of the Senate and House of Commons."

11 Pursuant to Standing Order 108 of the House of Commons (Article 106-2). See www.parl.gc.ca/About/House/StandingOrders/chap13-e.htm (consulted on March 28, 2014).

12 Information taken from the OAG website: www.oag-bvg.gc.ca/internet/English/admin_e_41.html (consulted on February 10, 2015).
13 The number of chapters inventoried includes those on "Other Audit Observations" and chapters on specific organizations or problems. The reports presented by OAG as "Other Audits" are not included.
14 The debates examined in this chapter are solely those that occurred at the PACP. This scandal generated many other debates in the House of Commons that are not considered here.
15 See PACP website: www.parl.gc.ca/CommitteeBusiness/AboutCommittees.aspx?Cmt e=PACP&Language=E&Mode=1&Parl=41&Ses=1&View=CH (consulted on April 3, 2014).
16 This allocation of discussion time among the 30 topics is as accurate an estimate as possible of the duration of the meetings held by Parliamentarians and the attribution of these durations to specific chapters. Nonetheless, with the measures taken during the creation of the database, the coding and control of the quality of the coding and the tabulation done, errors, if any, should not have influenced the conclusions of the study.
17 Information taken from the website: www.oag-bvg.gc.ca/internet/English/mr_2010 0514_e_33882.html (consulted on April 14, 2014).
18 Information taken from the website: www.oag-bvg.gc.ca/internet/English/osm_2010 0615_e_33897.html (consulted on April 14, 2014).
19 At the request of the Minister of Public Works and Government Services on March 19, 2002, AG Fraser had made an audit of three contracts worth a total of $1.6 million awarded to Groupaction between 1996 and 1999. This audit had significant consequences on the Liberal Government, one of it being the triggering of the audit of the Sponsorship Program. On May 30, 2002, when addressing to the PACP, AG Fraser would say:

> Our audit showed major shortcomings at all steps of the contract management process. Government files on the three contracts are so badly documented that many key questions regarding the selection of the contractor and the method used to establish the price and scope of services stipulated in the contracts remain unanswered. In our opinion, the government did not receive everything it contracted for.
> The nature of the findings is such that I referred the matter to the Royal Canadian Mounted Police, and as you know, it decided to open a criminal investigation. I have also decided to undertake a government-wide audit of advertising and sponsorship programs. We plan to report on the results of this audit by the end of 2003.
>
> Website: www.parl.gc.ca/HousePublications/Publication.
> aspx?DocId=653535&Mode=1&Parl=37&Ses=1&Language=E#Int-261463
> (consulted on April 30, 2014)

20 Supreme Audit Institutions (SAIs) that promote the role of catalyst for change and improvement in Administrations and express the goal of extending their actions beyond accountability include: National Audit Office, www.nao.org.uk/about-us/ (England); Australian National Audit Office, www.anao.gov.au/About-Us (Australia); Office of the Auditor-General, www.oag.govt.nz/about-us (New Zealand); Northern Ireland Audit Office, www.niauditoffice.gov.uk/index/about-niao/purpose_statement. htm (Northern Ireland); Audit Scotland, www.audit-scotland.gov.uk (Scotland); and the US Government Accountability Office, www.gao.gov/about/index.html (United States). Websites consulted May 28, 2013.

References

Auditor General of Canada (2002a) "Placing the Public's Money Beyond Parliament's Reach," Chapter 1, April Report of the Auditor General of Canada. Website: www.oag-bvg.gc.ca/internet/English/parl_oag_200204_e_1133.html (retrieved on April 28, 2014).

Auditor General of Canada (2002b) "Department of Justice – Costs of Implementing the Canadian Firearms Program," Chapter 10, December Report of the Auditor General of Canada. Website: www.oag-bvg.gc.ca/internet/English/parl_oag_200212_10_e_12404.html (retrieved on April 1, 2014).

Auditor General of Canada (2003) "Government-Wide Audit of Sponsorship, Advertising, and Public Opinion Research – Overall Main Points" (Chapters 3, 4 and 5), November Report of the Auditor General of Canada. Website: www.oag-bvg.gc.ca/internet/English/parl_oag_200311_e_1126.html (retrieved on March 17, 2014).

Auditor General of Canada (2006a) "Government Decisions Limited Parliament's Control of Public Spending," May Report of the Auditor General of Canada. Website: www.oag-bvg.gc.ca/internet/English/parl_otp_200605_e_14966.html (retrieved on April 1, 2014).

Auditor General of Canada (2006b) "Canadian Firearms Program," Chapter 4, May Status Report of the Auditor General of Canada. Website: www.oag-bvg.gc.ca/internet/English/parl_oag_200605_04_e_14961.html (retrieved on April 2, 2014).

Auditor General of Canada (2006c) "Pension and Insurance Administration – Royal Canadian Mounted Police," Chapter 9, November Report of the Auditor General of Canada. Website: www.oag-bvg.gc.ca/internet/English/parl_oag_200611_09_e_14977.html#ch9hd3a (retrieved on April 2, 2014).

Auditor General of Canada (2011) "G8 Legacy Infrastructure Fund," Chapter 2, Spring Report of the Auditor General of Canada. Website: www.oag-bvg.gc.ca/internet/English/parl_oag_201104_02_e_35221.html#hd3a (retrieved on April 15, 2014).

Auditor General of Canada (2012) "Report of the Auditor General of Canada to the Board of Internal Economy of the House of Commons," June. Website: www.oag-bvg.gc.ca/internet/English/parl_otp_201206_e_36890.html#hd3a (retrieved on April 15, 2014).

Brown, Tom A. (2007) "Value for Money Accountability in the UK Government: Is there a Gap?" *The Irish Accounting Review*, 14(1): 31–50.

Franks, C. E. S. (Ned) (2006) "A Canadian Solution," in Restoring Accountability – Research studies – Volume 3 – Linkages: Responsibilities and Accountabilities. The Public Service and Transparency, Commission of Inquiry into the Sponsorship Program and Advertising Activities, pp. 207–17. Ed.: Her Majesty the Queen in Right of Canada, represented by the Minister of Public Works and Government Services.

Gendron, Y., Cooper, D. J. and Townley, B. (2001) "In the Name of Accountability: State Auditing, Independence and New Public Management," *Accounting, Auditing & Accountability Journal*, 14(3): 278–310.

Gomery, John. H. (2005a) "Who Is Responsible? Summary," Commission of Inquiry into the Sponsorship Program and Advertising Activities, Ed.: Her Majesty the Queen in Right of Canada, represented by the Minister of Public Works and Government Services, 84 pp. Website: http://epe.lac-bac.gc.ca/100/206/301/pco-bcp/commissions/sponsorship-ef/06-03-06/www.gomery.ca/en/phase1report/summary/index.asp (retrieved on March 17, 2014).

Gomery, John. H. (2005b) "Who Is Responsible? Facts Finding Report," Commission of Inquiry into the Sponsorship Program and Advertising Activities, Ed.: Her Majesty the

Queen in Right of Canada, represented by the Minister of Public Works and Government Services, 708 pp. Website: http://epe.lac-bac.gc.ca/100/206/301/pco-bcp/commissions/sponsorship-ef/06-03-06/www.gomery.ca/en/phase1report/ffr/index.asp(retrieved on March 17, 2014).

Gomery, John H. (2006) "Restoring Accountability – Recommendations," Commission of Inquiry into the Sponsorship Program and Advertising Activities, Ed.: Her Majesty the Queen in Right of Canada, represented by the Minister of Public Works and Government Services, 245 pp. Website: http://epe.lac-bac.gc.ca/100/206/301/pco-bcp/commissions/sponsorship-ef/06-03-06/www.gomery.ca/en/phase2report/recommendations/cispaa_report_full.pdf (consulted on March 3, 2014).

Lonsdale, Jeremy and Bechberger, Elena (2011) "Learning in an accountability setting," in Jeremy Lonsdale, Peter Wilkins and Tom Ling (eds.), *Performance Auditing – Contributing to Accountability in Democratic Government*, Chapter 13, pp. 268–88, Cheltenham: Edward Elgar.

Malloy, Jonathan (2004) "An auditor's best friend? Standing committees on public accounts," *Canadian Public Administration/Administration publique du Canada*, 47(2): 165–83.

Malloy, Jonathan (2006) "The Standing Committee on Public Accounts," in Restoring Accountability – Research studies – Volume 1 – Parliament, Ministers and Deputy Ministers, Commission of Inquiry into the Sponsorship Program and Advertising Activities, pp. 62–100. Ed.: Her Majesty the Queen in Right of Canada, represented by the Minister of Public Works and Government Services.

Morin, Danielle (2000) "La vie après une mission de vérification de l'optimisation des ressources: le point de vue des gestionnaires" (Life after value for money audit: the auditees' standpoint), *Administration publique du Canada/Canadian Public Administration*, 43(4): 432–52.

Morin, Danielle (2003) "Controllers or Catalysts for Change and Improvement: Would the Real Value for Money Auditors Please Stand Up?" *Managerial Auditing Journal*, 18(1): 19–30.

Morin, Danielle (2008) "Auditors General's universe revisited: An exploratory study of the influence they exert on public administration through their value for money audits," *Managerial Auditing Journal*, 23(7): 697–720.

Morin, Danielle (2011) "Serving as magistrate at the French Cour des comptes: Navigating between tradition and modernity," *Accounting, Auditing & Accountability Journal* (Australia), 24(6): 718–50.

Murphy, Shawn (2007) "Restoring the Honor of the RCMP: Addressing Problems in the Administration of the RCMP's Pension and Insurance Plans," Report of the Standing Committee on Public Accounts, December, 39th Parliament, 2nd session.

Murphy, Rex. (2010) "MPs' attitude doesn't add up," *National Post*, A4, May 21.

Pollitt, Christopher, Girre, X., Lonsdale, J., Mul, R, Summa, H, and Waerness, M. (1999) *Performance or Compliance? Performance Audit and Public Management in Five Countries*, Oxford: Oxford University Press.

Power, Michael (1997) *The Audit Society: Rituals of Verification*, 2nd edn, New York: Oxford University Press.

Radcliffe, V. S. (2008) "Public Secrecy in Auditing: What Government Auditors cannot Know," *Critical Perspectives on Accounting*, 19(1): 99–126.

Roberts, Simon and Pollitt, Christopher. (1994) "Audit or evaluation? A National Audit Office VFM study," *Public Administration*, 72: 527–49.

Skaerbaek, Peter (2009) "Public sector auditor identities in making efficiency auditable:

The National Audit Office of Denmark as independent auditor and modernizer," *Accounting, Organizations and Society*, 34: 971–87.

Sossin, Lorne (2006) "Defining Boundaries: The Constitutional Argument for Bureaucratic Independence and its Implication for the Accountability of Public Service," in Restoring Accountability – Research studies – Volume 2 – The Public Service and Transparency, Commission of Inquiry into the Sponsorship Program and Advertising Activities, pp. 25–72. Ed.: Her Majesty the Queen in Right of Canada, represented by the Minister of Public Works and Government Services.

5 Danish public sector performance audit

An SAI and PAC tango

Peter Skærbæk and Mark Christensen

Introduction

The Danish Public Accounts Committee (DPAC) is amongst the world's oldest parliamentary account oversight committees, having been established in 1849 and enjoying constitutional recognition in each of Denmark's five successive Constitution Acts since 1849. The longevity of the DPAC's existence and the strength of its continued importance during that history are testaments to its significance in a society that now prides itself as being highly transparent (Williams, 2014). This chapter analyses how the DPAC and the National Audit Office of Denmark (NAOD) interrelate with each other in the acquittal of transparency of government in the performance audit regime.[1] Within this field we find an intricate interface between political controversy and audit independence concepts that displays a tango of relations and identities around the enduring complexity of how Supreme Audit Institutions (SAI) and oversight bodies behave – sometimes with the pace of a fast tango dance. In their joint behaviours we observe intricate connections between SAI independence, audit quality and parliamentary oversight of the audit function. In providing this analysis, a contribution is made to understandings of institutional arrangements between parliamentary transparency mechanisms in a sophisticated constitutional democracy.

The singularly important concept in this discussion of the DPAC and NAOD (and indeed this book) is that of SAI independence. Since the INTOSAI 'Mexico Declaration' regarding independence, good practice has been prescribed by ISSAI 10 (INTOSAI, 2007). However, as noted in various studies, compliance to ISSAI 10 is not uniform and at least 60 variables (Robertson, 2013) can be tested to assess compliance so achievement of absolute independence can be considered as a 'holy grail' for auditors, auditees and oversight bodies. Nevertheless, the degree of executive influence over exercise of audit powers is the core of independence and Thomas (2003: 297) identifies five structural features of independence in a parliamentary system that can assist to narrow our focus:

- the nature of the mandate of the agency, including how it is defined initially and how it is updated periodically;

- the provisions respecting the appointment, tenure and removal of the leadership of the agency;
- the process for deciding budgets and staffing for the agency;
- whether the agency is free to identify issues for study and whether it can compel the production of information; and
- the reporting requirements for the agency and whether its performance is monitored.

For the purposes of assessing SAI independence, Thomas's five features can be distilled into three primary issues, as are reflected in many Auditor-General Acts around the world. For example, these three features are captured in Section 7 of the Western Australian Auditor General Act, 2006: 'the Auditor General is not subject to direction from anyone in relation to whether a particular audit is conducted, how it is conducted or what is included in an audit report.' One further issue that can be added to the three aspects is that SAI avoids involvement in systems change within the auditee institution in order to be free of consequential bias for future audits (INTOSAI, 2010: 8). In the DPAC–NAOD relationship, we see institutional elements that are not in the normative prescription for SAI independence and as a result we set out to determine if public sector performance audit in Denmark is affected by issues related to the NAOD's independence.

The chapter utilizes the following structure: first it presents an overview of the DPAC and its relationship with the NAOD; second, having identified potential reasons to question the independence of the NAOD, the chapter examines evidence relevant to that issue and does so using a macro-view of the performance audit portfolio before examining secondary sources in a form of meta-analysis of relevant literature; a discussion is then provided to better understand how the tango of relations impacts on the reality of practice within Danish performance audit; finally, the chapter concludes and provides some suggestions for fruitful further research.

A Danish conquest: an oversight capture of independence

'According to the Danish Constitution, Parliament appoints the members of the Public Accounts Committee (PAC) to carry out the audit of the Danish public accounts' (Statsrevisorerne, 2012: 3). This extract from the Preamble of the DPAC's official English-language overview of itself provides a simple encapsulation of the DPAC's vision that it is the ultimate auditor of the Danish public sector. Indeed, in contrast to other PACs where members are given the title of 'Commissioner' or 'Member', the DPAC is constituted of 'State Auditors' (in Danish: *Statsrevisor*); this title has been in place since the PAC's inception in 1849 including when first incorporated under the Danish Constitution. The concept of the DPAC being an integral part of the Danish audit function is further elaborated by the DPAC:

> *the Danish public audit organisation* comprises 2 independent institutions under Parliament: the PAC and the Auditor-General's Office. The Auditor-General's

Office carries out the majority of the audit work. The Auditor-General's Office reports to the PAC in the form of reports and memoranda. The *PAC is the only authority with the right to direct the Auditor General to carry out specific audit activities.*

(Statsrevisorerne, 2012: 12, emphasis added)

The explicit inclusion of the DPAC in the singular 'Danish public audit organisation' is a characteristic that demands attention in this chapter. However, other elements of what makes up the DPAC are notable and are explained below.

The DPAC consists of six State Auditors elected by Parliament with the six largest political parties each electing one State Auditor. These State Auditors do not necessarily need to be Members of Parliament and the present Chair who has served the DPAC for 22 years (16 years as Chair) is not a Member of Parliament. Each State Auditor is elected for a four-year term but can be re-elected without maximum term. The Chair is the State Auditor with the longest serving DPAC membership (Knudsen, 2001) and is typically not a member of the main political party supporting the government, and perhaps this is related to two further interesting features of the DPAC's workings:

1   A principle of consensus: 'Individual PAC members often express views on audit reports and upcoming investigations to the media and the public. However, such views are always based upon unanimous decisions in the PAC' (Statsrevisorerne, 2012: 12). The principle of consensus in particular 'applies in cases where the PAC makes the request that specific investigations be carried out by the Auditor General' (Statsrevisorerne, 2012: 11).
2   In camera meetings with only associated staff (the DPAC has a staff of three) and the NAOD: during these meetings State Auditors have confidence that they will be heard on confidential matters before having to comply with the unanimous decisions of the DPAC (Christensen, 2009).

Holding meetings in camera and maintaining its principle of consensus may be seen as tactics to minimize political gamesmanship within the DPAC. As a result the DPAC argues that it has high credibility (Statsrevisorerne, 2012) and this claim is supported by J.G. Christensen (2009). The DPAC's credibility within the overall political process of Denmark is a fragile achievement belied by its more benign and uncontroversial four-part mission as stated in the 1849 Danish Constitution:

1   to verify that all revenue is correctly reflected in the accounts and that all expenditure has been paid in accordance with the legislation;
2   to verify that the accounts are correct;
3   to assess whether the public funds have been managed properly; and
4   to submit the audited public accounts for parliamentary approval.

(Statsrevisorerne, 2012: 1)

Notwithstanding the apparent account and accounting foci in that mission, the more politically contentious performance audits bring the DPAC into unavoidably controversial areas. Attached to those controversies come a range of consequential questions such as whether a performance audit is appropriate, whether the audit's scope and terms of reference are suitable, whether the conduct of the audit is professional, whether the audit of one matter eventuates in the omission of other matters from the performance audit portfolio (given constrained resources) and so on. It is those questions and their ilk that potentially can lead to attacks on the functioning of the DPAC as well as the alleged independence of the NAOD.

The DPAC's relationship with the NAOD begins with its role in the appointment of the Auditor-General since the DPAC nominates an individual to the Speaker of Parliament for appointment. However, from that point the relationship becomes one of interdependency, which can be seen at the beginning of a performance audit mandated by the DPAC. The DPAC provides draft terms of reference for the NAOD to consider and in turn the NAOD responds with a memo indicating the terms of reference to be adopted. Further negotiation can take place but rarely is that seen in a public forum. At the other end of the audit process – the provision of a report – the DPAC holds another power over the NAOD, which is not empowered to release its reports to the public or media. Instead, NAOD reports are forwarded to the DPAC, which in turn presents them to Parliament and does so with an accompanying commentary and recommendations for ministerial action. These aspects of the DPAC–NAOD relationship, together with the power of the DPAC to mandate NAOD conduct of specific performance audits, form some of the most important aspects of the DPAC–NAOD relationship. However, given the nuances of the relationship between an oversight committee and an SAI, it remains an empirical question as to whether the NAOD's independence is limited in the Danish pursuit of audit supervision. It is to that question that we turn next.

The empirical corpus of this chapter is captured in Table 5.1 as discussed in the remainder of the chapter.

Dimensions of the NAOD's independence

In this section we assess whether the NAOD is unfettered in its performance audit planning. We present an overview of the relative importance of DPAC-mandated performance audits compared to the remaining audits that are programmed by the NAOD. The importance of this is found in ISSAI 10 Principle 3, requiring a broad mandate and full discretion for the SAI in its functions, as is sympathetic to the prescriptions of Thomas (2003).

Relative importance of DPAC-mandated performance audits

Since performance audits are by nature variable in their terms of reference size, impact or precedence, it is challenging to assess the significance of a specific

Table 5.1 Overview of empirical corpus

Independence characteristic	Evidence drawn upon	Source
NAOD ability to determine its audit portfolio plan	Statistical analysis of the source of past audit topics	NAOD audit reports for 1998 to 2013
Freedom to determine an audit's terms of reference	Police reform audits (2008–2010)	Skærbæk and Christensen (forthcoming)
Audit report writing without external influence	Audits of Ministry of Foreign Affairs (2001–2002) and Ministry of Transport (1998–2004)	Justesen (2008); Justesen and Skærbæk (2005; 2010)
Impartiality: avoidance of decision making involvement	Audits of Defence (1989–2006) and Denmark's Radio Controversy (2001–2008)	Skærbæk (2009); NAOD and DPAC public announcements

collection of audits (for example, those audits not mandated by the NAOD in their portfolio of audits). However, it can be presumed that as the number of performance audits mandated by the DPAC increases as a proportion of the total number of performance audits, other things being equal, it is likely that the level of interference in the NAOD's independence may be higher. In accordance with this presumption we have extracted data (Table 5.2) showing the number of audits mandated by the DPAC under Section 8.1 of the Auditor General's Act (Rigsrevisorloven 2011).

Table 5.2 Quantum of performance audits mandated by the DPAC, 1998–2013

Year	Audits mandated by DPAC	Audits not mandated by DPAC	% of annual audit programme mandated by DPAC
1998	5	8	38
1999	4	13	24
2000	7	8	47
2001	5	12	29
2002	6	11	35
2003	6	8	43
2004	6	12	33
2005	6	11	35
2006	5	10	33
2007	7	11	39
2008	7	11	39
2009	8	9	47
2010	2	13	13
2011	8	12	38
2012	5	12	29
2013	5	22	19

From Table 5.2 it is notable that in ten separate years, a third or more of the NAOD's performance audit topics were chosen by the DPAC. On a simple measure of topics, it would seem that the NAOD cannot argue that the first simplified feature of independence (that is, unfettered freedom to choose audit topic) is met. In no single year has the NAOD been able to determine more than 87 per cent of its performance audit programme and so it can be concluded that a materially significant number of topics or devotion of audit resources are not of the choice of the NAOD.[2] Clearly, Section 8.1 of the Auditor General's Act, which empowers the DPAC to interfere in the NAOD's audit programme, is not a hollow power but instead is operating to ensure that party political forces have an active say in what issues are subject to performance audit.

The NAOD's unusual legislated framework has led to independent commentary of the NAOD on issues of independence (NAOD, 2006a) in a peer review conducted with the assistance of INTOSAI. That peer review noted that the legislative framework 'makes the NAOD unique, compared to other SAIs' (NAOD, 2006a: 6). Further, the review noted that the NAOD has a need to enhance its 'ability to set the correct long-term priorities in performance audit' (p. 9). These comments recognize the dual interference in audit planning quantum and timing that means the NAOD is significantly challenged in its ability to determine an audit portfolio plan on any timeframe.

Arising from oversight interference in the NAOD is its inability to follow its desired audit plan, since it can be disrupted at any time and to any extent decided by the DPAC. The difficulty of this situation is noted by Knudsen (2001: 141):

> The Auditor-General has to find a balance between requested audits and self-determined audit work. This requires that the resource consumption to the various tasks is made explicit. This also requires that the Auditor-General draws attention to circumstances where requested work becomes an impediment to other tasks.

However, to date there is no known public expression of dissatisfaction by the Auditor-General – including in the years 2000, 2003 and 2009 when the DPAC mandated 47 per cent, 43 per cent and 47 per cent of the whole performance audit regime. It is difficult to contemplate how a planned programme of performance audits can absorb such magnitudes of unplanned audits without weakening the audit plan in regard to its topics or its depth of audit. Thus the issue of priority setting in determining the programme of performance audit is clearly an issue with which the NAOD must grapple given the annual and ad hoc mandated audits directed by the DPAC and given the inability of the NAOD to expand its resources (budget or manpower) at short notice.

Whilst the Auditor General's Act allows DPAC mandate of audit, there is evidence that the powerful Parliamentary Finance and Budget Committee also directs the NAOD to conduct audits. This evidence is found in a report by the consulting firm Rambøll, noting that 'The Parliament's Finance and Budget Committee is also requesting *more* reviews to be done' (Rambøll, 2009: 35, emphasis added). Although the magnitude of such requests is unknown, Skærbæk and Christensen (forthcoming) also document an instance of direction from the Finance and Budget Committee to the NAOD via the DPAC for conduct of a performance audit.

Given the NAOD's inability to fully programme its audit plan, it faces difficult choices in resource allocation, and indications are that one choice is to make the audit less deep and/or less wide. That is, an observed tendency to compliance audit rather than performance audit has been documented by peer review (NAOD, 2006a) and agreed by the NAOD (NAOD, 2013). This tendency means that the NAOD's performance audit programme has less emphasis on efficiency and effectiveness (NAOD, 2006a) than would be expected of a truly independent SAI. Arising from this observation is an interest in the other aspects of independence, to which we turn next.

Freedom to determine an audit's terms of reference

Crucial to an independent SAI is the ability to focus planned performance audits on specific matters where justified by the Auditor's-General judgement on materiality and risk without external pressure to include or exclude certain matters. The final expression of that judgement is the audit specification documented in terms of reference defining the scope of the audit. Implicit in good performance audit practice is the understanding that the auditor will determine the audit's terms of reference and other aspects of the audit's specifications (INTOSAI Professional Standard Committee, 2010).

In order to understand the NAOD's situation with respect to audit specification, it is necessary to consider the process by which a performance audit is conceived, planned, executed, reported upon and subsequently audited. That process is depicted in Figure 5.1, wherein it is shown that NAOD performance audits are subject to a routine draft of an audit specification which needs to be agreed to by the DPAC before the commencement of the audit.

In this section, we review evidence that audit specifications do not always comply with ISSAI Principle 3. Rarely can we see behind the closed doors of the DPAC and NAOD in their audit planning, but in the case of multiple performance audits of the Danish police reforms from 2008 to 2010, revealing data is produced. As documented by Skærbæk and Christensen (forthcoming), draft terms of reference were prepared by the NAOD after receiving a DPAC notice of requirement of a performance audit. The draft terms of reference were sent to the DPAC with the Auditor's-General request: 'If the DPAC wants, I can initiate the investigation in accordance with the sketched above' (NAOD, 2008: 4), and final audit specifications were approved by the DPAC and the audit commenced forthwith (Rigsrevisionen, 2009). In a major performance audit, the specification was narrow, such that instead of a performance audit in which evaluations of economy, efficiency and effectiveness would be reached there was a 'decision to focus on the management of the reform (which) framed the audit and this can be identified as an instance of

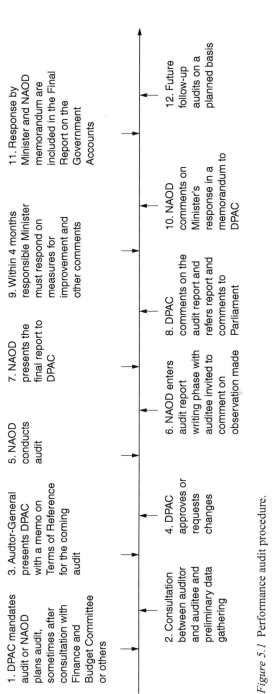

1. DPAC mandates audit or NAOD plans audit, sometimes after consultation with Finance and Budget Committee or others

2. Consultation between auditor and auditee and preliminary data gathering

3. Audtor-General presents DPAC with a memo on Terms of Reference for the coming audit

4. DPAC approves or requests changes

5. NAOD conducts audit

6. NAOD enters audit report writing phase with auditee invited to comment on observation made

7. NAOD presents the final report to DPAC

8. DPAC comments on the audit report and refers report and comments to Parliament

9. Within 4 months responsible Minister must respond on measures for improvement and other comments

10. NAOD comments on Minister's response in a memorandum to DPAC

11. Response by Minister and NAOD memorandum are included in the Final Report on the Government Accounts

12. Future follow-up audits on a planned basis

Figure 5.1 Performance audit procedure.

blame purification provided by the auditing profession' (Skærbæk and Christensen, forthcoming).

Whilst the police reform audits can be considered to be a single case where political controversy was extreme (see Skærbæk and Christensen, forthcoming), it is notable that the formalized process of determining terms of reference as shown in Figure 5.1 is apparently designed to ensure that the NAOD does not commence a performance audit with only its independent judgement determining the issues to be subject to audit. A review of DPAC requests for audits under Section 8.1 of the Auditor General Act reveals that the DPAC uses a standard format in which it specifies questions or issues to be investigated which subsequently appear in the audit's terms of reference. Indeed, it is documented that the DPAC holds its meetings with the Auditor-General waiting outside the meeting room in case he (now she) is required for discussions with the DPAC (Rambøll, 2009: 29). The consequential smooth flow of non-documented directives from the DPAC directly to the NAOD does not reinforce the image of the Auditor-General exercising absolute independence. Further, there is no evidence of a lack of unanimity between the DPAC and the NAOD on the terms of reference for performance audits. Instead, it seems that the process is designed to privilege political influence over the NAOD's judgement and in contravention of ISSAI Principle Number 3.

Performance audit report writing without influence external to the NAOD

Performance audit reports are invariably controversial in their findings. Such controversy raises issues of political risk to government, agencies and senior managers such that there is heightened sensitivity to the written word of the eventual audit output: a final report. It is in that context that INTOSAI (2007) has pointed to the importance that the SAI is not subject to influence in writing of the performance audit report. It is within that issue we now consider evidence arising from the NAOD's recent activities.

The extant literature reveals strong evidence that the NAOD subjects its audit reports to a degree of co-authoring. For example, Justesen (2008) presents an in-depth study of the writing of a performance audit regarding the Ministry of Foreign Affairs. She finds that a 'multiplicity of authors' (p. 214), such as the press, DPAC members, MPs, auditee representatives, etc., give birth to audit reports that are attributed solely in the name of the NAOD.

Comparable to the analysis of Justesen (2008), Justesen and Skærbæk (2005; 2010) analyse a series of audit reports between 1998 and 2004 in the Ministry of Transport (MoT) portfolio and identify instances of co-authoring of audit reports. In that six-year period, the DPAC mandated seven audits related to specific issues arising in the MoT's responsibilities. These audits can be seen as a series in which issues from prior audits influenced audit reports in the subsequent audits. By recognising the *seriatim* nature of these reports, Justesen and Skærbæk (2010) point out that the ways in which media, politicians and auditee managers have treated prior reports seem to be influencing subsequent report writing and selection of future audit topics. Whilst perhaps being recognition of the importance of public commentary on performance audits, this observation is interesting since it signals that audits conducted in *seriatim* need to be considered as a package rather than individually. However, unlike the application of this concept in a judicial context where *seriatim* is known to all parties to proceedings, the DPAC's ability to 'extend' performance reviews, without warning or planning by issuing sequential demands for audits, leaves the auditee and the NAOD unprepared for the consequential demand on resources.

In the package of information presented by Justesen and Skærbæk (2010) it is notable that the series of audits reached a culmination in a DPAC-mandated audit on the 'corporate management' responsibility of the MoT Secretariat (Rigsrevisionen, 2004). The evidence suggests that the DPAC had targeted the cause of its concerns regarding transport issues across multiple agencies over a six-year period: the senior managers. Both these managers and the NAOD were aware that media reaction to audits is positively correlated with the extent of criticism expressed in the audit reports and so the number of rounds of report revision seemed to increase as the *seriatim* audits emerged. In the latter audit report writing, six drafts were discussed before the NAOD felt confident to provide the DPAC with its report (Justesen and Skærbæk, 2005: 334). Such an incidence of drafting indicates a degree of co-authoring or negotiation rather than the prescribed 'check for accuracy' process whereby an auditee is invited to comment on a draft report. As Justesen and Skærbæk (2005: 334) note: an 'important external factor that influenced the process was the PAC who initiated the writing of the report (and) ... in this sense the PAC is clearly an active co-writer in this particular audit process'. Thus, the ideal image of an audit report being an unbiased and independent output of a scientific process of enquiry is damaged by Justesen's (2008) and Justesen and Skærbæk's (2010) demonstration of co-authoring and the determination of audit targets in a series of progressive audits.

Decision-making involvement

Sound arguments are provided by ISSAI 10 and ISSAI 12 as to why auditors should avoid involvement in the management or decision-making processes of auditee entities. A solid principle is that such involvement will necessarily reduce the SAI's independence if conducting future audits in those affected entities. In this regard, we sought to identify whether there is evidence of the NAOD breaching this good practice whereby auditors should 'not be involved or be seen to be involved, in any manner, whatsoever, in the management of the organizations that they audit' (ISSAI 12: 5).

At the time of the cases referred to in Table 5.1, the NAOD English-language webpage unintentionally revealed the potential for danger in regard to involvement in decision-making. It sought to establish a twin identity which, if implemented, would bring the NAOD close to involvement in auditee decision making. The webpage stated that NAOD's mission covered both a 'control' and an 'encourage' role (NAOD, 2005); however the NAOD did not seem to recognize the inherent contradiction between controlling auditees without having involvement in management or decision-making – as would be the case if change was 'encouraged'.[3] Whilst that inherent contradiction was present, a 'trap' seemed to be present for NAOD auditors such that their enthusiasm for change might blind them to the dangers attached to auditors becoming too closely associated with planning and/or implementation of new systems. It is to that danger that we turn in this section.

At least two documented cases exist where evidence points to NAOD auditors being accused of involvement in management decision-making within an auditee entity. One case is documented by Skærbæk (2009) and relates to the Danish Defence Force (DDF) in a series of eight audits conducted by the NAOD from 1989 to 2006. Over such a large number of audits it is shown that the NAOD's desire to see management accounting reform resulted in their exposure to decision-making about the precise design of that reform. Thus one interviewee recalled when the decision was being made to implement the new accounting system named DeMars: 'the NAOD was sitting at the end of the table when DeMars was decided' (quoted in Skærbæk, 2009: 981). Further, in the Auditor-General's 1996 annual report to Parliament, he assured them that DeMars 'will solve all significant problems' (quoted in Skærbæk, 2009: 981). In this evidence we see the NAOD assuming an identity not consistent with ISSAI Principle 3 since it became active in the DDF as a 'modernizer' rather than an independent auditor. The modernizer was keen to support and implement what it considered to be improvements to the DDF's accounting system. Consequential to that, the DPAC expressed concern that the NAOD 'was involved with the DeMars project as a consultant giving advice' (Skærbæk, 2009: 981).

The NAOD's exposure to a self-inflicted impairment to its independence in the DDF audits did not act to prevent it from much greater reputational damage in 2006 when it became embroiled in criticism of its active support of management decision-making in Denmark's Radio (DR) building cost-overrun scandal. Although peer-reviewed analysis of the NAOD's involvement in the DR scandal is yet to appear, we rely here on source documents that reveal matters relevant to our endeavours in this chapter.

Denmark Radio is Denmark's national broadcaster and the case here emerged from serious cost overruns that developed as DR was managing the construction of a new headquarters intended by the government to be a major piece of infrastructure underpinning a new urban extension of Copenhagen on previously undeveloped land. The new building and concert hall was to be a landmark and thus was politically important from the beginning of its conception. During the construction phase, the NAOD made annual financial audits and various commentaries 'on a running basis' (KPMG and Grant Thornton, 2008: 161) on the DR construction project between 2002 and 2006. Indeed, to do so, the NAOD's allocated staff frequently attended the premises of DR during the construction management period. From this close relationship between the NAOD and DR management one eventual result was that the NAOD was challenged as to whether it had breached the impartiality principle of avoiding decision-making in auditee entities.

The controversy surrounding the very large cost overruns (around 600 million DKK in 2006) of the DR project led to growing commentary in the Danish media. The amount of money involved became a political embarrassment and the NAOD responded by announcing in early September that it would conduct a major review of the DR project. However, this action generated criticism that the NAOD lacked impartiality because it had previously supported budget allocations, with advice to the DR Board in April 2006 that those allocations encompassed known risks. That is, commentators drew attention to the NAOD's lack of independence on the matter of DR's management as a consequence of its provision of *advice* regarding future eventualities. The severity of this criticism motivated the Parliament's Culture Committee to seek advice from Parliament's Legal Secretariat as to the reality or appearance of the NAOD's lack of impartiality, independence or competence to audit the DR. In December 2006 the Secretariat brought its report to Parliament, noting that the NAOD had provided advice and support to the DR in its management of the construction project (Folketingets Lovsekretariat, 2006); however, a case of partiality sufficient to warrant dismissal of the Auditor-General was not found. Nevertheless, the Auditor-General decided to cancel the proposed audit and instead KPMG and Grant Thornton were commissioned, by the Ministry of Cultural Affairs, to conduct a performance audit of DR from which they eventually produced a 389-page report.

The notable outcome of the DR case, from the audit point of view, was that it produced a very rare moment the long history of Denmark's DPAC: the DPAC issued a criticism of the NAOD. Even though the extensive KPMG/Grant Thornton report concluded that DR's management could not rely only on the NAOD's advice, the DPAC's secretariat was more damning in its conclusion that 'there was an expectations gap ... (we) had expected that the NAOD had audited the budgetary assumptions and had compared them to the degrees of actual accomplishment' (Statsrevisorerne Sekretariat, 2008: 8). Further, the DPAC noted that it found it 'unsatisfactory that the NAOD for a number of issues had not carried out its audit task on the DR's construction (project)' (Statsrevisorerne, 2008: 1). This observation of the DPAC reveals an expectation that the NAOD could in some way have prevented the cost overruns. Such an expectation appears to be reflective of a faith in the power of audit which is clearly beyond what can be delivered and, if it were possible, would imperil the NAOD's impartiality. As will be noted, the DPAC would achieve more if it invoked other arms of government machinery to implement change where the DPAC perceived that change was required.

The DR case is enlightening, not simply for its alert to the NAOD of the importance of independence. Additionally, it revealed that the decision to conduct performance audits in Denmark, at that time, was a political outcome and that the DPAC is superior to the NAOD. Further, it revealed involvements of Parliamentary Committees beyond the DPAC and Finance and Budget Committee in the selection of audit topics and the crafting of terms of reference (even after the commencement of the audit, since the NAOD audit was altered by request of the DPAC and the Culture Committee, after the audit had commenced and before it was later aborted) (NAOD, 2006b). These observations are consistent with aspects of the abovementioned Police and Defence audits.

Conclusion: 'something rotten in the state of Denmark', or an open and transparent society?

The above discussion presents evidence that the relationship between the NAOD and the DPAC leaves the NAOD in a situation of weakened or impaired independence. The NAOD cannot determine its audit plan without interference by the DPAC and other Parliamentary bodies; the audit specifications are negotiated and eventually approved by the DPAC; audit reports are the consequence of a co-authoring process and subject to overarching comment by the DPAC before being released for public consideration; and there are known instances of the NAOD providing advice to auditee entities where that advice relates to management decision-making which may be subject to future audit. Each of these matters is in contradiction to ISSAI standards or good practice.

The evidence noted questions the Danish institutional arrangements for public sector audit. However, an arguable case can be made that the Danes have established legislative and precedential conventions that make open (or relatively open) what happens by way of hidden reality in most other countries. That is, it is naive to expect that audit oversight bodies do not exert varying levels of influence over SAIs in terms of their performance audit planning and in terms of interpretation of the audit results, including crafting of a politically sensitive audit report (for a comparable example, see Radcliffe, 2008). By legislating the DPAC's right to mandate audits and by creating the convention that audit terms of reference are influenced and approved by the DPAC, Denmark has made open the fact that SAIs cannot operate with absolute independence whilst Parliament remains supreme. Of course, the 'balancing act' that is required is for Parliament to ensure that the Executive does not turn Parliament into a 'rubber stamp' approving body. In that regard, the Danish mechanism of the six largest political parties electing one individual each (and not necessarily a Parliamentarian) means that audit oversight is enacted by a political mix close to that which characterizes Parliament, and not the government, which is constituted by the single largest political party or a coalition commanding a majority of votes.

Against the efficacious design features of the DPAC–NAOD 'tango' can be noted some risks which demonstrate that Denmark could nevertheless improve matters related to public sector audit. In particular there is a risk of impartiality impairment as the tenures of the DPAC Chair and the Auditor-General stretch into long – sometimes decades-long – concurrent tenures. In the period from 1998 to 2012 the same DPAC Chair and the same Auditor-General held their respective roles and during that period it is notable that the degree of

DPAC-mandated audits rose to 50 per cent of the total performance audit programme. Such proportions cannot be seen as conforming to the right of the SAI to determine *what* is audited but they may indicate that the relationship between DPAC Chair and Auditor-General had reached levels of mutual confidence and understanding that do not serve the interests of Parliament, nor of independent audit. In such a close relationship, it is possible that both institutions begin to rely on each other's support to the point where mutual co-dependency causes dysfunctions in the acquittal of independent audit. Thus we observe the NAOD failing to preserve its impartiality in cases such as the DR audit and we observe the DPAC involving itself in audits as they proceed even to the effect of altering terms of reference during an audit.

The time-honoured principle of ensuring auditors do not develop a close personal relationship with auditees could be equally applied to the tango of relations between a DPAC Chair and an Auditor-General. In order to obviate the likelihood of co-dependency reaching levels comparable to nepotism, it would seem desirable to set maximum terms of Chair tenure for the DPAC in a manner similar to that imposed on the Auditor-General in the 2011 amended Act (Rigsrevisorloven, 2011). Such a system would be a contrast to the current arrangement whereby the DPAC Chair is the longest-serving State Auditor (Knudsen, 2001); thus there is no mechanism to prevent a long-serving Chair from serving a concurrent period with a long serving Auditor-General. In fact, the current arrangements guarantee the DPAC Chair and the Auditor-General will work closely together for long periods unless either relinquishes their appointment. Thus we see that the current DPAC Chair and the previous Auditor-General were in their respective positions concurrently for 14 years. Given the controversial nature of public sector audit it seems likely that a series of 'crises', in which the performance of both the DPAC and the NAOD come under pressure and scrutiny, may result in the DPAC Chair and the Auditor-General, as individual human beings, being compromised by favours, exchanges and administrative accommodations that will necessarily arise. This observation leads to another that also arises from the examination of DPAC and NAOD relations: the concern as to how the NAOD's activities are influenced by the NAOD's subservient relation to the DPAC.

The NAOD appears to have become a tool of investigation for the DPAC, which also acts as its administrative supervisor and conduit to Parliament. Whilst the NAOD is administratively a rather recent institution (commencing in 1976), the DPAC is remarkably long-standing with its history, dating from 1849 (Statsrevisorerne, 2012). These comparative histories add to the exercise of control by the DPAC over the NAOD with respect to performance audits. However, that control, at least under the 14-year period of concurrent tenures of the current DPAC Chair and the previous Auditor-General, has seen the NAOD performance audit criticized by peer review for excessive focus on compliance at the expense of considerations of efficiency and effectiveness (NAOD, 2006a). It has also seen up to 47 per cent of the NAOD's annual audit programme being determined by the DPAC (see Table 5.2) and evidence of other bodies' influence over the NAOD's audit programme is also found. These findings are coupled with the finding that Danish public sector performance audits arising from the political process are characterized as exercises in blame (Skærbæk and Christensen, forthcoming) in which that blame turns focus on to individuals and thus diverts attention from system issues of efficiency and effectiveness. As a result it is observed here that the NAOD's performance audit function is less effective than is possible.

In addition to the above-mentioned observations with respect to the NAOD's performance, this chapter concludes with the observation that the DPAC is itself not well served by its control over the NAOD. First, the DPAC has a confidence in the power of audit that exceeds the reality of audit: instead of invoking the use of relevant arms of government (such as the Ministry of Finance), the DPAC seems to rely on the NAOD for accounting expertise. Second, the disservice to the DPAC results from the manner in which the DPAC has diminished the NAOD's independence such that the oversight of the NAOD is also diminished. Since the DPAC Chair and the Auditor-General are likely to spend a number of years in close cooperation over controversial matters of intense interest to the political parties of Denmark, the DPAC's oversight of the NAOD is also compromised. As a result, instances of NAOD transgression of normal audit principles designed to preserve impartiality have been shown to arise. Perhaps with a less compromised oversight, the NAOD's service to the DPAC would be improved. Indeed, the significant drop in DPAC-mandated audit in the first full year of the new Auditor-General (see Table 5.2, 2013 data) may indicate that the new Auditor-General has observed the dangers pointed out above and has also been able to persuade the DPAC of her need to control the NAOD's audit programme in order to preserve her independence. Another interpretation of this limited data emergence is that the previous DPAC Chair and Auditor-General tango also allowed the NAOD to use the cover of the DPAC mandate to persuade agencies that the necessity for a performance audit – and its timing – in their realm of responsibilities was 'independently' determined from outside the NAOD. In doing so, the room to negotiate timing and scope of the audit would be eliminated since the legislative and political power of the DPAC would overwhelm any considerations that an agency might be able to marshal.

A final comment is worthy here: the above-mentioned cases and data relate to the Danish public sector audit tango of relations between SAI and audit oversight body, yet these observations can throw light on the generics of this difficult relationship. Clearly, SAI independence is crucial. However, SAIs do not have some god-like existence but they are drawn necessarily into the human and non-human networks within which they must operate. As a result, they need to preserve their reputation and identity as experts with the purity that is associated with independence and impartiality, yet they also need to have allies in government and in the public sector. To marshal support will sometimes require being supported and, perhaps later, being supportive. Such 'deals' can thus influence the context within which SAIs necessarily operate – including their relationships with the parliamentary oversight of their operations. The Danish situation may be uniquely Danish with its unusual legislative framework and its long history, but it does involve principles that are necessarily unavoidable in most SAIs.

Acknowledgements

The assistance of Dr Rolf Elm-Larsen, Dr Lise Justesen, Dr Tim Neerup Themsen, two anonymous reviewers and Professor Zahirul Hoque is kindly acknowledged. With additional empirics and analysis, this chapter has emerged from a project undertaken for publication in the Danish language monograph *Offentlig Revision i det 21st Århundrede*.

Notes

1 The term 'performance audit' (*forvaltningsrevision* in Danish) is described by the NAOD's website as including 'large audits' and 'progressive audits'. We do not pursue that distinction but instead limit our enquiries to non-financial audits.
2 Without wishing to be too forceful on this point, it is acknowledged that there is the possibility that the NAOD might have reached similar conclusions on the need for the conduct of a performance audit without the intervention of the DPAC. Nevertheless, the NAOD's audit planning is disrupted as a result of the DPAC's reactive interventions.
3 Sometime between 2012 and the time of writing, the NAOD revised its webpage and removed the words 'control' and 'encourage' from its mission. The more recent mission statement is: 'Rigsrevisionen audits the government accounts on behalf of the Danish Parliament and supports the development of efficient administration in order to create maximum value for the citizens' (NAOD, 2014).

References

Christensen, J. G. (2009) 'Notat vedr. Statens revision', Aarhus Universitet. Available at: www.ft.dk/Statsrevisorerne/Arbejde/~/media/Statsrevisorerne/Statens_revision%20 pdf.ashx. Accessed on 26 September 2014.
Folketingets Lovsekretariat (2006) Notat om Rigsrevisionens habilitet som undersøger af DR's byggeprojekt i Ørestaden. Available at: www.ft.dk/samling/20061/almdel/kuu/ bilag/94/333503/index.htm. Accessed on 26 September 2014.
International Organisation of Supreme Audit Institutions (INTOSAI) (2007) Mexico *Declaration on the Independence of Supreme Audit Institutions*.
INTOSAI Professional Standards Committee (2010). *ISSAI 3100 Performance Audit Guidelines – Key Principles*. Copenhagen: PSC Secretariat. Available at: www.issai. org/media/13220/issai_3100_e.pdf. Accessed on 20 September 2014.
Justesen, L. (2008) 'Kunsten at skrive revisionsrapporter. En beretning om forvaltningsrevisionens beretninger', PhD thesis, Forskerskolen i Ledelsesteknologier, Copenhagen Business School.
Justesen, L. and Skærbæk, P. (2005) 'Performance auditing and the production of discomfort', in S. Jönsson and J. Mouritsen (eds) *Accounting in Scandinavia: The Northern Lights*, pp. 321–43, Kristianstad: Liber and Copenhagen Business School Press.
Justesen, L. and Skærbæk, P. (2010) 'Performance auditing and the narrating of a new auditee identity', *Financial Accountability and Management*, 26(3): 325–43.
Knudsen, T. (2001) 'Statsrevisorerne i dag,' in K. Brandt and H. Rasmussen (eds) *Statsrevisorerne – 150*, Copenhagen: Schultz Erhvervsboghandel.

98   P. Skærbæk and M. Christensen

KPMG and Grant Thornton (2008) *Revisorundersøgelse af DR's byggeprojekt I Øresta-den*, 19 June, Copenhagen: Kulturministeriet.

NAOD (2005) *Værdigrundlag*. Available at: www.rigsrevisionen.dk/composite-13.htm. Accessed on 14 November 2005.

NAOD (2006a) *Peer Review Report: National Audit Office of Denmark*. Available at: www.rigsrevisionen.dk/media/102463/peer_review.pdf Accessed on 18 September 2014.

NAOD (2006b) 'Administrationsnotat til statsrevisorerne om Rigsrevisionens udtræden af undersøgelse om DR's byggeri i Ørestaden'. Available at: www.rigsrevisionen.dk/media/1881202/adm03–06.pdf. Accessed on 29 September 2014.

NAOD (2008) 'Notat til Statsrevisorerne om tilrettelæggelsen af en større undersøgelse af implementeringen af politireformen'. Available at: www.rigsrevisionen.dk/media/1914341/a406_08.pdf. Accessed on 30 September 2014.

NAOD (2013) 'Management's action plan to follow up on peer review suggestions'. Available at: http://uk.rigsrevisionen.dk/about-us/development/managements-action-plan-to-follow-up-on-the-review-suggestions. Accessed on 19 September 2014.

NAOD (2014) *Mission and Strategic Objectives 2012–2015*. Available at: http://uk.rig-srevisionen.dk/about-us/strategy-and-performance-targets/mission-and-strategic-objectives. Accessed on 26 September 2014.

Radcliffe, V. (2008) 'Public secrecy in auditing: What government auditors cannot know', *Critical Perspectives on Accounting*, 19: 99–126.

Rambøll Consulting (2009) *Rigsrevisionen – Kundeundersøgelse*, Rigsrevisionen rapport Oktober. Available at: www.rigsrevisionen.dk/media/102342/kundeundersogelse_2009.pdf. Accessed on 24 September 2014.

Rigsrevisionen (2004) *Beretning om Justitsministeriets Økonomistyring*. Beretning 9 March.

Rigsrevisionen (2009) *Beretning til Statsrevisorerne om politireformen*. August. Available at www.rigsrevisionen.dk/media/1831642/16-2008.pdf Accessed 3 November 2014.

Rigsrevisorloven (2011) *Bekendtgørelse af lov om revisionen af statens regnskaber m.m* Available at: www.retsinformation.dk/forms/r0710.aspx?id=140272. Accessed on 10 February 2015.

Robertson, G. (2013) *Independence of Auditors General*, Melbourne: Victorian Auditor-General Office.

Skærbæk, P. (2009) 'Public sector auditor identities in making efficiency auditable: The National Audit Office of Denmark as independent auditor and modernizer', *Accounting, Organizations and Society*, 34: 971–87.

Skærbæk, P. and Christensen, M. (forthcoming) 'Auditing and the purification of blame', *Contemporary Accounting Research*.

Statsrevisorerne (2008) 'Statsrevisorernes bemærkning til Rigsrevisionens revision af DR's byggeri i Ørestaden'. Available at: www.rigsrevisionen.dk/media/1918721/jur01_08_sr_udtalelse.pdf. Accessed on 10 February 2015.

Statsrevisorerne (2012). *The Public Accounts Committee of the Danish Parliament*. Available at: www.thedanishparliament.dk/About_the_Danish_Parliament/Institu-tions_of_the_Danish_Parliament/~/media/Pdf_materiale/Pdf_publikationer/English/The_Public_Accounts_%20Committee_of_the_%20Danish_Parliament.pdf.ashx. Accessed on 19 September 2014.

Statsrevisorerne Sekretariatet (2008) 'Gennemgang af Rigsrevisionens revisionsplaner og revisionsprotokollater vedrørende DR's byggeri i Ørestaden', 10 October. Available at: www.statsrevisorerne.dk. Accessed on 22 September 2014.

Thomas, P. (2003) 'The past, present and future officers of parliament', *Canadian Public Administration*, 46(3): 87–314.

Western Australian Legislation (2006) *Auditor General Act 2006*. Available at: www.slp. wa.gov.au/legislation/statutes.nsf/main_mrtitle_63_homepage.html. Accessed on 3 November 2014.

Williams, A. (2014) 'A global index of information and political transparency', University of Western Australia Business School Discussion Paper 14.07. Available at: www. business.uwa.edu.au/__data/assets/pdf_file/0004/2478928/14-07-A-Global-Index-of-Information-and-Political-Transparency.pdf. Accessed on 16 September 2014.

Part II

Public Accounts
Committees in Europe

6   The Public Accounts Committee of the House of Commons

Anthony Staddon

Introduction

The PAC is responsible for the non-partisan audit of public expenditure. Created in 1861, it has long been viewed as one of the Parliament's most powerful committees (Chubb, 1952; Flegmann, 1979). Rush (2005: 208) described the PAC as 'one of, if not the, most effective of parliamentary committees', while Peter Hennessey crowned it as 'the queen of the select committees … [which] by its very existence exerted a cleansing effect in all government departments' (Public Accounts Committee, 2007). The PAC's reputation is enhanced when compared with Parliament's continued weakness in *ex ante* decision-making power (Wehner, 2003). Scrutiny of government spending proposals is one of the weakest areas of parliamentary scrutiny in the UK and the House's power over expenditure has been described as close to a 'constitutional myth' (Select Committee on Procedure 1999: para 5).

The creation of departmental select committees in 1979 enabled the PAC to act as *primus inter pares*, with its long history, tradition of consensus and non-political reputation and support of the National Audit Office (NAO) crucial to its success. Comparative studies across the Commonwealth (Stapenhurst *et al.*, 2005; Pelizzo *et al.*, 2006), have examined what makes PACs work effectively and the good practice identified – such as whether the PAC is chaired by an Opposition member and the activity of the committee – and such studies have tended to reinforce the UK PAC's reputation.

At home, however, the PAC's standing vis-à-vis the other committees has been affected by the increased profile given to the Liaison Committee, consisting of the chairs of all the select committees in the House of Commons, particularly now that the Prime Minister appears before the committee to give evidence on matters of public policy three times a year. The Joint Committee on Human Rights, established in 2001, undertakes thematic inquiries on human rights issues and scrutinises all government Bills for human rights implications and has also developed a strong reputation in its short existence. Meanwhile the departmental select committees, which unlike the PAC consider the merits of policy rather than its implementation, have matured with the introduction of core tasks and heightened public expectation. The welcome development of legislative oversight capacity may have led to increased competition for attention across the various parliamentary committees, but this study will demonstrate that the PAC continues to receive great attention.

Wider changes across the political landscape have also impacted upon the PAC. The Westminster PAC no longer has a role in scrutinising much of the expenditure in the devolved parts of the UK. Before devolution in 1999, audit in the UK was concentrated from the centre and carried out by the NAO and the PAC. Audit devolution was developed administratively through the operation of distinct procedures in the UK PAC at Westminster (in line with other distinct procedures established at Westminster for Scotland and Wales). Devolution has seen the creation of separate audit bodies for Scotland, Wales and Northern Ireland and the establishment of PACs in each legislature.[1] The amount of time spent on public audit has therefore dramatically increased and provides further evidence for what Power (1994) describes as an 'audit explosion' within the UK.

This chapter examines the structures, responsibilities and working practices of the committee, drawing on the response to a questionnaire that was sent to the UK PAC House of Commons by the World Bank Institute in 2008/9 as well as a literature and press review of its work and modus operandi. Achieving good value for public money has always been important, but the aftermath of the financial crisis and the budgetary cuts across most government departments make this an opportune time to re-examine the PAC's role and performance, particularly since the leadership of the committee is now undertaken by its first directly elected chair. The analysis highlights the growing importance of the NAO and PAC, partly because of increased access rights and partly as a result of the actions taken by the committee in the current Parliament.

Heightened PAC visibility has led, in turn, to some criticism and a greater focus on the PAC itself. The NAO's evidence-based findings have long been important for the PAC, but this relationship has now become even more critical with the NAO's reports serving as a shield for the PAC. For its part, the PAC can operate at a more visible and political level than the more circumspect and cautious NAO, taking a sword to waste and inefficiency across the public sector. Finally, the study argues that measuring the impact of the PAC in terms of financial savings and the number of recommendations implemented is likely to undervalue the committee's actual influence.

Powers and responsibilities

Operating under the authority of the Standing Orders of the House of Commons, principally No. 148, the PAC's remit is 'the examination of the accounts showing the appropriation of the sums granted by Parliament to meet the public expenditure, and of such other accounts laid before Parliament as the Committee may think fit'. The committee has the unrestricted right to access government agencies, statutory authorities, government-owned corporations and government service providers. It can summon officials from any publicly funded body to which the NAO has access and can summon representatives of anybody involved in the spending of public money by virtue of the power, common to all select committees, of calling for 'persons, papers and records'.

The PAC has the right to examine public accounts and financial affairs and can consider issues of efficiency, economy and effectiveness of programme implementation as well as the effectiveness of policy implementation. The PAC does not look at the merits of policy: this falls to the departmental select committees. Indeed, the PAC today seldom looks at the accounts of government departments. This is partly because the programme of value for money (VFM) studies is so intensive and partly because the departmental select committees are now expected to carry out this role (although the extent to which they do so varies). However, the PAC still has the right to take evidence about them, and regularly examines, for example, aspects of the accounts of the Revenue and Customs.

One of the differences across the UK concerns a PAC's access to local government. The Welsh PAC has an unrestricted right of access to local government while the scrutiny of local councils in Scotland falls within the responsibility of the Accounts Commission which forms part of Audit Scotland, but reports to Scottish ministers. England has a separate Audit Commission charged with the oversight of both local government and a range of other locally active bodies and an NAO for central government operations. In other words devolution has enabled Scotland and Wales to adopt alternative audit arrangements which differ from those pursued in England. However, the extent of divergence should not be exaggerated as there are also pressures to converge. In 2007, the five UK audit agencies (the Audit Commission, Audit Scotland, the NAO, the Northern Ireland Audit Office and the Wales Audit Office) jointly launched a set of indicators through the Public Audit Forum with the aim to create consistency across the audit bodies.

England is facing the loss of one of its audit bodies with the Audit Commission expected to close in 2015, 30 years after it was established, with the expectation that independent audit committees will be created within the local authority to ensure the independence of the audit relationship and protect the principle that public bodies should not appoint their own auditors. One of the key justifications for contracting out local government audit to private firms is to bring the public sector audit regime into line with the private sector: arrangements for the monitoring of audit quality will be aligned with those in place for audits of private-sector companies carried out under the Companies Act. Whether this is a positive change for local government is a matter for debate; one issue raised is that the audit of public bodies generally requires a broader scope than the audit of financial statements for private companies.

A further interpretation of the decision to abolish the Audit Commission is that it signals a retreat from the idea of a regulatory state with the centre setting objectives and targets and the local government devising the delivery methods. Indeed, the Coalition Government has justified the end of the Commission as part of its commitment to localism and a move away from a 'command and control' approach to central–local government, particularly evident under New Labour. As a 2014 PAC report highlighted, local authorities were given £36.1 billion in 2013–14, 'of which £32.9 billion had no specific conditions attached as to how local authorities could use it, other than that spending was lawful' (PAC 2014: 5).

There does, however, appear to be an inconsistency in the Coalition Government's approach and rhetoric. On the one hand there is an attempt to extend the local scrutiny function; on the other local authorities remain dependent on central government and central taxpayers. From a local democracy perspective, the argument that the national legislature, and bodies reporting to Westminster, should have a role in addressing accountability at the local level is controversial. Yet this may be inevitable if money is raised and distributed from the centre as the national legislature has a duty to ensure such money is spent wisely. This view is supported by a 2014 inquiry into local government funding as the Department for Communities and Local Government was unable to confirm that local authorities achieve value for money with government funding (PAC 2014: 3). This may justify why some of the Audit Commission's functions will transfer to the NAO, but it is hardly an argument for localism.

The Comptroller and Auditor-General (C&AG) will be given the Audit Commission's role of preparing the Code of Audit Practice which sets out the framework within which local auditors carry out their work, and will also be empowered to produce guidance to local auditors. A second provision of the Bill increases the NAO's capacity to undertake examinations regarding the 'value for money' with which local public bodies have used their resources. This was previously the statutory duty of the Audit Commission which, unlike the NAO, had an explicit duty to scrutinise government policy. The hope is that this change will inform Parliament and add value at the local level, but it is worth noting that the government promoted this change without prior consultation with Parliament. The NAO's examination of local government will focus on studies across local government instead of the workings of individual authorities. However, the current Chair of the PAC, Margaret Hodge, has indicated that the Committee would in future seek to look at individual councils' performance (Keeling, 2013). The result is a degree of confusion and uncertainty across local government on the approach and reach of national bodies.

The demise of the Audit Commission and extension of the work of the NAO is evidence of a third trend: the broadening of the UK NAO and PAC's access rights. In response to Lord Sharman's 2001 report on audit and accountability in central government, the C&AG was given the right to carry out public-sector audits of the accounts of certain non-departmental public bodies that are registered companies, as well as their subsidiary companies. This was a response to the fragmentation of public services. Civil list expenditure and the BBC's accounts are also now subject to NAO and PAC scrutiny, and the PAC has used this new access to release critical reports on high-profile issues such as the Duchy of Cornwall accounts (PAC, 2013a) and the BBC's relocation expenses as part of its move to a new centre in Salford (PAC, 2013b).

Government departments continue to contract work to the private and third sectors and there are still demands for access to further bodies to ensure appropriate oversight and accountability. The current PAC Chair is in favour of giving the C&AG the right to examine the accounts of those private businesses which are delivering public contracts and she is also pushing for the government to sign an openness clause when signing a contract with the public sector.

The C&AG and NAO

The C&AG is appointed by The Queen on a motion in the Commons in the name of the Prime Minister (PM) with the agreement of the Chair of the PAC. For the appointment of the current C&AG, the PAC Chair presided over a small appointments panel, including the Permanent Secretary at the Treasury (representing the PM) and the incumbent C&AG, as an independent observer. A name was then put to the PM, who approved the nomination. The then Chair of the PAC defended the involvement of the PM as follows:

> [T]here is a need for the Government to have confidence in the person appointed because that person has unlimited access to all private papers and persons of the Government ... the current situation ... in which both the Prime Minister and the Opposition Chairman of the PAC have to agree is not unreasonable. I say that as long as the Government appreciate the difference between selection and appointment, they need to be involved in the appointment, but not in the selection. That should be the job of the House.[2]

The PAC as a body has no formal role in the selection of the C&AG, but it did hold a hearing with the current postholder before he was formally appointed. This is part of a broader trend from 2007 towards pre-appointment hearings which are non-binding on ministers. It has since been agreed the C&AG-designate will appear before the PAC once a name has been announced, but before the debate on the motion for the appointment. The Liaison Committee (2011: 3) has described pre-appointment hearings as 'a modest step forward in securing democratic accountability of ministerial decision-making'. However, it could potentially put the committee at odds in future with both its Chair and the PM.

Previous C&AGs have been appointed for life (or until they have decided to retire), to protect the independence of the position. The term has now been limited to a non-renewable ten-year term. This brings the UK in line with most other European and Commonwealth Parliaments – the AG in Scotland is appointed to a single, non-renewable term of eight years and the Welsh National Assembly can fix the period of office at the time of appointment. A motion passed by both Houses of Parliament is required to dismiss a C&AG, but neither the Chair of the PAC nor the committee as a whole has a statutory role in this. The UK PAC therefore has less formal power than those PACs that are required by law to approve the C&AG's appointment and any motion to remove him of her from office. However, this may underestimate both the informal power and involvement of the committee through the pre-appointment process and the actual powers and influence of the PAC Chair.

Once appointed, a close working relationship has traditionally existed between the PAC Chair and the C&AG. The C&AG, or his representative, is present at all evidence sessions and can be questioned by members and can also question witnesses at the discretion of the Chair. The NAO also produces the first draft of a PAC report. The clerk then considers the report, before being forwarded to the chair for comment (the normal practice in most other jurisdictions is for the PAC secretariat to draft the report). The C&AG has complete discretion in the choice of the NAO's programme of value for money studies, but is obliged by statute to consult the PAC. It should also be noted that the NAO (2012: 6) is seeking to be more responsive by producing rapid investigations following concerns raised by MPs, whistleblowers and the public.

The non-party aspect of the PACs work, and preference for unanimity – long thought essential for any PAC – is greatly assisted by its ability to draw on the factual, comprehensive and evidence-based reports of the C&AG. Similarly, the PAC increases the authority of the reports of the C&AG, by adding the necessary political weight; the government is formally obliged to respond to PAC but not to NAO recommendations. A plus-sum relationship is the result. The PAC can also provide more strident criticisms than the more sober assessments released by the NAO. Sharma (2007) documents how NAO Value for Money reports can be altered before final publication and Dunleavy *et al.* (2009: 44) raise the question of a possible regulatory risk whereby the NAO may have 'a tendency to "pull its punches" in terms of its comments on departments and agencies, especially in not criticising most departmental figures and reasoning … because of the difficult departmental clearance process, which each report must go through'. Yet this risk is mitigated by the fact that NAO staff can provide private oral briefings to the PAC and by the work and criticisms of the PAC itself. The NAO provides the ammunition for the PAC to fire, and working together they are both better equipped to force departments to justify their actions when spending public money.

The Budget Responsibility and National Audit Act 2011 created the statutory basis for the NAO's governance, by establishing the NAO as a corporate entity, with a statutory board. The Public Accounts Commission, a parliamentary committee separate from the PAC but with overlapping membership, is formally responsible for the appointment of the non-executive members of the NAO Board and the external auditor of the NAO. The Commission is also responsible for scrutinising the NAO's budget: the NAO appears before it twice a year – once to consider the NAO's three-year strategy and once to consider the NAO's estimate. The PAC gives an opinion on the budget, but the decision remains one for the Commission and it is voted on directly by Parliament as a separate line in the requisitions of the parliamentary vote.

The arms-length approach between the PAC and NAO is justified because of fears that the PAC may have a vested interest in maximising resources to the Audit Office. Yet the resources of the NAO have increased in recent years to cope with its broadened mandate: in 2007 the NAO's budget was £90 million – almost double its budget in 2001.[3] The NAO (2013: 20) is reducing costs by 15 per cent by 2014–15, but it is notable that support for Parliament is increasing – both to the PAC and to select committees – and now acts as about 10 per cent of the NAO's total cost base (Public Accounts Commission, 2013: 13). This is understandable given that the Chair of the PAC is a member of the Public Accounts Commission and her predecessor is the current Chair of the Commission. The operational links between the NAO and the PAC therefore remain strong even though these are formally exercised through the Commission.

Membership and leadership of the PAC

The typical size of a PAC in the Commonwealth is 11 members (McGee, 2002: 61). This level of variation is comparable to the relative size of the Parliament and similar differences exist across the UK, where the Westminster PAC is the largest with 14 members (reduced from 16 in the previous Parliament). The committee's political legitimacy and independence are assisted by its balanced representation and the exclusion of government ministers (Pelizzo and Stapenhurst, 2008: 121). One of the government members on the committee is a Treasury Minister, but this is only a formality and the Minister plays no active part.

Membership of the PAC is proportionate to party membership in the House (again this is the practice – the Standing Orders are not prescriptive as they are in Northern Ireland, Scotland and Wales). Members of the PAC are appointed for the length of the life of the legislature, although the potential exists for members to be reassigned during the term. Permanent membership over the course of a Parliament offers stability and will normally assist committee effectiveness, and it is therefore a little concerning that almost half of the current PAC has changed since the start of the Parliament. However, the Clerk and the C&AG can also provide continuity.

The PAC consists of both experienced and relatively new members. In the 2005–2010 Parliament, the Father of the House of Commons – the member with the longest unbroken service in the Commons – was an active member. Over half of the current committee were first elected in 2010, but it also includes one member elected in the 1970s and two members in the 1990s (including the chair). This mixture of experienced and inexperienced members is valuable as it offers an important training opportunity for the latter, and the former are more likely to understand the ethos of the civil service.

One encouraging trend is that attendance by MPs at PAC committee sessions has increased dramatically (Table 6.1). This may be a result of the pressure on political parties to arrange for their own members of select committees to be elected in a transparent and democratic way. The application of the 60 per cent attendance rule (where any member of a select committee whose cumulative attendance during a Session is below 60 per cent should be automatically discharged at the end of that Session) may be a further factor. Improved attendance may also be a reflection of the high-profile work the PAC is pursuing under its new Chair.

The PAC has always been a busy committee and members face a heavy workload. It meets twice as often as most other committees and the range of subjects

Table 6.1 PAC Select Committee activity

Session of parliament	Total number of meetings	Average PAC members' attendance (%)	Turnover of membership (%)	Number of reports
2007–2008	63	47	38	60
2008–2009	46	46	13	56
2009–2010	26	43	0	33
2010–2012	108	68	36	88
2012–2013	60	67	21	44

Source: Prepared by the author based on House of Commons Session Returns 2007–2013.

reported on is impressive. This results in a great deal of work for members, with the expectation in the 2005–10 Parliament that members would come to at least half the sessions. This appears to have had an impact on attendance. The 2005–10 PAC worked on the basis that each member has ten minutes for questions, so it is likely that the reduction in the size of the committee has created further demands and opportunities for individual members on the committee. The number of PAC meetings may increase in future as the current PAC was granted the power in the 2010–12 session to allow the committee to sit when the House is adjourned, a power available to other select committees. This will give the PAC further flexibility when arranging its schedule. The PAC has also continued the practice of its predecessor committee by meeting occasionally outside London in an effort to move away from a predominantly London-centric approach.

Chairing the Committee

The Chair is required by convention and statute to act on the Committee's behalf in a number of respects and the PAC is invited to agree at the beginning of each Parliament a resolution recognising those special responsibilities. These normally include dealing with any correspondence received (or delegating to staff) and being consulted by government departments on issues such as contingent liabilities, and on matters of great sensitivity the Chair has an *ex officio* statutory role.

By convention and now set down in the Standing Orders (122B) the Chair of the PAC is always a member of the main Opposition Party. This reflects the practice across the Commonwealth, where 67 per cent of chairs are Opposition members (McGee, 2002: 97). While the members of the Committee used to formally choose the Chair, the practice was for the Opposition whips to select the candidate. Since May 2010, however, the Chair of the PAC, alongside the majority of Select Committee chairs, is elected by MPs in a secret ballot under the Alternative Vote System. There were six candidates for the PAC Chair position (the most candidates for any select committee position, which may well reflect the PAC's reputation as being Parliament's pre-eminent committee). The ex-minister Margaret Hodge won the secret ballot, beating her nearest rival by six votes in the fifth round of voting. Although all MPs were entitled to vote in the ballot for each Chair, only members of the Labour Party were eligible to stand as candidates for the PAC position.

Ms Hodge cites two main reasons for her election: she is the first woman to hold the position of PAC Chair; and her high-profile campaign to defeat a fascist candidate at the 2010 General Election.[4] It is interesting that her previous government experience was not presented as an asset. The importance of executive experience is an under-researched area when evaluating the impact of Select Committee chairs and this is potentially even more important for a PAC as it scrutinises a much broader area of government machinery. Of course a Chair's own record as a Minister may cause some issues of conflict of interest, especially if the time lag is not great between a ministerial post and a committee chairmanship. Indeed the very first hearing under Ms Hodge's chairmanship was on a programme she had initiated in government.

There can be little doubt that the PAC has raised its public profile under Ms Hodge's leadership. A recent analysis of the most important UK press database (run by LexisNexis) shows there has been a substantial increase in press coverage of House of Commons Committees since 2008 with four committees, including the PAC, being the main reason for this increase (Dunleavy and Muir, 2013). Russell and Benton's (2011: 22) research assessing the performance of select committees in the UK found that fewer than one in ten select committee reports could be considered 'agenda setting', but the PAC has been successful in setting the agenda on matters concerning the issue of tax avoidance of companies,[5] for example, and changing the terms of political debate in relation to the costs of high-speed rail.

The number of PAC reports also provides an illustration of the PAC's workload, and it is perhaps not surprising that the UK PAC produces more reports than other UK select committees given the support of the NAO. As a guide, the PAC produces a similar number of reports per session to what the Health and Home Affairs Select Committees produced over the period from 1997 to 2010 (Russell and Benton, 2011: 18). Figure 6.1 does suggest that the number of PAC reports has reduced somewhat. As the activity of the PAC is not decreasing, this may be a reflection that the PAC is taking longer in its inquiries as well as of the increased focus on follow-up (see below).

One result of the increased public profile is increased attention – and criticism – of the PAC and Ms Hodge's abrasive style of questioning. Ms Hodge's campaign to tackle company tax avoidance, involving bringing Starbucks, Google and Amazon before the PAC to answer questions, was highly regarded, but there have been criticisms from business witnesses and anonymous briefings from within the Treasury that the prospect of public humiliation at a public hearing will make businesses think twice about where to invest (Mason, 2014). The Chancellor of the Exchequer, George Osborne, has broken the convention that ministers do not criticise outright the conclusions of a PAC report by publicly censuring the PAC and its Chair for its critical report on the way that the royal

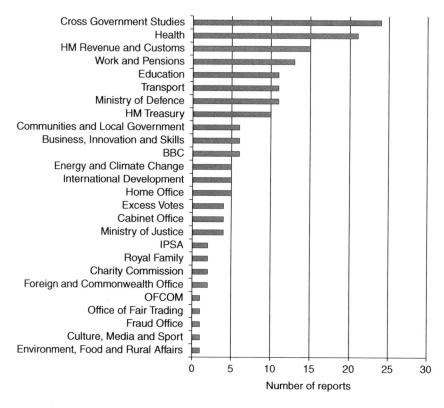

Figure 6.1 Total PAC reports by department/subject 2010 to February 2014.

household is controlling the Queen's finances. This may be one of the consequences both of giving the PAC chair a personal mandate and of the involvement of the PAC in high-profile cases of public concern. Given the increased focus on the PAC, the importance of the evidence-based findings of the NAO is likely to become ever more apparent as it will be difficult to dismiss the PAC if it is grounded on the NAO's investigatory work and the committee continues to be non-partisan. There is no evidence of any criticisms from within the PAC (nor from the NAO). Such criticisms would have more serious consequences for the PAC's reputation.

A further criticism of the PAC was made by the former Cabinet Secretary, Lord O'Donnell, who expressed concern at the way the PAC questions and treats civil servants following a decision by the committee to take evidence from one official under oath. There is certainly a very robust approach to questions under the current committee and a readiness to challenge individual civil servants. Ms Hodge has introduced the practice of calling back civil servants who have changed jobs to answer for actions taken in a previous position. Further changes introduced include calling witnesses from private companies who provide public services and questioning the senior responsible officer within a department rather than the Permanent Secretary/Accounting Officer. This is a welcome improvement on previous practice, which saw many public servants escape accountability to Parliament.

The PAC has also expanded its work from measuring financial impact in terms of savings to also include consideration of actual service delivery from the feedback of clients. The NAO has included extensive material on quality of service and client feedback for several years, but the PAC has recently begun calling additional witnesses so the committee can hear from those experiencing programmes delivered by public money.[6] An examination of the Sessional Returns for this Parliament (2010/13) shows that the number of appearances of 'other' witnesses – a rather unhelpful description – jumped to 36 per cent from 12 per cent in the 2005–10 Parliament. The percentage of appearances by officials from, or representatives of, government departments has remained steady (49 per cent compared to 51 per cent), as has the proportion of appearances of officials from executive agencies (2.2 per cent and 4.3 per cent). The biggest decrease has been the number of witnesses of officials from or representatives of public bodies and non-ministerial departments (12 per cent and 43 per cent). The PAC is also seeking to innovate and take on matters under their remit which are separate from the C&AG's value for money reports and the Standing Orders were amended in the 2010–12 session to allow it to appoint specialist advisors, alongside the other select committees.

PAC reports

A study (Dunleavy *et al.*, 2009: 27–28) of the previous Parliament found that some departments (for example the Departments of Health and Education) were reported on by the PAC much more than others. The same study found that 72 per cent of NAO reports go to the PAC, but the take-up rate was comparatively low for the cross-governmental value for money (VFM) studies. The study concludes that PAC members tend to find such studies 'too abstract or not meshing with their constituents' experiences … [or not] very newsworthy'. There were 20 cross-government reports issued by the PAC between 2003 and 2009, fewer than reports on the Departments of Health, Education, Defence and similar to the Home Office, Department for Work and Pensions, Transport and Environment, Food and Rural Affairs.

An examination of PAC reports in the current UK Parliament (May 2010 to February 2014) shows that cross-government studies have become the most common subject reported upon (Figure 6.1). The NAO reports that many within government have welcomed comparative work between departments and it has responded by increasing the number of cross-government studies and by organising and applying its expertise to clusters of departments that face similar strategic issues. For example, one cluster covers three departments which have almost all the major contracting and long-term project activities in government (Defence, Transport and Environment) and it is hoped that this cross-scrutiny will encourage government to compare results and learn lessons across departments (Public Accounts Commission, 2013).

A further method of reporting across sector and cross-government studies is the examination of an issue, such as procurement, over a period of time using a consistent framework. The NAO has also adapted its approach towards an examination of how government is operating in the present, including how projects and programmes are set up, instead of the traditional focus on the recent past. The value of this approach is that the NAO/PAC can point to issues while they can still be corrected, and focus on forward planning. For example, on the basis of a report by the C&AG, the PAC examined the Department for Culture, Media and Sport and the Olympic Delivery Authority on the progress that had been made in preparing for the Games, and the areas of risk that needed to be managed (PAC, 2007). Such studies boost the timeliness of PAC activity and will raise its profile in the media.

PAC recommendations and follow-up

In 2012/13 the government wholly or partially accepted 82 per cent of all the recommendations of the PAC (NAO, 2013: 17), which is a substantially higher number than the 40 per cent of select committee recommendations accepted by government (Russell and Benton, 2011: 7) and the 70 per cent of cases accepted by governments across the Commonwealth (Stapenhurst *et al.*, 2005: 145). The higher success rate of PAC recommendations is partly explained by the fact that NAO audit reports are agreed with departments, making it difficult for the government to ignore the PAC. Also, PAC recommendations relate to improving the implementation of policy, which are easier to implement than the recommendations produced by many of the other select committee on the actual merit of policy. However, these are still impressive figures and it should also be noted that PAC reports are often more hard-hitting and critical than both NAO and departmental select committee reports.

Having recommendations accepted is important – but measuring implementation is even more important to demonstrate actions and outcomes from the audit process. The government implemented 58 per cent of recommendations in the 2010–12 Parliamentary session, with the final figure expected to be 90 per cent (NAO, 2013: 22). Again this is a higher implementation rate than most departmental select committees, and one crucial variable to determine the success of recommendations identified by Russell and Benton (2011) is basing reports on clear evidence and new research. Such findings reinforces the significance of the NAO's value for money studies and financial audit work.

There is now evidence of a more formal process to monitor and follow up the implementation of government responses to PAC recommendations in the UK. The NAO has a practice of producing comments for the Committee on all government responses and, as mentioned above, a number of issues are now considered regularly. The PAC does often write to departments to follow up poor performance, for example a recent chain of letters on civil service reform was cited in the PAC's session on 7 July 2014 on the Centre of Government. A practice has also been introduced in the current Parliament where the PAC has a recall session twice a year to study the implementation of PAC recommendations. The fear of recall acts as an incentive for departments to implement recommendations, and there are plans to strengthen recall by randomly selecting reports for scrutiny.

Evaluation of performance

One criticism of PACs is that they can be too critical and discourage innovation and risk. This may be exacerbated by the media's tendency to focus on reports that are critical of departments and permanent secretaries. The PAC does attempt to give praise where it is due: for example its post-Games review into the London 2012 Olympic Games and Paralympic Games praised the way government departments worked together and with other bodies to deliver complex programmes. However, most of the coverage concerned the one negative aspect of the report relating to the planning for venue security. It is right that the PAC should act as an incentive to better performance in government, but the PAC may have to make more effort to publicise examples of good practice to balance the media's focus on criticisms and to maintain the confidence of government departments.

A common performance measure used by Supreme Audit Institutions and PACs is the amount of money saved through its value for money reviews. In 2012–13 60 value for money reports were published at an average cost of £197,000, against a target of £218,000. The NAO (2013: 14) reports in the UK cost more than £100,000 each to produce, but its work led to savings to the public purse of almost £1.2 billion. These are significant savings at a time of financial pressures and both the NAO and the PAC are justifiably credited for helping the government to save public money.

It is difficult to divorce the impact of the PAC from the NAO. Three traditional measures used to assess impact are the implementation of PAC recommendations; the views of senior public servants who are most affected by the PAC; and the quality of press coverage of PAC hearings and reports. Assessing the views of senior public servants offers a different methodological approach by looking at relationships and anticipated reactions. Russell and Benton (2011) provide a broader definition of select committee influence, including contributing to debate, drawing together evidence, spotlighting issues, brokering between actors in government, improving the quality of government decision-making through accountability, exposing failures, and 'generating fear'. It is not difficult to apply such influence to the work of the PAC today.

In short, the number of PAC recommendations accepted and implemented, though impressive when compared with other select committees, may actually understate the PAC's impact on those entities which are answerable before it. Flegmann (1979: 169) describes the committee as having a 'continuous influence on departmental administration [and they] make every effort to reduce the number of occasions which make it necessary for the Permanent Secretary to appear in front of the PAC'. The fear factor is also illustrated by Drewry's (1989) comment that the PAC is 'the one select committee before which even the most exalted Permanent Secretary can be made to tremble'.

Lonsdale (2000) adds a further dimension by arguing that reports by NAO and PAC have an impact on Parliament itself by providing information that can inform select committees' work. There is certainly evidence that other select committees are making more use of the NAO. As mentioned earlier, the money budgeted by the NAO to Parliament is increasing while other budgets are shrinking. The NAO responds to queries from select committees and individual MPs, and some of these queries eventually lead to a full value for money report. The NAO also produces performance briefings to assist select committees' annual oversight of departments' performance; during 2012–13 the NAO provided 15 select committees with an overview of their work to assist the committee in their annual review of the relevant government department. This included a review of charity regulation for the Public Administration Select Committee and a review of sustainable procurement in government for the Environment Audit Committee (NAO, 2013: 17).

Despite some improvement, the NAO's own figures show a considerable number of departmental select committees are still not making use of the NAO in any capacity. It is worth restating that any UK select committee can take evidence on a NAO report if the PAC does not wish to do so. Dunleavy (1990) has proposed that the PAC should leave single-department reports to the relevant select committee and focus instead on cross-departmental issues in a more focused way. This has not happened to date and there does not appear to be any systematic attempt to encourage select committees to examine NAO reports on individual departments. The assumption and working practice is that the PAC remains the most appropriate committee to undertake inquiries based on NAO reports. However, there is also an argument that departmental select committees should make use of the NAO's sector reports to identify and learn from general issues in that sector and to assist their examination of main estimates, annual expenditure and annual resource accounts. It remains to be seen how effective passing responsibility to the departmental committees would be in practice and it would probably depend on the willingness of the members of each committee, and the chairs in particular, to undertake the task. This could be something to attempt on a trial basis with cooperative committees in a future Parliament.

Finally, few PACs adopt a formal mechanism for measuring their performance, and this is usually only carried out in an annual review/sessional report or reported directly to corporate body/internal management. The PAC is perhaps guilty, alongside other select committees, of not addressing the criticisms of Brazier and Fox (2011) by not reviewing and assessing the way in which they discharge their work. A strategic plan at the start of each Parliament would bring greater accountability of its own work and enable the PAC to make a judgement on their own effectiveness, successes and failures over the course of the Parliament. The PAC chair may find such work useful if she decides to seek re-election in the next Parliament, but it would also be a useful device in its own right – particularly given the PAC's increased public profile. A further option would be to produce a 'legacy' paper at the end of the Parliament – this will be easier to arrange in a fixed-term Parliament – as this has proved to be a useful tool for passing on experience to successor committees in Scotland.

Conclusion

This chapter has examined the work and performance of the PAC following recent changes and trends in public audit and wider changes across the UK. The committee now has a reduced role in scrutinising only those items of expenditure in Scotland, Wales and Northern Ireland which have not been devolved. At the same time there has been a broadening of access rights, most recently in relation to the BBC and civil list expenditure. A further significant change, not without controversy, concerns the imminent closure of the English Audit Commission and the transfer of some functions to the C&AG and NAO. The PAC and its vocal chair are keen to push the PAC into new areas that have hitherto escaped scrutiny. As access rights increase, care will need to be taken not to take the NAO/PAC into the policy arena.

The relationship between the PAC and NAO remains strong, with the PAC Chair having a leading role in the selection process and the pre-appointment hearing which will now take place with a prospective C&AG before the formal appointment. While the committee may have less formal power than other PACs in the election and dismissal of C&AG, the pre-appointment process and the actual powers and influence of the PAC Chair (now directly elected) are considerable. It is difficult to imagine a C&AG accepting the position without the support of the committee. In terms of the operational links between the NAO and PAC, the current Public Accounts Commission – the body with responsibility to examine the NAO Estimate and lay it before the House – is chaired by the former Chair of the PAC and all the members (bar one) are former or current members of the PAC (including the current PAC Chair). Therefore, it is rather misleading to say that the PAC is removed from operational oversight of the NAO.

The members of the PAC continue to be appointed for the term of the Parliament, and this longevity of membership together with the maintenance of a non-partisan culture (there has not been a division on a PAC report since the 1960s) has always strengthened the committee. There is a good mix of experienced and newly elected MPs on the committee, although one area of concern is the high degree of turnover of PAC members. This is balanced by improved attendance at PAC meetings in the current Parliament.

The PAC has also increased its public profile under its first directly elected chair, who has been successful in setting the agenda in areas such as tax avoidance and areas of topical political debate. She has used her membership of the Liaison Committee to raise PAC-related issues in questions to the Prime Minister. The changes made to the way the PAC operates – questioning the senior responsible officer within a department rather than the Permanent Secretary/Accounting Officer and calling back civil servants who have changed jobs to answer for actions taken in a previous position – have dealt with some of the frustrations expressed by previous committees when trying to enforce accountability across the public sector.

The PAC's higher visibility has led to a great deal of praise as well as some criticism of the committee. The non-party aspect of the PAC's work, and preference for unanimity, has always been a great asset to the committee, as has its ability to draw on the factual and comprehensive reports of the C&AG. These practices and relationships become even more crucial following the PAC's move towards new areas of scrutiny. It is also likely that the PAC's own performance will become subject to greater scrutiny. The NAO's evidence-based reports will not prevent all criticism (nor should they) but it does act as a shield for the PAC. Similarly, the PAC acts as a sword to attack waste and poor performance across the public sector as the committee can be much more critical and forthright than the NAO and provide the necessary political weight to the C&AG's reports. An enduring working relationship is the result as the two bodies enjoy an interdependent relationship. Against this backdrop, it is not surprising to learn that the NAO's support for Parliament is increasing at a time of cuts and savings elsewhere within the organisation. It is in the NAO's interests that the PAC maintains its effectiveness.

The reports of the NAO/PAC now range from the traditional value for money sector reports to an increasing number of cross-government studies. Two further approaches are also evident: repeat studies that track performance over a period of time, and examinations of how government is operating in the present, rather than in the recent past. In terms of impact, the NAO and PAC can point to impressive statistics in terms of the agreement and implementation of recommendations, even more so when compared with other select committees. This is likely to be a result of reports being based on clear evidence and the fact that NAO reports are agreed with departments.

The savings to the public purse through the value for money reviews are impressive – especially during a time of financial austerity – but the fact that the NAO/PAC are expanding their work to include consideration of actual service delivery from the feedback of clients shows that measuring impact can be broadened from a narrow and traditional focus on savings and implementation of audit recommendations. The new practice of recall sessions is likely to increase the fear factor, for example, and the PAC's work and reach across Whitehall supports recent research showing that select committee influence is often felt in more subtle ways, such as contributing to debate and anticipated reactions.

There is still much the PAC can do to improve its performance and to avoid the committee appearing too protective about its relationship with the NAO. The committee should review and assess the way in which they discharge their work and publicise the results, perhaps through a legacy report at the end of this fixed-term Parliament. As part of this strategy, the PAC could also encourage other select committees to make more use of NAO reports, perhaps by encouraging other committees on a trial basis to take evidence on single-department reports, leaving the PAC free to focus in more depth on cross-departmental issues and issues of priority. By looking inward as well as outward, the PAC may be able to cement its status as the committee *primus inter pares* among select committees of the House of Commons.

Notes

1 PACs have also been established in two British Crown dependencies: Guernsey and Jersey, with the latter also introducing the position of an Auditor-General (AG). A third Crown dependency, the Isle of Man, has also recently restructured its PAC and passed legislation agreeing that an AG function should be introduced. The three countries are not part of the UK but are self-governing dependencies of the Crown.
2 HC Deb 23 Jan 2088: c1527.
3 Commons Hansard, 19 April 2007, col. 494–495.
4 Speech given by Margaret Hodge MP at the third Westminster Workshop: The Public Accounts Committee, 24–27 June 2013.
5 It can do this work because the NAO has the right to examine the role of tax authorities in deciding how much private companies paid in tax.
6 Speech given by Margaret Hodge MP at Westminster Workshop, March 2012.

References

Audit Commission. (2011) 'Future of local public audit', Department for Communities and Local Government Consultation: Audit Commission Summary Response, Audit Commission, London.

Brazier, A and Fox, R. (2011) 'Reviewing Select Committee Tasks and Modes of Operation', *Parliamentary Affairs*, 64 (2): 354–369.

Chubb, B. (1952) *The Control of Public Expenditure*, Oxford, Clarendon Press.

Comptroller and Auditor General (2013) *Financial Management in Government*, Session 2013–14, HC 131, National Audit Office, June 2013.

Drewry, G. (1989) 'Select Committees and Backbench Power', in J. Jowell and D. Oliver (eds) *The Changing Constitution*, 2nd edn, Oxford: Oxford University Press.

Dunleavy, P. (1990) *Reinventing Parliament: Making the Commons more effective, Part 2: Practical reforms to make the Commons more effective*, London: Charter 88.

Dunleavy, P and Muir, D (2013) 'Parliament bounces back – how Select Committees have become a power in the land', *Democratic Audit*, www.democraticaudit. com/?p=1106 (accessed 27 November 2014).

Dunleavy, P., Gilson, C., Bastow, S. and Tinkler, J. (2009) 'The National Audit Office, the Public Accounts Committee and the risk landscape in UK public policy', URN 09/1423. The Risk and Regulation Advisory Council, London, UK.

Flegmann, V. (1979) 'The public account committee: a successful select committee?' *Parliamentary Affairs*, 33(1): 166–172.

House of Commons Communities and Local Government Select Committee (2011) 'Audit and Inspection of Local Authorities', House of Commons, Fourth Report of Session 2010–2012, Volume I, HC 763, London: The Stationery Office, 7 July 2011.

House of Commons Committee of Public Accounts (2007) *Preparations for the 2012 Olympic Games and Paralympic Games – Risk Assessment and Management*, Thirty-ninth Report of Session 2006–07, HC 377, 10 July 2007.

House of Commons Committee of Public Accounts (2013a) *The Duchy of Cornwall*, Twenty-fifth Report of Session 2013–14. HC475, London: The Stationery Office, 5 November 2013.

House of Commons Committee of Public Accounts (2013b) *The BBC's move to Salford*, Twentieth Report of Session 2013–14, HC293, London: The Stationery Office, 16 October 2013.

House of Commons Committee of Public Accounts (2014) *Local Government Funding: Assurance to Parliament*, thirteenth report of Session 2013–14, HC456, London: The Stationery Office, 12 September 2014.

House of Commons Liaison Committee (2011) *Select Committees and Government Appointments*, First Report of Session 2010–12, HC1230, 4 September 2011.

House of Commons Select Committee on Procedure (1999) *Procedure for Debate on Government Expenditure Plans*, Sixth Report, HC 295 of 1998–1999, para.5.

House of Commons Public Accounts Commission (2013) 'Oral evidence taken before the Public Accounts Commission, NAO's Estimate for 2013–14', www.publications.parliament.uk/pa/cm201213/cmselect/cmpubacc/uc1058-i/uc105801.htm (accessed 2 March 2014).

Keeling, R. (2013) 'MPs to haul in councils for questions', *Local Government Chronicle*, 18 October 2013.

Lonsdale, J. (2000) 'Developments in Value-For-Money Audit Methods: Impacts and Implications', *International Review of Administrative Sciences*, 66(1): 73.

McGee, D. (2002) *The Overseers: Public Accounts Committees and Public Spending*, London: Pluto Press.

Mason, C (2014) 'Treasury Anger over Margaret Hodge "Grandstanding"', *BBC News*, 23 January 2014.

National Audit Office (2014) *Annual Report and Accounts 2013–14*, HC-170, London: The Stationery Office.

National Audit Office (2013) *Annual Report and Accounts 2012–13*, HC-62, London: The Stationery Office.

National Audit Office (2012) *Our Strategy 2013–14 to 2015–2016*, National Audit Office (November).

Pelizzo, R. and Stapenhurst, F. (2008) 'Public Accounts Committees', in F. Stapenhurst, F. Pelizzo, D. Olson and L. von Trapp (eds) *Legislative Oversight and Budgeting: A World Perspective*, Washington DC: World Bank Institute.

Pelizzo, R., Stapenhurst, F., Saghal, V. and Woodley, W. (2006) 'What makes public accounts committees work? A comparative analysis', *Politics and Policy*, 34(4): 774–793.

Power, M. (1994) *The Audit Explosion*, London: Demos/White Dove Press.

Public Accounts Committee (2007) *Holding Government to Account: 150 Years of the Public Accounts Committee*, London: Public Accounts Committee.

Public Accounts Commission (2013) 'Oral Evidence NAO's Strategy 2014/15–2016/17, 5 November 2013', www.parliament.uk/documents/commons-committees/publicaccountscommission/tPAC-transcriptamended-5Nov2013.pdf (accessed 28 January 2015).

Rush, M. (2005) *Parliament Today*, Manchester: Manchester University Press.

Russell, M. and Benton, M. (2011) *Selective Influence: The Policy Impact of House of Commons Select Committees*, London: UCL, The Constitution Unit.

Sharma, N. (2007). 'Interactions and Interrogations: Negotiating and Performing Value for Money Reports', *Financial Accountability & Management*, 23(3).

Sharman, Lord of Redlynch (2001) *Holding to Account: The Review of Audit and Accountability for Central Government.*

Stapenhurst, F., Vinod, S., Woodley, W. and Pelizzo, R. (2005) *Scrutinizing Public Accounts Committees: Assessing the Performance of Public Accounts Committees in Comparative Perspective*, Policy Research Working Paper 3613, Washington DC: World Bank.

Wehner, J. (2003) 'Principles and Patterns of Financial Scrutiny: Public Accounts Committees in the Commonwealth', *Commonwealth and Comparative Politics*, 41(3): 21–36.

7 In the absence of a Public Accounts Committee

The Swedish experience

Louise Bringselius

Introduction

Public accountability is a cornerstone of modern democratic governance, helping both citizens and parliaments to oversee government activities (Diamond and Morlino, 2005; Przeworski *et al.*, 1999). A key arena, where these accountability issues are typically played out, is the Public Accounts Committee (PAC). The PAC helps to balance the power of the government and the opposition, but it also has a symbolic function, representing a willingness among these parties to cooperate in matters of accountability (Pelizzo and Stapenhurst, 2008). This is an important function, given the incentives of the PAC members – typically Members of Parliament (MPs) – to instead act in a partisan interest.

Thus, PACs may foster a political culture of cooperation and transparency, downplaying partisan hierarchy and authority. However, PACs may also foster the opposite culture: they may create conflict by holding policy-makers accountable and seeking headlines, instead of focusing on the subject matter and on how issues can pragmatically be resolved (Bowerman *et al.*, 2003; Travers, 1999). One reason for such an approach could be that the auditing bodies also need to show that they themselves provide value for money (Talbot and Wiggan, 2010; Lonsdale, 1999). The easiest way to achieve this is to consistently point out problems and show that these are grave, although this may curb both objectivity and quality (Pollitt and Summa, 1997; Bowerman *et al.*, 2003; Bringselius, 2013).

Brian Landers, formerly Chief Internal Auditor at Sainsbury's and Financial Director of the British Prison Service Agency, has described his experience from the British PAC. In his account he describes the PAC as a feared institution consisting of overly critical backbenchers and people with 'a vested interest in scoring points' (Landers, 1999: 206). When the British National Audit Office (NAO) was formed, it became equally critical as the PAC, and equally interested in creating headlines, as maintained by Landers (1999: 201).

Thus it is obvious that the system with PACs comes with a set of risks. Yet, for many countries, a political system without a PAC would be hard to imagine. Sweden, however, has chosen another trajectory. The Swedish reluctance to introduce a PAC may be viewed as surprising, in particular, considering that the

Swedish Supreme Audit Institution, the SNAO (Swedish National Audit Office), was formed as late as 2003, through a reform which provided excellent opportunities to align with the model of many other European countries.

The Swedish experience with the absence of a PAC is interesting not only to understand alternative models of democratic governance, but also to understand the relation between these models and the national political cultures. This chapter analyses why some countries chose not to have a PAC, building on the Swedish experience from two (non-PAC) models for the channelling of SNAO performance audit reports to the Swedish Parliament. The chapter is the result of a review of documents and administrative law, but it also builds on data from a longitudinal case study of the SNAO, stretching from 2002 to 2013. This study includes 102 interviews and extensive document studies (for further details, see Bringselius 2008, 2013, 2014).

The chapter makes two main contributions. First, it suggests a framework to analyse and compare the relations of SAIs with parliaments and auditees. Second, it argues, based on findings from the Swedish case, that the choice not to have a PAC may be best understood in relation to the national political culture. In Sweden, there is a political culture focused on informality and pragmatic cooperation. This can be contrasted with countries where the political culture is more focused on accountability issues. In these countries PACs are common. Although PACs may downplay partisan interest (Pelizzo and Stapenhurst, 2008), they are still focused on confrontation in relation to the auditee, and this is not an approach that all countries are fully comfortable with.

The chapter is organised as follows. First, there is an introduction to Supreme Audit Institutions (SAIs). In this section, an analytical framework is also developed. The research design is then outlined. After this, the Swedish administrative model is introduced, with a special focus on the Swedish National Audit Office (the SNAO). A more thorough account of the Swedish case, lacking a PAC, is provided in the next section. A discussion follows and the chapter is finally closed with conclusions.

Supreme Audit Institutions

Every modern democracy has a Supreme Audit Institution (SAI), responsible for providing independent accounts on the performance of the executive branch of government. Using this information, the citizenry and Members of Parliament can hold responsible members of government to account, in particular in the public debate, parliamentary hearings and public elections. However, the scope of SAI audits, the methods adopted, and the relations between the SAI and its external stakeholders can sometimes differ rather substantially between countries. Often, audit reports from the SAI are channelled through a PAC. However, this is not always the case, as we shall see.

The SAIs typically conduct both financial audits and performance audits. The latter can also be referred to as Value for Money audits (VFM audits), a concept commonly used, for example, in the United Kingdom. Whereas a financial audit is highly focused on compliance with formal financial standards and regulations, there is much more room for interpretation in VFM audits. The international standard-setting organisation for SAIs, the INTOSAI, defines performance audit as follows.

> While financial audit tends to apply relatively fixed standards, performance auditing is more flexible in its choice of subjects, audit objects, methods, and opinions.... [Performance audit] is by nature wide-ranging and open to judgments and interpretations. It must have at its disposal a wide selection of investigative and evaluative methods and operate from a quite different knowledge base to that of traditional auditing. It is not a checklist-based form of auditing.
>
> (INTOSAI, 2003: 12)

Because different interpretations can be made, the judgements of performance auditors will play a major role, leaving the auditee vulnerable, in particular considering that audit results can have a major impact for both institutions (agencies, ministries, political parties, etc) and individuals (policy-makers, Director-Generals and others).

Value for Money (VFM) audits can be positioned in different ways in relation to both auditee (the executive) and the principal (Parliament). First, in the literature, the importance of independence in the relationship between the SAI and the executive branch of government has often been emphasised (e.g. Mohan and Sullivan, 2007; Gendron *et al.*, 2001; Jacobs, 1998; English and Guthrie, 2000; Funnell, 1994, 1998; and White and Hollingsworth, 1999). In this relation, performance audits can focus either on confrontation or on collaboration. Or, as Travers (1999) asks, 'Should the inspector be a bruiser?' With confrontation, accountability is emphasised. With collaboration, local and pragmatic improvement is emphasised. In reality, audits will have a combined purpose, including both these aims. However, different SAIs will tend to emphasise one over the other to some degree, and when there is a PAC, audits will tend to focus more on accountability than on collaboration – to settle who is accountable for the identified performance issues is even the key role of the PAC.

Second, in relation to Parliament, the legislative branch of government, the areas for performance audits can be determined more or less independently. At some SAIs, most audits take the form of direct assignments, leaving very little independence to the SAI itself in this regard. At other SAIs, audit areas are determined with no involvement whatsoever from the principal (Parliament), meaning that there is a high degree of independence. Between these extremes, there can be various blended forms. For example, there can be *collaboration*, with some direct assignments and some audits focused on areas determined by the SAI itself. There can also be *dialogue*, meaning that suggestions from Parliament are encouraged, but the SAI preserves the right to choose whether or not to meet these suggestions.

A framework with these two dimensions is outlined in Figure 7.1. This figure also suggests that SAIs with a PAC would typically be positioned in the box

		Primary goal in relation to the executive (auditee)	
		Confrontation	Collaboration
Choice of audit areas/ relation to Parliament (the principal)	Integration (almost exclusively direct assignments)		
	Cooperation (some direct assignments)	SAI with PAC	
	Dialogue (suggestions are encouraged)		
	Total distance (contact avoided)		

Figure 7.1 Analytical framework to compare relations between SAIs with a Public Accounts Committee (PAC) and SAIs without a PAC.

combining a confrontational approach to the Executive (auditee), and a cooperation approach to Parliament (principal). Again, this is a simplified way of illustrating some of the positions that the SAI can take in these two key relations. In reality, boundaries will not be this sharp. Figure 7.1 will serve as an analytical framework in this study.

To understand why some countries chose not to have a PAC, this study focuses on the following two research questions.

RQ1. How, for example, can results from performance audits at the SAI be channelled to the national Parliament, without a PAC? What is the experience from these models?

RQ2. How can we understand why some countries chose to have a PAC?

Research design

This chapter is based on data from a longitudinal study of the Swedish SAI, the Swedish National Audit Office (SNAO) and its stakeholders. Sweden is an interesting case partly because policy-makers, despite pressures from international comparisons, have refused to form a PAC to handle SAI reports. The Swedish case is also interesting because two different non-PAC models have been adopted, with somewhat different outcomes.

The study of the SNAO and its stakeholders began in 2002 (with preparations for the forming of a new SNAO in 2003) and it was closed in 2013. The case study includes 102 interviews and extensive document studies. Some of the results from the study can be found in two books (Bringselius, 2008, 2013) and in a journal article (Bringselius, 2014). None of these publications, however, focus on the same topic as this chapter.

This specific chapter builds in particular on studies of laws and regulations, and on documents indicating the experience of the SNAO stakeholders. This includes reports on how officials in the governmental offices and Members of Parliament perceive the (non-PAC) process used to channel SNAO reports to Parliament, and also attitudes relating to the value of these reports. Documents also include two reports from a special committee under the Riksdag, assigned to evaluate the SNAO reform and how the SNAO has developed over the years from 2003 to 2008 (Sveriges riksdag, 2008/09: URF1, URF3). These reports led to judicial changes, implemented in January 2011.

Because other types of data from the longitudinal study of the SNAO are not being used much in this chapter, I will not go into detail here on matters such as interview guide, choice of interviewees, survey methods, etc.

The Swedish administrative model

Sweden is a parliamentary representative democracy and a constitutional monarchy. The Swedish Constitution dates back to 1975. Before this, Sweden was formally governed under the 1809 Constitution. However, Sweden had a de facto parliamentary system from 1917, when the Swedish King agreed to abandon any claims to political power.

Today, the executive power is exercised by the government (the Cabinet). This is headed by the Prime Minister of Sweden and includes 22 Ministers, who are responsible for the ministries.

The legislative power is exercised by both the Cabinet and the Riksdag (Parliament), meaning that legislation may be initiated by any of these. The unicameral Swedish Riksdag has 349 Members of Parliament (MPs), appointed for a period of four years. The Riksdag can alter the Constitution of Sweden, but only with approval by a supermajority and confirmation after the following general elections.

In practice, many decisions in the Swedish Riksdag are resolved in the standing parliamentary committees, at meetings preceding parliamentary sessions. These committees are also authorised to take the initiative to make legislative changes. Committee chairs are distributed proportionally among the parliamentary parties. The areas of specialisation of the standing committees are similar to the jurisdictions of government ministries. These parliamentary arrangements in Sweden aim to facilitate a 'consensual style of policy-making' (Bergman, 2003). Rather than accountability, this culture is focused on informality (Jacobsson, Pierre and Sundström, 2015; Page, 2012), pragmatic improvement (Anton, 1969; Heckscher, 1984) and an anticipatory and pro-active, rather than reactive, policy-style (Ruin, 1982). Furthermore, rather than focusing on single decisions or issues, the Swedish political culture tends to focus on *systems* of decision-making, meaning general norms and structures:

> [B]y emphasizing relationships expressed as norms and limits instead of goals, and by focusing on relatively stable role expectations instead of the heroic actor-individual, it underlines the structural determinants of behavior without denying the rational calculations of individuals in structured situations; and by insisting on the significance of information – communication, it offers a systematic account of the sources of stability and change in system environment relationships.
>
> (Anton 1969: 91)

In an article in a major Swedish newspaper, Professor Steve Kelman (2013) argues that the sense of kindness and consensus in Swedish politics is a rare thing, and that this has been a factor in the success of major political reforms. In the same article, Kelman argues that it is imperative for Sweden to be able to preserve this culture in the future, in order to also secure the success of coming reforms.

For accountability purposes, the Swedish Parliament has a number of instruments at hand to control the actions of the Cabinet, its ministries and the executive agencies. These instruments, typically referred to as the 'parliamentary control' (Instrument of Government, in Swedish *Regeringsformen*, Chapter 13), are the following.

1   Swedish National Audit Office (SNAO)
2   Questions to Ministers
3   The Parliamentary Ombudsmen
4   The Committee on the Constitution
5   No-Confidence Votes

The five instruments have different roles. For example, the Committee on the Constitution is responsible for checking for compliance with the Constitution (the four fundamental laws, in Swedish *grundlagarna*), whereas the SNAO is responsible for checking the yearly financial accounts of agencies and auditing the performance of the executive branch of government.

Most of these instruments have an advisory function, meaning that they do not force the executive to take action in any regard. For example, reports from the Committee on the Constitution often lead to a long debate in the Swedish Riksdag – yet these debates almost always end with the report being put aside. With the No-Confidence Votes, an absolute majority can bring down the whole Cabinet (Instrument of Government, Chapter 12, §4), but these votes can also be directed towards individual ministers. No-confidence votes are rare, however, and they are seldom successful when they take place. The Parliamentary Ombudsmen audit how the decisions and actions of public agencies and their staff comply with laws and other statutes. Although their decisions tend to lead to action, formally they only have the status of recommendations. Also, SNAO reports include recommendations, but the Cabinet is obliged to return to Parliament explaining what actions have been taken in response to criticisms.

The SNAO was formed in 2003, in a reform preceded by lengthy political deliberations (see Bringselius, 2008, 2013). In legal terms, it was formed as a totally new institution. In terms of organisation, it was implemented as a merger of the previous two institutions for state audit: Riksrevisionsverket (RRV) and the Parliamentary Auditors. Although both these offices had important merits, neither of them had been fully autonomous: RRV reported to the Ministry of Finance, and the Parliamentary Auditors actually consisted of a group of MPs, assisted by a secretariat of circa 25 non-partisan auditors. Building on the merits of RRV and the Parliamentary Auditors, but adjusting the legal conditions under which it served, the new SNAO was expected to be state-of-the-art among SAIs.

The reform was preceded by a debate on the lack of a PAC in the Swedish Riksdag, and some requested that a PAC ought to be formed. It was finally agreed, however, that the SNAO would instead report to an independent 'board'. This board was formally tied to the SNAO, but it consisted of MPs, representing each of the political parties in Parliament. I shall explain further below how this model worked. It was also agreed that *three* Auditor-Generals, instead of one, would head the SNAO.

Two non-PAC models in Sweden

Instead of introducing a PAC into the Swedish political system, two different models for the dissemination of SNAO reports to the Riksdag have been tested. The first model was introduced as the SNAO was formed in 2003. The second model was introduced after two highly critical reports from a committee under the Swedish Parliament, and effectuated in January 2011. In the following two sections, the two models are described and the Swedish experience from each model is reported.

The first model: the SNAO board

As explained, instead of a PAC, an independent board was formed and tied to the SNAO in 2003. The members of this board were MPs, representing each of the parties in the Riksdag. One of the responsibilities of the board was to select the specific reports to be passed on to the Riksdag (Instrument of Government, Chapter 12, §7). In doing this, they also determined if a parliamentary decision was called for, or if the report was primarily 'for information'. Apart from this, the board had a supervisory function, but without any tools for sanctions or a mandate to override the decisions of the Auditors-General. This way, the Riksdag wished to ensure that the SNAO was not subjected to partisan interests.

After reports had been finished, they were sent to both the SNAO board and the Cabinet. Each year, the Cabinet had to account for the measures they had taken as a consequence of the SNAO audit reports and they chose to do this in connection with the yearly budget bill.

This model led to a number of problems. In particular, the SNAO became dependent upon the media to attract attention to its reports and increase the chances for these reports to gain some degree of impact in Parliament (Bringselius, 2014). Typically, these reports were otherwise put aside rather swiftly. In parallel with this, the first set of Auditors-General requested that the SNAO should adopt a new approach in performance audits, in comparison to the one developed by their predecessors (RRV and the Parliamentary Auditors). Instead of the traditional 3E (Economy, Efficiency and Effectiveness; see INTOSAI, 2003: 11) audit, they explained that audits should be focused on formal norms and aim to define which individual or institution was accountable for specific issues (Bringselius, 2013). Professional autonomy was strongly curtailed; furthermore, a study (Grönlund *et al.*, 2011) shows that audit reports became highly focused on compliance in the years from 2003 to 2007.

These changes led to protests from SNAO performance auditors. The relation between them and the three Auditors-General became increasingly tense. Auditors complained that

- professional autonomy was too heavily curtailed;
- the SNAO had become too focused on attracting media attention, rather than presenting substantial and interesting results;
- performance audit at the SNAO was gradually transformed from a broad, interpretive practice (as recommended also by ISSAI 3000–3100) into a compliance audit;
- audit reports were too focused on accountability and conflict in relation to the Riksdag, rather than pragmatic support.

The relation between the SNAO and Parliament was tense, partly as a consequence of the Auditors-General demanding that Parliament act in accordance with their suggestions in reports.

After a parliamentary committee had been initiated in 2007, to evaluate the performance of the SNAO from a parliamentary perspective, this gradually changed. This may be one reason why the number of reports requesting a parliamentary decision diminished during the years 2008 to 2010, as compared to the years 2004 to 2007. During the period between 2008 and 2010, a majority of the reports sent to Parliament were instead meant to be only informational (see Table 7.1). The board also chose to put a considerable number of reports in the archive, instead of passing them on to Parliament. The reason why Table 7.1 does not include the years 2011 to 2012 is that a new model was introduced in 2011, as we shall see.

Many MPs were critical of the path that the SNAO had taken. Some argued that the SNAO was becoming too involved in policy issues. A respondent in a stakeholder survey from 2006 explained:

Table 7.1 Decisions at the SNAO board, concerning performance audit reports, in the years 2004 to 2010

	2003	2004	2005	2006	2007	2008	2009	2010
To Parliament, suggesting a parliamentary decision		12	10	17	14	7	5	7
To Parliament, for information		5	11	7	8	17	17	23
To the archive		4	9	9	3	8	6	8
Total number of reports	1	21	30	33	25	32	28	28

Source: Collected from SNAO yearly reports.

> The SNAO appears keen to take on an increasingly political role and profile itself by different moves.
>
> (Demoskop, 2006: 53)

This argument was repeated in a stakeholder survey the year after (Gullers Grupp, 2007). It was raised as a risk that the SNAO would become the tool of the opposition, instead of a *non-political* driver of improvements. Some respondents compared the SNAO to the tabloids, explaining that these auditors were only looking for issues to complain about.

> The hyperbolized statements are a weakness. They have a negative approach, they are actually only looking for errors. Instead, when you work in central government, the shared mission should be to improve operations.
>
> (Gullers Grupp, 2007: 9f.)

Respondents from the Riksdag complained that the SNAO board had positioned itself as an obstacle between the SNAO and the parliamentary committees (Gullers Grupp, 2007). For example, they saw it as problematic that the SNAO board modified suggestions from audit reports and instead, they wished that the standing parliamentary committees themselves could choose what parts of these reports to build on.

The second model: standing committees

In 2008 and 2009, a parliamentary investigation presented two highly critical reports (Sveriges riksdag, 2008/09: URF1, URF3) concerning the SNAO. This included concerns regarding the lack of a solid response to SNAO reports, but also concerns pertaining to the internal problems (high overhead costs, low productivity and employee distrust) at the SNAO and the relevance of the areas the Auditors-General chose to audit. The two parliamentary reports showed how the SNAO had chosen to audit many areas that were of minor financial interest to the Riksdag, in comparison to their part of the state budget. About the same time, a research study (Grönlund *et al.*, 2011) showed that SNAO performance audit had become primarily oriented towards compliance audit during the years since the reform, as opposed to traditional performance audit, as outlined by the INTOSAI (3E). The reports highlighted that this was problematic and questioned the Auditors-General's focus on accountability issues. Instead of identifying someone to be held accountable, they asked for a state audit focused on pragmatic support and improvements.

The parliamentary investigation suggested a number of changes to legislation, aimed to improve SNAO performance and align it more with parliamentary requirements. Suggestions were accepted by the Committee on the Constitution and the Parliamentary Board, with only minor changes. This means that there was broad political support in the Riksdag for the criticisms raised in the two reports.

In the deliberations that took place in the parliamentary committee, some people argued again that a PAC should be formed. It was, however, agreed otherwise and, from 2011, SNAO reports have instead been sent directly to the standing committees in the Riksdag. The Riksdag then passes them on to the Cabinet. For example, reports concerning Swedish defence are today sent to the parliamentary committee on defence. By sending reports to the concerned committee, it is expected that reports will have a genuine impact in the relevant channels and raise discussions among those who are specialised in the specific topic. Furthermore, this means that those MPs responsible for policy-making in the area also have to address feedback on the same policies. Since 2011, the Swedish Cabinet has also been obliged to respond to criticism in SNAO reports within a four-month period.

It is interesting to note that the two reports from the parliamentary committee also resulted in a rare change to Swedish legislation: a section stating how SNAO performance audit should be defined was included. This stated that SNAO performance audit should be focused on traditional '3E' performance audit (Act 2002: 1022 on state audit, in Swedish *Revisionslagen*, §4).

The parliamentary reports also requested that the SNAO should focus on support, rather than accountability. The first set of Auditors-General had been very explicit internally (Bringselius, 2008, 2013, 2014) about their aim to ensure that all performance audit reports from the SNAO pointed out not only problems, but also a person or institution that the Riksdag could – and should – hold as being accountable. This focus on being held accountable is rare in the political culture of Sweden, which is characterised rather by pragmatism, informality and pro-activeness, as I have explained.

Preliminary findings (e.g. Gullers Grupp, 2011) indicate that the new model for the dissemination of SNAO reports to the Riksdag works rather well. The standing committees can now address feedback from the SNAO, on policy problems and the performance of executive agencies in their area, in a pragmatic way. Committee members are specialised in the relevant area and therefore they typically have the necessary know-how to relate to reports. The relation between the Riksdag and the Auditors-General has also been improved with the new model, partly because they meet regularly for presentations and discussions. However, there is a high awareness on the side of both parties that the Riksdag is not allowed to decide what areas the SNAO should audit.

A problem is, however, that the response from the Cabinet tends to be of a rather general character. One reason for this may be that four months is too short a time to be able to actually plan any major changes, following criticism from the SNAO.

As I have explained, the relationship between the SNAO and the Riksdag became increasingly tense during the first five to seven years. Since the changes implemented in 2011, with a new model for the dissemination of SNAO reports to the Riksdag, this relationship has gradually improved. Today, it is less formal and less focused on accountability. This is the result of a deliberate effort from the side of the SNAO, where the SNAO, for example, has arranged meetings and seminars for all parliamentary committees, in order to improve its dialogue with them (Bringselius, 2013).

Discussion

How does the Swedish model(s) compare to a model with a PAC? This chapter describes how it is possible for legislatures to handle their oversight function without a PAC – and how there also may be benefits from these alternative models. The Swedish case offers experience from two different models for the channelling of results from SNAO audits to the Riksdag.

The first model, with an independent body between the SNAO and the Riksdag, called a 'board', did not turn out to be very successful. This was partly because neither the Riksdag nor the Cabinet had strong incentives to respond to reports, or even bring them up on the political agenda. The SNAO reports became increasingly critical during these years, partly aiming to attract more public interest, but this led to criticism from the Riksdag and other stakeholders, where the SNAO was accused of being 'overly critical' (Bringselius, 2014). There was very little personal contact between the Riksdag and the Auditors-General.

The second model has proved to have more merit, although its effects will need to be explored further. This model, which has been valid since 2011, means that reports are sent to the relevant standing parliamentary committees in the Riksdag. Accordingly, reports are always included on the political agenda and in the relevant context, to those with a vested interest in the area in question. This model makes the Cabinet obliged to respond to SNAO reports within four months, thus also giving the Cabinet incentives to take action following criticism from the SNAO. With this model, the SNAO has become less focused on accountability and moved more into the supportive function that the Riksdag has requested (in particular in the two highly critical reports from 2008 and 2009, Sveriges riksdag 2008/09: URF1, URF3).

One of the aims behind the Swedish trajectory has been to ensure that SNAO reports are being used – yet without introducing an accountability-focused polit-ical culture. This cultural aspect is more important, this study suggests, than what is generally acknowledged in the literature on PACs and other systems for state oversight. As I have explained, the Swedish 'policy style', or political culture, is characterised by informality (Jacobsson, Pierre and Sundström, 2015; Page, 2012), a consensual and pro-active style of policy-making (Bergman, 2003; Ruin, 1982; Kelman, 2013) and by pragmatic improvements (Anton, 1969; Heckscher, 1984). This includes a focus on improving systems, rather than holding individuals or institutions accountable, as noted by Anton (1969). The decision to avoid forming a PAC in Sweden can be understood as a consequence of this culture.

This political culture is functional for many actors, since they can avoid conflict, but yet have administrative improvements and carefully work to develop public policy. This may be one reason why it has persisted, despite the excellent opportunities that were provided for the introduction of a PAC, first in the SNAO reform in 2003, and then in the legislative changes implemented in 2011.

This does not mean, however, that any country could manage without a PAC. In Sweden, social trust, including citizen confidence in the performance of the public administration, is higher than in many other countries (Inglehart, 1999). With this trust as a foundation, it is easier to enter pragmatic and informal discussions, following criticism in state audits, such as those conducted by the SNAO. There is an assumption that officials, managers and policy-makers want to do a good job, rather than an assumption that they must risk being held accountable in order to achieve this performance.

Finally, it is interesting to reflect on how PACs affect the audit approach of, for example, Supreme Audit Institutions. With their focus on accountability, it may be hypothesised that PACs lead to more compliance audit, compared with the traditional performance audit (focused on the three Es). On the other hand, this may be the consequence also of a model that cannot secure that audit reports gain some degree of impact. This was the case at the SNAO until a new model was introduced in 2011 (see also Bringselius, 2014, on SNAO relations with the media). Since the changes implemented in 2011, also explicitly stating the acts under which the SNAO should serve, this audit approach has changed.

Today, there is much more of a collaborative culture between the SNAO and the Riksdag, with its standing committees as a key actor. Thus, we conclude that the parliamentary oversight function can work well also in the absence of a PAC. Under the influence of globalisation and harmonisation within the EU, however, Sweden is likely to experience increasing pressures to form a PAC.

Finally, returning to the analytical framework presented in the first part of this chapter, the Swedish non-PAC models can be positioned according to Figure 7.2. Before the reform in 2003, the Swedish SNAO was focused on collaboration with the auditee and cooperation with the principal, i.e. the Ministry of Finance. Again, at this time, the SNAO did not enjoy full autonomy, but took assignments from the ministry, although they also initiated some studies themselves. During the period from 2003 to 2010, the SNAO took on a position of confrontation in relation to the auditee and total distance in relation to the principal (Swedish Parliament). Lacking a PAC, they had to turn to the media to make sure that audit reports gained some attention and could have some impact (see also Bringselius, 2014). After the judicial changes implemented in 2011, the

		Primary goal in relation to the executive (auditee)	
		Confrontation	Collaboration
Choice of audit areas/ relation to Parliament (the principal)	Integration (almost exclusively direct assignments)		
	Cooperation (some direct assignments)	PAC	Sweden before 2003
	Dialogue (suggestions are encouraged)		Sweden 2011–
	Total distance (contact avoided)	Sweden 2003–2010	

Figure 7.2 Models for the channelling of results from the SNAO to Swedish Parliament during the period 2000–2014, as compared to a model with a PAC.

SNAO has moved to a position where it collaborates more with the auditee and also with the concerned parliamentary committees. Initiatives from these committees are encouraged and there is an ongoing contact between the SNAO and these. In Figure 7.2, this is referred to as *dialogue*. There is still no PAC in Sweden, but with the new position, it appears as if the SNAO has finally taken on the position that Parliament once hoped for when forming it in 2003 – namely a position of pragmatic collaboration with the auditee and equally pragmatic dialogue with Parliament and the different subject committees. Of course, it requires extensive work to maintain a running dialogue with all these committees, as compared to what would have been the case with only one PAC, but Sweden has chosen that it is still worth maintaining this model.

Conclusions

For many countries, the Public Accounts Committee (PAC) is an important democratic institution, and it would be hard to imagine a political system without it. Yet this is the case in Sweden. When the (new) Swedish National Audit Office (SNAO) was formed in 2003, many people expected that a PAC would be formed. Instead, an independent body with Members of Parliament was formed and was prescribed to choose which specific SNAO reports should be passed on to Parliament and with what recommendation. This model led to a number of problems. It was replaced by a new model in 2011. The body with Members of

Parliament was abandoned, but still no PAC was formed. Instead, SNAO reports are now being sent directly to the standing committees in Parliament. Today, the Cabinet is also obliged to respond to each report within a four-month period.

This chapter has primarily made three contributions. First, it has depicted the Swedish experience from two non-PAC models, showing that it is possible to make use of audit reports without the accountability debates typical of PACs. In particular, this aims to avoid the auditor becoming 'a bruiser', as Travers (1999) argues in a common temptation. Second, it has also suggested a framework to compare how SAIs related to the auditee and to Parliament in performance audits. Third, to explain the Swedish choice of a non-PAC model, the chapter has argued that there is a correlation between the political culture and the existence of a PAC. In Sweden, there is a political culture focused on collaboration and pragmatic improvement, rather than confrontation and accountability debates. By turning to the standing committees, building a working relationship with these, the Swedish culture can be preserved at the same time as audit results are disseminated to those who are most interested. It should be noted that some of these also will be found among the auditees – the executive agencies. To estimate the impact of audits, in a pragmatic politico-administrative culture, it may be equally important to consider the (sometimes informal, subtle or longitudinal) actions taken by these, following audits, as it is to understand to what extent Parliament takes action. Findings emphasise the importance of a fit between political culture and systems for accountability.

References

Anton, T. J. (1969) 'Policy-Making and Political Culture in Sweden', *Scandinavian Political Studies*, 4: 88–102.

Bergman, T. (2003) 'Sweden: From Separation of Power to Parliamentary Supremacy – and Back Again?', in K. Strøm, W. C. Müller and T. Bergman (eds) *Delegation and Accountability in Parliamentary democracies*, Oxford: Oxford University Press.

Bowerman, M., Humphrey, C. and Owen, D. (2003) 'Struggling for supremacy: The case of UK public audit institutions', *Critical Perspectives on Accounting*, 14(1–2): 1–22.

Bringselius, L. (2008) *Personnel Resistance in Public Professional Service Mergers: The merging of two national audit organizations*, Lund: Lund Institute of Economic Research.

Bringselius, L. (2013) *Organisera Oberoende Granskning: Riksrevisionens första tio år'*, Lund: Studentlitteratur [book on the first ten years of the SNAO].

Bringselius, L. (2014) 'The dissemination of reports from Supreme Audit Institutions: Independent partners with the media?' *Financial Accountability & Management*, 30(1): 75–94.

Diamond, L. J. and Morlino, L. (2005) *Assessing the Quality of Democracy*, Baltimore: Johns Hopkins University Press.

English, L. and Guthrie, J. (2000) 'Mandate, Independence and Funding: Resolution of a Protracted Struggle between Parliament and the Executive Over the Powers of the Australian Auditor-General', *Australian Journal of Public Administration*, 59(4): 98–114.

Funnell, W. (1998) 'Executive Coercion and State Audit: A Processual Analysis of the Responses of the Australian Audit Office to the Dilemmas of Efficiency Auditing, 1978–84', *Accounting, Auditing and Accountability Journal*, 11(4): 436–459.

Funnell, W. (1994) 'Independence and the State Auditor in Britain: Constitutional Keystone or a Case of Reified Imagery', *Abacus*, 30(3): 175–195.

Gendron, Y., Cooper, D. J. and Townley, B. (2001) 'In the Name of Accountability: State Auditing, Independence and New Public Management', *Accounting, Auditing & Accountability Journal*, 14(3): 278–310.

Grönlund, A., Svärdsten, F. and Öhman, P. (2011) 'Value for money and the rule of law: the (new) performance audit in Sweden', *International Journal of Public Sector Management*, 24(2): 107–121.

Gullers Grupp (2007) *Omvärldens syn på Riksrevisionen: en intervjuundersökning med 23 viktiga intressenter* [stakeholder survey for the SNAO], Stockholm: Gullers Grupp.

Gullers Grupp (2011) *Bilden av Riksrevisionen: en kvalitativ intressentanalys'*. [stakeholder survey for the SNAO], Stockholm: Gullers Grupp.

Heckscher, G. (1984) *The Welfare State and Beyond: Success and problems in Scandinavia*, Minneapolis: University of Minnesota Press.

Inglehart, R. (1999) 'Trust, well-being and democracy', in M. E. Warren (ed.) *Democracy and Trust*, Cambridge: Cambridge University Press.

INTOSAI (2003) *ISSAI 3000–3100, Performance Audit Guidelines*, www.issai.org.

Jacobs, K. (1998) 'Value for Money Auditing in New Zealand: Competing for Control in the Public Sector', *British Accounting Review*, 30(4): 343–360.

Jacobsson, B., Pierre, J. and Sundström, G. (2015) *Governing the Embedded State: The Organizational Dimension of Governance*, Oxford: Oxford University Press.

Kelman, S. (2013) 'Sveriges framtid behöver kompromissviljan', *Dagens Nyheter*, 30 December.

Landers, B. (1999) 'Encounters with the Public Accounts Committee: A personal memoir', *Public Management*, 77(1): 195–219.

Lonsdale, J. (1999) 'Impacts', in C. Pollitt, C. Xavier, J. Lonsdale, R. Mul and M. Waerness (eds) *Performance Audit and Public Management in Five Countries*, Oxford: Oxford University Press.

Mohan, R. and Sullivan, K. (2007) 'Managing the Politics of Evaluation to Achieve Impact', in Promoting the Use of Government Evaluations in Policymaking', *New Directions in Evaluation*, 112.

Page, E. C. (2012) *Policy without Politicians: Bureaucratic Influence in Comparative Perspective*, Oxford: Oxford University Press.

Pelizzo, R. and Stapenhurst, R. (2008) 'Public Accounts Committees', in R. Stapenhurst, R. Pelizzo, D. M. Olson and L. von Trapp (eds) *Legislative Budgeting and Oversight: A world perspective*, Washington DC: World Bank Institute.

Pollitt, C. and Summa, H. (1997) 'Comparative and International Administration Reflexive Watchdogs? How Supreme Audit Institutions Account for Themselves', *Public Administration*, 75(2): 313–336.

Przeworski, A., Stokes, S. C. and Manin, B. (1999) *Democracy, Accountability, and Representation*, Cambridge: Cambridge University Press.

Ruin, O. (1982) 'Sweden in the 1970s: Policy-Making Becomes More Difficult', in J. J. Richardson (ed.) *Policy Styles in Western Europe*, London: Allen and Unwin.

Sveriges riksdag (2008/09: URF1) *Uppföljning av Riksrevisionsreformen I: Riksrevisionens styrelse, ledning och hanteringen av effektivitetsgranskningar.* [Report from parliamentary investigation].

Sveriges riksdag (2008/09: URF3) *Uppföljning av Riksrevisionsreformen II: Effektivitetsrevisionen, den årliga revisionen och den internationella verksamheten. Slutbetänkande av Riksrevisionsutredningen.* [Report from parliamentary investigation].

Talbot, C. and Wiggan, J. (2010) 'The public value of the National Audit Office', *International Journal of Public Sector Management*, 23(1): 54–70.

Travers, T. (1999) 'Should the Inspector be a Bruiser?' *Public Finance*, 19 November.

White, F. and Hollingsworth, K. (1999) *Audit, Accountability and Government* Oxford: Clarendon Press.

Part III

Public Accounts Committees in Australia and the Pacific

8 Pragmatism, black letter law and Australian Public Accounts Committees

David Gilchrist and Kylie Coulson

Introduction

The Australian federation, in the context of public financial management, is complex largely as a result of its history and its constitutional settlement. Notwithstanding the inheritance of the Westminster legacy in all Australian jurisdictions, the overlay of Washington-style constitutional nuances, combined with a natural tendency toward pragmatic political arrangements, has meant that the unwritten aspects of the various constitutions are often played down to the detriment of parliamentary sovereignty. Combining this preference for pragmatism with the country's almost insoluble problem of vertical fiscal imbalance has meant that there is increasing emphasis on the executive, thus reducing parliamentary sovereignty. The role of the Australian Public Accounts Committees (PACs) in defending parliamentary sovereignty – and the Westminster Model of parliamentary government that is constantly referred to by commentators and politicians alike – is not well documented, particularly in relation to the Australian jurisdictions.

The scrutiny of public finances is a complex activity in any country, regardless of the style of government put in place. The need to examine the proposals of the executive, its execution of policy objectives and the efficiency with which it pursues its objectives are all necessary activities. However, traditionally, these activities have been undertaken by different committees; usually the Estimates Committee in relation to *ex ante* analysis and the PAC in relation to *ex post* analysis. In the Australian environment, the Westminster Model is referred to constantly for both historical explanation and for legitimacy in terms of the actions of parliaments and executives. Ranged against this traditional view of the Westminster Model generally and of PACs specifically are the pragmatic political actions of the members of committees and the development of PACs over the last 160 years or so of Responsible Government in most Australian states. Our interest in this chapter is to describe the 'purist' Westminster Model PAC, to examine the extent to which the purist Westminster PAC is the template from which Australian PACs are drawn, and to consider the Australian experience in relation to the various proxies used to denote the existence of PAC independence and effectiveness.

In this chapter, we examine the PACs in place in Australian jurisdictions, the pressures that combine to ensure the Westminster Model is not adopted in a pure sense in each jurisdiction, and the extent to which the identified proxies taken to represent PAC effectiveness are present in each jurisdiction. The chapter is divided into six sections. In section two we examine the extent to which PACs are considered a part of the Westminster Model of parliamentary government. In section three we review the idea of Australian parliamentary actors as pragmatists while in section four we identify the components of a 'purist' model of a PAC's establishment in order to compare this to the Australian experience of PACs in section five. In section six we provide some concluding remarks.

Public Accounts Committees as Westminster Model apparatus

It is axiomatic that the British Empire bequeathed a number of institutions to those countries that made up its empire. Chief amongst these, and most often cited, is the Westminster System or Model of government. In the Anglophone world at least, the Westminster Model has become one of the two major systems recognised as appropriate for the constitutional organisation of democratised countries, the other being the Presidential System created first upon the establishment of the United States. The Westminster Model bequest has been argued by many to be a significant and lasting contribution to the political structure of developed and developing countries alike and has been a foundation upon which political science and public administration have been moulded over the last century or so in these countries. Of course, the Westminster Model evolved over a period of centuries, and most readers will have at least a general appreciation as to the trajectory of the development of this important institution.

What is often not well recognised is the fact that the mature Westminster Model is really a relatively new institution, one which developed during the course of the establishment and political settlement of the major settler colonies of the British Empire – Canada, Australia, South Africa and New Zealand (see for instance Bunn and Gilchrist, 2013; James, 1997). As these settler colonies were being granted Responsible Government and worked toward independence, the United Kingdom was developing its constitutional frameworks so that, by the end of the Victorian era, the institution that we would recognise as the Westminster System was in place in the United Kingdom and had been adopted, with local variations, throughout the settler colonies of the Empire. As such, while we talk in terms of the bequest of the Westminster Model, the constitutional arrangements of the settler colonies were significantly influenced by the British model but evolved concomitantly with those of the United Kingdom, rather than afterwards. The adoption process, still continuing today in developing countries with historical attachments to the British Empire, is undertaken by countries generally seeking to take the best from the system in the context of local cultural, historical and political arrangements (see Coulson and Gilchrist, Chapter 10 of this volume).[1] It is to the development of the Australian colonies to which we now turn. In terms of Australia, the focus of this chapter, the relatively late federation of the various colonies in 1901 meant that the Founding Fathers were in a position to take the best of the Westminster Model and incorporate elements of the Presidential System, such that the Australian federal constitutional settlement incorporates aspects of both systems, leading us to consider the extent to which Australia actually operates under the Westminster Model.

Indeed, Rhodes (2005: 130, 132) argues that while Australia does not technically follow the Westminster Model, in the psyche of many of the Founding Fathers it adopted the British system of parliamentary government. In his view, the federal model in Australia is at best a mutated version of the Westminster Model with the adoption of judicial review and the separation of powers acting as an addendum to the British model. However, Rhodes (2005: 129, 133–4) does identify that the phrase 'Westminster Model' serves two purposes in Australian discourse; a historical explanatory purpose and a normative purpose. The former purpose serves as historical shorthand for explaining the current system in Australia, while the latter serves as a source of legitimacy for governments and procedures. In this chapter it is the normative use that we are interested in. That is, the utilisation of the term 'Westminster Model' to provide legitimacy to functions, procedures and structures on the basis that they conform to the Westminster Model. Public Accounts Committees are specifically described by Balls (1963) as constituting a part of the Westminster Model, and he traces a cogent trajectory of the development of this institution as a critical part of the development of the Westminster Model itself. Therefore, in discussing the role of PACs in Australian parliaments, we are interested in the extent to which those institutions form part of the Westminster Model and to what extent they are informed by ideas that revolve around the model.

The PACs support the cardinal principle of the British parliamentary system that Parliament should exercise supreme financial control (Balls 1963: 15). Developing his description of the trajectory of the development of the Westminster Model, Balls (1963: 15–17) describes the deficiency which was felt to exist during the course of the first half of the nineteenth century, resulting in the establishment of the first PAC of the Westminster Parliament in 1856, sponsored by Prime Minister Gladstone. That is, as a result of Parliament approving taxation and proposed expenditure (via the estimates process) but not considering the issue of assurance, the 'circle of control' was not closed. Arrangements were in place to authorise the raising of funds, to authorise the proposed expenditure of funds but not to check whether those funds had been expended as intended and that the executive delivered what we would today call value for money in pursuit of its policies. The establishment of the first PAC in Britain was undertaken at virtually the same point in time as the Australian colonies of New South Wales, Victoria, Tasmania and Queensland were afforded Responsible Government and the PAC found its way into the *modus operandi* of these new states, as did many of the other aspects of the Westminster Model (Bunn and Gilchrist, 2013). As such, in the minds of the colonial founders, the adoption of the Westminster Model was an essential aspect of creating local government in the effigy of the Imperial government at 'Home'.

Each of the colonies in Australia achieved responsible government before they federated in 1901. Therefore, their constitutions are, albeit generally covertly,[2] more purely Westminster in nature than the constitution that was developed to enable federation. The various founding fathers of each colony did not believe that there was a need to consider alternatives to the Westminster Model as it stood in the mid-nineteenth century. This attitude was probably reinforced by the fact that the gift of Responsible Government rested with the Imperial Parliament; there was little political incentive to agitate for an alternative system. Additionally, each colony was a unitary state in itself. The 'warping' of the Westminster Model upon federation was required in order to induce the prospective member states to join.

Ensuring states' rights were maintained so that the interests of all states (regardless of size by population or resources) were protected, that an umpire existed to ensure the federal Parliament did not encroach on those rights or seek to serve one or more states to the disadvantage of another or others (the High Court), and the retention of a number of residual powers by the states meant that the federal constitutional arrangements were a mix of Westminster and Presidential models. However, the Westminster Model 'tag' is most recognised and most deployed in order to achieve the normative validity sought for actions and procedures within the current system.

While Rhodes (2005: 131) describes federalism as a 'weak' model, it is sufficient to say here that the timing of federation combined with the normative ascription of the Westminster Model to all Australian sovereign governments, places PACs, which are established in all modern Australian parliaments, in the category of Westminster Model institutions. In that line, Balls (1963: 19–25) describes a number of aspects relating to the establishment and operation of the British PAC that serve in the minds of many as a normative description of the requirements of a successful PAC. These include that the chair of the PAC is to be a member of the Opposition, the membership of the committee should be established such that the parties represented are recruited in proportion to the political make-up of the House of Commons (i.e. the popular house), that the statutory auditor should work closely with the PAC, and that the PAC should confine its deliberations to issues of financial control. In other words, the PAC should not be drawn on the efficacy of the policies being funded but, rather, on whether those policies have been pursued in accordance with the appropriation, efficiently and effectively – that is, whether the executive has been efficient and effective in pursuit of its policy agenda. This last normative statement is, of course, a major focus of discussion surrounding PACs and the political nature of their members.

Indeed, Woolmer (1998: 42) indicates that the PAC has responsibility for ensuring that the Parliament has sufficient information to scrutinise the government's management of the public purse. In Woolmer's view, the PAC must assess the economy, efficiency and effectiveness of financial management; and review the financial reports of the government and the reports of the statutory auditor in order to undertake this task. Degeling *et al.* (1996) have reported that, in their view, PACs in Australia have achieved varying degrees of success over time. In their review of the performance of the Federal PAC between 1914 and 1932, they considered that the performance of the PAC was variable and sound performance seemed to 'go in waves' (Degeling *et al.*, 1996: 30–1). They indicated that PACs are often described in terms of what they should be doing rather than what they are doing, and that they are institutions which are seen as 'underwriting' the financial accountability of the executive to parliament (p. 44). Of course, role descriptions do not necessarily mean the role will be carried out in the way described or in the spirit intended – political pragmatism overrides constitutional niceties.

Pragmatic realities of Australian Public Accounts Committees

While Balls has set out the key structural elements that should ensure a PAC operates appropriately, there are other considerations that are clearly impacting the effectiveness of PACs in Australia. For instance, while Degeling *et al.*'s study considered a period of the Federal PAC's operations that occurred over 60 years ago, the review undertaken and the results reported are as relevant today as they were when this early PAC was sitting. The realities of the political environment remain the same. For instance, their findings that the PAC's effectiveness was undermined by 'a lack of parliamentary interest and resources' are anecdotally supported today. Further, the enduring reality of the political environment means that the forces impacting PACs will always ensure that the capacity for it to remain focused on the ideal of a policy neutral, efficiency and effectiveness scope of operations is highly difficult.

This enduring reality seems to have a certain inevitability to it. For instance, Bennett (1980: 972) identified that the provision of an account is a standard procedure undertaken by political actors in seeking to influence the response to their actions. The way political problems develop depends on how political opponents respond, and so the presentation and acceptance of budgets, accounts and outcomes statements is critical to an executive retaining political acceptance – whether within the House or within the electorate. As such, the executive will always have a significant interest in trying to guide the debate and findings of any committee set up by the Parliament, including the PAC, because the political drivers are the same in any age.

Benton and Russell (2012) expand on this argument by highlighting that the capacity of PACs to achieve what is expected of them is also retarded due to the members being inexpert and relatively party-dominated. We shall return to the issue of expertise shortly. However, at this point we wish to focus on the issue of party domination and political focus – indeed, what we believe drives the Australian predilection for pragmatic action. In Australia it has long been recognised that governments and politicians (and the community for that matter) prefer pragmatic rather than ideological responses to issues (Gilchrist, 2013; Rhodes, 2005; Metin, 1977 [1901]). This pragmatism has developed into an ideology in its own right (Rhodes, 2005: 136).

Indeed, Rhodes (2005) has indicated that reform in Australian PACs (as with any other aspect of parliamentary machinery) has not been undertaken unless there was a good, pragmatic reason for it. Such pragmatic rationales are usually constituted by politically charged reasons rather than functional, machinery improvement reasons. To be sure, most Commonwealth countries have deviated in some way from the Westminster Model (Balls, 1963: 25). In Australia, however, PACs have become politicised because the PAC itself constitutes a platform for pursuing political interests and concerns important to the individual members. This outcome is reflective of the fact that it is extremely difficult to separate the policy framework from financial scrutiny (Degeling *et al.*, 1996: 40, 47).

Monk is a little more straightforward in his assessment of the situation. Quoting O'Keefe (1992), Monk (2010: 3) considers that parliamentary committees are made up of politicians behaving politically. Behaving politically in the Australian context – as in the context of many other countries – equates to behaving pragmatically in the interests of party and personal political advancement. As such, if we recognise the Australian penchant for pragmatic action, we must necessarily consider another element of the Westminster Model that, arguably, has not been translated into the parliamentary arrangements of many Commonwealth countries, namely that of parliamentary sovereignty.

Parliamentary sovereignty is an important consideration here because the 'classical' role of the PAC is to close the financial control circle by administering the assurance necessary to ensure the executive has raised taxes and expended money in accordance with expectations, and as efficiently as possible. Parliamentary sovereignty is built on financial control. Additionally then, if the Parliament is sovereign, the political power of Parliament will be of value in ensuring the PAC does what is expected of it – not necessarily that which is pragmatic for its members, the government or some other sub-set of interests to undertake. The unique Australian constitutional settlement does call into question the extent to which Parliament is sovereign and various commentators have raised this issue in considering a number of aspects of parliamentary operation, including that of PACs.

Rhodes (2005: 141) considers that parliaments in Australia are not supreme but, rather, a 'popular sovereignty' is the cornerstone of Australian democracy. Asserting that it is more precise to describe 'citizens [as] no longer members of a political community but part of a chain of principal-agent contracts', Rhodes (2005: 142–3) considers that Neo-Liberalism has replaced our conceptions of citizenship with a sort of purchaser/provider relationship with governments supported or deposed at elections depending on whether they have delivered to the satisfaction of voters. Given this commercial way of representing the political arrangements in modern Australia, the actions of a duly elected Parliament which might include a hostile Senate rejecting a government measure or the effects of a High Court decision rejecting the capacity of a government to do a certain thing will more likely result in cries of outrage because an elected government is being restricted from governing. Certainly, the leadership of the party in power will cite its mandate for pursuing the particular measure that was rejected. In the case of the federal government being thwarted by such actions, justifications such as states' rights, constitutional incapacity or the policy assertions of minority parties controlling the Senate do not, generally, accrue much sympathy from citizens.

While Australian citizens do not necessarily understand the constitutional arrangements establishing the federal political settlement in Australia, the argument that a principal/agent relationship is the appropriate description of the political reality raises two further issues. Firstly, there is considerable complexity and difficulty in seeking to introduce Agency theory into the political arena. As Pilcher *et al.* (2013) have identified, this complexity and difficulty arises out of the sheer number of relationships that exist in the political arena and the overlapping nature of economic and political interests that arise. It is argued by Pilcher *et al.* (2013) that there are direct and indirect agent/principal relationships including but not limited to: the relationship between parliament and the voters; that between the Parliament and the executive; and that between the executive and the public service. Second, this complexity combined with the apparent lack of understanding within the electorate mean that voters expect – and, therefore, politicians are rewarded for – pragmatic action aimed at resolving issues rather than having a predisposition toward constitutional correctness.

If the pragmatic actions of politicians are rewarded as a result of the expectations of voters, if the constitutional framework is not of great significance to Australian voters as Rhodes would have us believe and, if parliamentary sovereignty is on the wane as Goldsworthy (2010: 2) suggests, then it is likely that the PAC in any jurisdiction will operate pragmatically and in the interests of the political persuasion that has control of the Parliament and forms the government. This will occur unless a minority government is formed or the parliamentary conventions are so strong that it is simply not feasible to ensure the government members have control of the PAC. While the latter is the case with respect to the Westminster Parliament, the continued reversion to the Westminster Model normative description which is used in order to provide the necessary legitimacy does raise a question with regard to the extent to which the model implemented in Westminster Model jurisdictions is commensurate with that implemented in Westminster itself.

In the case of PACs, there is diversity amongst the Australian jurisdictions which will be discussed in detail below. This diversity is maintained not only by a reversion to pragmatism but also by virtue of the super-infrastructure that is in place and which supports this diversity – namely the Commonwealth Parliamentary Association (CPA) and the Australasian Council of Public Accounts Committees (ACPAC). This super-infrastructure is not a formal part of the constitutional arrangements of countries which are members of these associations, but it does have a significant role to play in legitimising diversity within the Westminster 'club'. It helps to maintain and reinforce the situation where diversity is acknowledged and relative effectiveness in the operations of infrastructure, such as PACs, is the sole concern and province of the particular parliament, and their straying from the wholesome Westminster Model (amongst other things) is not to be commented upon by other jurisdictions. Di Francesco (2013) puts this neatly when discussing public sector reform generally; he argues that 'Westminster can be seen as a kind of reversible political cloak that clothes public service reform – sometimes as a critique of conventional practice, other times as a defence against unwanted change'.

This reality is reinforced by the super-infrastructure in place surrounding Westminster Model parliaments and their offshoots. The CPA[3] has been in existence for over 90 years and has served to bring together Commonwealth parliaments across 175 jurisdictions – both national and sub-national. The CPA looks to mature parliaments in developed and developing countries, provide fellowship in a non-political environment, and, importantly, provide professional development and networking opportunities. Equally importantly, it is a vehicle for supporting developing nations within the membership via the contributions of developed nations which are also members and their parliamentary staff. The ACPAC, on the other hand, is a reasonably loose affiliation of PACs operating in parliaments in the Australasian Region. The CPA is an association founded upon the relationship existing between Commonwealth countries, their mutual legal and political history and the influence of the Westminster Parliament. The ACPAC is similarly based on the shared history and Westminster foundations of many of its members but it is not a requirement of membership that members operate under some form of Westminster constitutional settlement but, rather, that they are part of the geographic region.

In terms of diversity within the CPA and the ACPAC, Pelizzo (2011: 532) identifies that there is great diversity amongst the PACs of countries constituting the CPA. For instance, he identifies that it is commonly believed that the committee size, the political orientation of the chair and the number and expertise of staff supporting the PAC are significant determinants of the effectiveness of the PAC. In examining a number of PACs in operation globally, he identifies that Singapore has no Opposition Members of Parliament in its PAC, while Grenada has no Government Members of Parliament on its PAC. He does indicate that the majority of PACs he reviewed where chaired by members of the Opposition and that the Opposition numbers of those PACs outnumbered those of the government. He also confirms that a vast array of activities is undertaken by PACs and that they are served to varying degrees of effectiveness by staff (Pelizzo, 2011: 534–43). The CPA and the ACPAC do not develop and disseminate policy positions with regard to the appropriate constitution, organisation or operation of a PAC. Notwithstanding, in the case of the ACPAC, the chief major activity undertaken is the holding of a conference on a biennial basis where practice and other elements affecting PACs are examined.

The ACPAC represents an opportunity for cross-pollination and development to the advantage of developing and developed nations (Woolmer, 1998: 44) and the biennial conference is the chief means by which this opportunity is realised. Each conference is held in a different location and is attended by members of PACs, staff and interested commentators and others, including academics. These conferences regularly present speakers and topics related to the efficient and effective operation of PACs. A review of the papers for a recent conference highlights topics such as 'Opposition-led Committees', 'Parliamentarians and Politicians' and 'Engaging the Public' (Legislative Assembly, Western Australia, 2011).

However, the lack of a policy position taken by ACPAC related to these types of issues has the effect of reinforcing the diversity between PACs in each jurisdiction. That is not to say that it is either practical or desirable to have a policy position articulated by CPA or ACPAC in relation to such aspects of PAC organisation as the chairmanship or the membership's political persuasion. However, the acceptance of diversity and the lack of an identification of preferred or better practice arrangements mean that diversity is accepted and reinforced. This is especially the case in Australia. The existence of a range of diverse practices with respect to PACs operating in the Australian jurisdictions – which are discussed in detail below – is reinforced by the acceptance of all that the actual organisation and operation of PACs and other parliamentary and integrity infrastructure is a matter for the local players. This is at least a curious position given the strong cultural, historical and political ties enjoyed by the Australian jurisdictions.

However, there are a number of strong arguments that support this lack of policy direction in relation to the organisation and operation of PACs. For instance, the practical constitutional arrangements in place differ in their particulars in each jurisdiction, the population size of each jurisdiction relative to the numbers of members of parliament differ, the roles of the PACs themselves differ, and the basis of the establishment of that role also differs. For instance, some PACs have a legislated responsibility while others have a set of responsibilities that have evolved over time.

While these differences are patent, and the practical difficulty of organisations such as ACPAC developing policy positions in relation to the operation of PACs is clear, one thing is certainly the case. All of these institutions refer to the Westminster Model of government in their defence of their right to establish their own *modus operandi* and to parliamentary sovereignty as their guardian against outside influence. However, all acknowledge that there is a 'classical' model relative to the establishment and operation of a PAC.

A purist model

The PAC is the 'apex of financial scrutiny' in the Westminster Model (Wehner, 2010: 21). While we are interested in the diversity of Australian PACs and what that diversity might mean for PAC effectiveness within jurisdictions, there is a general agreement as to what elements will support PAC effectiveness. Further, though, it is also acknowledged that it is very difficult to measure PAC effectiveness, and so we tend to consider elements of organisation that we believe would constitute attributes of successful PACs notwithstanding that we cannot necessarily prove that they are critical to ensuring PACs are in fact successful. Further, there is limited evidence that these elements do affect the capacity of PACs to do their job (Monk, 2010; Pelizzo, 2011).

Notwithstanding, there are a number of 'classical' attributes that most commentators believe would support the establishment and operation of an effective PAC. A number of these have been touched upon above. However, it is useful to confirm these before considering the Australian experience in some detail. In essence, the effective scrutiny of public finances requires the Parliament to undertake an *ex ante* and *ex post* evaluation of expenditure and to consider the extent to which the executive has carried out its policy programme efficiently and effectively (Whemer, 2010: 23–4). To be effective, not only does the PAC need to consider its role in conjunction with other standing committees, especially the Estimates Committee if one exists, but the Parliament also needs to be involved and engaged with the findings of the PAC. This engagement can be hard to attain. Monk (2010: 1–3) argues that the work of PACs has become 'routine and without effect'; while ministers would find that the committee's work is useful it does not tell them anything that they don't know. However, Wehner counters that, if the work of the PAC is effective, the recommendations of the committee can often inform future budgets and other financial arrangements even if they are not of interest to the current executive. Wehner calls these processes 'virtuous cycles of improvements in public spending' (2010: 24).

Alongside this need for parliamentary engagement with the PAC, there have been identified a number of other attributes that are said to enhance the capacity for the PAC to remain focused on financial expenditure and efficiency. These include the PAC to be chaired by an Opposition member, close attention to be paid to the reports of other finance committees – especially the Estimates Committee – together with a close liaison with the statutory auditor, and for the PAC to focus on matters of efficiency and effectiveness rather than policy (Balls, 1963; McGee, 2002; Wehner, 2010; Pelizzo, 2011). Finally, the resourcing of PACs is said to be a proxy for effectiveness as the committee needs to be adequately resourced by appropriate numbers of appropriately qualified staff. In the next section, we will consider the Australian experience and the extent to which a number of these attributes apply in Australian jurisdictions.

Australian experience

A PAC's overall objective has been identified as being to close the financial control circle by providing assurance that the money appropriated to the executive for the reasons cited in the executive's budget, and the taxes raised to provide the funds to support that budget, have been collected and expended as efficiently as possible in order to effectively achieve the executive's policy objectives. In essence, the PAC is identified within the Westminster Model as having a remit to examine the extent to which the executive has achieved value for money in pursuit of its policy objectives. Given that the membership of the PAC will (usually) be Members of Parliament – some members of the governing party and some of the Opposition or independents – there will always be a political imperative for differing emphasis in the work of PACs in Australia.

In considering the experience of the Australian PACs, we have reviewed their current arrangements, status and key attributes against a number of elements which we have identified as proxies likely to be representative of pragmatism exercised by the committees and reflected in their organisation and operations. These attributes are: (1) whether a PAC exists; (2) whether it is chaired by an Opposition member; (3) how many Opposition and independent members are members of the committee; (4) what house the committee resides in; (5) what the PAC's relationship to the statutory auditor is; and (6) whether there are any specific legislated responsibilities or arrangements that are likely to enhance or retard the capacity of the PAC to address the key objective of reporting on efficiency and effectiveness. We have reviewed each committee in each jurisdiction that has a finance focus. Therefore, we have concentrated on finance committees rather than purely PACs. Additionally, where a Parliament has more than one finance committee dealing with those aspects of financial oversight that are traditionally dealt with by a PAC, we have included analysis of these committees as well.

By and large, the Australian Parliaments fall into two broad categories. They are either original states' Parliaments or Federal Territory Parliaments. In the case of the former, the PACs existing in each Parliament have, by and large, operated in some way, shape or form, since the commencement of Responsible Government. As indicated above, most colonies received Responsible Government in the middle decades of the nineteenth century while all had received it prior to federation. In the case of the latter, the Parliaments and other constitutional arrangements put in place have been established in recent history and are provided at the pleasure of the federal Parliament. In the case of the former group of Parliaments, their form of Westminster Model, including the development of PACs within their jurisdictions, developed alongside that of the Imperial Parliament. In the case of the latter, the arrangements put in place, including those relating to the establishment and operation of PACs, were developed out of recent experience and the perceived needs of relatively small jurisdictions.

Each of these jurisdictions considers itself a Westminster Model jurisdiction and argues the importance of the PAC in the context of the Parliament's oversight role.[4] In considering these jurisdictions, each of which is a member of CPA and ACPAC, we can see that, at a macro level, the aims and objectives of each committee remain constant – to oversee and report on the efficiency and effectiveness of the executive and its pursuit of its policy priorities. However, below this apparent uniformity, there are considerable differences between jurisdictions and also between Australian PACs and the Westminster Parliament's 'template' model. Superficially, only five of the 11 committees studied have a committee named the Public Accounts Committee or some close derivation. A number of committees are named to more fully reflect their purpose and status within the Parliament. For instance, the Victorian Parliament has established a joint committee entitled the Public Accounts and Estimates Committee to more accurately reflect its wider remit, including more than a purely *ex post* evaluation role.

In terms of chairmanship, of the 11 committees examined, at the time of writing, only four committees had a chairman whose party was in opposition. One committee had an independent member as chair while the remaining six committees had government members as chair. Interestingly, where a Parliament had more than one finance committee, it might have a differing response to the issue of who chaired each committee. For instance, in Western Australia, where three finance committees were examined, it was found that one had a government member as chair (importantly this was the Public Accounts Committee in the Popular House) and two had Opposition chairs – one, a joint committee, by virtue of the fact that the standing orders held that the chair must be appointed by the Legislative Council and the other a Legislative Council committee. Therefore, both were chaired by Opposition members by virtue of the fact that the Legislative Council was not controlled by the government.

The received wisdom regarding the chairmanship of committees generally is that there needs to be a separation between the government and Opposition members in order that the interests of the Parliament are preserved. It appears axiomatic that the preservation of the chairmanship of committees – especially the PAC – in the hands of the Opposition will ensure the Parliament's interests are protected in accordance with the accepted Westminster Model. Independence from the executive is, then, an important aspect of this discussion. While independence is apparently preserved in relation to the majority of PACs in Australia, there is an instance where the PAC's role and the interests of the executive are concomitant. In the case of the Northern Territory's PAC, the minister has the power to direct the committee to examine a particular issue. This is unique in Australian Parliaments and would seem to fly in the face of the PAC's role in preserving the primacy of Parliament within the Westminster Model. There are cogent arguments for such arrangements from a pragmatic perspective.

First, in small jurisdictions the capacity for adequately separating functions is limited due to resource priorities. However, it might also be argued that, given Goldsworthy's (2010: 9) observation regarding the fading away of parliamentary sovereignty, there is both a pragmatic political incentive for the executive to create such an arrangement as well as a natural response to the changing nature of the relationship between the voters and the Parliament. In short, perhaps the executive deserves the capacity to direct such committees, as it will be the executive that is punished by the voters.

As to staffing arrangements, this was a difficult aspect to analyse in a number of respects. First, a number of jurisdictions – especially the smaller ones – do not allocate permanent staff to committees. Therefore, the quantity and quality of the staffing complement is difficult to pinpoint. Second, the vast array of topics pursued by the committees mean that even the committees with an apparently suitable complement of staff were unable to cover all of the experiential requirements necessary to address all of the areas of interest to the committee. An example of the skills mix and potential deficiencies here includes the experience of the Western Australian Legislative Council in 2012.

Briefly, the Standing Committee on Public Administration *inter alia* reported on its difficulties in obtaining information from the state's statutory auditor. While this experience and its aftermath are better left to another day, one of the issues raised was that related to the expectation gap between what auditors (statutory or otherwise) do and what the recipients and readers of their reports think that they do. Essentially, the issue here is the expertise gap and capacity of committee staff and members to respond to the information they are provided (Legislative Council, Western Australia, 2012; Martin, 2013). Overall, the average number of staff specifically allocated to a PAC or similar committee in Australian jurisdictions floated around three.

With regard to an overt role in the examination of the entire financial cycle, the smaller jurisdictions had identified specific responsibility for examining estimates, accounts and the reports of the statutory auditor. This makes some sense given the size of these jurisdictions. However, there is also some logic in the deployment of a committee that is resourced and charged with the full ambit of financial oversight. Wehner (2010: 24) has pointed out that there seems to be a trade-off between a committee holding *ex ante* and *ex post* power. However, if we can close Balls' (1963) circle of expenditure, we can consider what was intended and what was achieved with minimal translation effects between estimates committees and PACs.[5] Of the 11 committees examined, only two had an overt responsibility for examining estimates and the accounts while three had a remit that could capture the full financial cycle if the members were of a mind to. As to the assurance arrangements, PACs also have a role in the oversight of statutory auditors and in receiving and considering such auditors' reports.

Auditors-General have been appointed in all Australian jurisdictions.[6] Each of the committees examined had some role with respect to the statutory audit of the jurisdiction. The relationship of the PAC or finance committee with the Auditor-General varied from one jurisdiction to the next. Substantively, the roles of the PACs ranged from simply examining the Auditor-General's reports through to actively considering the role and resources of the Auditor-General and his audit plans from time to time. For instance, in the South Australian context, the PAC has a role of interviewing the Auditor-General; in Tasmania the PAC and the Auditor-General have established a Memorandum of Understanding as to their relationship; and the Victorian PAC has a role of consulting with the Auditor-General in developing the annual audit programme. Additionally, three PACs have an overt role in assessing and considering the resources provided to the Auditor-General while, in the case of Western Australia, the PAC has a very limited role which has been largely superseded by the recent establishment of a Joint Audit Committee. Additionally, in terms of the relative closeness of the Auditor-General and the PACs, it is noteworthy that the Victorian PAC staffing levels incorporate a position occupied by an intern from the Auditor-General's office. Clearly following up Auditors-General's reports is also a major area of operation for a number of PACs.

When considering the role of the Auditor-General in providing reports to the Parliament that identify shortcomings and make recommendations, there is also a significant need for those reports to be followed up in order to assess the extent to which the Auditor-General's comments and recommendations have affected the operations of the executive. In terms of the Australian experience, it was identified that two PACs were specifically required to follow up the Auditor-General's reports, while a further five PACs were charged with examining the Auditor-General's reports. At the other end of the spectrum, while the Western Australian PAC retains a responsibility for the examination of the Auditor-General's reports, the establishment of the Joint Audit Committee does suggest that this aspect of the operations of the PAC is now redundant.

Concluding remarks

As one would expect, given that the Australian sub-national jurisdictions developed their constitutional arrangements concomitantly with the substantive development of the Westminster Model during the second half of the nineteenth century, the various constitutional settlements in each state are different in their particulars. At a superficial level, each jurisdiction, including the federal juris-diction, considers that it follows the Westminster Model precepts of parlia-mentary government, and this consideration extends to the operation of the PACs in each jurisdiction.

Indeed, each jurisdiction uses the Westminster Model both as a historical refer-ence point and, importantly for our analysis, as a means to obtain the necessary legitimacy required in relation to its organisation, actions and the outcomes achieved. While there are a number of elements that we have identified as repre-senting proxies for effectiveness in relation to a PAC's operations, there is little if any evidence as to the extent to which these proxies are truly reliable for such a consideration. While most argue for the establishment of these elements within the arrangements of a PAC, there are a number of people who consider that such arrangements are either not effective or not necessary. For instance, the extent to which having an Opposition member as chair of a PAC will mean the PAC retains its focus on financial rather than policy matters is probably questionable. However, it is probably better to have an Opposition member as the chairman with the requisite political interest in attacking the executive than a government member who has little interest in pointing out the deficiencies of government action.

Overall, the development of Westminster Model parliamentary government in Australian jurisdictions has been commensurate with the development of such systems in similar countries, while the mixing of elements of the Presidential System with those of the Westminster Model have seen the Australian jurisdic-tions more likely to succumb to the pragmatic interests of political players than has the original Westminster Parliament. The limited resourcing and the reduced importance of Parliament itself in the minds of voters and the Members of Par-liament combine to ensure that the Australian tradition of pragmatic action over constitutional niceties will always be at the fore. Therefore, the contribution of this study is to highlight the importance of vigilance in maintaining parlia-mentary sovereignty in a developed, democratic nation and to show that all actors must take responsibility for maintaining the democratic arrangements established.

Appendix

Table A8.1 Websites – Public Accounts Committees

Parliament	Committee name	PAC website
New South Wales	Public Accounts Committee	www.parliament.nsw.gov.au/publicaccounts?open&refnavid=CO3_1
Victoria	Public Accounts and Estimates Committee	www.parliament.vic.gov.au/paec
Western Australia: Legislative Assembly	Public Accounts Committee	www.parliament.wa.gov.au/Parliament/commit.nsf/WCurrentNameNew/4EEE9871F206653648257B6C00165610?OpenDocument
Western Australia: Legislative Council	Estimates and Financial Operations Committee	www.parliament.wa.gov.au/Parliament/commit.nsf/WCurrentNameNew/4BD7BB81ED2067B848257831003B03A4?OpenDocument
Western Australia: Joint Audit Committee	Joint Audit Committee	www.parliament.wa.gov.au/Parliament/commit.nsf/WCurrentNameNew/75BC87F7B36B83BD48257B8A001157E6?OpenDocument
Queensland	Finance and Administration Committee	www.parliament.qld.gov.au/work-of-committees/committees/FAC
Tasmania	Standing Committee of Public Accounts	www.parliament.tas.gov.au/ctee/Joint/pacc.htm
Australian Capital Territory	Standing Committee on Public Accounts	www.parliament.act.gov.au/in-committees/standing_committees/Public-Accounts
South Australia	Economics and Finance Committee	www.parliament.sa.gov.au/Committees/Pages/Committees.aspx?CTId=5&CId=173
South Australia	Budget and Finance Select Committee	www.parliament.sa.gov.au/Committees/Pages/Committees.aspx?CTId=3&CId=187
Northern Territory	Public Accounts Committee	www.nt.gov.au/lant/parliamentary-business/committees/public%20accounts/publlic-accounts.shtml
Commonwealth Parliament	Public Accounts and Audit Committee	www.aph.gov.au/Parliamentary_Business/Committees/House_of_Representatives_Committees?url=jcpaa/about.htm

Notes

1 Interestingly, anecdotally a number of countries that became protectorates of the British Empire rather than being annexed in a formal way as part of the Empire consider that they might have endured imperial control without the benefits of the formal adoption of the institutions that other countries enjoyed. An example here is the Maldives, an Indian Ocean island nation that was 'protected' by Britain but to which Britain failed to transfer its popular institutions.

2 Most state constitutions were developed with the expectation that the Westminster Model would be adopted and so explicit description of the model was not necessary. It is important to note though that the constitutions of the Territories (the Australian Capital Territory and the Northern Territory) were created very recently and may be said to reflect more modern considerations of constitutional law within models that are considered appropriate for a territory of the Commonwealth. In other words, they are not sovereign to the same extent that the original states of the federation are considered to be.

3 The comments related to the CPA have been published on the Association's website at: www.cpahq.org/cpahq/mem/default.aspx (accessed 28 January 2015).

4 Websites for all committees are provided in the appendix to this chapter.

5 Wehner (2010: 24) goes on to argue that there is a focus on *ex ante* control in the Presidential Model while in the Westminster Model the focus is on *ex post* control, while he exemplifies the German Bundestag as having a balance between both.

6 External territories such as the Indian Ocean Territories and Norfolk Island do not appoint Auditors-General. The Norfolk Island legislature does operate a PAC while the Indian Ocean Territories are essentially appended to the Northern Territory's jurisdiction.

References

Balls, H. R. (1963) 'The Public Accounts Committee', *Canadian Public Administration*, 6(1): 15–34.

Bennett, W. L. (1980) 'The Paradox of Public Discourse: A Framework for the Analysis of Political Accounts', *The Journal of Politics*, 42: 792–817.

Benton, M. and Russell, M. (2012) 'Assessing the Impact of Parliamentary Oversight Committees: The Select Committees in the British House of Commons', *Parliamentary Affairs*, 66: 772–97.

Bunn, M. and Gilchrist, D. J. (2013) 'A Few Good Men: Public Sector Audit in the Swan River Colony, 1828–1835', *Accounting History*, 18(2): 193–209.

Degeling, P., Anderson, J. and Guthrie, J. (1996) 'Accounting for Public Accounts Committees', *Accounting, Auditing and Accountability Journal*, 9(2): 30–49.

Di Francesco, M. (2013) 'Under Cover of Westminster: Enabling and Disabling a Public Service Commission in New South Wales', *Australian Journal of Public Administration*, 72(4): 391–6.

Gilchrist, D. J. (2013) 'Refinement and Refutation: N. G. Butlin's 1959 Monograph "Colonial Socialism in Australia" and Explanations of Colonial Socialism, 1850 to 1890', accepted for presentation at the History of Economic Thought Society Conference at the University of Western Australia, 2013.

Goldsworthy, J. (2010) *Parliamentary Sovereignty: Contemporary Debates*, Melbourne: Cambridge University Press.

James, L. (1997) *The Rise and Fall of the British Empire*, London: Abacus.

Legislative Assembly, Western Australia (2011) *ACPAC 2011: A Report on the 11th*

Biennial Conference of the Australasian Council of Public Accounts Committees, Report No. 11, 38th Parliament, Perth, Western Australia.

Legislative Council, Western Australia (2012) *Standing Committee on Public Administration Special Report*, 38th Parliament, Perth, Western Australia.

McGee, D. G. (2002) *The Overseers: Public Accounts Committees and Public Spending*, London: Commonwealth Parliamentary Association in Association with Pluto Press.

Martin, W. (2013) 'Forewarned and Four-Armed – Administrative Law Values and the Fourth Arm of Government', Address for the 2013 Whitmore Lecture, Sydney.

Metin, A. (1977 [1901]) *Socialism without Doctrine*, trans. R. Ward, Chippendale: Alternative Publishing Co-operative Ltd.

Monk, D. (2010) 'A Framework for Evaluating the Performance of Committees in Westminster Parliaments', *The Journal of Legislative Studies*, 16(1): 1–13.

Pelizzo, R. (2011) 'Public Accounts Committees in the Commonwealth: Oversight, Effectiveness, and Governance', *Commonwealth & Comparative Politics*, 49(4): 528–46.

Pilcher, R. A., Gilchrist, D. J., Singh, H. and Singh, I. (2013) 'The Interface between Internal and External Audit in the Australian Public Sector', *Australian Accounting Review*, 23(4): 330–40.

Rhodes, R. A. W. (2005) 'Australia: The Westminster Model as Tradition', in H. Patapan, J. Wanna and P. Weller (eds) *Westminster Legacies: Democracy and Responsible Government in Asia and the Pacific*, Sydney: University of New South Wales Press.

Wehner, J. (2010) 'Principles and Patterns of Financial Scrutiny: Public Accounts Committees in the Commonwealth', *Commonwealth & Comparative Politics*, 41(3): 21–36.

Woolmer, L. (1998) 'Public Accounts Committee – Checks and Balances Queensland Style', *Accountability & Performance*, 4(1): 41–51.

9 Making a Public Accounts Committee effective

A Chair's perspective from the State of New South Wales, Australia

Jonathan O'Dea MP

Background

In Westminster-style parliaments, the elected arm of government is well placed to keep the executive arm of government in check, holding it to account in the period between the ultimate public accountability of elections. It can do so through a range of instruments and forums, including committees. In Australia, Public Accounts Committees (PACs)[1] are powerful and valuable safety mechanisms to ensure greater accountability and scrutiny of the executive. In the author's experience, seven key factors especially influence how well PACs perform.

Public Accounts Committees date back over 150 years to England and are known by various names in different Australian jurisdictions. While titular and operational variations exist between jurisdictions,[2] these committees have common functions. Each PAC scrutinises the actions of an executive on behalf of the Parliament, recommending improvements to the efficiency and effectiveness of Government activities and helping to ensure appropriate use of public funds and resources.

In addition to government oversight, PACs also play an important role overseeing financial overseers such as an Auditor-General and their Audit Office. In New South Wales (NSW) this extends to oversight of a Parliamentary Budget Office (PBO) pursuant to the Parliamentary Budget Officer Act 2010.

The existence of a PAC in New South Wales dates back to 1902. The NSW PAC has responsibilities to inquire into and report on activities of government that are reported in the Total State Sector Accounts and the accounts of the State's authorities. The functions of the PAC are specified in Section 57 of the Public Finance and Audit Act 1983. In practice, the NSW PAC focuses on examining and reporting on the Auditor-General's opinions and reports. It undertakes regular inquiries relating to all performance audit reports as well as repeated recommendations in financial audit reports of the Auditor-General. The NSW PAC can also follow up its own reported conclusions and recommended improvements. It meets at least once every parliamentary sitting week.

In NSW we are fortunate that the PAC is adequately empowered with statutory authority under a legislative framework. Mindful that this empowerment cannot be taken for granted in all jurisdictions, what other key success factors impact on a PAC's practical success?

Seven key success factors[3]

Impartiality

In some Australian jurisdictions opposition parties appoint 'WasteWatch' co-ordinators or committees to highlight government waste and mismanagement. These entities operate with far less structure and fewer resources than PACs, and attract no administrative support from the Parliament. They will be more directly critical of perceived waste and mismanagement within a relevant government and its executive. Such party-based entities do not attempt to be impartial and generally have overt and unapologetically political agendas.

In contrast, PACs operate in a more bipartisan way, on behalf of parliaments and their electors. They have cross-party membership and generally formulate consensus recommendations. A formal committee structure exists within a statutory framework providing powers and obligations. There is also support from a Parliamentary Secretariat. These features enable fuller consultation, with more opportunity for balanced debate, proper research, public hearings and evidence from relevant experts. The committee's agenda is predominantly based on helping achieve good public outcomes and value for money.

While the NSW PAC's six members include the Shadow Treasurer and an independent member its majority comprises backbench government members. This reflects the composition of the current Legislative Assembly (Lower House) as elected by the people. Even if PAC members were drawn from both Houses of the NSW Parliament,[4] it is unlikely to ever be controlled by an Opposition.

The aim of PACs should be appropriate balance rather than simply adversarial competition. They should complement as well as confront; support as well as scrutinise; and co-operate as well as challenge. In this way, they can better promote good governance and democratic process, with the executive and Parliament generally more balanced. Where balance is missing or a government is dysfunctional, the separate role of the Opposition can enhance balance by criticising a government, for example through a WasteWatch function.

A discussion point attracting significant comment in recent years is whether a PAC is best chaired by a member of the government (as mostly occurs in Australia, including NSW) or Opposition (as in Britain and Canada). While there are valid arguments for both approaches, when a government is functioning effectively in a reasonably mature democracy, the author believes that PACs are best directed by a member of the government. This is because government members have advantages in terms of understanding, accessing and navigating relevant processes and personalities to deliver positive outcomes.

Situations may arise where there is a risk of tension between a Chair's loyalty to a government and the Committee's role in scrutinising the executive. However, Parliament's Standing Orders function to protect the committee's independence and support a Chair in fearlessly and fairly promoting a higher duty to the public. In any event, the personal characteristics displayed by the Chair and individual merit are more important than whether the Chair is part of the opposition or government of the day.

Despite the above comments, the current NSW PAC has recommended that when the next PAC is formed, the Deputy or Assistant Speaker of the new Parliament be considered as Chair with a view to lifting the position's status. To promote balance, it may also be appropriate to have a Deputy Chair from a different political party membership to the Chair. The motivation and capability of the Deputy Chair and other committee members is likewise crucial. They must be able to avoid acting on the PAC in a party-political fashion, despite also serving in a generally highly partisan legislature. The challenge is to act on the PAC more as a parliamentarian than as a politician.

Stage in political cycle

The risk of a lack of impartiality is heightened at certain stages in the political cycle. Further, whether consciously or not, the level of activity and focus of a PAC will often vary depending on the point in time within each individual parliamentary term as well as the total length of time a political party has been in power.

There is disincentive for any PAC with majority government representation (irrespective of the political alignment of the Chair) to undertake an inquiry potentially critical of the government in the immediate lead-up to an election, although less controversial issues might still be pursued. At such a time Committee members tend to be distracted by their desires to campaign for re-election.

The longer any government stays in power, the less likely it will be that a government-controlled PAC will aggressively pursue politically sensitive inquiries that may embarrass the executive. A properly functioning executive should welcome scrutiny and can deflect potential criticism through responding appropriately to issues highlighted, or blaming the cause partly on a previous government. However, it becomes more difficult for a government to deflect criticism if it has a long track record of scandal and mismanagement, as was the case in the final years of the NSW Labor Government's 16 years in power (1995–2011). So the executive and PAC working cohesively and positively is an ideal that may not always be a political reality, particularly as a government ages and becomes more defensive.

Resources available

There is a potential tension involved where funding for a PAC Secretariat and other resources are reliant on executive allocation. It is therefore important that treasurers and executives properly respect the oversight role of PACs and provide appropriate resource allocation.

Underactive PACs contribute to inappropriate resource allocations because they suggest fewer resources are needed to operate. Resourcing challenges can certainly threaten effective operation of a PAC. There have been issues with this in NSW, particularly after the 54th Parliament moved away from having a dedicated and permanent NSW PAC Secretariat with its own budget allocation.

While the current PAC in NSW is extremely active, there are a record number of other committees now competing for a common pool of staff and other resources. This restricts the scope for the PAC to innovate or to secure external expertise, and the author has pushed for a return to a largely dedicated Secretariat.

Internal resource limitations can be overcome to some extent through innovation. For example, in 2012 the NSW PAC initiated an innovative approach to obtaining public input on an inquiry related to energy generation. This involved a deliberative democracy process with two citizen juries meeting over five Saturdays in metropolitan and rural NSW. While limited parliamentary resources were available to support this valuable initiative, it was made possible with generous support from a charitable foundation.[5]

In addition to inadequate resources, high staff turnover can lead to a less consistently rigorous approach to fulfilling PAC functions. While the NSW PAC was well served by professional and competent staff, during the author's three-and-a-half years as PAC Chair, it was less than ideal to have five different committee directors (one on a temporary basis) in the Secretariat servicing the PAC.

Measurement of outcomes and benchmarking are fundamental to successfully managing available resources effectively and efficiently, whether within a PAC or a government. Evaluating the appropriateness of current staff and budgetary arrangements can be assisted by benchmarking resources and relevant committee outputs against other relevant jurisdictions and committees. This should occur at least once every eight years. At the time of writing it was overdue in Australia, with the most recent study published by KPMG in 2006.[6]

Parliament's level of interest

While parliaments trust PACs to perform a scrutiny function, there should also be a strong culture of accountability within each Parliament in promoting consideration and debate regarding PAC reports.

The NSW Parliament's Standing Orders[7] provide for Committee Chairs, at the end of Question Time, to table reports or advise the Parliament of any new inquiries being undertaken or referred. While this generates some interest, the reality is that Committee reports are not thoroughly read by most MPs, who have many competing demands for their attention and time.

In the 54th NSW parliamentary term, Committee reports were considered on a Friday, when there was no Question Time and many MPs did not even attend Parliament. As a consequence, there was generally inadequate consideration of Committee reports, with those members who sat on the Committee sometimes left to debate reports amongst themselves. In the 55th NSW Parliament, changing

Question Time to every sitting day ensured the presence of almost all MPs in the House on the day when Committee reports are listed for debate. This has promoted a better culture of accountability and improved attention to Committee reports. As a consequence, there has been an increased awareness of the important role of the PAC and a stronger focus on accountability.

For a PAC to be successful, it is therefore important that Parliament engages in the relevant processes and supports them as appropriate. There is an obligation in NSW for the government to at least respond to reports and recommendations within six months.[8] In practice, however, that response may not always be adequate or timely. For example, the NSW Labor Government in the 54th Parliament failed to respond to a PAC report on State Plan Reporting for almost two years. A response was only forthcoming when the matter was ultimately highlighted in Parliament and in the media (with the author playing a role in both as a then Opposition MP).

At the time of writing, there remained no formal mechanism to ensure a government follows PAC recommendations. The NSW PAC has recommended that the Parliament considers mechanisms to better follow up all committee reports and examine what action government agencies have taken to implement recommendations.

Level of media involvement

As NSW PAC Chair, the author has regularly issued PAC newsletters every four months to MPs, media and other stakeholders. Further transparency has been facilitated by ensuring that all NSW PAC public hearings are open to the media and other stakeholders. These measures help educate and promote constructive discussion. A desire for healthy media and community engagement is as important for committees as it is for the work of the House and can help promote better outcomes.

In pursuing improved government efficiency, effectiveness and cost control, PACs will sometimes need to rely on the media to convey crucial messages to a broader domain. This information dissemination can assist to engage public stakeholders and promote intelligent debate, which can create powerful expectations for the executive to act appropriately.

As a backbench MP and PAC Chair, the author found that a quality parliamentary speech on a tabled report will not always sufficiently communicate an issue of public importance. Issuing media releases and briefing journalists have their place in highlighting the need for issues to be addressed in the public interest.

Extent of interjurisdictional collaboration

An overriding common purpose of all PACs across the globe is to ensure public resources are expended effectively and efficiently, promoting financial accountability and integrity in public finances. In this way, they help improve governance and ensure a better quality of life for people in our societies.

Numerous international and regional groupings of PACs bring together and facilitate the exchange of ideas, information, experiences, concerns and examples of best practice. The value of this sharing is heightened as each PAC faces an increasingly complex financial, policy and technological environment.

One such forum for collaboration is the Australasian Council of Public Accounts Committees (ACPAC), the 12th biennial conference of which was chaired by the author in Sydney in 2013. The organisation consists of Public Accounts Committees throughout Australia, New Zealand, Papua New Guinea, the Solomon Islands and elsewhere in the Pacific. Visitor delegates often also come from further afield.

Formed in 1989, ACPAC provides a unique forum for the exchange of information and opinions relating to PACs. The forums provide opportunities to share and collaborate, with the aim of improving the quality and performance of PACs.

As well as their common purpose, it is appropriate to note the diversity of PACs. Represented at interjurisdictional forums such as ACPAC are people with different professional backgrounds, nationalities, native languages, political parties and philosophies.

As with unity of purpose, there is real strength in diversity of profile. Unity of purpose does not rely on having uniform profiles or opinions. The learnings of PACs will be enhanced by differences. Value-adding collaboration between jurisdictions should therefore draw on both the common purpose and the diversity of PACs.

Healthy relationship with Audit Office

Parliamentary committees are more effective in holding executives to account when they work closely with independent authorities charged with scrutiny functions. For example, the NSW PAC collaborates with the Auditor-General and his Audit Office.

A healthy relationship between the PAC and the Auditor-General in NSW is very important, as the two entities play complementary roles in promoting public sector accountability.

Fortunately, in recent years there has been a strong mutual respect between the Audit Office and the NSW PAC as part of an excellent collaborative relationship. Both entities are vitally interested in assisting each other to pursue the public interest objective of efficient and effective government. Both entities operate co-operatively and regularly discuss potential areas of inquiry that either might undertake.

A PAC complements the work of the independent office of an Auditor-General by following up aspects of Auditor-General audit reports to parliaments on administrative performance and financial matters. The PACs are able to use political force and expertise to subject the audits to greater parliamentary scrutiny and thus encourage government departments to properly respond to and act on Audit Office recommendations. In turn, as mentioned previously, the

PAC's reports are considered by Parliament and the executive is required to respond.

Other examples of collaboration between the NSW Audit Office and the NSW PAC include co-ordinated briefings of interested parliamentarians on relevant audit report topics as well as regular Audit Office participation in PAC inquiries.

While the NSW PAC is responsible for commissioning periodic reviews of the Audit Office, the two operate independently. The PAC also has a role in protecting the independence and integrity of the Auditor-General.

PACs overseeing financial overseers

Statutory Officers play a central role as financial overseers, helping to hold the executive arm of government, and potential alternative government, accountable for promised and actual expenditure of public funds.

The NSW Auditor-General (with their Audit Office) does this by providing an independent perspective on the performance and financial management of the executive arm of the NSW Government via the scrutiny of public sector agencies and entities.

The NSW Parliamentary Budget Officer (with their Budget Office) attempts to ensure that election promises during the run-up to a general election are costed accurately and quickly so that voters can exercise their voting responsibilities in an informed manner.

As part of the overall system of checks and balances, the PAC supervises these financial overseers in NSW to maintain a healthy level of accountability on behalf of the elected parliament. In doing so, it acts as both a scrutineer and a protector. It is useful to examine those dynamics and recent developments, particularly in a NSW context.[9]

The scrutiny of financial overseers is necessary and important. They have substantial power to oversee government, but should also be scrutinised themselves to ensure they operate as efficient and effective independent entities. Just as financial overseers question and challenge government agencies, it is appropriate to have measures which hold them to account.

Executive governments are sometimes reluctant to expose themselves to high levels of accountability from financial overseers and may seek to dilute the authority or power of financial overseers over time. The parliamentary oversight of financial overseers should therefore extend to vigilance in ensuring that the executive arm of government continues to be transparently overseen by independent, properly resourced bodies with appropriate powers.

So, the NSW PAC is not just a mechanism for ensuring the accountability of financial overseers; it is also a protector of them, helping to ensure that they, in turn, effectively hold the executive arm of government to account. In that sense the NSW PAC can be seen as both a protector's 'shield' and a scrutineer's 'sword' poised above the two relevant financial overseers in NSW – the Audit Office and the Parliamentary Budget Office.

The Audit Office

Discussions about Auditors-General's oversight generally boil down to themes of independence and accountability. It is also important that there be a collaborative relationship between Auditors-General (with their Audit Offices) and parliamentary committees such as PACs.

Certainly, any parliamentary oversight should aim to respect the independence of an Auditor-General or, adopting more useful terminology for present purposes, an Audit Office. While a level of parliamentary oversight of the Audit Office is needed, the key question is: what level and type is appropriate? This involves balancing the desirable dual objects of independence and accountability.

Australia's Commonwealth Joint Committee of Public Accounts and Audit (JCPAA)[10] has previously outlined a useful view on what was necessary to preserve the independence of an Auditor-General:

- a wide legislative mandate to audit the complete spectrum of Commonwealth functions;
- freedom to determine the audit programme, and to decide the nature and scope of audits to be conducted;
- unrestricted access to information in performance of the audit function, together with the right to report any findings to Parliament;
- personal independence in relation to appointment and tenure; and
- adequate resourcing to fulfil audit functions effectively.

None of these factors are compromised by the current nature of NSW PAC oversight. Current oversight powers include a right of veto over any new Auditor-General appointment (for a fixed term of eight years, recently increased from seven years in NSW). Also, perhaps most importantly, the PAC commissions independent quadrennial reviews of the NSW Audit Office's performance (recently changed from triennial), which is in alignment with the fixed four-year term of the NSW Parliament.

The NSW PAC completed one such quadrennial review in mid-2013, whereby it commissioned an independent review as required under the Public Finance and Audit Act 1983 (PFAA). It also undertook a complementary inquiry process itself, whereby it considered more qualitative aspects of Audit Office performance as well as issues relating to the Audit Office's scope of authority.[11]

The role of the PAC in this review process is different to that of other NSW committees that oversee statutory 'watchdog' offices such as the Independent Commission Against Corruption (ICAC) and the Police Integrity Commission (PIC). With the ICAC and PIC, there are less extensive but more regular reviews of annual reports by a parliamentary committee. For both commissions, there is also an independent statutory office of Inspector, whose role and function is to hold the ICAC and PIC accountable in the way they carry out their functions.

The PAC's report associated with its 2013 complementary inquiry confirmed the PAC's long-held opinion that the Audit Office was doing a very good job, providing value for money to NSW in delivering financial and performance auditing services. The report also made various recommendations for reform, including an increased scope of legislative authority for the Audit Office relating to compliance audits, as well as 'follow the dollar' powers to track use of public monies allocated to non-government organisations to deliver public outcomes. Such 'follow the dollar' powers already exist in most Australian jurisdictions.

Other potential Audit Office reform has also been considered, including in relation to PAC oversight. On being elected in March 2011, the current Government commissioned a review of the NSW public sector financial system and position (the Lambert Report). The Lambert Report made various recommendations, including some relating to the extension of the Auditor-General's powers and enhanced accountability measures.[12]

Proposals have been considered to enhance the Auditor-General's accountability, including by making the Auditor-General directly accountable to the PAC; and requiring the review of the Audit Office to be provided directly to the PAC rather than to the Auditor-General for passing on to the PAC.

As previously mentioned, an independent review of the NSW Audit Office is conducted every four years. However, in contrast with other Australian jurisdictions, NSW is the only jurisdiction where the Audit Office's independent reviewer has reported to the Auditor-General instead of directly to the PAC. This requirement in the PFAA is likely to change.

In terms of further improving the accountability of the Audit Office to Parliament, it should be noted that, despite the Auditor-General traditionally being seen as an Officer of the NSW Parliament, there is no formal accountability relationship to Parliament as exists in other jurisdictions. The Lambert Report proposed changing the PFAA to formalise the Auditor-General's relationship with the PAC and strengthen links to it as the agent of parliament. In particular, it proposed:

- empowering the PAC to undertake activities (hearings, submissions, etc.) and report on the performance of the Auditor-General;
- requiring the Auditor-General to confer with and have regard to the audit priorities of the PAC; and
- requiring the Auditor-General to submit an annual work plan to the PAC and allow for PAC comments.[13]

The Government's response to these proposals indicated that these measures should be formally put in place during 2015.

The Parliamentary Budget Office

It is easy for political parties on both sides to make big spending promises before an election, with taxpayers often left wondering how much these are going to cost and where the money is coming from to fund them. Independent Parliamentary Budget Offices help clarify the veracity of claims made.

In late 2010, in the dying days of the 54th NSW Parliament, legislation passed to establish a permanent Parliamentary Budget Office (PBO). Further legislation was passed in early 2013 to amend NSW's PBO model, limiting its operation to a nine-to-ten-month period surrounding the election, but improving transparency and accountability measures regarding election promises. This followed the recommendations of a Joint Select Committee that inquired into the future role and functions of the NSW PBO.[14]

Key features of the NSW PBO as provided for in the Parliamentary Budget Officer Act 2010 include:

- aligning the operation of the PBO to each election;
- submission of policies for costings is mandatory for the Leader of the Government and the Leader of the Opposition;
- comprehensive listing of reporting requirements to ensure that the Budget impacts are clearly reported by parliamentary leaders;
- allowing the PBO to release more than one budget impact statement prior to each election to capture any late policy announcements;
- parliamentary Budget Officer appointed by Presiding Officers of Parliament based on a recommendation from an independent panel;
- oversight by the NSW PAC, including post-election reporting arrangements for a parliamentary review of the PBO.

The operations of the PBO are limited to once every four years, and the PBO's sole function is to prepare election policy costings. This should help provide NSW taxpayers with more accurate, timely and independent information on the cost of election commitments. In considering the 2013 amendments, it was seen by Parliament that extra resources were not justified to permit the PBO to have a broader advisory role outside each election period.

The NSW Parliamentary Budget Officer's appointment starts on 1 September in the year prior to each State election and ends within three months after the election. The relevant role of Public Accounts Committee is set out in the Parliamentary Budget Officer Act, which states:

1   The Public Accounts Committee of the Legislative Assembly may monitor and review the operations of the Parliamentary Budget Officer appointed for a State general election and report to Parliament on any matter relating to that Officer.

2   The Parliamentary Budget Officer is to provide to the Public Accounts Committee a copy of the operational plan of the Parliamentary Budget Officer as soon as practicable after it is approved by the Presiding Officers.

3   The Parliamentary Budget Officer is required to furnish a report to the Public Accounts Committee as soon as practicable after the holding of the State general election for which he or she was appointed. The report may

include recommendations on operational arrangements and activities of the Parliamentary Budget Officer in respect of future general elections.[15]

As a statutory officeholder the Parliamentary Budget Officer obviously plays a valuable role in overseeing and scrutinising the election promises of the executive and the potential executive. However, there is further oversight of that overseer by the NSW PAC.

The NSW PAC is a bipartisan or non-partisan committee and operates in that fashion, even with the Shadow Treasurer as a member. There clearly is accountability and opportunity for the PAC to recommend changes if, having been tested, the system does not work properly.

No other Australian state or territory has a PBO, although the Commonwealth of Australia and numerous other countries do. The NSW PAC oversees both the NSW Audit Office and the NSW PBO in a similar way to that in which the Commonwealth Joint Committee of Public Accounts and Audit oversees both the Australian Audit Office and Commonwealth PBO.

One difference between the Australian and NSW jurisdictions is the post-election review process for the PBO. The NSW Act requires the budget officer to table a report after the election, which the PAC may review. The Commonwealth Act provides for its Committee to request an independent review of the PBO. The purpose of these two processes may be similar, but the mechanisms are slightly different.

As previously discussed, the parliamentary committee mechanism for overseeing Audit Offices is fairly universal across Australia and internationally. By comparison, the mechanism for overseeing Parliamentary Budget Office type institutions is far more varied across international jurisdictions than is the case for Audit Offices. For any jurisdiction entertaining establishing a new PBO, potentially with PAC oversight, the emerging nature and relatively recent history of PBOs make it worth examining oversight models in a number of different jurisdictions.[16]

Conclusion

It is clear that PACs have an important role as a mechanism of parliaments to help keep their executives in check. There are many elements that will impact on how successful PACs will be in performing this function. This chapter has examined seven key success factors in some detail: impartiality, the stage in the political cycle, resources available, Parliament's level of interest, the level of media involvement, the extent of interjurisdictional collaboration and a healthy relationship with the Audit Office.

Statutory officers, such as the Auditor-General or the Parliamentary Budget Officer, play a central role as financial overseers of government. While their independence is a vital ingredient in the recipe for success, it is also important that these officers and offices are properly accountable.

Parliamentary committees, such as the NSW PAC, provide effective means for statutory officers to be held accountable. As an overseer of the overseers, a

PAC has both a scrutiny and a protective function. It helps ensure that officers and organisations are efficient and effective; and that they remain independent, properly resourced bodies with appropriate powers.

The NSW PAC's oversight of the NSW Audit Office continues to evolve and reflects a common practice across numerous jurisdictions in Australia and internationally. In comparison, PAC oversight of PBOs is a relatively new development in Australia.

Whatever the mechanism at play, the fundamental needs are to ensure that these independent officers are scrutinised and held to account; as well as empowered to effectively hold government to account. This powerfully contributes to an effective democratic system.

Notes

1 While they have a variety of names, the generic term for them to be used in this article is Public Accounts Committee or PAC.
2 For example, unlike NSW, the Victorian PAC's functions extend to scrutinising the budget estimates process.
3 All but the sixth of these factors were initially identified by the author in a paper delivered to the 2011 conference of the Australian Study of Parliament Group.
4 As recommended by the Lambert Report, Michael Lambert, NSW Financial Audit 2011, NSW Treasury. It has been foreshadowed that this may occur in the next parliamentary term, after March 2015.
5 The newDemocracy Foundation, further information on which is available at www.newdemocracy.com.au.
6 This baseline study was published in 2006 by KPMG's Government Advisory Services for the La Trobe University Public Sector Governance and Accountability Research Centre.
7 Standing Order 299 of the NSW Parliament.
8 Under Standing Order 233 the government must indicate what action, if any, it proposes to take in relation to each recommendation.
9 These matters were initially addressed by the author in a paper titled 'Financial Overseers and their Oversight: A NSW Public Accounts Committee Perspective' delivered to the 2013 conference of the Australian Study of Parliament Group, available at www.aspg.org.au/conferences/perth2013/ (accessed 12 February 2015).
10 This view from October 1996 is referred to in the 2005 paper of Mr Tony Whitfield, NSW Deputy Auditor-General, 'Parliamentary Oversight: An Auditor-General's Perspective', *Australasian Parliamentary Review*, Autumn 2006, Vol. 21(1): 88–93.
11 This resulted in a report being tabled in September 2013, titled 'Efficiency and Effectiveness of the Audit Office of NSW'.
12 Michael Lambert, *The Lambert Report*, NSW Financial Audit 2011, NSW Treasury.
13 Ibid., p. 26.
14 Joint House Parliamentary Committee Inquiry into the Parliamentary Budget Office, NSW Parliament, December 2011.
15 Section 15 of the Parliamentary Budget Officer Act 2010.
16 Many international PBO type institutions, along with relevant oversight mechanisms, were examined in the author's paper to the 2013 conference of the Australasian Study of Parliament Group.

10 Public Accounts Committees in the Pacific – a PEFA perspective

Kylie Coulson and David Gilchrist

Introduction

Improvement in public sector finances, governance and accountability is a focus for many countries, with reforms under way in public financial management, machinery of government changes, and Parliamentary strengthening programmes. In order to identify, design and implement effective reforms, it is first necessary to understand what is not working well.

Some countries, particularly small island states, may require assistance to identify the strengths and weaknesses of their existing public financial management systems and processes, and also to design and implement reforms. This is particularly true in countries where the traditional operation of entities such as Public Accounts Committees and Offices of Auditors-General may be relatively new, or somewhat contradictory to the underlying culture of a country. Such issues may relate to the operation of the machinery of government in a purist sense, or in a local, traditional sense. Developing countries have particular challenges in attracting and retaining skilled staff, which can lead to less than satisfactory performance in public financial management, and inadequate fiduciary oversight provided through entities such as Public Accounts Committees.

This chapter surveys ideas regarding what constitutes effectiveness in the operation of Public Accounts Committees, and considers this in the context of small island states in the Pacific. Using the publicly available Public Expenditure and Financial Accountability (PEFA) reports, we have used this framework to assess the Public Accounts Committees extant in the sample.

Literature

Much of the recent literature regarding the activities and effectiveness of Public Accounts Committees refers to the 2002 book *The Overseers: Public Accounts Committees and Public Spending* by David McGee. This described the way Public Accounts Committees work, and identified good practices, but did not provide a detailed examination of the structures or conditions leading to this good practice (McGee, 2002).

Going some way to mitigating this gap, the powers and activities of Public Accounts Committees in Westminster-based Parliaments were the subject of a 2002 World Bank Institute survey. This data was used to examine the conditions required for effective scrutiny of public accounts in 51 Commonwealth countries, and has been used to inform several research papers including Stapenhurst *et al.* (2005) and Pelizzo *et al.* (2006).

There is consensus in the literature and by precedent that the role of the Public Accounts Committee is to focus on the efficient and effective financial implementation of government policy, rather than examining the objectives or intended outcomes of the policy itself. A review of standing orders of such committees will confirm their focus. This examination of the efficiency and effectiveness of government's finances is one of the elements contributing to the successful performance of a Public Accounts Committee, and is strengthened when the committee has the ability to examine all government expenditure, past and present, and can do so without political interference (Stapenhurst *et al.*, 2005; Pelizzo *et al.*, 2006; Hedger and Blick, 2008).

Another important condition for an effective Public Accounts Committee is the ability to prepare and publish recommendations, along with the ability to follow up on government's implementation of, or response to, those recommendations (Stapenhurst *et al.*, 2005; Pelizzo *et al.*, 2006; Hedger and Blick, 2008).

A Public Accounts Committee's effectiveness is also influenced by the information and technical expertise available to it, which in turn is often determined by available funding and resources. This expertise may be in the form of information and support provided by the public sector auditor, or from research staff (Stapenhurst *et al.*, 2005; Pelizzo *et al.*, 2006). The ability to prepare robust reports is impacted by the number of staff available in the context of the amount of review work to be undertaken, and a lack of expert staff is one of the biggest challenges for Public Accounts Committees in developing countries (Pelizzo, 2011; Hedger and Blick, 2008). It could be argued that financial independence from government, with enough resources to be adequately staffed, is a necessary pre-condition for an effective Public Accounts Committee. However, Pacific committees often lack funding and are understaffed (Rawlings, 2006).

Other key conditions contributing to the effective performance of Public Accounts Committees (as identified in Stapenhurst *et al.*, 2005; Pelizzo, 2010, 2011; Pelizzo *et al.*, 2006; Rawlings, 2006; and Hedger and Blick, 2008) include:

- the formal powers of the Committee – usually established via the Constitution, legislation, standing orders of Parliament;
- public interest and media scrutiny of activities and reports;
- bi-partisan and proportional representation of Committee members;
- the behaviour of Committee and its members; and
- the relationship with the Auditor-General, and the Auditor-General's relationship to the Parliament.

Pacific Islands context

To date, there has been limited research on the structure, activity and performance of Public Accounts Committees of Pacific Island states. Hardman (1984)
argued that the public administration of small island states which are members
of the South Pacific Forum, including approaches to budgeting and accounting,
tended to be a scaled-down version of larger states, often their former colonial
powers. By assuming that small island states had the same public financial management needs as other states, regardless of size, effective public administration
may be restricted.

Building on the 2002 World Bank Institute survey, a further survey was conducted in 2008–9, again by the World Bank Institute, with responses received
from seven Pacific Island jurisdictions. This data was used by Pelizzo (2010) to
examine the effectiveness of the seven Public Accounts Committees operating in
these jurisdictions, and the relationship between the formal or legislative powers,
and the actual activities and performance of the Public Accounts Committees.

Rather than focus on the conditions required for a successful Public Accounts
Committee, Pelizzo examined whether a Public Accounts Committee actually used
the powers available to it. He concluded that the legislative provision of formal
powers does not necessarily result in the successful performance of a Public
Accounts Committee, and provided an example by way of the Solomon Islands
Public Accounts Committee generating more reports than its equivalent in Samoa,
despite holding fewer meetings. Thus, high levels of activity (i.e. number of meetings held) do not automatically result in effective scrutiny of government accounts.[1]

Alternative sources of information

Given the small sample of Pacific Island countries included in the existing studies,
and the limitations of the data gathered through surveys, this chapter considers an
existing, alternative source of data regarding Public Accounts Committees in the
Pacific. We ask whether it is possible to build on previous knowledge regarding
the structure, activity and performance of Public Accounts Committees in the
Pacific by examining the publicly available reports of Public Expenditure and Financial Accountability (PEFA) assessments undertaken in various Pacific Island
countries. That is, whether the PEFA reports assist us in assessing the effectiveness of Public Accounts Committees in developing countries.

The PEFA framework

In 2001, the PEFA framework was established, via a partnership of seven donors
and international financial institutions, to develop a commonly accepted and internationally consistent method of assessing a country's public financial management
systems and processes, from which to identify a sequence of reform activities.

Prior to the development of the PEFA framework, numerous assessments and
analytics relating to public financial management were undertaken in many

developing countries by governments, donors and development partners. These assessments were often undertaken at the request of a donor or development partner to identify the strengths and limitations of public financial management systems and processes in a particular country. The burden on host countries could be significant, if multiple donors and development partners sought to undertake their own similar, but not identical, assessments. Therefore, the development of the PEFA framework potentially establishes a standard review framework and reduces the need for multiple review processes. Additionally, it can be used to enhance education and communication with respect to the key issues.

Therefore, as described in the PEFA framework documentation (2011), the objectives of the framework are to: provide reliable information on public financial management systems and processes performance over time; contribute to government reform processes; facilitate dialogue between donors and governments; provide a common, agreed, reliable public financial management assessment tool; and reduce transaction cost for governments by eliminating the need for multiple assessments.

The PEFA assessments are not designed nor intended to provide any commentary on government policies or reform priorities. The scope is limited to examining and documenting the existing public financial management systems and processes, rather than commenting on the policies which may be implemented using these systems and processes. Similarly, a PEFA assessment is designed to document, not explain, the processes used (Hedger and Blick, 2008). This draws parallels with the role of the Public Accounts Committees to examine the extent to which government policy has been implemented efficiently and effectively, rather than comment on the policy itself. Incidentally, generally this framing also delimits the role of the Auditor-General.

PEFA assessments and reports

Ideally, PEFA assessments are initiated or requested by recipient countries to establish an agreed benchmark of their public financial management systems and processes, to inform public financial management reforms and guide discussions with donors and development partners (examples in the Pacific region include Australian and New Zealand bilateral aid programmes, the World Bank, Asian Development Bank and European Community). In situations where a PEFA assessment has not yet been conducted, a donor or development partner may initiate the first assessment.

The PEFA assessments tend to be conducted by teams of approximately two to four people, ideally including one or more staff members from the recipient country's Ministry of Finance, or equivalent. The assessments can include a variety of methods to gather information, including workshops with relevant government officials, collation of documents, and consultation with donors, development partners and the private and not-for-profit sectors. Comprehensive templates and guidance on conducting the assessment, including the scoring methodology, are available from the PEFA secretariat in a variety of languages.

Each PEFA assessment team produces a standardised Public Financial Management Performance Report (PEFA report) containing an overview of the country's history, economy, legal arrangements and political settings. The reports then outline the assessment of the country's public financial management systems, processes and institutions against 28 performance indicators across six dimensions:

1   Credibility of the budget
2   Comprehensiveness and transparency
3   Policy-based budgeting
4   Predictability and control in budget execution
5   Accounting, recording and reporting
6   External scrutiny and audit.

Most PEFA assessments also contain an additional three performance indicators in a seventh dimension which examines donor practices. However, this additional dimension is not uniformly applied.

Each performance indicator is scored against better practice and international standards related to public financial management, with scores assessed on an A to D scale. Receipt of an A denotes better practice is in place/operating in that particular area while receipt of a D denotes that practice in the area is weak or non-existent. The scores can be used by countries to facilitate discussions with donors and development partners regarding areas of strength in existing systems and processes, and prioritise areas for improvement. Repeat PEFA assessments can be undertaken to document movements in scores over time.

It is noted that PEFA assessments are not intended to provide a basis for cross-country comparisons (Renzio, 2009). This means that a country that scores an A for a particular performance indicator is not necessarily 'better' than a country that scores a B for the same indicator. Individual country scores are provided at the end of this chapter solely to describe the performance of existing public financial management systems and processes in each country at the time of each assessment.

Scope and methodology of this study

This chapter focuses on the three performance indicators in dimension six, relating to external scrutiny and audit:[2]

*   Performance indicator 26: Scope, nature and follow-up of external audit;
*   Performance indicator 27: Legislative scrutiny of the annual budget law;
*   Performance indicator 28: Legislative scrutiny of external audit reports.

Each of these indicators has three or four sub-dimensions, and a scoring framework against good practices and international standards is provided in the PEFA framework (2011). A summary of the sub-dimensions, and the requirements for each of the A to D scores is provided in Table 10.1.

Table 10.1 PEFA performance indicators and scoring dimensions

Performance indicators and dimensions	Score	Minimum requirements
Performance indicator 26 – Scope, nature and follow-up of external audit		
i) Scope/nature of audit performed, including adherence to auditing standards	A	All entities of central government are audited annually covering revenue, expenditure and assets/liabilities. A full range of financial audits and some aspects of performance audit are performed and generally adhere to auditing standards, focusing on significant and systemic issues.
	B	Central government entities representing at least 75% of total expenditures are audited annually, at least covering revenue and expenditure. A wide range of financial audits are performed and generally adheres to auditing standards, focusing on significant and systemic issues.
	C	Central government entities representing at least 50% of total expenditures are audited annually. Audits predominantly comprise transaction level testing, but reports identify significant issues. Audit standards may be disclosed to a limited extent only.
	D	Audits cover central government entities representing less than 50% of total expenditures or audits have higher coverage but do not highlight the significant issues.
ii) Timeliness of submission of audit reports to legislature	A	Submitted within four months of the end of the period covered and in the case of financial statements from their receipt by the audit office.
	B	Submitted within eight months of the end of the period covered and in the case of financial statements from their receipt by the audit office.
	C	Submitted within 12 months of the end of the period covered (for audit of financial statements from their receipt by the auditors).
	D	Submitted more than 12 months from the end of the period covered (for audit of financial statements from their receipt by the auditors).
iii) Evidence of follow-up on audit recommendations	A	There is clear evidence of effective and timely follow-up.
	B	A formal, timely response, but there is little evidence of systematic follow-up.
	C	A formal response is made, though delayed or not very thorough, but there is little evidence of any follow-up.
	D	There is little evidence of response or follow-up.
Performance indicator 27 – Legislative scrutiny of the annual budget law		
i) Scope of the legislature's scrutiny	A	Review covers fiscal policies, medium-term fiscal framework and medium-term priorities as well as details of expenditure and revenue.
	B	Review covers fiscal policies and aggregates for the coming year as well as detailed estimates of expenditure and revenue.
	C	Review covers details of expenditure and revenue.e, but only at a stage where detailed proposals have been finalised.
	D	Review is non-existent or extremely limited, OR there is no functioning legislature.
ii) Extent to which the legislature's procedures are well established and respected	A	Procedures for budget review are firmly established and respected. They include internal organisational arrangements, such as specialised review committees, and negotiation procedures.
	B	Simple procedures exist for budget review and are respected.
	C	Some procedures exist for budget review, but they are not comprehensive and only partially respected.
	D	Procedures for the review are non-existent or not respected.

continued

Table 10.1 Continued

Performance indicators and dimensions	Score	Minimum requirements
iii) Adequacy of time for the legislature to provide a response to budget proposals, both detailed estimates and macro-fiscal aggregates earlier in the budget preparation cycle	A	The legislature has at least two months to review the budget proposals.
	B	The legislature has at least one month to review the budget proposals.
	C	The legislature has at least one month to review the budget proposals.
	D	The time allowed for the legislature's review is clearly insufficient for a meaningful debate (significantly less than one month).
iv) Rules for in-year amendments to the budget without ex ante approval by the legislature	A	Clear rules exist for in-year budget amendments by the executive, set strict limits on extent and nature of amendments and are consistently respected.
	B	Clear rules exist for in-year budget amendments, are usually respected, but they allow extensive administrative reallocations.
	C	Clear rules exist, but may not always be respected OR they may allow extensive administrative reallocation as well as expansion of total expenditure.
	D	Rules regarding in-year budget amendments may exist but are either very rudimentary and unclear OR they are usually not respected.
Performance indicator 28 – Legislative scrutiny of external audit reports		
i) Timeliness of examination of audit reports by the legislature (for reports received within the last three years)	A	Usually completed within three months from receipt.
	B	Usually completed within six months from receipt.
	C	Usually completed within 12 months from receipt.
	D	Does not take place, or longer than 12 months.
ii) Extent of hearings on key findings undertaken by the legislature	A	In-depth hearings take place consistently with all or most audited entities.
	B	
	C	In-depth hearings on key findings, may only cover some entities.
	D	In-depth hearings on key findings occasionally. No in-depth hearings conducted by the legislature.
iii) Issuance of recommended actions by the legislature and implementation by the executive	A	Legislature usually issues recommendation, generally implemented.
	B	Actions are recommended, some are implemented.
	C	Actions are recommended, but rarely acted upon by executive.
	D	No recommendations issues by the legislature.

Source: PEFA, 2011: 46–9.

We have reviewed the reports for each country and assessed the contents of each in relation to each of the performance indicators identified above. We then evaluate this data in the context of the indicators of Public Accounts Committee better practice.

The textual analysis of PEFA reports will focus on the context and background for each country, and the scoring and analysis of the above three performance indicators. This analysis will inform a conclusion about whether these reports contain enough robust and reliable information to contribute to the existing body of knowledge regarding Pacific Island Public Accounts Committees.

In this study we have reviewed publicly available PEFA reports with a view to assessing the extent to which these reports are useful in assessing the effectiveness of a sample of Public Accounts Committees. This sample of countries includes different cultures (Melanesian and Polynesian), different political and constitutional structures (including a kingdom, a constitutional monarchy and a self-governing state) and different relationships with multinational and bilateral donors. All are Commonwealth countries, and most have Parliaments based on the Westminster system.

We have not validated any information contained in these reports against other sources, and this may be undertaken as part of a future research programme.

Context and background – the countries in focus

This section provides an overview of the contextual and cultural information of the five countries in scope. We have provided here a general review of the demographics and geography, a brief description of the form of government, a brief introduction of the key legislation and a brief discussion relating to the Parliamentary oversight and audit arrangements.

Cook Islands

The Cook Islands has a total land area of 237 square kilometres, spread over 15 atolls and islands, spanning two million square kilometres across the South Pacific. The main economic activity in the Cook Islands is tourism, followed by the offshore banking industry.

The form of government is a self-governing Parliamentary democracy in free association[3] with New Zealand. As with most Pacific Island nations, there is no sub-national government. The Parliament has a 24-member Legislative Assembly, and the 1964 Constitution also allows for a House of Ariki, an advisory body of up to 14 traditional leaders that can advise on traditional matters.

Under Section 71 of the Constitution, the responsibility for external audit lies with the Audit Office, under the Public Expenditure Review Committee and Audit (PERCA). The PERCA Act 1995–6 outlines the duties and responsibilities of the Audit Office. All audit reports must be submitted to Parliament, and recommendations are to be followed up. Performance audits and other special reviews can be conducted if significant issues arise.

All public sector audits are overseen by the Audit Office, and are tabled in Parliament. The Public Expenditure Review Committee (PERC) reviews all audit reports, and the PERC's reports are also submitted to Parliament.

Samoa

Samoa has a population of approximately 180,000 and a total land area of about 2,900 square kilometres. Most of the population lives on the two main islands of Upolu and Savaii. The country's exports are dominated by nonu and coconut products, fishing and brewing. Private sector activities include agriculture, fisheries and tourism, with remittances from Samoans and their families living overseas contributing approximately 25 per cent of gross domestic product.

The Parliament comprises 49 members in the Legislative Assembly and the Head of State, each elected for a term of five years. The Head of State is elected by the Legislative Assembly, and appoints the Prime Minister.

The Public Financial Management Act 2001 outlines the legal framework for public financial management in Samoa. The executive is required to submit the annual budget to the Parliament before the start of the financial year.

A Finance and Expenditure Committee (formerly known as the Public Accounts Committee) has been established, with responsibility for oversight of public finances. This includes scrutiny of budget estimates, reports on government's annual financial statements by the Office of the Controller and Chief Auditor, and expenditure of ministries and other government bodies.

The Office of the Controller and Chief Auditor is established as a constitutional body, but does rely to some extent on funding from the government appropriation, which may be seen to compromise independence.

Solomon Islands

Almost 1,000 islands spread across nine provinces make up the Solomon Islands. Of the approximate population of 550,000, 85 per cent live in rural areas. The Solomon Islands gained independence on 7 July 1978, and is a constitutional monarchy. The unicameral Parliament comprises 50 members, each elected for a term of four years. The head of government is the Prime Minister, elected by the Parliament.

The Public Accounts Committee is a standing committee and has seven members. Importantly, a member of the Opposition is the Chair, and the Auditor-General acts as the Secretary. The responsibilities of the Public Accounts Committee include scrutiny of the draft budget estimates, reports on public accounts, and the Auditor-General's reports.

The Office of the Auditor-General is established as a public office under the Office of the Prime Minister. It is a member of both the Pacific Association of Supreme Audit Institutions (PASAI) and the International Organisation of Supreme Audit Institutions (INTOSAI). The role and responsibilities of the Office of the Auditor-General are outlined in the Constitution, the Public Finance and Audit Act 1978 and the State Owned Enterprise Act 2007.

Between them, these documents indicate that the Auditor-General is responsible for the annual audit and audit report for all ministries, offices, courts, authorities, state-owned enterprises and provincial governments. These reports are meant to be tabled by the Speaker within 12 months of the end of the relevant financial year.

Tonga

The Kingdom of Tonga comprises 169 islands, including 36 inhabited islands, and became a Polynesian kingdom in 1845. The Tongan economy is heavily reliant on remittances from Tongans living overseas, totalling about 30 per cent of gross domestic product in 2007–8. Another third of the economy is driven by exports of agriculture and fisheries, and 10 per cent of gross domestic product is contributed from official development assistance.

In 1875, it became a constitutional monarchy, and although it was a British protectorate from 1900 until independence in 1970, it was never colonised. The population is approximately 104,000, with about 70,000 living on the main island of Tongatapu.

The Legislative Assembly comprises 32 seats, of which only nine are determined by popular vote, and nine are selected by 33 nobles. The remaining 14 form the Cabinet, of which four are selected by the elected members of the Legislative Assembly and ten are appointed by the monarch for life. For those not appointed for life, members of the Legislative Assembly serve a term of three years.

The framework for public financial management in Tonga is established by the Constitution and the Public Finance Management Act 2002. Clause 78 of the Constitution makes it clear that the Legislative Assembly is responsible for establishing the estimates for public service expenditure each financial year. The Public Finance Management Act 2002 provides details on how budgets and appropriations are to be estimated and approved.

The Public Audit Act 2007 has improved understanding of the level of independence of the Audit Office, and clarified reporting arrangements to the Legislative Assembly.

There is an Expenditure Review Committee that meets regularly to discuss budget, revenue and economic policy matters. This is an administrative committee, rather than a Parliamentary committee, comprised of senior public servants and key ministers.

Vanuatu

Vanuatu, known as the New Hebrides until independence in 1980, is a chain of 83 islands with a population of approximately 205,000. Approximately two-thirds of the population rely on subsistence or small-scale agriculture. The other main economic contributors are fishing, offshore financial services and tourism.

Vanuatu is a republic, with the head of state elected by an electoral college comprising Parliament and regional councils. There are 52 members of the unicameral Parliament, plus the Speaker. Members of Parliament are elected for a term of four years, and are elected by universal adult suffrage.

Public financial management in Vanuatu is guided by the Constitution, which includes sections regarding public finances and the Auditor-General, as well as supporting legislation. The Public Finance and Economic Management Act 1998 outlines the requirements of economic and financial management, responsibility and reporting by government.

The Expenditure Review and Audit Act 1998 outlines the objectives, powers and functions of both the Public Accounts Committee and the Office of the Auditor-General. Although it does set out the requirement for an annual report on public finances, a timeframe for the submission of this report is not specified.

The Public Accounts Committee is the only standing committee of Parliament, and is chaired by a member of the Opposition. The committee has a maximum of six members, with equal representation from the government and Opposition.

Although the Office of the Auditor-General is a constitutional body with powers outlined in the Expenditure Review and Audit Act 1998, it also is required to act as the secretariat for the Public Accounts Committee. The Office's operational independence may be seen to be compromised due to a reliance on funding from the government.

Findings

This section provides a summary of the PEFA assessment for each country against the three relevant performance indicators. The detailed findings against each of the sub-dimensions can be found in the appendix to this chapter. Similar to the context and background section, the individual PEFA reports examined are the only source of information considered.

Cook Islands

The 2011 PEFA assessment in the Cook Islands found that the Parliamentary Procedures allow for the establishment of a select committee with the role and function of a Public Accounts Committee, namely the Finance and Economic Select Committee. However, in the period considered in the assessment, this committee was not selected or active.

Scope, nature and follow-up of external audit

The PEFA report states that the scope of external audits conducted in the period assessed was comprehensive, with annual audits conducted of all public entities and state-owned enterprises. The financial audits were conducted in accordance with New Zealand Auditing Standards, and cover assets, liabilities, revenues and expenditures.

Over the three year period of 2007–8 to 2009–10, more than 80 external audit reports each year were submitted to Parliament, and tabled within eight months of the period covered.

Any significant issues identified during the audit are outlined in a Management Letter to each ministry or line agency, and a response is required within 14 days. The PEFA report notes that although the formal management responses were generally received within this timeframe, there is little evidence of further follow-up, with recurrence of some key issues.

Legislative scrutiny of the annual budget law

The scope and procedures for budget scrutiny by the Parliament are outlined in the Parliamentary Standing Orders. A Committee of Supply considers the budget estimates at the time of the second reading of the Appropriation Bill (i.e. when the budget detail has been finalised). This committee is a Committee of the Whole House, rather than a separate committee, and does not appear to scrutinise the budget information in detail, but instead examines revenues and expenditure appropriations.

Parliamentary Procedures allow for the establishment of a select committee, known as the Finance and Expenditure Select Committee, with a mandate to review government finances in detail, but this Committee has not been active in the period assessed.

During this period, debate in Parliament regarding the budget has occurred within ten or fewer sitting days, with a maximum of ten days allowed by the Parliamentary Standing Orders. Detailed scrutiny of the budget may therefore be limited due to time pressures.

Legislative scrutiny of external audit reports

As described above, the Audit Office submits external audit reports to the Parliament. Under the Parliament's Standing Orders, the Finance and Expenditure Select Committee is required to review these audit reports, but as it has not been active for several years, this legislative scrutiny has not occurred.

The Public Expenditure and Review Committee (PERC) can and does review audit reports, but as it is not a legislative body, it is limited in its ability to conduct hearings and gather evidence.

Samoa

The scores for each performance indicator given for the 2006 and 2010 PEFA assessments in Samoa tended to differ. In each of the three performance indicators discussed below, the 2006 report contains generally higher scores than the 2010 report. This is explained in the 2010 report, which states that the scoring methodology was incorrectly applied in the 2006 assessment.

The two main issues identified in both reports were the timeliness of submission of financial statements to the Samoa Audit Office, with late submission making it difficult to complete external audits with 12 months of the end of the relevant financial year, and the short time provided for Parliamentary scrutiny of the budget estimates.

Scope, nature and follow-up of external audit

In addition to financial audits, the Samoa Audit Office's audit programme includes effectiveness audits against budgeted outputs, and systems audits in state-owned enterprises, including assessment of internal controls.

The 2010 PEFA report noted that in the period it considered, less than 50 per cent of central government agencies had completed financial audits. Delays in receipt of financial statements from the Ministry of Finance contribute to delays in tabling of audit reports in Parliament, though performance in this area had improved relative to 2006.

Management letters are provided by the Samoa Audit Office, and written responses are prepared by agencies. Although the process is in place, the timeliness of the audits may minimise the impact of any recommendations.

Legislative scrutiny of the annual budget law

A committee of the Legislative Assembly, referred to as the Public Accounts Committee in the 2006 report and the Finance and Expenditure Select Committee in the 2010 report, is required to spend at least 14 days reviewing the budget estimates. This process can include hearings.

Wider consideration by the Legislative Assembly of the budget estimates is only done after the Budget Address, when the details regarding revenue and expenditure have already been finalised.

Legislative scrutiny of external audit reports

The 2006 PEFA report states that examination of audit reports occurs within three months of receipt by the legislature, and therefore scored high on this element. The 2010 PEFA report noted that the audited financial statements for 2004, 2005 and 2006 were not tabled until January 2009, and that the review by the Finance and Expenditure Committee had not been completed, resulting in a significantly lower score.

Similar inconsistencies were identified regarding the extent of hearings regarding key audit findings. The 2010 report noted that although hearings are held by the Finance and Expenditure Committee, it only receives a copy of the audit opinion and the public accounts. With this summary level information, in-depth hearings are limited.

Solomon Islands

In contrast to Samoa, the two PEFA assessments conducted in the Solomon Islands have relatively consistent scores, with differences explained by changes in activities or performance, rather than application of scoring methodology.

During the period from 2001 to 2003, the Office of the Auditor-General comprised only three people, including the Auditor-General. With support from the Regional Assistance Mission to Solomon Islands (RAMSI),[4] capacity has increased, special audits were conducted to bring the programme up to date, and a normal audit programme resumed in 2006. In contrast, the Public Accounts Committee was not active in scrutinising audit reports between 2008 and 2011.

Scope, nature and follow-up of external audit

Since 2006, the scope of financial audits has increased to cover more than 75 per cent of total government expenditure. The 2012 PEFA report notes increases in the nature of the audits conducted by the Office of the Auditor-General, which now include performance, compliance and payroll audits, in addition to financial audits.

The timeliness of audits diminished between the 2008 and the 2012 PEFA reports, with tabling of audit reports stretching to more than 12 months from the receipt of the financial statements. A decision was taken to select only material and high-risk agencies to be audited for the 2011 Solomon Islands Government National Accounts. This will still result in more than 75 per cent of revenue and expenditure being covered by the audit, but is expected to reduce the timing of the audit report to eight months.

Follow-up on implementation of audit recommendations appears to be limited, with some findings and recommendations duplicated each year, suggesting little action has taken place to address the finding.

Legislative scrutiny of the annual budget law

The Public Accounts Committee is required under standing orders to examine and report on the annual budget estimates. The 2008 PEFA report noted that this process had occurred since the 1980s, but the quality of the scrutiny was diminished because it only occurs at the end of the budget process, and less than a week is usually taken by the Public Accounts Committee, with an additional week for review of the committee's report by the Parliament.

The 2012 PEFA report also identifies the weakness inherent in this limited time available for scrutiny of the annual budget. The Public Accounts Committee has recommended that at least one month be provided for review, but one week or less is usually provided, when Parliament is already in session. The responsible government agency, the Ministry of Finance and Treasury, intends to submit the draft budget estimates to Parliament three weeks prior to its sitting.

The quality of the budget scrutiny is also impacted by the regular turnover of the members of the Public Accounts Committee. However, new members are provided with ongoing training and advice, and committee members and staff are undertaking external training and partnering with other Parliaments to improve the effectiveness of the committee. In addition, the establishment of a Parliamentary Budget Office to assist with analysis of the budget estimates has been recommended by the Public Accounts Committee.

In early 2012, a new committee was created, known as the Public Expenditure Committee. It was also intended to introduce a new Standing Order which will allow the responsibility for budget scrutiny to be transferred to the new committee, with the Public Accounts Committee maintaining responsibility for the review and reporting of audit reports.

Legislative scrutiny of external audit reports

The 2008 PEFA report provided positive information and relatively high scores for this performance indicator, even though numerous disruptive events occurred during 2007 and 2008. The included a vote of no confidence leading to a change of government, and the death of the Auditor-General. Public hearings are conducted by the Public Accounts Committee, with media invited, along with senior officials from the relevant government agencies.

At the time of the 2008 PEFA assessment, only five reports had been tabled by the Office of the Auditor-General that were awaiting review by the Public Accounts Committee. Only one of these was more than 12 months old.

In contrast, the 2012 PEFA assessment contains very little information for this performance indicator, noting that none of the reports tabled by the Office of the Auditor-General since 2008 had been reviewed by the Public Accounts Committee, nor had any hearings been held since the previous PEFA assessment. Nine tabled reports remained outstanding.

Tonga

The 2010 PEFA assessment in Tonga does not provide any reference to a Public Accounts Committee or similar Parliamentary committee. There is no Supreme Audit Institution, with an Audit Office conducting both internal and external audits. All audit and budget scrutiny is conducted by the Legislative Assembly, often with extensive time lags in the tabling of reports. As the reports are at a summary level, the evidence of scrutiny and comment provided is limited.

Scope, nature and follow-up of external audit

Prior to the commencement in 2008 of the Public Audit Act 2007, there was no external auditor in Tonga. The audits subsequently undertaken by the Audit Office focus mainly on transaction-level testing, though capacity building to conduct performance audits is a focus for the Audit Office in the future.

Audit reports tend to be submitted to the Legislative Assembly more than 12 months after the end of the period covered. This delay is contributed to by the late receipt of financial statements from government ministries, agencies and statutory bodies.

Most audits conducted by the Audit Office are unqualified. If audit recommendations are provided, formal and timely responses tend to be provided, but these tend not to be comprehensive or followed up.

Legislative scrutiny of the annual budget law

Detailed budget estimates are provided to the Legislative Assembly once the budget proposals have been finalised, and often less than one month is provided for scrutiny. There was no evidence provided of any documented procedures of review to guide the Legislative Assembly in its debates.

Legislative scrutiny of external audit reports

The Audit Office submits a consolidated annual report of its audit findings to the Legislative Assembly, usually more than 12 months after the end of the relevant financial period. An example is provided of the 2007–8 annual report from the Audit Office being submitted to the Speaker of the Legislative Assembly in March 2009, and as at March 2010, it had not been tabled.

There appears to be no debate in the Legislative Assembly regarding the audit findings, and ministers are not required to respond to the findings or recommendations.

Vanuatu

The 2006 PEFA assessment in Vanuatu found that the National Audit Office was not conducting the required audits in a timely manner, nor was it conducting the full range and scope of required audits. The Public Accounts Committee had not been active since 2003.

Scope, nature and follow-up of external audit

The nature of audits to be conducted is outlined in the Expenditure Review and Audit Act 1998 and includes financial, compliance and performance audits. The scope of entities that are to be audited includes all central government, provincial and municipal agencies, state-owned enterprises and schools. The legislation requires that at least 20 per cent of all audits are to be contracted out.

The most recent audit reports submitted to Parliament were in 2000, and covered the period 1992 to 1997. At the time of the 2006 PEFA assessment, financial audits of central government departments for the period 1998 to 2004 were being completed. Audits of statutory bodies, state-owned enterprises and provincial governments were not prepared or submitted in the required timeframes.

For those audits that have been completed, there is little evidence of follow-up of audit recommendations. Signed management letters are not always provided.

Legislative scrutiny of the annual budget law

The scrutiny of detailed budget estimates and related budget documentation, such as financial policies and medium-term priorities, is the responsibility of the Public Accounts Committee. This has not occurred. The Appropriations Bill, however, was received and reviewed by Parliament, with at least one month allowed for debate of the budget estimates.

Legislative scrutiny of external audit reports

The Public Accounts Committee is responsible for reviewing external audit reports. The audit reports for the period 1986 to 1994 were reviewed in 2000.

Due to political instability, the Public Accounts Committee had not met since 2003, and had not issued any reports since 2000.

The 2006 PEFA report noted that a committee had recently been convened. As noted earlier, follow-up PEFA assessments were undertaken in Vanuatu in 2009 and 2013, but the reports are not publicly available, so it is unclear from available PEFA reporting whether the Public Accounts Committee is active and meeting its responsibilities.

Discussion

The literature review identified several key conditions and characteristics that contribute to the effective performance of Public Accounts Committees. Each of these will be briefly discussed in the context of the information contained in the PEFA reports examined, and a finding relating to the countries reviewed is provided.

Scope of activity, i.e. scrutiny of public expenditure, not policy

The scope of the activity considered by the legislature (not necessarily restricted to the Public Accounts Committee) is addressed by performance indicators 26 and 27. Achieving an 'A' score for performance indicator 27 requires scrutiny of fiscal policies, the medium-term fiscal framework and medium-term priorities, as well as detailed estimates of revenue and expenditure. If this activity is undertaken by a Public Accounts Committee, it could be argued that this goes beyond the scope required for an effective Public Accounts Committee.

Formal powers of the Public Accounts Committees, including the ability to scrutinise all public expenditure: past and present

The nature of the establishment of the Public Accounts Committees, whether by Constitution, legislation or standing orders, is usually addressed in the country context section of the PEFA report, though the level of detail and historical context varies between reports. The scope of financial activity able to be considered is addressed by performance indicator 26, regarding audited financial statements, and performance indicator 27, regarding annual budget law.

Prepare and publish recommendations, and ability to follow up

Performance indicator 28 contains information regarding whether the legislature issues recommendations, and if evidence exists that those recommendations have been acted upon by the executive. No information is provided regarding the outcome or result of any actions taken.

Adequate information, resourcing and staffing

There is limited, if any, information about Public Accounts Committee staffing and resourcing. The country context section of the report sometimes advised on the chair or secretariat of the Public Accounts Committee, but not the staffing arrangements, nor the process for funding the Public Accounts Committee.

Public and media scrutiny

There is no consistent and comprehensive information contained in the PEFA reports regarding whether or not the public and media have ready access to the reports issued by the Public Accounts Committee, and whether reports and recommendations are actively scrutinised and followed up.

Composition and behaviour of the Public Accounts Committee

The country context sections of the PEFA reports tend to provide details of the composition of the Parliament, but not the composition of the Public Accounts Committee. Performance indicators 27 and 28 describe the scope and timeliness of activities of the legislature, such as scrutiny of annual budget law and external audit reports. No information is provided about the behaviour of the Public Accounts Committee itself, such as whether it is bi-partisan, is chaired by a member of the opposition, or whether members are prepared for and active in meetings.

Relationship with the Auditor-General

The relationship between the Auditor-General and the legislature is usually documented in the country context section of the PEFA report, but the relationship with the Public Accounts Committee, including technical support provided, is not well documented.

Conclusions

The seven PEFA reports across five countries considered in this chapter provide a useful overview of the nature, role and activity of Public Accounts Committees in the Pacific. Each standardised report provides contextual information about the country and its political and legal framework. The three performance indicators relating to external scrutiny and audit provide information regarding the activities and performance of the Public Accounts Committee, and the relationship and interactions with the Auditor-General and the Parliament.

This information contributes to the existing body of knowledge by providing a summary of Public Accounts Committee structure and activities in these five countries. It also identifies a publicly available source of data that can be used to understand public financial management systems, processes and institutions in these and many other countries worldwide. As PEFA assessments are intended to be repeated over time, this will be a valuable source of information for future research.

As shown in the discussion section, the PEFA reports examined do not contain adequate information to address all of the commonly identified success factors for Public Accounts Committees from the literature. This is not surprising, given the scope and intent of PEFA assessments, and the lack of commonly agreed performance indicators and best practice standards for Public Accounts Committees.

Limitations, and opportunities for future research

The value of these findings is limited by three main factors. First, the quality and level of detail contained in the individual PEFA reports varies between countries and over time. The standardised nature of the assessments and structure and required content of the report does provide consistent information for each country. The varied composition and experience of the individual assessment teams, however, may mean that comparisons between countries may not be reliable. An example is the misapplication of the scoring methodology in the 2006 Samoa assessment. Additional guidance materials and training for PEFA assessors that have been made progressively available by the PEFA secretariat should continue to improve the quality and consistency of PEFA reports.

Second, the countries included in this assessment have been limited to those with publicly available PEFA assessments written in English, and then only the publicly available reports, as in the case of Tonga and Vanuatu. If those additional final PEFA assessments were made available by the respective countries, including Fiji, French Polynesia, the Federated States of Micronesia, Papua New Guinea, Tuvalu, and Wallis and Futuna, the publicly available information about Public Accounts Committees in the Pacific would be much more comprehensive. The 2012 PEFA report for New Caledonia is only available in French, and has therefore been excluded.

Similarly, draft reports have been prepared for PEFA assessments in Kiribati, Marshall Islands, Nauru and Niue, and a PEFA assessment is planned for Palau. As these reports are finalised, a more comprehensive assessment and comparison of Public Accounts Committees in the Pacific could be undertaken, and contribute further to the existing body of knowledge.

And finally, this chapter has relied on the information contained in the PEFA reports, and has not attempted to verify it against alternative sources of information. Further research could be undertaken to compare the findings of the PEFA assessments to other sources of available data, including Parliamentary records including Hansard, annual reports by Auditors-General, and existing surveys such as those conducted by the World Bank Institute.

Additionally, we have not attempted here to explain the results of the PEFA assessments with regard to the different cultural, political and historical contexts of each country. Further research will be pursued with a larger sample of PEFA assessments conducted over the years, and a broader range of countries, including those from Micronesia.

Appendix

Table A10.1 Summary of the PEFA assessment for each country by relevant performance indicators

Performance indicators and dimensions	Country	Year	Score	Comments
Performance indicator 26 – Scope, nature and follow-up of external audit				
i) Scope/nature of audit performed, including adherence to auditing standards	Cook Islands	2011	A	Rules for in-year budget amendments without *ex ante* approval exist; specifically, the Constitution specifies the limits on which in-year expenditures may exceed appropriations. However, there is evidence that these rules are not always followed (actual expenditures for individual MLAs that were above the voted appropriation (including the supplementary budget) as well as the Constitutional limit), and in some cases *ex post* approvals, e.g. through the approval of Supplementary Budgets after the end of the fiscal year.
	Samoa	2006	A	*Commentary is not consistent with score.*
	Samoa	2010	D	In the period under review, the focus has been on financial audits, the latest available audit report shows that <50% of central government entities were covered. Adherence to auditing standards including independence was recognised to be weak but with the ISP is improving.
	Solomon Islands	2008	B	Since 2006, the OAG has been carrying out traditional audits and covering all central government entities. Audits of extra budgetary funds take place when accounts are received. INTOSAI auditing standards are followed and significant issues clearly stated, but full independence has not been attained yet and no performance audits have been carried out.
	Solomon Islands	2012	B	Performance unchanged. Central government entities representing at least 75% of total expenditures are audited annually, at least covering revenue and expenditure. A wide range of financial audits is performed and generally adheres to auditing standards, focusing on significant and systemic issues.
	Tonga	2010	C	Central government entities representing at least 50% of total expenditures are audited annually. Audits predominantly comprise transaction level testing, but reports identify significant issues. Audit standards may be disclosed to a limited extent only.
	Vanuatu	2006	D	Audits of central government departments/ other institutions have taken place but do not represent a significant proportion of entities to be audited.

continued

Table A10.1 Continued

Performance indicators and dimensions	Country	Year	Score	Comments
ii) Timeliness of submission of audit reports to legislature	Cook Islands	2011	B	Over the last three years, audit reports have been tabled within eight months of the period covered.
	Samoa	2006	D	Audit reports are submitted to the legislature more than 12 months from the end of the period covered – delays in receipt of financial statements contributes to this delay.
	Samoa	2010	C	Audit reports and opinions on financial statements are issued within 12 months of year-end and/or receipt.
	Solomon Islands	2008	C	The OAG has successfully addressed the audit backlog and is now tabling audit of financial statements within nine months. For 2004 and 2005, the period was ten months and for 2006 three months, therefore an average of eight months. In addition to the composite status reports, for 2006 and 2007, annual reports summarising the activities of the OAG were also prepared for the period 2002–2006 and 2007, the former being tabled in latter being tabled in August 2008.
	Solomon Islands	2012	D	Performance diminished. Audit reports are submitted to legislature more than 12 months from the end of period covered (for audit of financial statements from their receipt by the auditors).
	Tonga	2010	D	Audit reports are submitted to the legislature more than 12 months from the end of the period covered (for audit of financial statements from their receipt by the auditors).
	Vanuatu	2006	D	The last audit reports and audited accounts tabled with Parliament were for the period 1994–1997. 1998–2001 accounts were sent to the Auditor General in 2003.
iii) Evidence of follow up on audit recommendations	Cook Islands	2011	C	The audit reports include formal management responses that are received within 14 days with some exceptions. There is little evidence of any follow-up after those management responses are received. Some key issues continue to arise in subsequent audits.
	Samoa	2006	A	The Audit Office advises that there is clear evidence of effective and timely follow up.
	Samoa	2010	B	A formal response is made to the management letter and follow-up is done by the SAO as indicated by the audit files, but given the delays in audits, this may not be done in a timely manner.
	Solomon Islands	2008	B	Audit plans are prepared, follow-up does take place but response varies across ministries
	Solomon Islands	2012	C	Performance diminished. A formal response is made by the management of audited entities, though delayed or not very thorough, but there is little evidence of any implementation of OAG recommendations.
	Tonga	2010	C	A formal response is made, though delayed or not very thorough, but there is little evidence of any follow up.

continued

Table A10.1 Continued

Performance indicators and dimensions	Country	Year	Score	Comments
	Vanuatu	2006	D	In the period under review there have been no clear responses to audits. Audit reports have not been issued. Signed management letters have not been routinely submitted to the auditee.
Performance indicator 27 – Legislative scrutiny of the annual budget law				
i) Scope of the legislature's scrutiny	Cook Islands	2011	C	Parliament considers the budget only after it has been finalised. The whole House (Committee of Supply) discusses only the appropriation lines for revenues and expenditures.
	Samoa	2006	C	The Parliament may only vote to reduce expenditure, not increase or transfer expenditure or revenue.
	Samoa	2010	C	The legislature only reviews detailed estimates at the end of the budget preparation process.
	Solomon Islands	2008	C	The legislature reviews the proposals at the end of the budgeting process.
	Solomon Islands	2012	B	Performance has improved. Starting in 2011, PAC is fully analysing budget submissions including budget strategies and fiscal policies.
	Tonga	2010	C	The legislature's review covers details of expenditure and revenue, but only at a stage where detailed proposals have been finalised.
	Vanuatu	2006	C	Although volumes 1–3 of the budget documentation submitted to Parliament include fiscal strategy, programme budget estimates and narrative. Legislative review concentrates on the detailed estimates and is not involved at a prior stage of the budget process.
ii) Extent to which the legislature's procedures are well established and respected	Cook Islands	2011	C	Parliamentary procedures for the review of the budget are clear in the Standing Orders but there appears to be gaps in their implementation (e.g. the functioning of the Finance and Expenditure Committee).
	Samoa	2006	B	*Comments not provided.*
	Samoa	2010	B	Simple procedures exist for the legislature's review and are respected.
	Solomon Islands	2008	B	The PAC's responsibilities are set out in a standing order and it is required to review the estimates and present a report to Parliament.
	Solomon Islands	2012	A	Performance has improved. Clearer rules and processes are in place as a result of the Parliamentary Strengthening Project that has helped to strengthen the capacity of PAC. Further improvement is expected as a result of the recently created PEC.
	Tonga	2010	D	Procedures for the legislature's review are non-existent or not respected.
	Vanuatu	2006		The PAC has not been carrying out its mandate with respect to the budget process, although review by the legislature has been followed.
iii) Adequacy of time for the legislature to provide a response to budget proposals, both detailed estimates and macro-fiscal aggregates earlier in the budget preparation cycle	Cook Islands	2011	D	Parliamentary Standing Orders indicate a maximum of ten sitting days for consideration of draft Estimates. In practice, this means that consideration ceases at the expiration of ten sitting days, significantly less than one month.

continued

Table A10.1 Continued

Performance indicators and dimensions	Country	Year	Score	Comments
	Samoa	2006	D	At least two weeks allowed to conduct hearings before the budget is tabled for approval.
	Samoa	2010	D	The committee must spend at least 14 days and in practice takes two to three weeks in reviewing the estimates. As the review period is less than one month, a D has been assigned.
	Solomon Islands	2008	D	PAC review is typically one week, with an additional week for the Parliament.
	Solomon Islands	2012	D	No change in performance. The amount of time allowed for Parliament to review the budget remains limited.
	Tonga	2010	C	The legislature has at least one month to review the budget proposals.
	Vanuatu	2006	C	The appropriation bill is submitted in October and debate starts in November, thus allowing at least one month for debate.
iv) Rules for in-year amendments to the budget without ex-ante approval by the legislature	Cook Islands	2011	D	Rules for in-year budget amendments without *ex ante* approval exist; specifically, the Constitution specifies the limits on which in-year expenditures may exceed appropriations. However, there is evidence that these rules are not always followed (actual expenditures for individual MLAs that were above the voted appropriation (including the supplementary budget) as well as the Constitutional limit), and in some cases *ex post* approvals, e.g. through the approval of supplementary budgets after the end of the fiscal year.
	Samoa	2006	A	*Comments not provided.*
	Samoa	2010	B	Clear rules exist for in-year budget amendments by the executive, but they allow extensive re-allocation.
	Solomon Islands	2008	C	Rules for the use of contingency warrants exist, but they have been used extensively in recent years.
	Solomon Islands	2012	C	No change in performance. Rules for use of contingency warrants exist, but they continue to be used under circumstances that are not necessarily urgent and unforeseeable.
	Tonga	2010	B	Clear rules exist for in-year budget amendments by the executive, and are usually respected, but they allow extensive administrative reallocations.
	Vanuatu	2006	B	Rules for in-year amendments to the budget without ex-ante approval by the legislature are set out in the financial regulations.

Performance indicator 28 – Legislative scrutiny of external audit reports

i) Timeliness of examination of audit reports by the legislature (for reports received within the last three years)	Cook Islands	2011	D	Evidence from Hansard indicates that Parliament does not generally examine audit reports except for special reports (e.g. the fuel farm review).
	Samoa	2006	A	*Commentary does not support the score.*
	Samoa	2010	D	Examination of the audited financial statements takes more than 12 months to complete. (D) Examination of CCA annual report has taken up to 12 months (C), although the latest review has not been completed.

continued

Table A10.1 Continued

Performance indicators and dimensions	Country	Year	Score	Comments
	Solomon Islands	2008	C	Only one of the outstanding reports is more than 12 months old and there are exceptional circumstances for this situation.
	Solomon Islands	2012	D	No examination of the audits took place since the last assessment. PAC is no longer active in reviewing audit reports.
	Tonga	2010	D	Examination of audit reports by the legislature does not take place or usually takes more than 12 months to complete.
	Vanuatu	2006	D	The last meeting of the PAC was in 2003 at which time it started the review of accounts for 1994–1997. Since the elections in 2004, the PAC has not been meeting; a new committee has, however, recently been convened.
ii) Extent of hearings on key findings undertaken by the legislature	Cook Islands	2011	D	In the absence of the Finance and Expenditure Committee, no in-depth hearings on key findings have been undertaken.
	Samoa	2006	A	The PAC conducts hearings for three to four weeks after the table of external audit reports. The PAC tables a report, and Cabinet has the responsibility of implementing recommendations.
	Samoa	2010	D	Hearings take place but the business committee only receives the annual summary of activity and the finance and expenditure committee only receives the audit opinion and the public accounts. Given the very limited information presented to them, their ability to carry out in-depth hearings is therefore limited.
	Solomon Islands	2008	B	Hearings do take place with most officials from the entities involved.
	Solomon Islands	2012	D	Hearings on key findings are yet to take place.
	Tonga	2010	D	No in-depth hearings are conducted by the legislature.
	Vanuatu	2006	D	No PAC meetings – no in depth hearings.
iii) Issuance of recommended actions by the legislature and implementation by the executive	Cook Islands	2011	D	There is no evidence of recommendations being issued by Parliament.
	Samoa	2006	B	The Office of the Chief Auditor reports on whether implementation has occurred.
	Samoa	2010	C	Recommendations are issued, but evidence of systematic implementation is not available.
	Solomon Islands	2008	B	Recommendations are made, there is evidence that some are followed but not universally and PAC does follow up but not systematically or in a timely fashion partly due to the limited number of parliamentary sessions.
	Solomon Islands	2012	D	No recommendations were issued, because no audit reports have been reviewed.
	Tonga	2010	D	No recommendations are being issued by the legislature.
	Vanuatu	2006	D	The PAC has not met since 2003 and no report has been issued since 2000.

Source: PEFA reports for the countries and years contained in the table.

Notes

1 Limitations of the data noted in this study include the imprecise wording of some questions, incomplete or seemingly inaccurate responses to some questions, and what appeared to be identical answers to similarly worded questions.
2 We acknowledge that some activities captured in other dimensions may affect these performance indicators. For example, performance indicator 25 examines the quality and timeliness of annual financial statements. Without timely and comprehensive financial statements, external scrutiny by the legislative auditor and the legislature is likely to be limited.
3 Cook Islanders have the right of access to New Zealand, and hold New Zealand citizenship.
4 RAMSI was established in 2003 following a request for assistance from the Prime Minister of Solomon Islands. A 15-country partnership, led by Australia and New Zealand and comprising all members of the Pacific Islands Forum, commenced providing police, military and civilian support. The programme includes public financial management support and Parliamentary strengthening.

References

Hardman, D. J. (1984) 'Public financial administration of microstates: South Pacific Forum', *Public Administration and Development*, 4: 141–54.
Hedger, E. and Blick, A. (2008) 'Enhancing accountability for the use of public sector resources: How to improve the effectiveness of Public Accounts Committees', background paper for the 2008 Triennial Conference of Commonwealth Auditors General, Overseas Development Institute, London.
McGee, D. G. (2002) *The Overseers: Public Accounts Committees and Public Spending*, London: Commonwealth Parliamentary Association & Pluto Press.
PEFA Secretariat (2009) *Issues in Comparison and Aggregation of PEFA Assessment Results over Time and Across Countries*, Washington DC: PEFA Secretaritat. Available at: www.pefa.org/en/content/methodological-guidance-and-practical-tools (accessed 29 January 2015).
PEFA Secretariat (2011) *PFM Performance Measurement Framework*. Available at: www.pefa.org/en/content/pefa-framework-material-1 (accessed 29 January 2015).
PEFA Secretariat (2012) *'Fieldguide' for undertaking an assessment using the PEFA performance measurement framework*. Available at: www.pefa.org/en/content/methodological-guidance-and-practical-tools (accessed 29 January 2015).
Pelizzo, R. (2010) 'Public Accounts Committees in the Pacific Region', *Politics & Policy*, 38(1): 117–37.
Pelizzo, R. (2011) 'Public Accounts Committees in the Commonwealth: oversight, effectiveness and governance', *Commonwealth and Comparative Politics*, 49(4): 528–46.
Pelizzo, R., Stapenhurst, R., Sahgal, V. and Woodley, W. (2006) 'What Makes Public Accounts Committees Work? A Comparative Analysis', *Politics and Policy*, 34(4): 774–93.
Rawlings, G. (2006) 'Regulating Responsively for Oversight Agencies in the Pacific', Targeted Research Paper for AusAID, State, Society and Governance in Melanesia.
Renzio, P. de (2009) *Taking Stock: What do PEFA Assessments tell us about PFM systems across countries?* Working Paper 302, London: Overseas Development Institute.
Stapenhurst, R., Sahgal, V., Woodley, W. and Pelizzo, R. (2005) 'Scrutinizing Public Expenditures: Assessing the Performance of Public Accounts Committees', World Bank Policy Research Working Paper 3613, Washington DC: World Bank.

Part IV

Public Accounts Committees in Asian regions

11 The development of the Public Accounts Committees of Bangladesh's Parliament

An overview

Sajjad H. Khan and Zahirul Hoque

Introduction

Regardless of the level of maturity of the public sector, good governance, with its principal attributes of accountability and transparency, is receiving increased attention from policy-makers, legislators, funding agencies and other stake-holders globally (Funnell and Cooper, 1998; Groot and Budding, 2008; Hossain, 2002; Lee, 2008; Lapsley, 2008). In many respects, the move toward New Public Management (NPM) has been a response to the perceived need for an increase in governance maturity within the public sector around the world. One of the important elements of any public sector governance process is the Parliament, which is often the heart of the modern democratic government system, including the Washington system. Further, the parliamentary committee system is an indispensable part of any parliamentary democracy (Stone, 1995).

Among all the parliamentary committees, the Public Accounts Committee (PAC)[1] is considered to be the most important (Jacobs *et al.*, 2007; McGee, 2002) as it plays a vital part in promoting transparency and accountability and in deterring corruption. The PAC is one organisational form of the parliamentary infrastructure through which parliament ensures the accountability of the government and its agencies that deliver services to the greater community (McGee, 2002; Wehner, 2003).

Jacobs and Jones (2009) argue that the PAC is a key example of an institution of audit, governance and regulation within the Westminster parliamentary system. Although it might not be considered a classical example of accounting practice, it has been required to exercise an accounting role through oversight and review of parliamentary spending. Therefore, the PAC has become a central element of the process of parliamentary and democratic accountability (Jacobs and Jones, 2009).

In 1972, Bangladesh introduced a parliamentary system based on the West-minster model. This system lasted until 1975. From 1975 to December 1990, military and quasi-military regimes ruled the country under a presidential form of government.[2] Again through a constitutional amendment in August 1991, Bangladesh adopted a Westminster-style parliamentary form of government, the *Jatiyo Sangshad* (BJS), with the Prime Minister as the head of the government and the President as the head of State, elected by members of the Parliament. Since the early 1980s, the successive governments of Bangladesh have initiated various reforms to modernise its public sector, including the PACs, to align its offices with the global trend and improve its performance in terms of efficiency and accountability. This chapter discusses the development of the PAC of Bangladesh.

Methodology

This chapter focuses on the functioning of the PACs of the seventh and eighth Parliaments (1996 to 2006). Institutional theory suggests that organisational structures or forms are the result of pressures from external constituents rather than the result of the internal efficiency choices of policy makers (Meyer and Rowan, 1977; Scott and Meyer, 1991; Scott, 1991). Such an external legitimacy grounded in the 'pressures' of environmental expectations and beliefs is said to have emerged through a process of 'coercive' isomorphism (DiMaggio and Powell, 1983). Coercive isomorphism results from both formal and informal pressures exerted on organisations by other organisations upon which they are dependent and by cultural expectations in the society within which the organisations function. DiMaggio and Powell (1983) note that in cases where alternative sources of finance are either not readily available or require effort to locate, the stronger party to the transaction can coerce the weaker party to adopt its practices in order to accommodate the stronger party's needs. Institutional theory indicates how organisations adopt certain practices and structures since they are compelled to do so by impinging external forces, or through more general social expectations. Our focus in this chapter is to discuss whether the Bangladeshi PAC adopted new governance modes and administrative procedures to increase its external legitimacy and survival prospects, independent of the immediate efficacy of the acquired practices.

Data for this study were collected through interviews, the review of archived documents and the observation of some PAC meetings. The interviewees were mainly from the Office of the Comptroller and Auditor-General (CAG) and the PAC. Interviews were conducted with the present CAG and three former CAGs, and with 13 members (out of 15) of the PAC. In addition, the former chairman of the seventh Parliament's PAC was interviewed. Three interviewees had been members of the PAC for both terms (seventh and eighth Parliaments). The interviews varied in length between 30 minutes and two and a half hours. Interviewees were asked follow-up questions subsequent to the main interview where additional details or clarification were needed.

Background of the PAC

Article 76 of the 1972 Constitution of the People's Republic of Bangladesh and Rules of Procedure of the Parliament governs the committee system in Bangladesh. The Constitution makes it mandatory for the Parliament to set up a PAC.

The functions of the PAC are outlined in the 1972 Constitution's Rules of Procedure of the Parliament (Section 233(2)) as follows:

> In scrutinising the Appropriation Accounts of the Government and the report of the CAG thereon, it shall be the duty of the Committee to satisfy itself that the money shown in the accounts as having been disbursed were legally available for, and applicable to, the service or purpose to which they have been applied or charged; that the expenditure conforms to the authority which governs it; and that every re-appropriation has been made in accordance with the provisions made in this behalf under rule framed by competent authority.

Following changes to arrangements made in 1991, the PAC is now empowered to report on the irregularities and lapses of different institutions of government and to suggest measures for rectification.

Section 234 of the Rules of Procedure of the Parliament (1972) stipulates that the Committee shall consist of no more than 15 members who shall be appointed by the House and that a member cannot hold a ministerial post. The representation of different political parties in the PAC is determined proportionately to the number of their members in the Parliament. The tenure of the PAC depends on the term of the Parliament, which is formed for five years. The Committee finishes its term when the Parliament dissolves.

The Office of the CAG submits audit reports to the President of the Republic through the Prime Minister. The President sends them to the Speaker, who then tables them in Parliament. It is the Parliament of Bangladesh's practice that the Speaker refers the yearly CAG's reports relating to the public accounts of the Republic to the PAC as soon as they are laid in the House to be acted upon.

The Chairman of the PAC sets up the date for meeting in consultation with members of the PAC and the Auditor-General to start its formal work. The Committee selects important paragraphs and comments from the audit reports for in-depth scrutiny. In making these selections the Committee is assisted by the Office of the CAG. The ministers' offices respond to any enquiries.

The PAC undertakes hearings on the audit reports submitted to the Parliament in the presence of the Secretary of the Ministry or Division, designated as the Principal Accounting Officer (PAO), the official representative of the Ministry and the CAG and his officers. On the basis of the hearings and review of the observations and comments of the audit reports, PAC members make recommendations and decisions on the irregularities mentioned in the CAG's reports. By precedent, the PAC's recommendations are required to be followed up by the government agencies and the ministries concerned. The PAC occasionally monitors the progress of implementation of its recommendations through follow-up and implementation meetings. The PAC publishes its own report, which is then submitted to the full House of Parliament incorporating meeting proceedings, compliance achieved, analytical comments and recommendations made thereon. Figure 11.1 outlines the PAC's procedures.

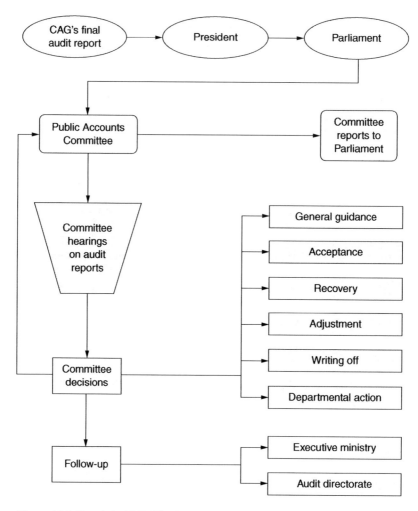

Figure 11.1 Bangladeshi Public Accounts Committee procedure (source: developed by the principal researcher based on Annual Report, OCAG of Bangladesh, 2001; this procedure is still followed by the PAC).

The PAC does not have any permanent office. Though the Chairman of the PAC has an office, it is not well equipped. The office does not have permanent staff. Instead, it hires staff from the Office of the CAG and the Parliament Secretariat. At present, there is no individual office room for the members of the PAC. Because of this, they feel devalued and unable to use their time and knowledge effectively. One PAC member commented: 'A permanent office is always an important thing to play a role in bridging the gap of time from one PAC to the other, which is not happening now. So, each PAC has to start from zero really'.

Interviews with PAC members revealed that working without organisational support was a problem. The Committee members store their reports and are forced to carry out the work with only very little assistance and without office space or access to reference materials. Interviews revealed that, at present, there is no systematic arrangement for the PAC to store the reports and other documents they work with. As a result, it is a challenge for PAC members to access and reference past records. Currently, there is no separate budget provision for the Committee. The Committee depends upon the Parliament Secretariat for all the budgetary and expenditure matters.

Changes in the PAC procedures and practices

Interviews with PAC members and the examination of PAC reports indicated that their procedures and practices have substantially changed since Bangladesh's independence in 1972. These changes have been around secretarial support, tripartite meetings, the implementation of recommendations, improvements to the Office of the CAG and performance audits. These changes are discussed in turn below.

Secretarial support for the PAC

Since 1997, the PAC has included a CAG Executive Officer who is able to identify the reports and issues related to the Office of the CAG to be discussed as a priority. He or she acts as a bridge between the PAC and the CAG. Initially, the Officer was seconded from the CAG's reserve post to support the PAC of the seventh Parliament. As a permanent and effective measure, the Committee requested that the CAG create a new section with at least one Grade 5 officer, two Grade 6 officers and two computer operators to ensure active PAC participation and administrative accountability (BJS, 1998b).

The third report of the fifth Parliament's PAC and the first report of the seventh Parliament's PAC drew attention to the urgent need to enhance secretarial support of the PAC to better deal with its increasing workload. Despite repeated request, the PAC of the seventh Parliament observed that no development had taken place in relation to secretarial and technological support to the Committee. Later, the first report of the eighth Parliament's PAC, in its extended thanks to the Strengthening Parliamentary Democracy Project funded by the United Nations Development Programme (UNDP) and the Financial Management Reform Programme (FMRP) under the Ministry of Finance, reiterated the need for technological support to the PAC.

Directives for tripartite meeting

There is an increasing number of audit reports waiting to be reviewed and discussed by the PAC. It is not possible to go through all the reports due to time constraints. The PAC has, however, taken steps to resolve this issue. The PAC of the seventh Parliament advised all ministerial offices to expedite the review of all audit objections and comments lodged in Parliament between 1972 and 1987 through bipartite or tripartite meetings with the audit directorates (BJS, 1998a). The outcome of the meetings was reviewed and discussed in the PAC and further instructions were given in the tenth meeting of the eighth Parliament PAC on 31 July 2004 to settle a large number of undiscussed audit observations up to 1989–1990 through bipartite and tripartite meetings and reports to the PAC within six months (BJS, 2005). At its 40th meeting, the PAC decided to extend the scope of this programme up to 1999–2000. All ministerial offices are required to give priority to this matter and apply necessary staff and other resources to processing these reports. Though this process only helps comment on reports rather than make decisions, the PAC will take final decisions on the disposal of these objections on the basis of the recommendations of the CAG.

Importance of implementation of recommendation

The PAC noted with concern that the responsible authorities were not mindful enough in implementing the recommendations and decisions of the Committee. The Committee believed that the decisions and recommendations are the formal expression of the will of the people. Therefore, the PAC of the seventh Parliament directed the concerned ministries or departments of the various government organisations to take necessary steps to implement the recommendations given in the last ten PAC reports within the following three months (BJS, 1997). The Committee formally held five meetings during its tenure to review the progress of the implementation of its recommendations. The PAC of the eighth Parliament also took a keen interest in implementing their recommendations and there was a regular follow-up agenda in the PAC meetings to see whether the executive agencies were implementing the PAC recommendations.

The PAC instructed all the ministries to provide the Committee and the Office of the CAG with a report on the implementation of the decisions and recommendations of the current and earlier PACs in the month of December every year (BJS, 2001a). Further, to review the directives for tripartite meetings, all ministries were requested to submit to the PAC and the Office of the CAG two reports on the progress of this review process in the month of April and September every year (BJS, 2001a).

Examination of the PAC reports indicated that the PAC had drawn attention to all the concerned authorities to implement their recommendations and decisions in promoting accountability and transparency in the public sector of Bangladesh. They wanted the interaction of respective actors in these processes to shape the public accountability issues. The PAC of the seventh Parliament published their reports in several languages, as they considered the reports to be of interest not only to their direct 'clients', but more broadly to the people of the Republic. One PAC member remarked: 'The PAC needs to communicate as much as possible. The more people are able to read these reports or get information from these reports, the better.'

The PAC of the seventh Parliament, in its second policy planning meeting, decided to refer the issues of non-compliance by ministries and individuals to higher bodies, such as the Cabinet and Parliament, recommending further discussions and the passing of a resolution condemning the offenders, as this seemed to operate as an important deterrent. The Chairman of the PAC of the seventh Parliament observed that the old habit of the ministries were gradually, although slowly, changing. He, however, also argued that without strong staff support, the Committee could not go much beyond a certain limit. The PAC Chairman remarked: 'Had there been provisions for better staff support, the Committee could have moved much faster.'

Improvement of the office of the CAG emphasised

The PAC of the seventh Parliament raised their concern that the Office of the CAG was structurally limited in its capacity to produce high-quality, modern audit reports. In order to receive effective and efficient audit reports, the PAC emphasised the need to improve some of the processes of the Office of the CAG.

The present organisational structure of the Audit Department is 25 years old. During the last three decades, there has been a massive change in the nature, objective and scope of audit. In many countries of the world, performance audit of government departments and organisations has been introduced in addition to financial and transaction audit. Equal importance has been placed on auditing the effective management of governments' revenue earnings, as well as on auditing governments' revenue expenditure. It was contended that the government's earnings could be greatly increased by identifying the prevalent faults and deficiencies of assessment and realisation of income tax and customs duties through this type of audit.

Members of the PAC felt that changing the structure and staff composition of the Audit Department was especially important to making audits more effective and efficient. The Committee suggested the formation of another committee comprising officials of the Finance Division, Ministry of Finance, Ministry of Establishment and Audit Department to make recommendations on structural changes to enable the Audit Department to undertake modern auditing and advise the Committee accordingly (BJS, 2001b). Further, the Committee advised the CAG to take steps to update the audit code and the audit manual of the Office of the CAG immediately and republish them.

Emphasis on performance audit

The PAC of the seventh Parliament believed that performance audit should be introduced along with the conventional audit systems now in use in the country in pursuance of worldwide modern audit systems. Specifically, in view of the large amount of development work, numerous projects and the free market economy, performance audit was very important in establishing transparency and accountability. In this context, the PAC of the seventh Parliament suggested the introduction of 'value for money' audit on a selective basis in various government organisations and projects. As a first step, it suggested that it might be introduced in one per cent of organisations annually audited by the CAG (approximately 22,000 organisations). The CAG had been requested to initiate organisational reforms as well as increase manpower, establish necessary support and logistics, and introduce human resources training and development as well as theoretical formulations. The Committee hoped that the Ministry of Finance and the Ministry of Establishment and others concerned would assist any such efforts of the CAG in developing the system of audit. The Committee confirmed they would support any legal or constitutional reforms of the audit system with appropriate recommendations of the PAC (BJS, 1998a).

The Committee was later informed that a performance audit cell had been created in the Office of the CAG and some performance audits were occurring in selected organisations. The Committee believed that this audit activity could not be continued or expanded with the existing auditors of the Office of the CAG. Performance audit is a complex, laborious and research-intensive activity. It is essential to involve executive officers. The Committee, therefore, requested the CAG to take necessary measures to create a performance audit directorate within the organisational structure of the Office of the CAG. The Committee also expected the Ministry of Finance and Ministry of Establishment to give priority to this matter by providing necessary assistance (BJS, 2001b).

Interviews with PAC members and examination of PAC reports indicated that the PAC had always been concerned about improving management practices and had given a number of directives and recommendations to ensure effective management practices in the public sector of Bangladesh.

Factors influencing the PAC's operations

The importance of the PAC stems from the fact that it is the most powerful parliamentary committee, as it is entrusted with the responsibility of overseeing the operation of public offices, and its creation is espoused by the Constitution. The CAG's audit is the mechanism through which such responsibility is normally discharged. As stated before, the Office of the CAG is empowered by the Constitution to prepare audit reports on all public offices, and these reports are formally referred to the PAC for review, scrutiny and final decisions. The PAC has powers to resolve all disputes of the Office of the CAG, on the standing audit objections raised by the CAG, about the government's executive agencies.

Close examination of interview data, the minutes of meetings and PAC rules reveal that the PAC and the CAG have a strong constitutional foundation and are closely linked in their important role in ensuring government accountability. Further, historical decisions and events have reinforced this interdependency (Jacobs *et al.*, 2007; McGee, 2002). The CAG carries out audits according to Article 128(1) of the Constitution of the People's Republic of Bangladesh and prepares and submits audit reports to Parliament that are acted upon by the PAC. The working of the PAC is dependent on the results of the audit and examination of the government's accounts carried out by the CAG. Though the CAG's audit is a legislative audit, unlike the PAC, it is not part of the Parliament. The CAG is the producer of audit reports, whereas the PAC is the principal user of those reports on behalf of the government. The PAC gives the overall guidelines and the Office of the CAG implements them and plans their activities according to PAC's suggestions. Although this relationship has not been formalised, one PAC member stated during an interview that 'There is a constant interaction because of the personal relationship between the CAG and the PAC, things do improve and have improved in the past. This is a continuous process.'

The Office of the CAG provides a range of support to strengthen the PAC's activities. For example, the Office of the CAG provided a mid-level officer (Additional Deputy CAG) to provide secretarial service to the PAC and help the Committee address technical issues. Staff from audit directorates also attend meetings to assist the CAG and the PAC. The PAC, in preparing to discuss reports, makes a number of recommendations, such as revisiting the auditees and re-verifying the audit paragraphs objections. Members of the PAC then sit with ministerial staff and the secretaries to identify people directly involved in mal-practice and discuss how to resolve matters amicably. The Office of the CAG implements these recommendations. Moreover, the Office of the CAG immedi-ately forms audit teams through its directorates and responds accordingly when the PAC recommends that certain kinds of audit should be done or certain insti-tutions should be audited in a particular way.

The PAC authorises the CAG to recommend the settlement of audit observa-tions after examining the relevant documents. The Office of the CAG follows the PAC's instructions as to which organisation to audit, but the Office has not yet put in place systems to discuss the plans or methods to be followed in audit-ing with the PAC. The PAC supports the Office of the CAG in their plans or requests for change. For instance, when the Office of the CAG required technical support for specific audits, the PAC took their request to the Minister of Finance.

The PAC formed sub-committees to conduct additional in-depth scrutiny on selected important issues and observations highlighted in the CAG's audit reports. The PAC of the eighth Parliament comprised ten sub-committees that dealt with observations pertaining to several ministries. These sub-committees often went on site visits to solve problems where they occurred and submitted their reports to the main committees. The Committee discussed sub-committees' reports along with their findings and recommendations. In many cases the Com-mittee summoned the accused persons before the Committee meeting for the hearings.

Since the PAC and the CAG are collectively responsible for conducting post-expenditure review of the public sector in Bangladesh, they need to work closely together to ensure that all activities of the government serve, protect and advance public interest. The existence of an effective relationship between the PAC and the CAG is vital as the accountability and transparency regime is absolutely dependent on it. Further, this is essential to a good democratic system.

Conclusion

The evidence discussed in this chapter suggests that the PAC has gradually shifted from an accounting focus to a policy focus. This is consistent with the views of Degeling *et al.* (1996) and Jacobs and Jones (2009). The above evidence suggests that the PAC has taken initiatives to support NPM ideals in promoting accountability and transparency in the public sector of Bangladesh (Hood, 1991, 1995). This is consistent with the view of Guthrie and Parker (1998: 55), who noted that the House of Representatives Standing Committee on Finance and Public Administration (HRSCPP) supported the introduction of private sector management and accountability systems in the public sector as a way of promoting efficiency of resource usage and the effectiveness of achieving organisational objectives.

There is clear evidence, particularly after Bangladesh's second phase of democratisation in 1991, that most chairmen are willing to spend more time than their predecessors in committee-related activities. However, their ability to work is largely constrained by practical problems, as committees in Bangladesh are less resourced and less informed than their counterparts, even in neighbouring countries. Without some kind of permanent, professional and expert assistance and institutional arrangements it will be difficult for committees to do what is expected of them (Spann, 1979). The limited amount of staff and other support currently available to committees in Bangladesh does not encourage the chairmen of the PAC and members to play a major proactive role.

In this chapter, we have argued that a set of role prescriptions does not guarantee their performance. They may be called into play more for their symbolic effect than for the rationales that lie behind them. The performance of a set of role prescriptions in the case of the PAC depends on the extent to which they are mobilised by organisational actors who have standing and power and find it in their interests to do so (Degeling *et al.*, 1996). The significance of the findings of this study is that the role of the PAC can be improved to better look into public accountability issues with the right kind of staff and support.

With this chapter, we have highlighted the importance of delegating authority. We argue that this would help save time and allow the PAC to discuss more recent audit reports. This chapter has also documented the importance of review and monitoring to achieve the desired results. The PAC case demonstrates that the PAC has formally held a number of review meetings to assess the status of implementation of decisions taken, which has, to some extent, changed the traditional practices of ministries unresponsive to requests to settle audit objections. This case has also highlighted the importance of communication in achieving the desired outcome. The PAC reports indicates that the PAC has drawn attention to all the concerned authorities to implement their recommendations and decisions in promoting accountability and transparency in the public sector of Bangladesh and has sought to interact with relevant actors in these processes to shape the public accountability practices.

Our findings revealed significant developments in internal governance structures, administrative and accountability practices in the Committee during the period between 1996 and 2006. These developments were predominantly driven by public sector reform policies – which changed the socio-political environments of the country – and external forces – namely donor agencies and international public sector training providers. Further, the findings of this study demonstrate the role of a country-specific changing socio-political environment in the form and operation of a government parliamentary accounting entity (Khan and Hoque, 2012).

Notes

1 This chapter uses 'the Committee' and 'the PAC' interchangeably, and the same with 'Office' and 'CAG' (Comptroller and Auditor-General).
2 The dictators took the title 'President' rather than the Washington system.

References

BJS (1997) *First Report of the Public Accounts Committee of the Seventh JS*, Parliament Secretariat, July, Dhaka.

BJS (1998a) *Second Report of the Public Accounts Committee of the Seventh JS*, Parliament Secretariat, March, Dhaka.

BJS (1998b) *Third Report of the Public Accounts Committee of the Seventh JS*, Parliament Secretariat, November, Dhaka.

BJS (2001a) *Fourth Report of the Public Accounts Committee of the Seventh JS*, Parliament Secretariat, January, Dhaka.

BJS (2001b) *Fifth Report of the Public Accounts Committee of the Seventh JS*, Parliament Secretariat, July, Dhaka.

BJS (2005) *First Report of the Public Accounts Committee of the Eighth JS*, Parliament Secretariat, Dhaka.

CAG (1997) *Annual Report*, Office of the Comptroller and Auditor-General of Bangladesh, Dhaka.

CAG (1998) *Annual Report*, Office of the Comptroller and Auditor-General of Bangladesh, Dhaka.

CAG (1999) *Annual Report*, Office of the Comptroller and Auditor-General of Bangladesh, Dhaka.

CAG (2000) *Annual Report*, Office of the Comptroller and Auditor-General of Bangladesh, Dhaka.

CAG (2001) *Annual Report*, Office of the Comptroller and Auditor-General of Bangladesh, Dhaka.

CAG (2002) *Annual Report*, Office of the Comptroller and Auditor-General of Bangladesh, Dhaka.

CAG (2003) *Annual Report*, Office of the Comptroller and Auditor-General of Bangladesh, Dhaka.

CAG (2004) *Annual Report*, Office of the Comptroller and Auditor-General of Bangladesh, Dhaka.

CAG (2005) *Annual Report*, Office of the Comptroller and Auditor-General of Bangladesh, Dhaka.

CAG (2006) *Annual Report*, Office of the Comptroller and Auditor-General of Bangladesh, Dhaka.

Constitution (1972) *Constitution of the People's Republic of Bangladesh* (updated up to 1998), Ministry of Law, Justice and Parliamentary Affairs, Government of Bangladesh.

Degeling, P., Anderson, J. and Guthrie, J. (1996) 'Accounting for Public Accounts Committees', *Accounting, Auditing and Accountability Journal*, 9(2): 30–49.

DiMaggio, P. J. and Powell, W. W. (1983) 'The Iron Cage Revisited: Institutional Isomorphism and Collective Rationality in Organizational Fields', *American Sociological Review*, 48(2): 147–60.

Funnell, W. and Cooper, K. (1998) *Public Sector Accounting and Accountability in Australia*, Sydney: University of New South Wales Press.

Groot, T. and Budding, T. (2008) 'New Public Management's Current Issues and Future Prospects', *Financial Accountability and Management*, 24(1): 1–13.

Guthrie, J. and Parker, L. (1998) 'Recent public sector financial management change in Australia', in O. Olson, J. Guthrie and C. Humphrey (eds) *Global Warming! Debating International Development in New Public Financial Management*, Oslo: Cappelen Akademisk Forlag, pp. 49–75.

Hood, C. (1991) 'A Public Management for all Seasons?' *Public Administration*, 69(1): 3–19.

Hood, C. (1995) 'The 'New Public Management' in the 1980s: Variations on a Theme', *Accounting, Organizations and Society*, 20(2/3): 93–109.

Hossain, S. Y. (2002) 'Reforms Initiatives in the Bangladesh Office of the Comptroller and Auditor General', *International Journal of Government Auditing*, 29(2): 14–23.

Jacobs, K. and Jones, K. (2009) 'Legitimacy and parliamentary oversight in Australia: The rise and fall of two public accounts committees', *Accounting, Auditing and Accountability Journal*, 22(1): 13–34.

Jacobs, K., Jones, K. and Smith, D. (2007) 'Public Accounts Committees in Australasia: The state of play', *Australian Parliamentary Review*, 22(1): 28–43.

Khan, S. H. and Hoque, Z. (2012) 'The role of a public accounts committee in promoting public sector accountability and performance: a case study', paper presented at the European Accounting Association Annual Congress, University of Ljubljana, 8–11 May 2012.

Lapsley, I. (2008) 'The NPM Agenda: Back to the Future', *Financial Accountability and Management*, 24(1): 77–96.

Lee, J. (2008) 'Preparing Performance Information in the Public Sector: An Australian Perspective', *Financial Accountability and Management*, 24(2): 117–49.

McGee, D. (2002) *The Overseers: Public Accounts Committees and Public Spending*, London: Pluto Press.

Meyer, J. W. and Rowan, B. (1977) 'Institutionalized Organizations: Formal Structure as Myth and Ceremony', *American Journal of Sociology*, 83(2): 340–63.

Scott, W. R. (1991) 'Unpacking Institutional Arguments', in W. W. Powell and P. J. DiMaggio (eds) *The New Institutionalism in Organizational Analysis*, Chicago: The University of Chicago Press, pp. 164–82.

Scott, W. R. and Meyer, J. W. (1991) 'The Organization of Societal Sectors: Proposition and Early Evidence' in . W. Powell and P. J. DiMaggio (eds) *The New Institutionalism in Organizational Analysis*, Chicago: The University of Chicago Press, pp. 108–42.

Spann, R. N. (1979), *Government Administration in Australia*, Sydney: George Allen and Unwin.

Stone, B. (1995) 'Administrative Accountability in the Westminster Democracies: Towards a New Conceptual Framework', *Governance: An International Journal of Policy, Administration and Institutions*, 8(4): 505–26.

Wehner, J. (2003) 'Principles and Patterns of Financial Scrutiny: Public Accounts Committees in the Commonwealth', *Commonwealth and Comparative Politics*, 41(3): 21–36.

12 The role of the Public Accounts Committee in enhancing government accountability in Malaysia

Zakiah Saleh and Haslida Abu Hasan

Introduction

There has been an increase, over time, in the public demand for government transparency and accountability. Haque (1994) wrote that accountability is crucial to safeguarding the public sector's image of serving the public interest. McGee and Gaventa (2010: 5) wrote that the field of government transparency and accountability is 'alive with rapidly emerging citizen-led and multistakeholder initiatives'. The International Federation of Accountants (IFAC) also published a policy paper urging governments to implement institutional arrangements necessary for the enhancement of public sector financial management transparency and accountability (IFAC, 2012). The Malaysian government has been very responsive to the increasing demand for greater government accountability and transparency. In 1998, the government implemented the Prime Minister's Directive No. 1, aimed at enhancing the integrity of management in government administration (Ahmad Badawi, 2004). The National Integrity Plan (NIP) and the Malaysian Institute of Integrity were launched in 2004 by then Prime Minister Abdullah Haji Ahmad Badawi to further realise Vision 2020's goal of creating an ethical and moral society. In 2009, Prime Minister Najib Abdul Razak introduced Ministerial Key Performance Indicators (MKPIs) focused on delivering results in the effort to enhance government accountability. Subsequently, in 2010, the Prime Minister formally announced the Government Transformation Programme (GTP). The GTP covers an initial six national key results areas (NKRAs), including an initiative to fight corruption (PEMANDU, 2010). The NKRAs were identified based on the evaluation of demands from the public obtained through surveys of citizens.

Administratively, the two main institutions responsible for public finance accountability in Malaysia are the National Audit Department (NAD) and the Public Accounts Committee (PAC). This chapter aims to introduce the PAC and its role in ensuring the accountability of Malaysia's federal government. In Malaysia, PACs are established by both federal and state governments. At the federal level, the PAC is established as a committee under Parliament, while at the state level, the PAC is established by the state's legislative assembly. Since more than 80 per cent of public revenue is collected by the federal government, the emphasis on accountability should be applied more on the federal government relative to other levels of government. Thus, the discussions in this chapter focus on the PAC at the federal level.

This chapter provides a description of the role, responsibility, authority, functions and performance of Malaysia's federal PAC. Published studies on PACs are referenced to provide a more complete understanding of their roles. Several studies conducted in various countries have assessed performance in terms of the factors that determine the efficiency and effectiveness of PACs. These include McGee (2002), Stapenhurst *et al.* (2005), Stapenhurst and Kroon (2011), Pelizzo (2011) and Makhado *et al.* (2012). McGee (2002) concluded that there are two important elements in a public accountability system: the office of the Auditor-General, and a parliamentary oversight committee (referred to as the PAC). Stapenhurst *et al.* (2005) extended the McGee (2002) study and identified 17 attributes of an ideal PAC that they believed deliver both efficiency and effectiveness. This chapter, in particular, uses the attributes developed by Stapenhurst *et al.* (2005) to assess whether Malaysia's federal PAC can be considered ideal or otherwise.

The remainder of this chapter is organised into five sections. The next section explains the context in which the PAC operates. Section 3 describes the methodology used to gather information about Malaysia's federal PAC. It is followed by findings and discussions in Section 4. Section 5 ends the chapter with a conclusion.

Context and background

This section starts with a brief description of Malaysia's government structure under the provisions of the Federal Constitution, followed by a discussion on the institutional arrangements related to ensuring government accountability. Malaysia is a member of the Commonwealth Association and gained its independence from the United Kingdom in 1957. Politically, Malaysia is a constitutional monarchy with an elected Parliament. The Malaysian public sector was established in accordance with the Federal Constitution, which established three tiers of government: federal, state and local governments. The federal government controls external affairs, defence, internal security, civil and criminal law, citizenship, finance, commerce and industry, shipping, education, health and labour. The Cabinet, headed by the Prime Minister, is the highest coordinating executive body of all government activities and interests. The Cabinet is collectively responsible to Parliament. Adopting the Westminster bicameral parliamentary system, Malaysia's Parliament consists of two houses: the Senate (upper house) and the House of Representatives (lower house). Article 43(2)(a) of the Constitution stipulates that the Prime Minister is appointed from members of the House of Representatives (Laws of Malaysia, 2010).

Unicameral systems exist at the state level, where an Executive Council headed by a Chief Minister is the highest coordinating body for state matters. The Council is responsible to the state's legislative assembly. The state secretariat and other state/central government departments assist the Executive Council in the administration of the state's affairs. Each of the states has its own constitution, which must be compatible with the Federal Constitution. Local governments, often referred to as local authorities, have been established under the jurisdiction of the state governments. Local authorities are primarily concerned with the environment, including providing services such as street cleaning, the collection and disposal of solid waste and sewage; the provision of public amenities such as parks and markets; and public health, including the licensing of hawkers and shops.

The significant role played by the public sector in the Malaysian economy can be determined by examining government expenditures as a percentage of gross domestic products (GDP). The 2013 public sector accounts reported consolidated operating expenditures of RM211.3 billion, representing almost 22 per cent of that year's GDP. The general government's development expenditures were reported to be RM42.2 billion, representing 4 per cent of GDP. Over the years, the government's total operating and development expenditures have remained at almost 25 per cent of GDP. In terms of employment, the expenditure on emoluments for the federal government's 1.4 million civil servants accounted for 28.5 per cent of operating expenditures (Ministry of Finance, 2014). The allocation of resources between governments in Malaysia is very centralised. The federal government accounts for around 83 per cent of the country's total public revenue. In terms of operating expenditures, the federal government spends a significantly larger amount that is slightly more than 90 per cent of the total general government operating expenditure (Ministry of Finance, 2014).

The Federal Constitution sets out the rules regarding financial provisions under Articles 96 to 112. The government must table an annual budget for approval by Parliament. Following is a summary of financial provisions contained in the Constitution:

1   There can be no taxation or loans without the consent of Parliament.
2   Consolidated fund: all public moneys must be put in one consolidated fund.
3   Parliamentary appropriation: no payment can be issued out of the consolidated fund except as authorised by Parliament.
4   Annual budgets must be tabled in and approved by Parliament.
5   Annual accounts must be prepared and audited, to be tabled and passed by Parliament.

The above discussions show the importance of parliamentary controls. Parliament enacts, repeals and amends laws related to financial matters. It controls expenditures through budgeting, and it requires the Accountant General's Department (AGD) to table annual financial reports in Parliament. These reports must be audited by an oversight body, which is the NAD. In addition, Parliament has established the PAC to ensure accountability. The administrative arrangements related to accountability are discussed next.

Administrative arrangements for accountability

The use of money by the public sector starts from the preparation of the budget at the Treasury, approval of the budget by Parliament, allocation of resources through central agencies to the various departments and agencies and the preparation of accounts. The accounts, prepared by the AGD, are audited by the Auditor-General. These audited accounts, are tabled together with the Auditor-General's report in Parliament. The Auditor-General will also brief the PAC on issues arising from his report. The federal government's accountability framework is shown in Figure 12.1.

The Accountant General's Department (AGD)

The AGD is a department under Malaysia's Ministry of Finance (MOF). It was set up in 1947, at which time the first Accountant General was appointed. In order to facilitate the control of financial transactions and ensure efficient and timely services (including the preparation of accounts), the AGD has 25 branches located throughout the country. As described in Section 3 of the Treasury Instructions (TI),[1] the Accountant General is the federal government's principal accountant, with authority over any issues related to accounting and the accounts of both the federal and state governments (Laws of Malaysia, 2008). One of the functions of the AGD is to prepare the financial statements of the federal government. In addition, the

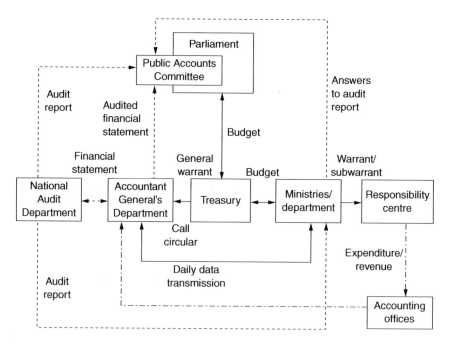

Figure 12.1 Financial accountability in Malaysia's Federal Government (source: prepared by the authors based on Saleh (2002)).

AGD also ensures that in preparing the financial statements of the state governments, the state treasurers or accountants comply with the regulations and provisions of the same constitution and legislation that apply to the federal government. The AGD manages accounting personnel for the government sector, including the appointment of state treasurers and accountants. They are, in turn, accountable to the Accountant General (Saleh, 2002).

The most recent development related to the AGD is the decision to move to accrual accounting. The decision was made in 2010, when accrual accounting was identified as one of the policy measures for public sector transformation. The new accounting system is expected to improve financial management – asset-liability management in particular – and subsequently enhance government accountability (Saleh, 2013). In the implementation of accrual accounting, the government has decided to adopt the International Public Sector Accounting Standards (IPSAS) and modify them to suit the Malaysian environment.

The National Audit Department (NAD)

The British administration set up the Auditor-General's institution in the early nineteenth century to strengthen government financial administration. The audit function mainly involves the certification of accounts and the maintenance of records (NAD, 2014b). After Malaysia's independence, the institution was renamed the National Audit Department. The NAD is responsible for ensuring accountability in the administration and management of public funds through the audit of the accounts and activities of the federal government, state governments, statutory bodies, local authorities, Islamic religious councils and other public entities. This is stated in Article 106 of the Constitution, and in Section 1 of the Audit Act 1957 (Revised 1972) (Laws of Malaysia, 2006a).

The Head of the NAD is the Auditor-General, who is appointed by the *Yang di-Pertuan Agong* (the ruler) in accordance with Article 105 of the Federal Constitution, which specifies:

1   There shall be an Auditor-General, who shall be appointed by the *Yang di-Pertuan Agong* on the advice of the Prime Minister, and after consultation with the Conference of Rulers.
2   A person who has held the office of Auditor-General shall be eligible for re-appointment, but shall not be eligible for any other appointment in the service of the Federation or for any appointment in the service of a state.
3   The Auditor-General may resign his office at any time but shall not be removed from office except on like grounds and in a like manner as a judge of the Federal Court.

The independence of the Auditor-General is ensured through the provisions of the Federal Constitution and the Audit Act 1957 (Revised 1972). The Auditor-General is appointed by the *Yang di-Pertuan Agong* and reports directly to

Parliament. Article 106 of the Constitution specifies the powers and duties of the Auditor-General as follows:

1   The accounts of the Federation and of the States shall be audited and reported on by the Auditor-General.
2   The Auditor-General shall perform such other duties and exercise such powers in relation to the accounts of the Federation and of the States and to the accounts of other public authorities and of those bodies which are specified by order made by the *Yang di-Pertuan Agong*, as may be provided by federal law.

Upon the completion of his audit of the financial statements of the federal and state governments, the Auditor-General must submit an audit report as specified in Article 107 of the Constitution:

1   The Auditor-General shall submit his reports to the *Yang di-Pertuan Agong*, who shall cause them to be laid before the House of Representatives.
2   A copy of any such report relating to the accounts of a State or to the accounts of any public authority exercising powers conferred by the State law, shall be submitted to the Ruler or *Yang di-Pertua Negeri* of that State, who shall cause it to be laid before the Legislative Assembly.

The scope of government auditing includes attestation, compliance and performance audits. The nature of an audit is specified in Section 6 of the Audit Act 1957, which states that the Auditor-General must ascertain:

1   whether all reasonable precautions have been taken to safeguard the collection and custody of public moneys or other moneys subject to his audit;
2   whether issues and payments of moneys subject to his audit were made in accordance with proper authority and payments were properly chargeable and are supported by sufficient vouchers or proof of payment;
3   whether due care has been taken to account for and to ensure proper use, control, maintenance and disposal of all public stores or other stores subject to his audit;
4   whether all accounts and other records have been and are properly and faithfully maintained;
5   whether in his opinion moneys have been applied to the purposes for which they were appropriated or authorised and the activities related to such purposes were carried out or managed in an efficient manner with due regard for economy and the avoidance of waste or extravagance;
6   whether the provisions of the Federal Constitution and the Financial

Procedure Act 1957, and any other written law relating to moneys or stores subject to his audit have been in all respects complied with.

It is noted that the Act does not refer to auditing standards. However, as a member of the International Organisation of Supreme Audit Institutions (INTOSAI), the NAD has adopted the International Standards of Supreme Audit Institutions (ISSAI 1000–1999) in performing its audit functions (NAD, 2014b).

Several initiatives have been undertaken by the Auditor-General and the NAD to enhance accountability. In 2008, the Auditor-General introduced the financial management accountability index (FMAI). The index ranks financial management practices of ministries, departments and agencies and should serve as a benchmark for self-improvement (Abu Bakar and Ismail, 2011). The Auditor-General tables two types of report: the AG's report on the financial statements and financial management, and the AG's report on the activities of the ministries, departments and agencies of the federal and state governments. As recommended by the GTP, the Auditor-General tabled his report on activities in a three-part series starting from 2013, and tables it as and when Parliament meets (NAD, 2014b). This allows for speedier follow-up on issues raised by the audit. The relevant ministry is expected to issue a feedback report containing its comments and outlining action taken on the issues raised by the auditor. Another NAD initiative to ensure accountability is the Accountant General's Dashboard. The Dashboard is an online monitoring channel that oversees and reports on the actions taken by government agencies on the audit report (Arukesamy, 2013). The above initiatives were hoped to enhance the transparency and accountability of the government.

Public Accounts Committee (PAC)

As a committee of Parliament, the PAC works closely with the NAD. It examines public accounts and responds to the Auditor-General's reports on issues involving the misappropriation of public funds, and government inefficiency and/or ineffectiveness. Detailed information on the PAC, including its establishment, membership, powers and functions is provided in the fourth section of this chapter. The Committee is identified here, however, in order to emphasise its role in the management of public sector finance. The next section briefly explains the methodology used to gather information about the PAC.

Methodology

The objective of this chapter is to describe the roles, responsibilities and performance of Malaysia's federal PAC. A pragmatic approach to data collection was used whereby the author did what was necessary to arrive at the objective of describing the PAC's roles and effectiveness. Data in this chapter were gathered through archival searches of government pronouncements, circulars, reports and articles. Documents collected for the purpose of this chapter came from several websites, including the PAC website (www.parlimen.gov.my/pac) and the NAD website (www.audit.gov.my). The PAC website provides official reports sum-marising its investigations and conclusions with respect to highlighted cases, as well as news related to issues and PAC action. The NAD's website supplies information on the audit reports it has issued, and highlights controversial areas in their investigations. The discussion concerning the roles and performance of the PAC in Malaysia is descriptive. A focus group discussion was held with parliamentary officers with responsibility for attending to the needs of the PAC. The discussion was conducted to confirm the information obtained from the archival searches and to gain insight into the roles and functions of the PAC.

The focus group discussion involved three parliamentary officers attached to the PAC. These officers hold responsibility for maintaining documents, arranging for PAC meetings, investigations and hearings, coordinating PAC investigations accord-ing to the available expertise in various government agencies (particularly the NAD), as well as recording and maintaining reports of activities undertaken. A list of ques-tions was emailed to the respondents prior to the discussion session so they could prepare beforehand. The questions prepared were based on the results of the archival search performed earlier. During the discussion, respondents were allowed to speak freely about their experiences and were prompted for additional information. The information obtained from the archival searches and focus group discussion was then analysed descriptively to generate the information presented in this chapter.

The effectiveness of Malaysia's PAC was examined using the attributes sug-gested by Stapenhurst *et al.* (2005), as the authors claimed that the attributes contribute to an ideal PAC. Stapenhurst *et al.* (2005) analysed data collected from 51 national and state/provincial parliaments in Commonwealth countries in Asia, Australasia, Canada and the United Kingdom. The 17 attributes of an 'ideal committee' were introduced based on their findings. The attributes cover two sets of factors deemed of great importance to understanding how the capa-city of PACs can be built. The two sets of factors are (i) institutional design of the PAC, and (ii) PAC functions and member behaviour. Institutional design includes the features, characteristics, power and mandate of the PAC, while PAC functions and member behaviour are best practices. The study also identified the following institutional factors that largely account for the success of the PAC: the focus on the government's financial activities rather than its policies, the power to investigate all past and present government expenses, the power to follow up on government action in response to its recommendations, and the Committee's relationship with the Auditor-General. Best practices associated with PAC members include that members must act in a non-partisan fashion and should try to have a good working relationship with each other, and that the PAC should always strive to achieve consensus among its members.

Findings and discussion

This section includes a description and discussion of Malaysia's federal PAC, and an assessment of the PAC using the attributes of an ideal committee defined by Stapenhurst *et al.* (2005).

Malaysia's Public Accounts Committee

The description and discussion of Malaysia's federal PAC is organised as follows: (1) authority and structure, (2) relationship and resources, (3) power, roles and practices, (4) meetings, reporting and follow-up, and (5) examples of cases investigated by the PAC.

Authority and structure

Malaysia's federal PAC is formed immediately after the beginning of each Parliament. The present Parliament, the 13th, began in July 2013. It also marked the appointment of PAC members who will hold office until 2018. The establishment of the PAC dates back to the first Parliament in 1959, although its role became prevalent only in the twenty-first century. The House of Representatives has five select committees, one of which is the PAC. Members of the PAC are selected from representatives in the House by another committee called the Committee of Selection. The Committee of Selection, comprised of the Deputy Prime Minister and the leaders of all main political parties with members in the House, selects members and forwards the names of its candidates to the Chairman of the House of Representatives. Members are selected based on their expertise and their ability to ensure the effectiveness of the PAC. In addition, the Committee of Selection works to ensure fair representation from both the government and the opposition. However, the appointment of the PAC's Chairman and Deputy is made through a motion brought by the Prime Minister and debated in the House of Representatives.

The regulations governing the PAC stipulate that it must consist of between six and 12 members, excluding the chair and deputy chair. The PAC, including the Committee appointed by the 13th Parliament, has always consisted of the maximum number of members. Although there is no specific requirement regarding which representatives may serve on the PAC, government ministers are not allowed to be selected. There is also no specific requirement in terms of the appointment of the Chairman of the Committee. The appointment is determined through the approval of the House, and the position could be occupied by a member from either the government or the opposition. However, by convention, the Chairman's position has gone to a member from the government while the Deputy Chairman has always been a member of the opposition. If the Chairman and Deputy Chairman are absent from a Committee meeting, the remaining Committee members shall elect any one member from among the remaining Committee members to act as a Chairman to preside over that meeting only. Even in this situation, a minister is still not allowed to be nominated or appointed to, or to act as a member or Chairman of the PAC.

The current PAC is composed of nine members from the government and five from the opposition. This reflects the composition of the House, where the majority of representatives are from the government. However, the 9 : 5 ratio has always been used, even when there were fewer opposition representatives in

previous parliaments. This adds to the credibility of the PAC's reports and conclusions and explains why PAC reports have rarely been challenged and have
been used as reference points for debates in Parliament. The PAC obtains its
authority and power through Parliament, and all rules regarding meetings,
reports and procedures that apply to Parliament also apply to the PAC. The PAC
shares facilities and resources, including human resources, with Parliament. At
present, only one full-time administrative staff member is dedicated solely to the
PAC, while other officers are shared with other offices of Parliament.

Relationship and resources

As indicated earlier, the financial accountability function of Parliament rests
with two institutions: the PAC and the NAD. Thus, this explains the close
cooperation between the PAC and the NAD. The PAC relies on the Auditor-
General's reports in initiating investigations of misconduct. The Auditor-General
is independent of the Cabinet and the PAC, thus the PAC cannot override the
Auditor-General's directives to staff within the NAD. The PAC maintains a
formal relationship with the NAD but it can utilise the NAD's staff and expertise
for its investigation and reporting tasks, as the PAC has only one full-time
administrative staff member of its own. For other tasks, the PAC has the authority to mobilise additional NAD staff. Besides the authority to utilise NAD staff,
the PAC also has power to summon government bodies and agencies to supply
them with information and assistance. Parliamentary staff and officers can also
be called upon to assist the PAC in its work, with regard to the arrangement of
meetings, investigations and related tasks.

In 1992, the Parliamentary Services Act 1963 (Act 394) was repealed by the
Constitution (Amendments) Act 1992 (Act A837). This abolished the PAC's
right to a financial allocation and control over its finances. Thus, at the present
time, the PAC has no control over its budget or of any funds allocated to it. The
position of the PAC as one of Parliament's select committees allows it to use
parliamentary resources, as well as the resources of other government agencies.
The members of the PAC are not entitled to any emoluments.

Power, roles and practices

The PAC obtains its authority and power through the constitutional provisions
enacted for Parliament. These provisions are called the *Peraturan-Peraturan
Majlis Mesyuarat Dewan Rakyat* (Standing Orders of the *Dewan Rakyat* of
Malaysia), and they provide the rules for the House of Representatives. The rules
were created by the House based on Part 62(1) of the Federal Constitution,
Section 77(1) Standing Orders (Parliament of Malaysia, no date), which outlines
the roles and responsibilities of the PAC, authorises it to inspect:

1   the accounts of the Federation and the appropriation of the sums granted by
     Parliament to meet the public expenditure;

2   such accounts of public authorities and other bodies administering public
     funds as may be laid before the House;
3   reports of the Auditor-General laid before the House in accordance with
     Article 107 of the Constitution; and
4   such other matters as the Committee may think fit, or that may be referred to
     the Committee by the House.

Based on the provisions of the Standing Orders, the PAC is responsible for
ascertaining that government ministries, departments and agencies ensure that:

1   all public moneys are accurately accounted for;
2   all payments are made based on approved legislation, have been correctly
     charged and are supported;
3   all assets are used, controlled and disposed of in accordance with specified
     rules;
4   all accounts and records have been correctly and accurately maintained; and
5   public moneys have been used according to approved provisions.

In fulfilling its responsibilities, and as one of Parliament's select committees, the
PAC has the power to summon witnesses and demand documents and information necessary for its investigations. It is an offence for an individual who has
been summoned by the PAC to be absent or to fail to supply relevant
information.

The PAC has the authority to comment on the implementation of any programmes or activities by government ministries, departments and agencies, with
respect to whether the initiatives are beneficial and achieving their intended
objectives. The PAC also has the power to provide advice on the use of public
funds, particularly when it suspects waste or excessive spending. The comments
and input provided by the PAC have always been used when the government
drafts its development plans and prepares a new budget.

The Auditor-General presents an audit report to Parliament three times a year.
Immediately after tabling the audit report in the House of Representatives, the
Auditor-General will brief the PAC on his findings. The PAC will then respond
to the Auditor-General's findings by mobilising the NAD, as well as the AGD's
staff, to assist in its investigation. The parliamentary officers attached to the PAC
will help to coordinate resources to meet the PAC's needs. This may involve,
among other things, arranging meetings of PAC members and summoning individuals to attend questioning sessions. The PAC also has the capacity to summon
any individual, officer or department to assist in its investigation.

Approximately 80 per cent of PAC investigations are based on the Auditor-
General's reports. The PAC also initiates enquiries and investigations that it
deems necessary to examine issues highlighted by various parties. Some of the
issues not in the Auditor-General's reports that the PAC has investigated in
recent years include reports dealing with the Port Klang Free Zone (PKFZ),
missing jet engines belonging to the air force and the collapse of a stadium. The

PAC's investigations extend beyond those related to financial issues and include performance reviews involving government ministries, departments and agencies. Nevertheless, the PAC is always careful to limit its investigations to the use of government and public money. There are instances where highlighted issues involve public listed companies; in such cases, the PAC has to draw the line between examining the use of public and private sector funds. In cases involving the private sector, the PAC would investigate through the central bank, Bank Negara Malaysia.

The PAC is obligated to report directly to the legislature. After the PAC is satisfied with its investigation and a consensus is reached by its members, a report will be submitted to the House of Representatives with recommendations for further action. However, the PAC can only make recommendations for follow-up by the relevant authorities. Its report also serves as a reference point for debate in Parliament.

Meetings, reporting and follow-up

It is compulsory for the PAC to meet after the Auditor-General presents an audit report. Subsequent to a briefing provided by the Auditor-General, the PAC will determine the issues raised by the report and the need for additional meetings. In addition, the PAC also meets when issues are raised either in Parliament or by the public. The Committee has been quite active, recording at least one PAC meeting every month. In 2009, the PAC recorded a record high of 40 meetings over the course of the year.

Prior to a full meeting of the PAC, a Pre-Council meeting will be held. The Pre-Council consists of the PAC's Chairman, Deputy Chairman and Secretary, together with the Auditor-General. The focus of the Pre-Council meeting is on issues highlighted in the Auditor-General's report. The Auditor-General will explain the issues and provide recommendations on relevant questions to ask the responsible officers during the PAC's investigations. The Auditor-General's involvement does not stop at the Pre-Council meeting: he also attends the full PAC meeting and may be requested to provide additional information when necessary. A PAC meeting includes all 14 committee members, representatives from the NAD, AGD, MOF, Economic Planning Unit (EPU) and the Public Service Department. The responsible officers from the respective ministries, departments and agencies will be called upon to explain the weaknesses or issues raised in the Auditor-General's report, and any remedial action their organisations have taken to address them. In the event that the PAC is not satisfied with an explanation provided, the PAC's Chairman can request further confirmation and suggestions from the Auditor-General.

It is compulsory for responsible officers to attend and respond at meetings and hearings when the PAC summons them. If a responsible officer fails to attend without providing a reasonable explanation, the PAC could choose to:

1   refuse to accept the submission of the representatives brought forward for investigation;

2   summon the official to provide a proper explanation of the inability to be present at the hearing; or
3   set another date for re-investigation of the respective officer.

The meetings, investigations and hearings of the PAC involve only Committee members and relevant individuals. As such, the meetings are closed to the public. All meetings, discussions and investigations are recorded verbatim; drafts of the transcripts of proceedings are reviewed and confirmed by the relevant parties before they are printed. After the end of a meeting, the PAC will prepare a PAC Meeting Report with the cooperation of the NAD. The Report will contain the issues raised, their cause, details of the investigation, explanations from the responsible officers under investigation, and the Committee's comments, recommendations, and decisions. The PAC's power extends to suggesting action to be taken by certain individuals, and government ministries, departments and agencies. The Report will then be presented to the House of Representatives. The PAC's reports are not debated in the House, as it is presumed that the content was properly deliberated during PAC meetings, which include a fair representation of members from the government and the opposition. Documentation and reports relating to ongoing investigations are not made available to the public; the public can only access summarised reports after an investigation has been concluded and closed.

Paragraph 304(b) of the Treasury Instructions stipulates that the following actions shall be taken after a PAC Meeting Report has been tabled in Parliament (House of Representatives):

1   The Treasury of Malaysia shall notify the responsible officers of the relevant ministries, departments or agencies of specific content concerning them and their organisations in the report.
2   The responsible officers shall embark on implementing the recommendations made by the PAC, and report to the Treasury on any action taken as well as on the current status of the issues concerned.
3   The Treasury shall prepare a final memorandum detailing the actions taken by the responsible officers in response to the issues raised, and forward this to the PAC. The memorandum shall be prepared immediately, and is tabled at the following PAC meeting for deliberation and further suggestions.

The above instructions show that the PAC does follow up on its recommendations through the final memorandum and enforcement of the Treasury. There is no requirement for the PAC to present an annual report or any other performance report to Parliament.

Examples of cases investigated

As indicated previously, the PAC investigates various cases highlighted in the Auditor-General's report, as well as cases raised by Members of Parliament involving ministers and top officials of ministries, departments and agencies, cases involving huge sums of money and fraud, as well as smaller cases. The following section cites investigations of several significant cases that have been officially published.

Port Klang Free Zone (PKFZ): In 1990, the government decided to upgrade Port Klang into a centre for regional loading and distribution. A 'Mega Distribution Hub' was established with a development project called the Port Klang Free Zone (PKFZ). The objective of the PKFZ was to develop the free zone concept by combining the activities of a Free Trade Zone and a Free Industrial Zone in one area. The project was developed on a 1,000-acre parcel of land that offered extensive distribution and manufacturing facilities. The PKFZ also offered various investment incentives to companies willing to locate in the zone. These incentives included tax exemptions on most products and services, subsidies, the participation of wholly foreign owned enterprises, free repatriation of capital and profits and incentives for research and development, training and export. The PKFZ was based on the model of the Jebel Ali Free Zone in Dubai and was launched in July 2004. However, in 2007, the Auditor-General's report on the Port Klang Authority (PKA) highlighted huge cost overruns amounting to RM 3.5 billion (US$1.1 billion) associated with the PKFZ. The original cost of setting up the integrated free zone was supposed to be RM1.8 billion, but this had increased to RM4.6 billion by the time the project was completed four years later. The PAC investigated the PKA and made recommendations, one of which resulted in an independent auditor being appointed in 2008 to conduct an audit. The auditor's PKFZ Position Review and Report were published in May 2009 and the audit report received huge coverage in the mass media. Further PAC investigations were held, resulting in the government's decision to form a special PKFZ Task Force in September 2009 to review the problems and make recommendations. The PAC then issued its final report with suggested actions on 27 October 2009. This resulted in the arrest of five people, who subsequently faced criminal charges for misconduct in administering and financing the PKFZ (PAC, 2009).

Malaysia International Tuna Port (MITP): The Fisheries Department of Malaysia built a complex for fish landing in Penang in 1979 and handed over the complex to the Malaysia Fisheries Development Authority (LKIM) in 1984. In 2002, LKIM's board of directors approved a proposal by Bindforce Sdn. Bhd. to build and operate an international tuna port at the site in collaboration with LKIM. A Memorandum of Agreement was signed in May 2002. In 2003, the government's Economic Planning Unit (EPU) approved the privatisation of the port, resulting in the formation of a new company, Malaysian International Tuna Port Sdn. Bhd. (MITP Sdn. Bhd.). However, the Auditor-General's report in 2009 raised the issue of the abandonment of the project after the government had spent RM95 million. The PAC started an investigation shortly thereafter by calling on several parties responsible for the project. The Committee also conducted a site visit in 2011. In this case, the PAC assessed the amount of possible loss for the government, highlighted weaknesses in the due diligence assessment conducted by the EPU, and indicated that the EPU should be held responsible. The PAC also highlighted the negligence of LKIM's management and representatives, and reported that the LKIM director should have carefully observed the project to protect the government's interest. The PAC also pointed out conflict of interest issues in the project's management that had been overlooked. The PAC's report resulted in action being taken against MITP Sdn. Bhd. and various responsible parties involved in the project (PAC, 2011).

Rawang to Ipoh Electrified Double Tracking Project: The main components in this project involved building an electrified rail system and upgrading existing track for the use of fast trains with a top speed of 160kph. The Ministry of Transport (MOT) acted as the project's implementing agency, with the responsibility for appointing contractors, organising financial provisions and ensuring that the government's interests were protected during project planning and execution. Malayan Railway Limited (KTMB), the end user of the resultant infrastructure, was responsible for preparing a Statement of Needs. The management and oversight function was undertaken by Syarikat Kinta Samudera-Opus Consortium (KS-Opus), a project management company appointed by the MOT. In 2008, the Auditor-General's report highlighted numerous weaknesses found in the project. It mandated the PAC to investigate and, in particular, to justify the project's value for money as the project involved huge expenditures. In January 2010, the PAC reported abnormalities in the terms of the contract between the government and the main contractor. The PAC suggested that several facilities be redistributed, and that the MOT take stern action against the project managers who failed to supervise or oversee the project. The PAC also urged the MOF to blacklist companies involved in the project that failed to live up to their obligations to the project (PAC, 2010).

The Auditor-General's 2012 report also identified many concerns that the PAC is currently investigating (NAD, 2013). Among others, the PAC will call on top officials to explain (i) weaknesses found at the Ministry of Education over the financial management of security control services, (ii) the National Film Development Corporation's (FINAS) 'patchy and inconsistent' financial management from 2009 to 2012, and (iii) the surge in the cost of the Kuala Lumpur International Airport 2 (KLIA2) project (NAD, 2014a).

Assessment of PAC performance

Every year the Auditor-General's report highlights cases of misappropriation of funds, potential civil servant fraud and government overspending. These incidents result in the public questioning of government accountability, and criticism of the role played by the PAC. The Parliamentary Committee of Selection, in addressing the criticism, exercises care in selecting PAC members by ensuring that the Committee comprises members of diverse expertise, including those with an accounting background. Although Malaysia's PAC has been actively pursuing issues raised by the Auditor-General, it has been criticised for (among other things) failing to tackle issues of graft and financial misappropriation, taking a long time to investigate and conclude issues, and lacking the power to probe into cases raised. However, these criticisms have been raised mainly on the internet and by social media. In order to assess whether the PAC is effective, the data gathered, described and discussed in the previous section were compared to the 17 attributes of an ideal PAC developed in Stapenhurst *et al.* (2005). An assessment based on these 'ideal committee' attributes would help to establish the credibility of Malaysia's federal PAC. Table 12.1 illustrates the attributes of Malaysia's PAC.

As evidenced in Table 12.1, Malaysia's PAC possesses 13 out of the 17 attributes of an ideal committee. The PAC is relatively small, excludes government ministers, and is appointed for the full term of Parliament. Abiding by regulations, the PAC's maximum number of members is 12, government ministers are not permitted to serve on the committee, and the appointment of members is aligned to the full term of Parliament.

As indicated previously, the PAC meets frequently (at least once a month), and a Pre-Council meeting precedes the full committee meeting to ensure that important issues and related matters are properly covered. The roles, responsibilities and powers of the PAC and its members are stipulated clearly in the Standing Orders of the *Dewan Rakyat* (House of Representatives). In general, 80 per cent of the PAC's investigations result from issues raised in the Auditor-General's report, while the remaining cases are initiated by current issues raised by Members of Parliament. The PAC issues a formal report to Parliament after completing its investigation and obtaining the consensus of its members. Although the Treasury Instructions require the Treasury of Malaysia to conduct a follow-up and report back to the PAC, actual practice requires other government ministries, department and agencies to also report directly to the PAC on the results of their own follow-up.

Although the PAC has never been chaired by a senior opposition figure, the Deputy Chairman comes from the opposition and the two top positions are determined in a parliamentary debate. In addition, senior opposition members do receive appointments to the PAC. Malaysia is not the only country where senior opposition members do not typically chair the PAC. Stapenhurst *et al.* (2012) highlighted that Australia also represents an interesting exception, as the country considers it advantageous to have a government member as chairman to better assist with the implementation of the PAC's recommendations. From 1992 onwards, the PAC has not had its own budget. Instead, it shares resources with Malaysia's Parliament. Although the PAC does not have many resources of its own, several parliamentary officers are tasked with the responsibility of assisting the PAC. The PAC also has the power to summon resources, expertise, documents and other support from various government entities. While PAC meetings are not open to the public, a full verbatim transcript of meeting and hearing proceedings is submitted to Parliament, and summaries of the PAC's reports are published on the PAC's website. Parliament, however, does not hold annual debates on the work of the PAC.

Therefore, it is evidenced that the Malaysian federal PAC has the attributes needed to be effective. The recurring issues highlighted in the Auditor-General's

Table 12.1 Assessment of the effectiveness of Malaysia's Federal PAC

No.	Attributes	Yes/No
1	The committee is small; committees seem to work well with 5–11 members, none of whom should be government ministers.	✓
2	Senior opposition figures are associated with the PAC's work, and probably chair the committee.	✗
3	The Chair of the committee is a senior parliamentarian, fair-minded and is respected by Parliament	✓
4	The committee is appointed for the full term of the Parliament.	✓
5	The committee is adequately resourced, with an experienced clerk and a competent researcher(s).	✗
6	There is clarity on the committee's role and responsibilities.	✓
7	The committee meets frequently and regularly.	✓
8	Hearings are open to the public; a full verbatim transcript and summary minutes are quickly available for public distribution.	✗
9	A steering committee plans the committee's work in advance and prepares an agenda for each meeting to the full committee.	✓
10	The typical witness is a senior public servant (the 'accounting officer') accompanied by the officials that have detailed understanding of the issues under examination.	✓
11	The Auditor's Report is automatically referred to the committee and the auditor meets with the committee to go over the highlights of the report.	✓
12	In addition to issues raised by the auditor, the committee occasionally decides to investigate other matters.	✓
13	The committee strives for some consensus in its reports.	✓
14	The committee issues formal substantive reports to Parliament at least annually.	✓
15	The committee has established a procedure with the government for following up its recommendations and is informed about what, if any, action has been taken.	✓
16	In all its deliberations, the committee uses the auditor as an expert advisor.	✓
17	Parliament holds an annual debate on the work of the committee.	✗

Source: Stapenhurst *et al.* (2005: 25).

report are not the result of an ineffective PAC, but may be due to various other reasons such as an inability to take action and limited resources in conducting investigation and research. In addition, since the PAC's power is limited to investigating and forwarding its findings and recommendations to other parties, it is up to these parties (including the judiciary) to take further action – including penalising offenders.

Conclusion

This chapter's discussion and conclusion are based on publicly available archival documents, as well as on a focus group discussion with three officers from Parliament. It covers only the appreciation of the PAC's role and performance, and an evaluation of whether or not it is considered an 'ideal committee'. Based on the findings, Malaysia's PAC has been actively pursuing issues highlighted in the Auditor-General's report, as well as other issues involving government entities. Notable cases, such as the Port Klang Free Zone and the Rawang–Ipoh electrified double tracking project, have been discussed here. Malaysia's PAC is considered almost ideal since it possesses 13 of the 17 attributes of an ideal committee. The four attributes that the PAC does not possess include: the Committee does not have a senior member of the opposition as its chairman; the Committee does not have its own budget; the Committee does not hold public hearings; and there is no annual debate in Parliament on the work of the Committee. However, the findings show that the lack of these four attributes has not hampered the work of the PAC; recurring problems uncovered by the Committee, such as the misappropriation of government funding, are due to a lack of enforcement by other responsible agencies.

This chapter has examined the PAC at the federal government level in Malaysia. Future research could look into the PAC at the state level, and could explore the factors that influence the PAC's effectiveness. Research involving interviews with members of the PAC, Members of Parliament and officials from government ministries, departments and agencies to gain further insight into the effectiveness of the PAC and improving government transparency and accountability would also be worthwhile.

Note

1 The Treasury Instructions (TI) provide details on financial and accounting procedures. They encompass the regulations to be adhered to in the management of government funds. As stated in Section 4 of the Financial Procedure Act 1957, 'Every accounting officer shall be subject to this Act and shall perform such duties, keep such books and render such accounts as may be prescribed by or under this Act or by instructions issued by the Treasury in matters of financial and accounting procedure not inconsistent therewith' (Laws of Malaysia, 2006b).

References

Abu Bakar, N. B. and Ismail, S. (2011) 'Financial Management Accountability Index (FMAI) in the Malaysian public sector: a way forward', *International Review of Administrative Sciences*, 77(1): 159–90.

Ahmad Badawi, A. (2004) 'Message', in *National Integrity Plan*, Kuala Lumpur: Integrity Institute of Malaysia, pp. vii–ix.

Arukesamy, K. (2013) 'AG's Dashboard to ensure accountability', *theSundaily*. Available at: www.thesundaily.my/news/844897 (accessed 13 March 2014).

Haque, M. S. (1994) 'The Emerging Challenge to Bureaucratic Accountability: A Critical Perspective', in A. Farazmand (ed.) *Handbook of Bureaucracy*, New York: Marcel Dekker Inc., pp. 265–85.

International Federation of Accountants (IFAC) (2012) 'Public Sector Financial Management Transparency and Accountability: The Use of International Public Sector Accounting Standards', *IFAC Policy Position 4*, New York: IFAC.

Laws of Malaysia (2006a) *Audit Act 1957 (Revised 1972) Incorporating all amendments up to 1 January 2006*. Available at: www.agc.gov.my/Akta/Vol.%202/Act%2062.pdf (accessed 26 August 2014).

Laws of Malaysia (2006b) *Financial Procedure Act 1957. Incorporating all amendments up to 1 January 2006*. Available at: www.ilkap.gov.my/download/pekeliling/agc/Act61.pdf (accessed 15 September 2014).

Laws of Malaysia (2008) *Arahan Perbendaharaan* [Treasury Instructions]. Available at: www.treasury.gov.my/pdf/arahan_perbendaharaan/arahan_perbendaharaanpdf (accessed 29 January 2015).

Laws of Malaysia (2010) *Federal Constitution. As at 1 November 2010*. Available at: www.agc.gov.my/images/Personalisation/Buss/pdf/Federal%20Consti%20(BI%20text).pdf (accessed 26 August 2014).

Makhado, R. A., Masehela, K. L. and Mokhari, R. W. (2012) 'Effectiveness and Efficiency of Public Accounts Committees (PACs) in Enhancing Oversight and Accountability in the Public Sector', paper presented at the 2012 SALSA Development Seminar, East London, Eastern Cape, South Africa. Available at: www.sals.gov.za/devseminar/2012/rmakhado.pdf (accessed 21 December 2013).

McGee, D. (2002) *The Overseers: Public Accounts Committees and Public Spending*, London: Pluto Press.

McGee, R. and Gaventa, J. (2010) 'Review of Impact and Effectiveness of Transparency and Accountability Initiatives', Transparency and Accountability Initiative, London. Available at: www.ids.ac.uk/publication/review-of-impact-and-effectiveness-of-transparency-and-accountability-initiatives (accessed 16 September 2014).

Ministry of Finance (2014) *Economic Report 2013/2014*. Available at: www.treasury.gov.my/index.php?option=com_content&view=article&id=2735:economic-report-2013-2014&catid=262&Itemid=2478&lang=en (accessed 4 September 2014).

National Audit Department (NAD) (2013) *Laporan Ketua Audit Negara Persekutuan 2012*. Available at: www.audit.gov.my/index.php?option=com_content&view=article&id=414:laporan-ketua-audit-negara-persekutuan-2012-3&catid=108&Itemid=474&lang=ms (accessed 18 September 2014).

National Audit Department (NAD) (2014a) *Liputan Media*. Available at: www.audit.gov.my/images/media/Liputan_Media/The_Star/2014/the%20star-jan%202014.pdf (accessed 18 September 2014).

National Audit Department (2014b) *Malaysian Public Sector Auditing – At A Glance*.

Available at: www.audit.gov.my/images/pdf/2014/Pengauditan/bi buku malaysian public sector auditing at a glance_opt.pdf (accessed 15 September 2014).

Parliament of Malaysia (no date) 'Standing Orders of the *Dewan Rakyat* of Malaysia' [*Peraturan-peraturan Majlis Mesyuarat Dewan Rakyat*]. Available at: www.parlimen. gov.my/images/webuser/news/PM_DR_BI.pdf (accessed 4 January 2014).

Pelizzo, R. (2011) 'Public Accounts Committees in the Commonwealth: Oversight, effectiveness, and governance', *Commonwealth & Comparative Politics*, 49(4): 528–46.

Performance Management and Delivery Unit (PEMANDU) (2010) *Government Transformation Programme – The Roadmap.* Available at www.pmo.gov.my/GTP/index.php (accessed 17 September 2014).

Public Accounts Committee (PAC) (2009) *Laporan Jawatankuasa Kira-Kira Wang Negara Terhadap Projek Pembangunan Zon Bebas Pelabuhan Klang.* Available at: www.parlimen.gov.my/images/webuser/pac/LapPAC-PKFZ.pdf (accessed 18 September 2014).

Public Accounts Committee (PAC) (2010) *Laporan Jawatankuasa Kira-Kira Wang Negara Mengenai Projek Landasan Berkembar Elektrik Antara Rawang dan Ipoh.* Available at: www.parlimen.gov.my/pac/review/docs-53-49.pdf (accessed 18 September 2014).

Public Accounts Committee (PAC) (2011) *Laporan Jawatankuasa Kira-Kira Wang Negara Mengenai Pengurusan Pembangunan Pelabuhan Antarabangsa Tuna Malaysia MITP.* Available at: www.parlimen.gov.my/pac/review/docs-56-52.pdf (accessed 18 September 2014).

Saleh, Z. (2002) 'Governmental Accounting in Malaysia', unpublished PhD thesis, Cardiff University.

Saleh, Z. (2013) 'Financial administration II: Accounting and reporting', in N. A. Siddiquee (ed.). *Public Management and Governance in Malaysia: Trends and Transformations*, Abingdon: Routledge, pp. 121–39.

Stapenhurst, R. and Kroon, C. (2011) 'Public Accounts Committee Profiles and Performance in Canada', Canadian Study of Parliament Group. Available at: www.studyparliament.ca/English/pdf/ongoing/CPSG_World_Bank_on_PACs.pdf (accessed 21 December 2013).

Stapenhurst, R., Pelizzo, R. and O'Brien, M. (2012) '*Ex Post* Financial Oversight: Legislative Audit, Public Accounts Committees … and Parliamentary Budget Offices?' OECD Parliamentary Budget Fiscal Councils and Independent Fiscal Institutions, 4th Annual Meeting, OECD Conference Centre, Paris. Available at: www.oecd.org/gov/budgeting/49778002.pdf (accessed 16 September 2014).

Stapenhurst, R., Sahgal, V., Woodley, W. and Pelizzo, R. (2005) 'Scrutinizing Public Expenditures: Assessing the Performance of Public Accounts Committees', Policy Research Working Paper #3613. Available at: http://wbi.worldbank.org/wbi/Data/wbi/wbicms/files/drupal-acquia/wbi/Scrutinizing%20Public%20Expenditures.pdf (accessed 18 September 2014).

13 Responses to the Public Accounts Committee of India

A textual analysis

Bikram Chatterjee, Alistair Brown and Victoria Wise

Introduction

The Public Accounts Committee of India (PACI) has a long history dating back to 1921. The Committee has undergone major reform since India's independence in 1947. Initially the Finance Minister held the position of Chairman of the committee; however, in 1967 a member of the oppositional political party was appointed to this position for the first time. To uphold free expression of views and critical evaluation of executives, the tradition of appointing a member of the Opposition as the Chairman of the committee has been continued.

Previous research pointed out the primary aim of Public Accounts Committees (PACs) worldwide is to attain economy and efficiency rather than service provision (Degeling *et al.*, 1996), and contrasting interests of PACs between managerial and financial accountability with political accountability (Funnell, 2003; Gray and Jenkins, 1993). There is no existing study analysing the activities of PACI despite India being the world's largest democracy in terms of population. Due to concerns over PACs worldwide and a dearth of studies in India, the aim of this study is to analyse the responses of Ministries and Government Departments to recommendations, suggestions and comments to the reports of PACI to determine whether there is a general need for strengthening of regulation, monitoring and oversight of public administration practices in India. The research method includes a textual analysis of 50 PACI reports and responses to those reports across the period from 2009 to 2011. This study contributes to existing knowledge by evaluating the present legislation and outlining directions for future developments in the area of public administration.

The remainder of this chapter proceeds as follows. In the next section a review of the literature outlining relevant perspectives on parliamentary and democratic responsibility and accountability is presented. This is followed by an overview and evaluation of the legislation and country context of PACI. Then the theoretical framework within which the study proceeds and a discussion of the research method and information analysis is provided. The next section includes a discussion of the results presented within the underlying themes identified in the textual analysis. Finally a set of concluding remarks is presented which summarizes how Ministries and Government Departments appear to be managing the legitimization of their practices through their responses to PACI reports.

Literature review

A PAC is a committee of selected members of Parliament, whose role is to review the audits generated by the Comptrollers and Auditors-General on behalf of Parliament (Jacobs and Jones, 2009; Jones and Jacobs, 2006, 2009; Jones, 2006; McGee, 2002). Across the globe, PACs have 'become a central element of the process of parliamentary and democratic accountability' (Jacobs and Jones, 2009: 14), by introducing a form of external scrutiny (Mulgan, 2000) of public accountability (Normanton, 1971). The literature on PACs dwells on many aspects of accountability raised by these legislative oversight boards. Financial accountability draws on economic and legal rationalities emphasizing the PAC's accountability for probity, internal control adequacies, economies and efficiency (Gray and Jenkins, 1993). In contrast, managerial accountability, drawing on legal, economic and technical rationalities, emphasizes the PAC's accountability for integration, consistency of service provision, economies and efficiency, while accountability codes of professions invoke social rationalities emphasizing service, accessibility, quality, equity and client power (Gray and Jenkins, 1993). Those PACs that operate in a high-income economy seldom achieve all levels of accountability (Mulgan, 2000). For example, some executive governments may focus more on managerial and financial accountability rather than political accountability to accommodate the prevailing socio-political milieu of the day (Funnell, 2003; Gray and Jenkins, 1993).

In exploring the link between public sector accountability and the Joint Committee of Public Accounts of the Commonwealth of Australia (JCPA), Spann (1979) and Reid (1968) observed that the JCPA provided only fact-finding and reporting duties. This narrowness of scope was also found in other studies of PACs. For the period 1914 to 1932, Degeling *et al.* (1996) found that the JCPA was used 'as a mechanism for infusing financial and economic rationalities into the day to day operations of government departments and instrumentalities' (Degeling *et al.*, 1996: 45)

Further, PACs have used accounting and economic discourses within parliamentary administration in ways that provide a narrow form of managerial legitimacy of the system.

> PACs contribute to reframe meaning in public policy circles in ways which cause administrators and service providers to attend to economy and efficiency and displace concern for other values such as equity, access, service appropriateness and client empowerment.
>
> (Degeling *et al.*, 1996: 45)

The capacity of PACs to promote accountability and reduce corruption has been questioned by Jacobs (2013). Jacobs (2013) referred to a KPMG (2006 cited in

Jacobs, 2013) report on the performance measurement criteria of the Victorian Public and Estimates Committee, including the percentage of the PAC's reports accepted by the government and the number of completed reports and responses received by the PAC. Jacobs (2013) noted that the internal performance review system of JCPA included the speed and responsiveness of government's responses to JCPA's recommendations. The author expressed concern about such performance measurement criteria, specifically the number of PAC recommendations accepted by the government, as such a performance measurement criterion may not lead to better public administration.

Jones and Jacobs (2006) argued that PACs veer towards managerial accountability rather than political accountability, as the latter form of accountability is overwhelmed by the personal political interest of committee members. Although PACs are a source of legitimacy of parliamentary entities (Jones and Jacobs, 2009) and a visible symbol of the democratic process (Pelizzo *et al.*, 2006), their external scrutiny is considered vulnerable (Jacobs and Jones, 2009) and brittle in some contexts (Brown, 2011).

Wehner (2003) examined the role of Commonwealth country PACs in parliamentary financial scrutiny and found that PACs could play a potentially useful role in scrutinizing public spending but needed to find innovative ways to better attain affordability and effectiveness in pursuing financial scrutiny. A key finding from Wehner's study was that PACs across the Commonwealth vary in terms of the political context and financial resources and thus in their ability to achieve an appropriate level of financial scrutiny. Some PACs, for example, were operating in an environment of substantial public sector economic reform and were blessed with a pool of independent and expert human resources. Other PACs, particularly in developing countries, simply did not have the requisite human resources and accounting expertise to carry out their expected duties. Some PACs operated in restrictive political climates in which freedom of speech and open accountability were discouraged (Pelizzo, 2010; Brown, 2011).

Samsuddin and Mohamed (2009) reviewed the working of PACs in all 11 states in Peninsular Malaysia. The authors reported that the 2005 PAC reports of all the states were outdated and related to audited financial statements of much earlier financial years. The time lag between the Auditor-General (AG) report and PAC reports ranged from two to eight years. Some PACs conducted a combined review of five years' financial statements. Following these findings, Samsuddin and Mohamed (2009) suggested that the relevance of PAC reports was at stake in Malaysia.

Montano (2009) identified one of the major issues for PACs in Trinidad and Tobago as the backlog in examining reports, the number of which was large. Okpala (2013) investigated the effectiveness of the PAC oversight function of audited reports of federal government in Nigeria in the context of financial indiscipline and wastages in the public sector. Their study included the administration of a survey questionnaire distributed to members of the National Assembly and Ministers. Their study revealed a disturbing situation wherein Ministries and

Commissions did not respond to audit queries and no measures were taken in response to issues raised.

Pelizzo (2010) analysed the activities of the PACs of six Pacific Island countries, including the Fiji Islands, Kiribati, Papua New Guinea, Samoa, Solomon Islands, and Vanuatu, and of the autonomous jurisdiction of Bougainville and found that:

> The Parliament of Kiribati provides no indication as to any type of PAC activity, the Parliament of Fiji Islands does not say whether the Fijian PAC ever held any hearing in the course of its meetings, while the Parliament of Bougainville suggested that the PAC had not conducted any activity in the first three years of its existence.
>
> (Pelizzo, 2010: 127)

The reasons for PAC's inaction is unclear from Pelizzo's (2010) study but according to Brown (2011), in certain Pacific Island countries PACs are viewed as an intrusive foreign product that ignores embedded chief-centric hierarchical systems of traditional government. The lack of passion for PACs in this Pacific region is exemplified by the listlessness of PAC meetings:

> The PAC in the Fiji Islands is allowed, in spite of the military rule, to meet, its meetings are held on a daily basis and yet, they do not produce any reports. In Vanuatu, the PAC has not accomplished anything in the meetings that it held. And if one compares the data for Samoa and the Solomon Islands, one finds that the PAC in the Solomon Islands holds fewer meetings and generates more reports than its Samoan counterpart. This means that the successful performance of a PAC – that is, its ability to scrutinize government accounts and to promote good governance – may not be a simple consequence of the amount of activities.
>
> (Pelizzo, 2010: 127–8)

Indeed, in the context of Vanuatu, Brown (2011) found not only a paucity of annual reporting by the Auditor-General's Office (AGO), and thus no auditing or examination of the government of Vanuatu and its public sector entities, but also that any reports produced by the AGO were effectively ignored by the PAC. There is a need to consider the geographic, economic, political and cultural difference of the context in which PACs operate. Using a historical institutionalist perspective, Jones and Jacobs (2009) argue that the relevance of PACs can be understood by analysing their evolution.

The previous studies discussed in this section outlined the contrasting interests of PACs worldwide, between managerial or financial accountability and political accountability (Funnell, 2003; Gray and Jenkins, 1993) as well as economy and efficiency versus service provision (Degeling *et al.*, 1996). There is a dearth of studies investigating PAC activities in emerging economies. Previous studies on emerging economies reported significant time lags between

Auditor-General and PAC reports (Samsuddin and Mohamed, 2009; Montano, 2009) and a poor response to PAC reports (Montano, 2009). Following such concerns raised in previous studies and the significance of India as the world's largest democracy, the present study analyses responses by Ministries and Government Departments to reports of the PACI. Analysis of PACI reports provides insights into exemplary areas and priority areas for development, and can be used to interpret the effectiveness of PACI.

India: country context

The geographic, economic, political and cultural context of India offers a unique landscape in which to examine the mechanics of the PACI. India is recognized as the largest democracy by population in the world with a population of 1.2 billion (Census of India, 2011). However, its Gross National Income (GNI) per capita is relatively low compared to Organization for Economic Cooperation and Development (OECD) nations, with a GNI per capita of about US$1,580 (The World Bank, 2012).

Based on the Westminster system of government, the PACI is one of many parliamentary committees that attempt to inform the administrative accountability of India's parliamentary system. The PACI has its origins in 1921, when it was part of the Montagu–Chelmsford reforms. In 1950, when the Constitution of India came into force, the PACI functioned under the control of the Speaker of the House with a non-official Chairman appointed by the Speaker from among the Members of the Lower House of the Parliament of India (Lok Sabha – 'House of the People') elected to the Committee (PAC of India, 2014). The PACI is constituted annually under Rule 308 of the Rules of Procedure and Conduct of Business in Lok Sabha, and consists of up to 22 members comprising 15 members elected by Lok Sabha (PAC of India, 2014).

The PACI examines accounts showing the appropriation of sums granted by Parliament for the expenditure of the Indian government and the government's annual financial accounts. The involvement of the PACI is particularly significant considering that the government of India exceeded 90 per cent of its annual expenditure target in the first eight months in the financial year 2013 (India Country Monitor, 2014), suggesting the need for more stringent economic control and financial accountability. The spending on public health as a percentage of Gross Domestic product (GDP) declined from an already low 1.05 per cent in 1985–6 to about 0.90 per cent in 2003–4. The central government health expenditure is below comparable developing countries and far below the amount required to provide basic acceptable healthcare for the population according to the Economic Research Foundation (2006). The PACI declared that it needed to ensure that account money was disbursed properly, that expenditure conforms to governed expectations and that appropriations were in accord with the rules framed by the competent authority (PAC of India, 2014). The PACI generally examines any expenditure on a service that exceeds an amount for that service granted by Parliament. It is also interested in examining cases that involve losses, unusual expenditures, internal control problems, apparent extravagances and finan-cial irregularities. If these events are detected, the relevant Ministry or Department is asked to explain what action will be taken to prevent its recurrence.

The PACI relies upon the audit report of the 'Accounts' of the Union Govern-ment conducted by the Comptroller and Auditor-General. They conduct govern-ment entity audits, paying particular attention to accountancy, regularity, appropriation, propriety and efficiency-cum-performance (PAC of India, 2014). The government entity responding to the PACI is required to advise the PACI about its actions or proposals and an 'action-taken' report is presented to Parlia-ment. The PACI may accept or reject such responses and ask the Ministry or Department to further consider issues outlined in its initial report. This provides for accountability of the Executive to Parliament and enables Parliament, and the public it represents, to appraise government replies and PACI recommendations.

Theoretical framework

The assumption that legitimacy is one of the central purposes of public account-ability systems was mooted by Bovens (2005). Jacobs and Jones (2009) sup-ported this proposition and demonstrated that legitimacy was critically important to the start-up of PACs for state and federal governments in Australia. This was particularly crucial in times of political and financial crises, during which the need for legitimacy through the set-up of PACs helped establish a form of legis-lative oversight. Jacobs and Jones (2009) noted that in establishing a stand-alone PAC in the state of Victoria in Australia, the Victorian state Parliament copied practices and procedures from the Westminster system of the United Kingdom. In turn, the Australian federal Parliament copied the Victorian state Parliament's PAC practices and procedures.

The need for legitimacy may vary across jurisdiction. Brown (2011), for example, found that the legitimacy practices and procedures of the UK West-minster system were considered in Vanuatu to be a foreign intrusion rather than meeting a local need. In the case of India, there is considerable rhetoric sur-rounding the importance of the PACI and whether this importance is reflected by actual practice.

By focusing on PACI reports, the analysis presented in this study provides a first attempt to evaluate the actual practice concerning Ministerial and Govern-ment Department responses to PACI recommendations, suggestions and com-ments. Further, we identify some developments and outline directions for future development in the area of public administration in India. Specifically, a categor-ization of the observed responses within a textual analysis framework is pro-vided (see Table 13.1 for descriptive statistics) and the responses are discussed and rationalized through the lens of legitimacy theory. Accordingly, in the fol-lowing section we present and discuss details of the research method and the technical analysis employed in this study to address the question of whether the rhetoric about the importance of the PACI is reflected in actual practice and performance.

Research method and information analysis

This study used textual analytical approach to interrogate the comments of the PACI and the responses from various Ministries and Government Departments. Textual analysis focuses on the underlying theme of a text and is used to evaluate the contextual nature. The approaches taken in textual analysis may include semiotic, narrative or rhetorical, and the text is presented as evidence to the argument. Textual analysis differs from 'content analysis', as the latter is quantitative in nature and includes the coding of text into units for analysis. In contrast, 'textual analysis' is used to identify latent meanings in the text including assumptions and omissions (Fursich, 2009).

Textual analysis includes in-depth analysis of meaning to bring out latent meanings (Fursich, 2009). It belongs to a cultural-critical paradigm and includes a strategy of deconstruction that illuminates underlying assumptions of the text by investigating internal inconsistencies and drawing on linguistic, rhetorical and semiotic strategies. The technique is also described as text-based analysis, thematic analysis, ideological analysis and critical discourse analysis. For example, the critical discourse perspective views text as tools to present arguments in order to convince an audience that their perception of the theme of the text will be enriched if they choose to view the text similarly to the critic. Textual analysis may also involve concentrating on specific aspects such as genre analysis or cultural analysis (Pawsey *et al.*, 2013).

Textual analysis is open-ended, enabling the identification of underlying meanings and themes, and underlying positions and contradictions (Dow, 1996). Text communicates myths, rituals and archetypes. Higgins (1986) suggests that textual analysis embodies the messiness of the world and confronts the perceived rationalized reality.

Following previous literature using textual analysis (Entman, 2003; Shah and Nah, 2004; Steeves, 1997; Pawsey *et al.*, 2013), PACI reports were categorized to elicit latent dominant themes. This study includes an analysis of 50 PACI reports from November 2009 to December 2011 (available on the Parliament of India website, 2014).

Results and discussion

Of the 50 reports of PACI, ten containing PACI comments were subsequently addressed by respective Ministries and Departments, resulting in 40 reports for analysis. Of these, 18 reports were pending a response, and 22 included a response to PACI comments.

The 18 pending reports included 268 pending comments requiring a response. Of the 268 pending comments, 22 were general observations and statements of PACI resulting in 246 comments for analysis in this study.

The remaining 22 reports included 328 responses to PACI comments. In 240 of these PACI accepted the comments. In 32 observations, PACI was satisfied with responses resulting in no further necessary action by the Ministries and

Table 13.1 Descriptive statistics relating to the PACI recommendations, comments, responses and outstanding actions required

Total PACI reports	50
Less: Reports containing comments addressed by Ministries	(10)
Reports for analysis	40
Less: Reports pending a response	(18)*
Reports which included a response to PACI comments	22**
Pending reports*	18
Included:	
Pending comments for response	268
Less: General observations	(22)
Comments for analysis	246
Reports inclusive of a comment**	22
Included:	
Responses to PACI comment	328
Less: Comments accepted by Ministries	(240)
PACI satisfied by Ministries' responses	(32)
PACI rejected Ministries' responses, requiring further action	(46)
Interim responses requiring further update	10

Departments, and 46 of the responses were not accepted, which required Ministries and Departments to take further action regarding the identified issues. Finally, interim replies were provided to ten PACI comments, resulting in further updates due to PACI. Table 13.1 provides the descriptive statistics relating to the PACI recommendations, comments, responses and outstanding actions required.

In the following section, the themes in 'pending reports' and 'responded reports' are outlined.

Pending reports

The 18 pending reports include concerns raised by PACI in regard to (1) monetary, (2) operational, and (3) PACI (audit) related issues.

Monetary

Approximately one-third of pending comments were 'monetary' in nature. These monetary issues can be broadly sub-categorized into 'procedural issues' 'monitoring' and 'revenues and expenditure'.

Procedural issues

Approximately one-third of monetary issues were procedural. These included suggestions and queries on enhancing financial management including budgeting for future projects and programmes to contain comprehensive, realistic costing of activities, price fluctuations, and detailed outlines of activities and associated costs to avoid misclassification of amounts when comparing actual with budget.

In cases where funds were allocated to other parties such as state governments, the PACI suggested that the other party should bear the cost of excess expenditure over budget resulting from delays in completion of projects.

Monitoring

Approximately two-thirds of monetary issues were monitoring-related. These included suggestions by the PACI to reduce excess expenditure over budgeted expenditure, the timely presentation of accounts to Parliament for authorization in cases where excess expenditure occurred, and providing detailed reasons for delays in responding to PACI queries. In the case of expenditure on pensions, the PACI requested the use of new information technology to reduce excess expenditure over budget. Ministries and Departments were frequently asked to provide details of corrective action undertaken to reduce excess expenditure. The PACI also asked for firm and stern measures to avoid excess future expenditure such as by reducing future departmental budgets by the amount spent in excess in the current year if the excess amount resulted from non-adherence to rules and guidelines.

The PACI has suggested adequate funds be released so that Ministries and Departments can meet their costs. It also raised concerns that appropriate duties were not being collected in accordance with guidelines, and requested updates on recovery amounts. The PACI stressed the need for monitoring the use of funds in cases where funds are paid to external groups such as Village Health and Sanitation Committees. It also expressed concerns about limited funds being released to support programmes such as the National Rural Health Mission (NRHM) so that these programmes could be rolled out without delay in order to achieve their objectives. The PACI stressed the need to appropriately plan projects and monitor the release of funds to state governments. Further, it expressed concern in regard to the non-utilization of some state government funds such as the Non Lapsable Central Pool of Resource Scheme, as withholding diminishes the progress of projects. Importantly, the need to monitor projects for time and cost over-run was raised by PACI in many reports. Concern was raised specifically in regard to the Ministry of Railways' huge excess expenditure. The PACI also requested that data be collected in regard to defaulting departments, expressed concern about missing files and records, and suggested the need for recovery of such records.

Revenues and expenditure

Only a few comments on the state of revenue and expenditure of Ministries and Departments were made. The PACI often commented on the general benefit to the population of planned expenditure on programmes. For example, the PACI asked Ministries to increase their budget for the NRHM so that rural household expenditure on health is reduced. In regard to doctors in rural areas, the PACI suggested that the relevant Ministry or Department should consider providing monetary incentives so that doctors have a strong reason to stay in rural areas. In cases of medicine manufacturing, the PACI stressed the need to direct funds to research and development. Again, the PACI emphasized the need for Ministries, particularly the Ministry of Railways, to investigate ways to reduce costs.

Operational issues

Operational issues raised by the PACI mainly included queries and suggestions on policy and programmes, procurement-related matters, monitoring of departmental operations, updating of data and data storage, and infrastructure-related concerns. Other comments addressed staff-related issues, safety, operational evaluation and quality assurance.

'Policy and programmes' issues included new programme suggestions, including an empirical study to investigate the effect of yoga on health, new legislation to contribute towards water pollution as an offence, building the capacity of states to better co-ordinate projects, and a review of existing provisions for the extension of the storage life of Indian Army rations to address food quality.

'Procurement-related' matters included PACI suggestions to organize efficient and timely supply, regularly review suppliers, impose penalties when suppliers do not meet the terms and conditions of their contract, the need for comprehensive evaluation before procurement is arranged, and streamlining of the procurement process. For example, the PACI recommended that the Ministry of Railways should make effective arrangements with suppliers of spare parts to enhance smooth operations. It stressed the need for a clearly delineated purchase procedure in the case of procuring medicines to promote timely procurement. Importantly, the PACI stressed the need to monitor medical suppliers and impose penalties where suppliers do not meet the terms and conditions stated in their contracts. It also recommended the expeditious introduction of a centralized procurement agency for medicines.

'Monitoring of departmental operations' included oversight of timely project completion and the validation of data supplied by Ministries and Departments. The PACI recommended that the validation of some data should be conducted by external independent verifiers such as in cases of special economic zones and units. It also asked that feedback be provided when requested such as in the case of the NRHM.

'Updating of data and data storage' included suggestions from the PACI that data entry be streamlined, data be updated, and ease of access to data be improved. For example, it identified a need for the updating of data in regard to medicines and hospital procurements. The PACI also suggested that data be stored in centralized databases to improve access. The PACI requested updated data in many cases including from the Department of Water and Sanitation in regard to habitation matters. Similarly, it recommended the introduction and retention of data in relation to food rations for the Indian Army as information about feeding strength is currently unavailable.

'Infrastructure' comments included identifying new infrastructure needs. For example, the PACI stressed the need to develop railway infrastructure, including new bridges and terminal facilities; the need for information technology systems to support the coding of conventional medicines; the need for export infrastructure; and upgrading technology for health diagnosis in villages.

Additional comments relating to staff included that Ministries and Departments should appoint a level of staff necessary to efficiently implement programmes such as the National Rural Employment and Guarantee Act (NREGA), monitor staff, including their work hours, through systems as simple as job cards, delegate specific responsibilities to staff, take stringent actions against staff who engage in malpractice, and appoint external human resource experts. The PACI also recommended the equalization of pay between doctors of traditional natural Indian medical practice, that is Ayurveda, Yoga and Naturopathy, Unani, Siddha and Homeopathy (AYUSH), and mainstream doctors with Bachelor of Medicine and Bachelor of Surgery (MBBS) qualification; and the communication and importing of good practices of one department to the other. Comments related to safety included worrying concerns raised by the PACI relating to railways. These included the recent increase in carrying capacity of rail wagons without a thorough evaluation. The PACI asked the Ministry of Railways to introduce monitoring of illegal overloading through installing newer technology. It also suggested that punitive action be taken against individuals involved in illegal overloading and called for the updating of incident records. Operational evaluation suggestions included a review of the Special Economic Zones Act 2005; while quality assurance comments included addressing and ensuring the quality of goods and services. For example, the PACI suggested that the quality of Indian Army rations should be independently verified by an external agency.

PACI issues

Pending responses related to the non-response by Ministries and Departments to PACI issues and queries., the Committee urged more timely collection of data so that the timeline for response could be met, and it often reiterated the revised timeline within which Ministries and Departments were required to report to the PACI. In the context of frequent and significant delays, the PACI often asked to see plans and the details of procedures for responses to PACI queries.

In the next section we discuss the acceptances by Ministries and Departments of PACI concerns.

Responded reports

The following section outlines responses accepted by PACI, as well as those PACI comments accepted by Ministries and Departments, interim replies awaiting further update, and the responses of Ministries and Departments that have not been accepted by PACI.

PACI comments, accepted by Ministries

Monetary

Monetary concerns included 'procedural' and 'monitoring' and 'others'.

Procedural issues

Approximately one-quarter of monetary comments were procedural in nature. These included the need to follow appropriate procedures regarding payments to contractors; standardized procedures in case of natural disasters so that state governments are sure about the amount of compensation from the central government; following set procedures to issue grants; and auditing of excess expenditure of Departments over budget through Parliament. For example, the PACI suggested that the payment of a significant amount of advances to Educational Consultants of India (EdCIL) by the University Grants Commission (UGC) was contrary to set procedure. Other excess expenditures over budget occurred in relation to civil, defence, postal services and railways.

Responses to PACI observations mainly included plans for future improvements. In most cases the auditing of excess spending has already been conducted.

Monitoring

More than half the monetary comments related to monitoring. This included monitoring expenditure, maintaining records and related staff responsibility delegations, diversion of funds from one use to another, oversight of reasons behind significant excess expenditure over budget, monitoring of payments to contractors so that extra amounts are not paid beyond those stated in contracts and set procedures, timely recovery of money from defaulting contractors, underutilization of funds, appropriate allowance of subsidies, and the timeliness of funds disbursement for project completion. An example of 'monitoring of expenditure' is the case of food grains, where the PACI recommended reimbursing the states only for the amount that is essential for such purpose, thus avoiding unnecessary expenditure. The PACI asked that the Delhi Development Association (DDA) recover money from defaulting contractors, and generally expressed significant concern about excess expenditure as it has become a repetitive phenomenon. An example of the under-utilization of funds occurred in relation to a programme for nutritional support to primary education (the 'midday meal') where the slow release of funds impeded this programme.

The response of Ministries in most cases was to accept the PACI's views, and some future improvements to enhance monitoring have already taken place or are planned.

Others

The remainder of the comments addressed budgeting, changes in compensation amount, loss of revenue due to slow decision-making, and recommendations to increase revenue to meet cost. Concern regarding budgeting included the effect of no budgeting for projects, and questionable estimates for needed funds on upcoming projects. For example, the PACI recommended the introduction of an incentive/disincentive scheme for electricity distribution. It observed that the Ministry of Railways did not make appropriate budget projections, resulting in a shortage of funds to complete projects. A recommendation to increase revenue to meet cost was recommended by the PACI in the context of the Ministry of Railways' argument that the railways mainly serve social goals.

Operational

'Operational' comments mainly related to procurement, policy and programmes, infrastructure and safety. Other comments included suggestions for research, the monitoring of staff, departments and associates, effective data storage, internal audit and facilities, as well as staff-related comments such as the need for staff training, staff promotion policies, communication of good practices to departments, attaching specific accountability to staff, statements of staff duties, efficient and timely updating of data, responses from Ministries and Departments to operational enquiries of PACI and general operational efficiency.

'Procurement' related comments emphasized the timely completion of projects by contractors. It also suggested the drafting of an appropriate procedure for the speedy supply of resources in case of natural disaster, preparing performance guidelines to measure the delivery of projects, simplification of procurement procedures, appropriate consideration of procurement alternatives such as buy versus make, a long-term procurement plan, and the monitoring of timelines for receipt of goods and services.

'Policy and programme' related suggestions from the PACI related to the introduction of newer programmes such as a programme to meet energy shortages. In case of natural disaster it recommended that difficulties in planning future programmes be addressed. Also addressed were joint programmes between the central and state governments such as for the prevention of improper funds usage particularly in the case of natural disasters, and the timely finalization of programmes to reduce adverse environmental impacts.

'Infrastructure' related suggestions included upgrading existing infrastructure, such as radar technology and village telephone systems, periodic evaluation of existing infrastructure such as telecom networks, appropriate maintenance of infrastructure, and safeguarding infrastructure by installing electronic surveillance systems, aimed for instance at preventing train vandalism. 'Safety' related comments included taking steps to avoid accidents such as on highways under construction, and to develop plans for responding to major incidents such as railway accidents.

The Ministries and Departments have accepted these suggestions, and are either working on these issues or have already addressed them.

PACI issues

Issues raised by the PACI focused on the poor or untimely response in regard to issues previously raised by the Committee. They suggested the introduction of comprehensive internal audit systems to avoid such delays in the future. The Ministries and Departments accepted these concerns, and many of the suggestions have already been implemented.

Response of Ministries, accepted by the PACI

Monetary

Responses to monetary queries raised by the PACI and requiring no further action were mainly procedural and procurement related. The PACI was satisfied with the Ministries' and Departments' explanations and positions, thus requiring no further action.

Operational

The operational queries raised by the PACI that were responded to and required no further action were mainly in regard to the monitoring of programmes and infrastructure related. Other comments and queries related to incentive schemes, suggestions for regular meetings, clear assignment of responsibilities, updated data, operational evaluation of programmes, and procurement. The PACI was satisfied with the explanations, positions and actions taken, thus resulting in no further action.

PACI issues

Four PACI issues were responded to and so required no further action. These were: incorrect observations of the PACI, and providing revised timelines for response to PACI queries. Where the PACI suggested assigning responsibility to individuals to avoid delays in responding to PACI comments, a Ministry responded that actions had been taken, but without specifying whether individual responsibility had been assigned. One of the PACI's concerns was not responded to by the Ministry of Railways. The Ministry of Railways provided a revised timeline for responding which was accepted by PACI.

Interim replies by Ministries

Monetary

Almost half of the cases where interim replies were provided by Ministries were monetary in nature. These included PACI queries about incidents concerning procurement cost and release of funds to state governments.

Operational

Around half of the cases where interim replies were provided were operational in nature. These included project monitoring, the need for new programmes, operational evaluation, and attaching responsibility to individuals for delays.

PACI issues

These related to lack of timely response to PACI concerns and pending concerns not yet responded to.

Ministries' responses, not accepted by PAC

Monetary

More than one-third of responses not accepted by PACI were monetary in nature and mainly in the areas of procedural, monitoring and budgeting issues. Procedural issues included the rationalization for providing excess advances to contractors contrary to those allowed under policies, rationalization of autonomous bodies funded by the government for not following standard procedure for approval of expenditure, and PACI suggestions to review existing systems such as the criteria for providing grants by the University Grants Commission. Budgeting-related issues included PACI dissatisfaction with budget over-runs and requests for realistic future budgeting, dissatisfaction about repeated misclassification of accounts, and the introduction of systems to reduce misclassification.

Monitoring issues included non-response to specific enquiries about project cost increases due to delays in execution of projects, non-imposition of penalties on contractors for delays in project delivery, rationalizations for not pursuing claims of government departments against other government departments (due to non-existence of records), shifting of responsibility to state governments for not achieving monetary targets of projects, and PACI suggestions that regular meetings be held to facilitate monitoring of expenditure throughout the year.

Operational

Most of the responses not accepted by PACI were operational and many related to monitoring of departments, programmes and staff, infrastructure and the use of resources. Operational issues included unsatisfactory responses from Ministries in regard to PACI operational suggestions, such as not including specifics of how operations would incorporate PACI suggestions, PACI requests for timely project delivery and for updates in this regard, PACI requests for improvement of facilities, and rejection by Ministries of recommendations to introduce separate departments to facilitate improvements such as the improved sanitation of railways, further development of infrastructure such as railway stations, and PACI suggestions to Ministries to address client grievances.

Monitoring issues related to Ministries and Departments not engaging and monitoring government-funded autonomous bodies such as the UGC, delays in project delivery where improvements were suggested by the PACI, lack of progress on programmes such as the eradication of bogus ration cards in spite of concerns raised by PACI about the importance of completing these programmes, lack of progress in achieving project targets, PACI dissatisfaction with the present state of facilities such as railway sanitation, suggestions that evidence of inspection of facilities such as by video recording be arranged, and directing Ministries to attach individual responsibility for issues such as engaging in procurement malpractice. The PACI recommended more effective use of resources such as the purpose of aircraft use by the Indian Air force and the under-utilization of aircraft.

PAC (audit) issue

The PACI expressed serious concern about the lack of assigning personal responsibilities for delays in responding to PACI concerns and delays in receiving responses, directed particularly at the Ministry of Railways.

Conclusion

The results of this study suggest that, while the parliamentary system appears legitimate in form, there remain gaps in legitimacy in substance. The Ministerial and Departmental responses to the PACI in most cases are generic rather than detailing what specific improvements have resulted from PACI recommendations. Often the responses are the PACI recommendations that have been accepted by the Ministries and Departments, suggesting that only a veneer of legitimacy is exercised. Given the lack of details about specific improvement in processes there does not appear to be evidence of deep-seated legitimizing practice.

Regarding financial scrutiny, it appears that some procedural improvement has taken place in regard to the channelling of funds and payments. However, a key finding of this study is that budget over-runs and lack of routine inclusion of comprehensive cost data in budgets still present major concerns. In regard to the monitoring of expenditure it appears that improvement has taken place in regard to the timely regularization of excess spending compared to budget. However, excess expenditure is still a regular occurrence, together with significant cost over-runs resulting from delays in the completion of projects. The PACI has made suggestions for firm measures to be introduced in order to avoid excess expenditure.

The results of the analysis of reports conducted in this study suggest that marginal, if any, improvement exists in regard to poor monitoring practices over staff, suppliers, projects and programmes. It also appears that the identified needs for timely completion of projects and updated data are outstanding issues contributing to operational inefficiencies. Further, there is little evidence of endeavour by Ministries and Departments to evaluate projects or programmes.

While many of the PACI's comments were addressed by Ministries in a timely manner, there is still a clear need for improvement. There were significant delays in some cases. This finding is similar to the results of earlier studies undertaken in emerging economies (for example Montano, 2009). India, however, has a significant economy and this situation cannot be tolerated; the PACI needs to find innovative ways to encourage the Ministries and Government Departments to embrace a more disciplined and consistent approach to providing timely responses, otherwise the relevance of the process may be threatened. The government entity responding to PACI is required to advise of its actions or proposals, and untimely responses or non-response raise important concerns over the appropriate acquittal of the accountability of the Executive (Ministries and Departments) to Parliament, and cast doubt over the legitimacy of those arms of government.

It appears from the results of this study that while PACI has been successful in scrutinizing government accounts and making recommendations, suggestions and comments aimed at promoting good governance, it has not yet been successful in achieving important tangible improvements in all areas. While the PACI report and response process can be seen to have enhanced the monetary accountability of government, it has had a much lower impact on improving operational efficiency. Overall it appears that, specifically in regard to the integrity of data – that is, monitoring, collection, maintenance and updating of data, the assignment of responsibilities to individuals, and general operational efficiency – the PACI's success has been limited. This is all part of an evolutionary process, but unless firm action is taken, the performance and public accountability of some Ministries (in particular Railways) and departments will remain less than satisfactory. Hence future regulation is suggested to attribute direct monitoring power to PACI. There does not appear to be such an opportunity for PACs in other countries to directly monitor government departments. Hence, this suggestion has implications for strengthening the authority of the PACI and for further development of PACs in other countries.

Finally, this study is limited to an analysis of 50 PACI reports. Future studies in this area could use a larger sample. Interviews and surveys of Ministers, Ministry and Departmental staff and PACI members are also likely to provide insights into deep-rooted causes behind the present state of the PACI's success.

References

Bovens, M. (2005) 'Public accountability', in E. Ferlie L. Lynn and C. Pollitt (eds) *Public Management*, Oxford: Oxford University Press, pp. 182–208.

Brown, A. M. (2011) 'The milieu of government reporting in Vanuatu', *Pacific Accounting Review*, 23(2): 165–84.

Census Info India (2011) www.censusindia.gov.in/2011census/censusinfodashboard/index.html (accessed 24 April 2014).

Degeling, P., Anderson J. and Guthrie, J. (1996) 'Accounting for public accounts committees', *Accounting, Auditing and Accountability Journal*, 9(2): 30–49.

Dow, B. J. (1996) *Prime-time Feminism: television, media culture, and the women's movement since 1970*, Philadelphia: University of Pennsylvania Press.

Economic Research Foundation (2006) *Government Health Expenditure in India: A benchmark study*, New Delhi: MacArthur Foundation.

Entman, R. (2003) *Projections of Power: Framing news, public opinion and U.S. foreign policy*, Chicago: University of Chicago Press.

Funnell, W. (2003) 'Enduring fundamentals: constitutional accountability and auditors-general in the reluctant state', *Critical Perspectives on Accounting*, 14: 107–32.

Fursich, E. (2009) 'In defence of textual analysis', *Journalism Studies*, 10(2): 238–52.

Gray, A. and Jenkins, W. (1993) 'Codes of accountability in the new public sector', *Accounting Auditing and Accountability Journal*, 6(3): 52–67.

Higgins, J. (1986) 'Raymond Williams and the problem of ideology', in J Arac (ed.) *Postmodernism and Politics*, Minneapolis: University of Minnesota Press.

India Country Monitor (2014) *Country Intelligence: Report: India.*, http://web.a.ebscohost.com/ehost/pdfviewer/pdfviewer?vid=12&sid=201ca182-2c65-4fea-b6fd-226d8ed0b1c0%40sessionmgr4002&hid=4209 (accessed 2 February 2015).

Jacobs, K. (2013) 'The capacity and performance of public accounts committees', Australasian Council of Public Accounts Committees Conference, Sydney, Australia.

Jacobs, K. and Jones, K. (2009) 'Legitimacy and parliamentary oversight in Australia: the rise and fall of two public accounts committees', *Accounting, Auditing & Accountability Journal*, 22(1): 13–34.

Jones, K. (2006) 'Exactly on all-fours with the English precedent – establishing a public accounts committee in the Antipodes', *Victorian Historical Journal*, 77(2): 194–211.

Jones, K. and Jacobs, K. (2006) 'Governing the government: the paradoxical place of the public accounts committee', *Australian Parliamentary Review*, 21(1): 63–79.

Jones, K. and Jacobs, K. (2009) 'Public accounts committees, new public management, and institutionalism: a case study', *Politics & Policy*, 37(5): 1023–46.

McGee, D. (2002) *The Overseers: Public accounts committees and public spending*, London: Pluto Press.

Montano, D. (2009) 'Financial accountability: enhancing the functions of the public accounts Committees in Trinidad and Tobago', *The Parliamentarian*, 3: 232–5.

Mulgan, R. (2000) 'Accountability: An ever-expanding concept?', *Public Administration*, 78 (3): 555–73.

Normanton, E. L. (1971) 'Public accountability and audit: a reconnaissance', in B. R. L. Smith and D. C. Hague (eds) *The Dilemma of Accountability in Modern Government: Independence versus control.*, New York: St Martin's Press.

Okpala, K. E. (2013) 'Public accounts committee and oversight function in Nigeria: a tower built on sinking sand', *International Journal of Business and Management*, 8(13): 111–17.

Parliament of India (2014) *Committee Reports*, http://164.100.47.134/committee/reports_
page.aspx (accessed 6 March 2014).

Pawsey, N., Brown, A. and Chatterjee, B. (2013) 'The potential adoption of IFRS for U.S.
Issuers: A textual analysis of responses to the proposal', *Asian Journal of Business and
Accounting*, 6(1): 59–93.

Pelizzo, R. (2010), 'Public Accounts Committees in the Pacific Region', *Politics &
Policy*, 38(1): 117–37.

Pelizzo, R., Stapenhurst, R., Sahgal, V. and Woodley, W. (2006) 'What Makes Public
Accounts Committees Work? A Comparative Analysis', *Politics & Policy*, 34(4): 774–93.

Reid, D. (1968) 'The Parliamentary Joint Committee of Public Accounts', in W. Jay and
R. Mathews (eds), *Government Accounting in Australia*, Melbourne: Cheshire.

Samsuddin, R. S. and Mohamed, N. (2009) 'The magnitude of public accounts committee's (PACs) work in reviewing and reporting on state governments' financial statements', *Malaysian Accounting Review*, 8(2): 1–15.

Shah, H. and Nah, S. (2004) 'Long ago and far away: how U.S. newspapers construct
racial oppression', *Journalism*, 5(3): 259–78.

Spann, R. N. (1979) *Government Administration in Australia*, Sydney: George Allen &
Unwin.

Steeves, H. L. (1997) *Gender Violence and the Press: the St. Kizito story*, Athens: Ohio
University Centre for International Studies.

The World Bank (2012) 'GNI per capita, Atlas method', http://data.worldbank.org/indic-
ator/NY.GNP.PCAP.CD (accessed 24 April 2014).

Wehner, J. (2003) 'Principles and patterns of financial scrutiny: Public Accounts Committees in the Commonwealth', *Commonwealth and Comparative Politics*, 41(3): 21–36.

14 Promoting public sector accountability in Indonesia

A historical overview

Bambang Setiono and Chandra Ery Prasetyo

Introduction

After the fall of President Suharto in 1998, Indonesia ran free and fair legislative elections in 1999, which led to the establishment of democratic rule. Today, Indonesia is the world's third most populous democracy, the world's largest archipelagic state, and the world's largest Muslim-majority nation (CIA, 2014). Despite Suharto never having formally been convicted, for health reasons, his fall was allegedly due to corruption. Suharto, who became president after the first Indonesian President, Sukarno, governed Indonesia with authoritarian rule under the political system called the 'New Order'. It was thought that corruption was endemic under Suharto's regime because of the country's lack of democratic rule. Since then, it has become apparent, however, that increasing democracy in Indonesia did not lead to increased accountability of politicians and corporations in managing public funds and other interests.

Despite successfully running three peaceful presidential and legislative elections, the democratic Indonesian government has failed to stop corruption. Indonesia is today a democracy and the 16th largest economy in the world, but corruption remains endemic (Cochrane, 2013). Several members of the Indonesian Parliament, *Dewan Perwakilan Rakyat* (DPR) have been charged in relation to significant corruption cases and some are still under investigation by the Indonesian anti-corruption commission, *Komisi Pemberantasan Korupsi* (KPK). High-level government officers, including police officers and judges, have also been implicated in corruption cases. Most of these cases are in relation to misused government funds. There is a discussion of cases handled by KPK later in the chapter.

Under these political, economic and social conditions, DPR created a state financial accountability agency, the Indonesian Public Accounts Committee – *Badan Akuntabilitas Keuangan Negara* (BAKN). It was established in August 2009, under Law No. 27, Article 110, and was created to follow up on audits from the Indonesian Supreme Audit Institution, *Badan Pemeriksa Keuangan Republik Indonesia* (BPK-RI), and inform members of DPR of their findings to help prevent the misuse of state funds and assets, stop its reoccurrence and improve government financial systems. More specifically, BAKN's mission was to:

1   review BPK audit reports presented to DPR;
2   present the result of their review to each commission in DPR;
3   follow up on DPR commissions' recommendations to executive members of government after the hearing on BPK's audit report; and
4   give recommendations to BPK-RI about annual audit planning, difficulties in performing audits as well as presenting quality of audit reports.

The BAKN committee was expected to respond appropriately and quickly to BPK-RI audit findings. For members of DPR to get the full benefits of their services, it was important for BAKN to have the capacity to understand and analyse issues raised in BPK-RI audit reports and provide timely information to members of DPR on their audit findings. It was also important for BAKN to be independent. This was a challenging mission that called for an 'ideal committee'.

The purpose of this chapter is to present a review of BAKN's capacity to improve public accountability and perform its mandate under the law. For this review, data analysed included BAKN's policy document and interviews with a member of BAKN and several general administrative staff. The findings reported in this chapter add to an increasing body of literature regarding the structure and operations of Public Accounts Committees (PACs) around the world (Jacobs and Jones, 2009; Jacobs *et al.*, 2007; Pelizzo and Stapenhurst, 2004; Stapenhurst *et al.*, 2005; Gay and Winetrobe, 2003; Wehner, 2003; McGee, 2002).

The rest of this chapter is organised as follows. In the next section, we outline the Indonesian political and economic environment. The third section presents a review of studies identifying the role of PAC in promoting public accountability. Section four summarises the method used for assessing the capacity of BAKN to promote public sector accountability. The fifth section presents our study's findings about BAKN's ability to perform its mission. Section six discusses the relationship between our findings and the abolition of BAKN in 2014. The chapter ends with our concluding remarks.

Indonesian context

Indonesia, located between two big countries, Australia and China, is the third most populated country in the world. Its population was 234.6 million in 2010 and has been growing at a rate of 1.32 per cent per year for the past five years. By the end of year 2025, the country's population is expected to reach 274 million.[1] Since 2008, Indonesia has been part of the lower middle-income countries. Its income per capita was US\$3,448 in the third quarter of 2013 (Badan Pusat Statistik, 2011). The Indonesian economy grew at a rate of 5.9 per cent during the third quarter of 2013 and, for the period from 2010 to 2014, grew at 6.28 per cent per year (Kementerian Keuangan, 2014).

After the resignation of long-time authoritarian president Suharto in May 1998, Indonesia launched fundamental constitutional reforms to promote democracy. These reforms led to changes to the constitutional law, *Undang-Undang Dasar* (1945), which allowed people to form political parties and civil organisations. The changes also allowed for direct elections of the President and Vice President as well as members of DPR. Other reforms included the creation of a second house of national legislature to represent the interests of the provinces – *Dewan Perwaki-lan Daerah* (DPD) – and a new court to judge the constitutionality of laws and referee election disputes. The new constitutional law also abolished the legislative seats previously set aside for high-ranking military members. Since 1999, Indonesia has also embarked on an ambitious decentralisation programme. This resulted in the direct election of provincial governors and district heads in 2005 (Carter Center, 2005).

Today, Indonesia is a unitary state in the form of a republic. By July 2013, there were 539 regional governments in Indonesia, consisting of 34 provincial governments, 412 district governments (*Kabupaten*) and 93 city governments (*Kota*).[2] The president holds the government's executive power while the Parliament has the power to create laws in discussion with the executive government. The president ratifies laws passed by DPR. The operations of DPR are structured as follows (Sherlock, 2007b):

1   The Leadership of the House (the Speaker and four Vice Speakers);
2   The Steering Committee (*Badan Musyarawarah*) that decides the agenda of the annual sessions;
3   The *Komisi* that exercises the power of DPR;
4   The Budget Committee (*Panitia Anggaran*) that determines the government's annual budget (APBN);
5   The Legislation Committee (*Badan Legislasi*) that prepares and drafts laws initiated by DPR;
6   The House Affairs Committee (BURT) that manages the budget of DPR activities;
7   The Committee for Inter-Parliamentary Cooperation (BKSAP) that is responsible for DPR's relations with foreign legislatures and international parliamentary organisations; and
8   The Public Account Committee (BAKN) that is responsible for assisting DPR in responding to BPK's audit reports.

In addition to the power to legislate, DPR also has the power to:

- select members of the Supreme Audit Board (BPK);
- deal with the results of BPK's investigations;
- approve the membership of the Judicial Commission;
- approve the membership of the Supreme Court as nominated by the Judicial Commission;
- select three out of nine candidates to be Constitutional Court Judge;
- give its opinion on the President's selection of ambassadors and receipt of foreign ambassadors; and
- approve the President's declaration of war or peace or signing of international treaties (Sherlock, 2007b).

The BPK-RI was set up as the Supreme Audit Institution (SAI) of the Republic of Indonesia to audit the management and accountability of state finance and to audit financial reports of the central and all regional governments.[3] It also has an obligation to annually audit financial reports of all state companies owned by the central government, *Badan Usaha Milik Negara* (BUMN), or owned by regional governments, *Badan Usaha Milik Daerah* (BUMD). By August 2013, the Indonesian government owned approximately 140 BUMN with total assets of IDR3,500 trillion – the equivalent of US$292 billion (Indonesian Corruption Watch, 2013). The audit reports of BPK-RI are submitted to DPR, the Regional Representative Council (DPD), provincial DPR and district DPR. The main role of DPD is to ensure laws are passed by DPR and that executive members of the government release regulations that support the country's regional autonomy.

Despite its being a democracy, corruption is still entrenched in Indonesia's political, social and economic environment. During the 2013 fiscal year, the KPK caught several government officials in the act of corruption. These government officials included Members of Parliament (DPR) arrested for bribery in the beef import quota policy, the Head of Oil and Gas Licensing Agency, *Satuan Kerja Khusus Pelaksana Kegiatan Usaha Hulu Minyak dan Gas Bumi* (SKK Migas), arrested for bribery in oil and gas licences, and the Head of the Constitutional Court, arrested for bribery in general election cases in several districts. The KPK also charged several other government officials with corruption, including the Governor of Riau province in relation to a forestry licence case and a national sport competition, *Pekan Olah Raga Nasional* (PON), and the Minister of Youth and Sport in relation to the development of Hambalang's sport centre case (KPK, 2014). Prior to 2013, KPK had also arrested a tax officer in relation to a million-dollar fraud case, members of DPR in relation to the selection of the central bank's governor, high-ranking police officers and state prosecutors for bribery in many investigations and prosecution cases, and other government officers in cases pertaining to public services. None of these corruption cases were originated by the work of BAKN. In most cases, KPK raised these cases based on their own investigations.

This is a challenging environment for any auditing body to perform its mission of promoting transparency and accountability. Corruption in Indonesia is common and has been more prevalent since Indonesia became a more open society (World Bank, 2003). The World Bank (2003) argues that corruption threatens democracy by destroying people's faith in formal rules and key organisations that are charged with safeguarding them. Corruption weakens a state's ability to deliver basic and essential public services and the rules that allow society to function effectively. It undermines the legitimacy and credibility of the state in the eyes of the people. Corruption, therefore, represents a significant threat to a successful political and economic transition for Indonesia from being regarded as a corrupt nation.

The PAC and public sector accountability

Audit is the crucial component of accountability, because it gives legitimacy to the information provided in financial reports or any report prepared for the purpose of accountability. Both the quality and the credibility of the audit determine the legitimacy of the information reported in the audited financial reports.

The public rely on the quality and credibility of auditors and the audit profession to assess the legitimacy of the information provided. There is, however, an 'expectation gap' between the auditing profession and the public's expectations (Koh and Woo, 1998; Godsell, 1992; Liggio, 1974). There is an expectation gap when auditors and the public hold different beliefs about auditors' duties and responsibilities and the messages conveyed by audit reports. For the private sector, the public, who depend on the audit report in making decisions about an organisation, expect no material error in the financial report prepared by the organisation. If, after the release of audit reports, an organisation collapses, the public are likely to blame the auditor for not informing them of the risk of collapse. However, auditors would argue that an organisation collapsing after the release of their audit report is not their responsibility. In the case of the public sector, the public will blame auditors if, after the release of audit reports, law enforcement officers find evidence of corruption by public officers. For example, Enron Corporation's shareholders sued the company's auditor, Arthur Andersen, following its collapse in 2002. The case brought down one of the then top five accounting firms in the world (Brown and Dugan, 2002). More recently, Fitzgerald (2014) reported the case of PricewaterhouseCoopers LLP, faced with a $1 billion lawsuit from the Federal Deposit Insurance Corporation, alleging that the accounting firm failed to detect and report on the massive fraud that led to the collapse of Colonial Bank, one of the largest bank collapses in US history.

In order to reduce the expectation gap, auditors need to improve their credibility and legitimacy of audit. According to Gendron *et al.* (2001), auditors' independence is an important factor to maintain the credibility and legitimacy of their practice. They argue that audit independence is socially constructed based on a range of sources, including audit and company laws, professional regulations, audit practices and education about civil society and democracy. The public are unlikely to perceive audit independence when auditors receive significant benefits or are under pressure from their auditees. Benefits can take many forms, including audit fees and management advisory fees, and can be difficult to trace when not directly linked to specific auditing jobs, such as presents or support for religious events. Pressure from clients or auditees can take a soft form, such as reducing benefits, or a hard form, such as physical and emotional threats.

Humphrey and Moizer (1990) found that people's perception of audit independence in the private sector was lower since private sector auditors were thought to be less able to withstand pressure from their clients. In that context, auditors were more seen as business consultants than as guardians of public interest. Power (1997) identified problems with audit independence in the public sector, especially when auditors reviewed the effectiveness of government policies. This was the case because auditors did not want to be seen to be challenging a political policy when making recommendations to improve the effectiveness of government policies. Thus, it is thought that auditors will not provide audit objective opinions as they ought to.

Accountability and transparency in the use of governments' funds are fundamental to the proper functioning of a democratic system (Funnell and Cooper, 1998). By making publicly available financial activities and transactions, political leaders and governments are held accountable for their actions. A PAC is set up primarily to improve the accountability of a democratic government's system (Stapenhurst and Kroon, 2011; Watson, 2004). It assists the parliament in assessing the proper use of government funds by its executive members. Under the Westminster system of government, the PAC is considered as one of many public initiatives aimed at reducing the influence of executive members of the government who have a monopoly on information about government functions (Watson, 2004). Generally speaking, the PAC is the oldest committee in the parliament and the most significant one (Stapenhurst and Kroon, 2011). The PAC is part of the parliamentary infrastructure that helps Members of Parliament ensure that executive members of government can account for their practices, policies and use of public resources (McGee, 2002).

The performance of PACs in improving the accountability of most democratic governments depends on reports from their Auditors-General. The PACs conduct detailed examination of the Auditor-General's reports. In general, they also have the power to initiate investigations themselves, or to respond to resolutions of the Parliament or references from ministers. The PACs generally investigate the way policy is implemented rather than the appropriateness of the policy. Since PACs do not question the appropriateness of a public policy, PAC reports usually present consensual conclusions. Because of this convention, PACs can rely on the cooperation of executive members when examining government financial decisions, and, thus, have more influence on the actions of the public sector than other Parliament committees (Watson, 2004).

A study on early operations of PACs recommended three ways of improving PACs' oversight functions (McGee, 2002). The functions of a PAC can be improved, first, by having the appropriate level of staffing and resources, training and access to information. Second, PACs should receive credible and legitimate reports from an independent non-partisan Auditor-General. Credible reports help PACs in ensuring executive members of government can account for all their programmes and projects. Third, PACs need to exchange information and ideas with executive members so that they can keep up to date with developments, changing standards and best practices. Stapenhurst *et al.* (2005) further developed McGee's study by evaluating the performance of PACs in Commonwealth countries and identified 17 attributes of an ideal or successful committee. They found that successful PACs focused on governments' financial activities rather than their policies, investigated all past and present government expenses, followed up on government actions in response to recommendations and managed a positive working relationship with auditors general.

The above studies suggest PACs play an important and legitimate role in keeping executive members of government accountable for their actions. They can work towards reducing information asymmetry between Members of Parliament and executive members of government on government matters that serve the public interest. The PACs can help Members of Parliament better understand audit findings about the activities of executive members of government. When the Parliament works towards the general public's interest, PACs can meet the public's expectations. What is then required is for PACs to have the capacity (e.g. staffing, skills and budget) as well as the authority to access a variety of information, including audit reports of the government auditors, and open up public discussion on their findings.

Method

Given PACs' general functions and ideal operations, this study analysed BAKN's capacity and role in improving the public sector's efficiency and accountability in Indonesia. To do this, we used the 17 attributes of an 'ideal committee' proposed by Stapenhurst *et al.* (2005), which include:

1   Small size;
2   Chaired by a senior opposition figure;
3   Chaired by a fair-minded and respected Member of Parliament;
4   Membership for the full term of the Parliament;
5   Adequately resourced with an experienced clerk and a competent researcher(s);
6   Clear role and responsibilities;
7   Meet frequently and regularly;
8   Hearings opened to the public;
9   Supported by a steering committee;
10   Able to question high-ranking government officers;
11   Automatically receive auditors' reports;
12   No limitation for investigation;
13   Able to get a consensus on recommendations;
14   Issue formal substantive reports to parliament at least annually;
15   Follow up on recommendations;
16   Partnership with the auditor;
17   Parliaments hold an annual debate on the work of the committee.

This study investigated BAKN's ability to deliver on its mission using 16 of Stapenhurst *et al.*'s (2005) attributes. Attribute no. 3 was excluded from this study as measuring levels of fair-mindedness and respect towards the Chair of BAKN was beyond our scope.

To measure the extent to which BAKN was an 'ideal' PAC, according to the 16 attributes, data were collected through interviews and by reviewing documents provided by BAKN as well as those available publicly. The interviews were conducted between September and December 2013 with four people: the head of audit experts, one audit expert and two consultants of BAKN. Of these, one was a politician and the others were professional employees. Semi-structured interviews based on the 16 attributes were conducted with the head of audit experts and one audit expert. With the consultants, we conducted unstructured interviews to better understand their role in increasing BAKN's capacity. The documents reviewed included BAKN's annual reports, journals and BAKN policy statements.

Findings

The main function of BAKN is to follow up on audit reports produced by BPK-RI for DPR on the use of state funds submitted.[4] Every year, DPR receives more than thousands of audit reports from BPK-RI. It is impossible for members of DPR to analyse all these reports properly without the support of BAKN. The results of BAKN's analysis of BPK-RI audit reports are submitted to DPR. It is expected that BAKN will improve the role of DPR in supervising the use of state funds. Every year, BPK-RI conducts a financial audit for all state government agencies including state-owned and local government owned companies, and BPK-RI also performs special audits to investigate issues of misuse of public funds as they or DPR see fit.

Given the environment and level of corruption in Indonesia, establishing BAKN was a big achievement for those concerned with public accountability; these included people in BPK-RI and several members of DPR. There was strong support for the establishment of BAKN from the former chief of BPK-RI, Mr Anwar Nasution, who felt that valuable information contained in audit reports was not being properly used by DPR. During his interview the head of the audit experts of BAKN on the history of establishing BAKN revealed that Mr Nasution, although not a politician, was able to influence members of DPR to establish BAKN because of his relationship with the Golkar Party – the second-largest political party in DPR. As the former Deputy Governor of the Indonesian Central Bank, Bank Indonesia, he was able to gain support from the Chairman of Golkar Party between 2004 and 2009, Mr Yusuf Kalla, and succeeded in persuading members of DPR to form BAKN. It should be noted that, unlike with the development of KPK, civil society groups or the public in general did not have a significant role in developing BAKN. However, BAKN did receive support from various organisations concerned with democratic accountability and transparency of public funds, such as the US Agency for International Development (USAID) and Australian National Audit Office (ANAO).

The request to establish PAC was in line with Article 69 Law No. 27 of 2009, which states that the Parliament has three functions: making laws (legislation), preparing budgets, and performing oversight.[5] For legislative function, DPR established *Badan Legislatif* (Baleg), and for performing the budgeting function it established *Badan Anggaran* (Banggar). However, DPR did not establish a committee to perform an oversight function until it established BAKN in 2009.

Since its inception, no major changes have been made to BAKN. The only changes have been in terms of committee members. The current committee of BAKN consists of nine people who are all Members of Parliament (DPR). The membership of BAKN is regulated under point 2 of Article 111, Law No. 27, 2009, which states that BAKN should have a minimum of seven members and a maximum of nine to be appointed at the beginning of parliamentary session based on nominations by fractions (*Fraksis*) in the parliament. The number and composition of committee members are considered 'ideal' according to Stapenhurst *et al.*'s (2005) criteria. Between December 2011 and November 2013, BAKN consisted of 9 members (see Table 14.1)

In the 2009 elections, nine political parties shared the 560 seats in DPR. The Demokrat Party had the majority of seats, controlling 148 seats, followed by the Golkar Party, with 108 seats. The PDI-P party held the third greatest number of seats, with 93 seats. Of these parties, PDI-P and Gerindra formed the Opposition, while the other seven parties formed a coalition government led by the Demokrat Party. Each party represented in DPR had a representative in BAKN. The chairwoman of BAKN was Mrs Sumarjati Arjoso, member of the opposition (Gerindra Party). In addition to the BAKN Chair, Mrs Sumarjati Arjoso, Mrs Eva Kusuma Sundari was also a member of the opposition (PDI-P Party). Interviewees considered both members to be influential senior representatives of their respective party with the capacity to be vocal and critical of executive members of government. Before December 2011, the chair of BAKN was Mr Ahmad Muzani (BAKN, 2011). He was a member of Gerindra, the opposition party. Thus, committee members were from both sides of the political spectrum and on occasion acted as representatives of their political party. This is consistent with practices in other countries and Stapenhurst *et al.*'s (2005) attributes of an 'ideal committee'.

The ability of BAKN to perform its mission is commensurate with political parties' commitment to assign their members to BAKN for a whole term of Parliament. This means that BAKN loses its ability to perform well when political parties only assign members for short terms. This has often been the case and is not an 'ideal' condition according to Stapenhurst *et al.* (2005). People can only

Table 14.1 BAKN (Indonesian PAC) members, November 2013

Name	Position	Political party
Dr Sumarjati Arjoso, SKM	Chairman	Gerindra
Mayjen TNI (Purn) Yahya Sacawiria, S.Ip., MM	Vice Chairman	Demokrat
Ir. H. Teguh Juwarno, M.Si	Member	PAN
Ir. Nur Yasin, MBA	Member	PKB
Drs Kamaruddin Sjam, MM	Member	Golkar
Drs H. Muchtar Amma, MM	Member	Hanura
Dr A. W. Thalib, M. Si	Member	PPP
Dra. Eva Kusuma Sundari M.A., MDE	Member	PDI-P
Fahri Hamzah	Member	PKS

serve as BAKN members when they are appointed by their *Fraksis* (representatives of the political parties in DPR). There are nine *Fraksis* in DPR, one per political party represented in DPR. A *Fraksi* is a parliamentary party similar to those in a Westminster Parliament (Sherlock, 2007b). If a political party has 11 members in DPR, it can form a *Fraksi* in DPR. Otherwise, it has to join a *Fraksi* established by another political party. Between 2009 and 2014, DPR organised into the following nine *Fraksi*:

1 *Fraksi* Demokrat Party
2 *Fraksi* Golkar Party
3 *Fraksi* PDI-P
4 *Fraksi* PKS
5 *Fraksi* PAN
6 *Fraksi* PPP
7 *Fraksi* PKB
8 *Fraksi* Gerindra
9 *Fraksi* Hanura

We found that BAKN was adequately resourced and budgeted for. It had an acceptable level of full-time staff (8) to perform administrative duties and was well was supported by experts in government auditing (5) previously working either at BPK-RI or the government internal auditor (BPKP). However, it would have required more research staff to meet the 'ideal' standard of PAC. Research staffs are important as they help improve BAKN members' ability to review audit reports and search for more substantive information relevant to issues raised by auditors.

The BAKN has a strong legal basis to perform its function. Under Article 113 of Law No. 27 of 2009 about MPR, DPR, DPD, and DPRD – usually called MD3 Law – and Article 70 DPR RI Regulation No. 01/DPR RI/I/2009–2010 regarding Order in the Parliament, the BAKN had four missions and five authorities to perform its missions. To perform the third mission, the BAKN is endowed with the authority to:

• request BPK-RI, government agencies, state-owned enterprises and other organisations managing state funds to appear before the BAKN;
• give recommendations to commissions to request BPK-RI to perform follow-up audits;
• periodically present its performance to the DPR leadership in DPR general assembly meetings;
• obtain support from accountants, experts, financial analysts and researchers; and
• be allocated a budget to perform its mission.

The BAKN is set up as an internal body of DPR to improve public accountability. It does not have the authority to report publicly on its review of BPK-RI audit reports, nor can it seek input from the general public to perform these reviews. Commissions of DPR are responsible for explaining to or getting inputs from the general public in relation to results of BPK-RI audit reports. The ability of BAKN to properly function is further limited by the fact that it has no steering committee. Ideally, a steering committee would help BAKN plan work in advance and prepare an agenda for each meeting with all its committee members.

Moreover, the general public has no access to summary reports from BAKN hearings. The BAKN expert leader interviewed stated that BAKN had two types of hearings: a closed hearing, *Rapat Dengar Pendapat* (RDP); and an open hearing, *Rapat Dengar Pendapat Umum* (RDPU). The general public may attend RDPUs only. Also, contrary to BAKN's statement, the general public has no access to minutes of meetings for both closed and open hearings.

The ability of BAKN to deliver on its missions would improve if it was able to produce quality reports. The quality of reports depends on whether BAKN can meet several criteria. First, BAKN would need to hold regular and frequent members' meetings. In practice, BAKN members meet once a week and, in general, most members attend these meetings. Second, BAKN would need to be able to bring before the committee relevant government employees to answer certain questions. The law provides BAKN with the power to call anyone in public office to appear before it. However, in practice, BAKN has experienced some difficulty in summoning heads of departments or ministers to appear before the committee, although it was successful in calling experts and deputy ministers as witnesses during hearings. Third, it would need full support from the auditor. In this case, the relation between BAKN and the auditor (BPK-RI) is positive as BPK-RI championed the establishment of BAKN. The BAKN experts communicate extensively with auditors of BPK-RI to gain a better understanding of audit findings. However, the auditor's reports can only go to BAKN once BPK-RI has presented the summary of audit findings to members of DPR. Indeed, the Chairman of BPK-RI passes the audit reports to the Chairman of DPR, who passes them to the Chairman of BAKN. Fourth, BAKN would need to be able to conduct its own investigation when audit reports are seen not to cover important issues. This has been done on occasions; BAKN has at times conducted its own investigation into matters not covered by audit reports. Fifth, the BAKN report to the DPR commission would need to present consensus in order to gain full political support in implementing their recommendations. By design, BAKN reports are the product of consensus amongst its members. Each BAKN member represents a different political party and there is only one member per political party. Sixth, results and recommendations to improve public services need to be traced and monitored. The BAKN works closely with DPR commissions to monitor recommendations given to executive members of governments (the working partners). Government agencies need to report on the progress of implementing recommendations to DPR commissions and BAKN. Finally, BAKN reports would need to be discussed with all members of DPR, and DPR usually organises debates or discussions about the work of the committee every semester or twice a year. Debates usually focus on reviewing BAKN's achievements and follow-up activities already undertaken by government agencies.

Discussion

Our analysis using Stapenhurst *et al.*'s (2005) criteria shows that BAKN was an 'ideal' PAC. It had the authority to improve public accountability and the ability to perform its legal mandate. It was a remarkable achievement for the public accountability movement in Indonesia given the political, social and economic conditions of the country and the lack of support for DPR. Unfortunately, the capacity of BAKN to perform its operations could not be fully assessed in this study because no BAKN annual or operating reports could be reviewed. However, as we argue below, the dismantling in July 2014 of BAKN might suggest that BAKN was successful in improving the government's accountability on their use of public funds.

In an unpopular move, members of DPR for the period 2010–14 revised the MD3 law under the People's Consultative Council (MPR), the house of people representatives (DPR), the House of Regional Representatives (DPD) and the Regional DPR (DPRD). This revised law resulted in: (1) the dismantling of the BAKN; and (2) the removal of the right of the winning party in the legislative election to lead DPR and any of its commissions, as was previously the case.

The abolition of BAKN was not seen as a controversial issue amongst members of DPR. This might be because DPR lacked a culture of public accountability, as suggested by Sherlock (2007b). The issue of BAKN's abolition was, however, raised by BPK-RI, its founding father, and by some NGOs, such as FITRA (Forum Indonesia Untuk Tranparansi Anggaran, the Indonesian Forum for Budget Transparency), concerned with public accountability. Despite their concern, they were not able to bring this issue to the attention of the general public.

This abolition was the result of several political forces. It is likely that members of DPR and executive members of the government, under pressure from BAKN's work, successfully influenced other members of DPR to dismantle the organisation. The abolition of BAKN was also the result of the need for DPR to address public criticism over the role of the Budget Committee (*Panitia Anggaran*). According to public opinion the standing committee was seen as corrupt and able to exercise too much power over the government's budget. Initially, politicians proposed to abolish all DPR standing committees, including the Steering Committee (Badan Musyawarah), the Legislation Committee (*Badan Legislasi*), the House Affairs Committee (BURT), the Committee for Inter-Parliamentary Cooperation (BKSAP) and BAKN. In the end, as an interview with a former BAKN's audit expert (August 2014) revealed, with the support of the Minister for Finance, parliamentarians decided to keep the Budget Committee and all other standing committees, but not the BAKN. During the follow-up interview with the head of audit experts, it was also revealed that BAKN was not supported by members of DPR or some executives due to the organisation's principles – to perform its mission based on an ideal concept of non-partisan public accountability and make recommendations to the Chairman of DPR based on technical audit findings.

With the abolition of BAKN, the powerful members of DPR have shown their lack of support for public accountability. As Sherlock has (2007b: 4) stated:

> [B]oth the members and the officials of the DPR largely remain captured by a culture that lacks transparency and accountability. Public access to information and documentation on the work of the DPR is virtually non-existent and is subject to the whim of individuals who trade on the power of control of information.
>
> (Sherlock 2007b: 4)

This lack of accountability of DPR is still the case despite increasing public involvement in the selection of members of DPR.

The second controversy in the unpopular move to revise the MD3 law was the removal of the right of members of the winning party in the legislative election to lead DPR or any of its commissions. This revision was supported by the coalition of dominant parties in the 2009 legislative election – who were defeated in both the 2014 legislative election and the presidential election. Under this revised law, by using the voting system the defeated political parties can still win leadership in each commission if they can form a coalition that has more voting rights than the coalition of parties led by the winning political party. Practically, this reduces the ability of the winning political party to influence decisions by DPR. In 2014, the PDI-P won in the legislative and the presidential elections against all the other six major parties. The revised MD3 law allows the opposition parties – currently the coalition of parties defeated in the last presidential election – to take on all the commission's leadership positions since they have more voting rights over the wining party and its coalition.

Between 2009 and 2014, DPR set up 11 standing committees, called Commissions (*Komisi*). Each commission has responsibility for a number of policy areas and a number of counterpart or partner agencies in the Executive (Sherlock, 2007a). The current commissions were created to deal with government functions pertaining to national defence and foreign affairs, public administration, law and order, forestry and environment, education, state finance, banking and monetary, among others. Except for the Chairman and the Vice Chairman of DPR, every member of DPR must be a member of one commission in DPR. The DPR regulation determines the number of commissions they can have, the number of government agencies that can be working partners with the commissions and the scope of work undertaken by the commissions. Members of DPR are assigned to commissions. One member can only join one commission. To be able to participate in a commission, a political party needs to be a member of *Fraksi* or Caucus in DPR.

Following the last revision of the constitutional law, DPR now holds significant power and is able to influence the government's functions. Indeed, if each *Fraksi* in DPR attempts to control each commission by putting a member of their

Fraksi as the leader of a commission, it is understandable that they will have a significant influence over decisions and matters determined by DPR. This is a challenge for Indonesia's democratic rule. But, as we learned from the establishment and abolition of BAKN, the influence of a powerful individual or organisation can be countered by initiatives that seek to pursue public accountability, especially when it has the general public's support.

Conclusion

The former Chairman of BPK-RI lobbied members of DPR to establish BAKN to improve public accountability. When the Chairman retired from his position, BAKN fell under the pressure of members of DPR who had little interest in public accountability. Contrary to the establishment of BAKN, the Indonesian public provided very strong support for the establishment of KPK, the anti-corruption agency. This lack of public interest in PAC in Indonesia needs to be better understood and constitutes an area for further studies. Though KPK has extraordinary judicial power, it has little understanding of the role of PAC in preventing and eradicating corruption.

The dismantling of BAKN and therefore of the Indonesian public accountability system will add pressure to the young Indonesian democracy. Champions of public accountability in Indonesia are fighting back. There is a judicial review process currently under way to bring the revised MD3 law to the Constitutional Court, involving civil society groups, the winning party of the 2014 general elections, DPD and KPK. They hope the judicial review will bring back BAKN to the public accountability system in Indonesia.

Notes

1 Indonesia long-term development planning, Law No. 17, 2007.
2 www.kppod.org/datapdf/daerah/daerah-indonesia-2013.pdf, accessed 3 July 2014.
3 Indonesian constitutional law, Undang-Undang Dasar (UUD) 1945, Article 23E, number 1.
4 www.dpr.go.id/id/bakn (accessed 10 November 2013).
5 Law No. 27, year 2009, regarding Majelis Permusyawaratan Rakyat (MPR), Dewan Perwakilan Rakyat (DPR), Dewan Perwakilan Daerah (DPD), and Dewan Perwakilan Rakyat Daerah (DPRD).

References

Badan Pusat Statistik (Statistics Indonesia) (2011) 'Penduduk Indonesia menurut Provinsi 1971, 1980, 1990, 1995, 2000 dan 2010', www.bps.go.id/tab_sub/view.php?kat=1&tabel=1&daftar=1&id_subyek=12&notab=1 (accessed 10 February 2014).

BAKN (2011) *Kinerja BAKN DPR RI selama periode 2010–2011*. Jakarta: Laporan BAKN DPR RI.

Brown, K. and Dugan, I. J. (2002) 'Arthur Andersen's Fall From Grace Is a Sad Tale of Greed and Miscues', *Wall Street Journal*, 7 June. Available at: http://online.wsj.com/articles/SB1023409436545200# (accessed 14 October 2014).

Carter Center (2005) *2004 Indonesia Election Report*, Atlanta: The Carter Center's Special Report Series.

Central Intelligence Agency (CIA) (2014) *The World Factbook*, 'Indonesia', www.cia.gov/library/publications/the-world-factbook/geos/id.html (accessed 30 January 2015).

Cochrane, J. (2013) 'Indonesian Strongman's Legacy Remains a Matter of Debate,' *New York Times*, 19 May.

Fitzgerald, P. (2014) 'Accounting Firm Must Face FDIC Suit Over Colonial Bank Failure, Judge Says PricewaterhouseCoopers Must Answer Government's Suit', *Wall Street Journal*, 16 July. Available at: http://online.wsj.com/articles/accounting-firm-must-face-fdic-suit-over-colonial-bank-failure-1405531036 (accessed 14 October 2014).

Funnell, W. and Cooper, K. (1998) *Public Sector Accounting and Accountability In Australia*, Sydney: UNSW Press.

Gay, O. and Winetrobe, B. K. (2003) *Officers of Parliament: Transforming the role*. London: The Constitution Unit, School of Public Policy, UCL.

Gendron, Y., Cooper, D. J. and Townley, B. (2001) 'In the name of accountability: State auditing, independence and new public management', *Accounting, Auditing & Accountability Journal*, 14 (3): 278.

Godsell, D. (1992) 'Legal liability and audit expectation gap', *Singapore Accountant*, 8: 25–8.

Koh, H. C. and Woo, E.-S. (1998) 'The expectation gap in auditing', *Managerial Auditing Journal*, 13(3): 147–54.

Humphrey, C. and Moizer, P. (1990) 'From techniques to ideologies: An alternative perspective on the audit function', *Critical Perspectives on Accounting*, 1(3): 217–38.

Indonesian Corruption Watch (ICW) (2013) 'BUMN Dalam Angka, Hasil penelusuran', Indonesia Corruption Watch – December.

Jacobs, K. and Jones, K. (2009) 'Legitimacy and Parliamentary Oversight in Australia: The Rise and Fall of two Public Accounts Committees', *Accounting Auditing and Accountability Journal* 22(1): 13–34.

Jacobs, K., Jones, K. and Smith, D. (2007) 'Public Accounts Committees in Australasia: the State of Play', *Australasian Parliamentary Review*, 22(1): 28–43.

Kementerian Keuangan (2014) *Arah dan strategi Pembangunan Kehutanan untuk Perubahan Iklim Dalam RPJMN 2015–2019*. Jakarta: Working Paper, Pusat Kebijakan Perubahan Iklim dan Multilateral (PKPPIM), Badan Kebijakan Fiskal.

KPK, 2014. *Laporan Tahunan tahun 2013*. Jakarta: Komisi Pemberantasan Korupsi.

Liggio, C. D. (1974) 'The expectation gap: the accountant's Waterloo', *Journal of Contemporary Business*, 3: 27–44.

McGee, D. G. (2002) *The Overseers: Public Accounts Committees and Public Spending*, London: Commonwealth Parliamentary Association and Photo Press.

Pelizzo, R. and Stapenhurst, R. (2004) 'Legislatures and Oversight: A Note', *Quaderni di Scienza Politica*, 11(1): 175–88.

Power, M. (1997) *The Audit Society: Rituals of Verification*, Oxford: Oxford University Press.

Sherlock, S. (2007a) *Parliamentary Indicators: Indonesia House of Representatives (DPR) and House of Regional Representatives (DPD)*, Jakarta: World Bank Institute.

Sherlock, S. (2007b) *The Indonesian Parliament after Two Elections: What has Really Changed?* Australia: CDI Policy Papers on Political Governance.

Stapenhurst, R. and Kroon, C. (2011) ;Public Accounts Committee Profiles and Performance in Canada', Ottawa: Canadian Study of Parliament Group.

Stapenhurst, R., Sahgal, V., Woodley, W. and Pelizzo, R. (2005) *Scrutinizing Public Expenditures: Assessing the Performance of Public Accounts Committees.* Policy Research Working Paper # 3613, Washington DC: World Bank.

Watson, D. (2004) 'The challenge for public accounts committees in evaluating public-private partnerships', *Australian Accounting Review*, 14 (2): 78–84.

Wehner, J. (2003) 'Principles and Patterns of Financial Scrutiny: Public Accounts Committees in the Commonwealth', *Commonwealth and Comparative Politics*, 41(3): 21–36.

World Bank (2003) *Combating Corruption in Indonesia: Enhancing Accountability for Development*, Jakarta: East Asia Poverty Reduction and Economic Management Unit.

15 The Public Accounts Committees in Thailand

A short note

Prapaipim Sutheewasinnon and Supot Saikaew

Introduction

Generally, in a democratic nation, the Parliament and the legislature are the most important institutions of the political system. The Parliament takes precedence over all other government institutions and its members have the power to legislate, vote to show confidence or not in the government and audit the government's budgets and expenditure (Tosaporn, 2003). The Parliament is the political institution that represents the public and supervises and monitors the public service's activities. The Constitution of Thailand gives Parliament the authority to approve the annual statements on expenditure by analysing, approving and apportioning the budget. The Thai Parliament is authorised to control the budget in two ways. First, it controls the budget before spending (pre-control) through an ad hoc committee appointed by the parliament. Second, it monitors the budget after spending (post-control) through the activities of a permanent committee called the Public Accounts Committee (PAC) (Tosaporn, 2003).

This chapter presents the role of the PAC in Thailand, considers the problems it encounters and outlines suggestions for the future. The method adopted to gather and analyse data presented in this chapter is a literature review of archives and other documents, such as internal reports, research publications and PAC information available online. This chapter proceeds as follows. The first section describes the role of the PAC in Thailand. Section two examines the problems regarding the operation of the PAC. The third section makes suggestions for the future.

The PAC in Thailand

The current 2550 BE[1] Constitution of the Kingdom of Thailand (2007) stipulates that Parliament consists of the House of Representatives and the Senate. Both entities directly control and audit the public sector's operations. One important role of the PAC is to ensure the implementation of the PAC's regulation of the legislation. The PAC consists of the Standing Committee and the Select Committee. The Standing Committee was established by the Parliament and comprises Members of Parliament and functions until the end of the Parliament's term. The Select Committee was also created under the auspices of the Parliament, and its members can be Members and non-Members of Parliament. The number of people on the Select Committee is determined by the Parliament, according to the nature of the special tasks or objectives set. The Select Committee will usually dissolve after the completion of its duties.

The authority of the PAC in Thailand

Since Thailand's Parliament is a bicameral legislature, the legislative committees are divided into two separate assemblies: the committees of the House of Representatives and the committees of the Senate. Consequently, the PAC in Thailand is divided into two boards: the PAC of the House of Representatives and the PAC of the Senate. The PACs in Thailand are appointed for the duration of Parliament and are then dismissed when Parliament is dissolved (Wattana *et al.*, 2008). Due to the recent political crisis in Thailand, the Parliament was dissolved in 2013. The National Legislative Assembly of Thailand (NLA) is a unicameral body comprising one unelected chamber, which was devised by the military under the auspices of the Interim Charter. The new PAC members were only recently appointed by the NLA in 2014.

Roles and responsibilities of the PACs

The PAC of the House of Representatives comprises 17 members who have the authority to investigate government budget policies and scrutinise the ways in which government agencies, departments and other state-owned enterprises spend the annual budget. It can also appoint a sub-committee to consider particular issues, appoint experts as consultants, specialists, academics and a secretary to the committee. Furthermore, the PAC of the House of Representatives can present opinions about the budget and ask relevant agencies to provide details about certain approved projects or initiatives that are presented to the Parliament. The PAC of the Senate consists of 15 members and it has the authority to review annual budget allocation policies, incomes and expenses as well as budget commitments over several years. In addition to this, the PAC has the authority to monitor the annual budget, including external funding arrangements and misconduct related to the budget. Furthermore, the PAC can seek to improve the performance of decentralised government agencies and local government offices. The PAC has the authority to make government officers comply with national development strategies and policies. Operations are monitored and a performance report is submitted to the Office of the Auditor-General in accordance with the Constitution. In summary, the PAC of the Senate compared to the PAC of the House of Representatives has more authority, because the former body has the power to both review the government's annual budget policies and monitor how it is spent.

Power and practices

The authority of the PAC is defined in Section 135 of the Constitution of the Kingdom of Thailand (2007):

> The Standing Committees have the authority to issue an order to retrieve documents from any person, issue an order to any person to give a statement of fact or opinion that might be useful for the investigation or auditing.

Therefore, the PAC has the power to summon witnesses and demand documents. In most cases, the financial documents submitted contain much unsynthesised raw data that take the PAC a long time to scrutinise. This creates time pressures and results in the PAC not being able to systematically scrutinise the government's implementation of its budget efficiently and effectively (Liisakul, 2007).

The PAC also uses hearings to seek answers from government agencies and other relevant bodies. The Secretarial Unit of the PAC sends an official letter to the relevant government agencies or individuals to clarify questions that are being asked regarding specific matters. Special seminars are also organised by the PAC inviting professionals and experts to discuss special or controversial issues with the PAC (Liisakul, 2007).

The PAC is empowered to appoint sub-committees to support some specific issues and report directly to the PAC. Each sub-committee comprises no more than ten people, which must be one-quarter of the main memberships of the PAC. The PAC has the authority to appoint professionals, academics and advisors, external to the government to work with the PAC (Sangdetch, 2010).

Reporting and recommendations

After completing the auditing and investigation processes, the Secretary will summarise the PAC's resolutions and report directly to Parliament. Secretarial staff are responsible for drafting evidence-based reports. The PAC's reports are sent to the government agencies implicated, are published on the PAC's website and then made freely available to the general public. The reports present the PAC's findings and include the resolutions and recommendations that the government should take in relation to the investigated matter. Reports are generally followed up by formal responses from the government agencies. However, in practice, the government does not always take appropriate or immediate action on the PAC's recommendations. Also, there are no formal follow-up procedures on government action regarding the PAC's recommendations or advice. Reports produced at the end of a PAC's investigation do not always require a formal response from the government.

The PAC's relationship with the Auditor-General and Audit Office

There is no coordination between the PAC and the Auditor-General. There is no exchange of data with each other. Any interaction between the PAC and other committees has tended to be limited (Liisakul, 2007; Wattana *et al.*, 2008). The PAC is free not to use the Auditor-General's reports to scrutinise public expenditures and generate useful and relevant information.

The PAC meeting

Typically, the PAC meets twice a week. The PAC's sub-committees meet three times a week. Thus, in total, there are five meetings held weekly. The number of attendees at each meeting must be at least a third of all members. Decisions do not have to be unanimous, but more than half of all members should reach a consensus on decisions reached (Liisakul, 2007). Therefore, in Thailand's case, a simple majority can make decisions, but there is no evidence to show that the minority group will express the views of dissenting members. The PAC's meetings are open to members to deliberate their opinions and ask questions of witnesses under the guidance of the meeting's chairperson. However, the public and the media are not formally allowed to attend meetings.

PAC resources

Currently, the PAC consists of a Secretarial Unit, with 11 full-time employees assigned specifically to the committee. The secretarial staff's functions include advising the PAC on procedural matters, preparing meeting agendas, drafting reports, and preparing notes, organising delegations and conducting study tours (Jitbun, 2012). According to an internal report by Jitbun (2012), there are not enough staff to manage the PAC's heavy workload. Also, staff members lack public administration and accountability knowledge to help them provide advice to the PAC (Liisakul, 2007; Sangdetch, 2010). Technical support, in the form of information technology and facilities, is still underdeveloped and the provision and quality of equipment needs be substantially improved. In terms of financial support, the PAC is independent. It has its own budget with which it can hire professionals, consultants and specialists to provide them with advice on issues and conduct study tours in and outside the country.

Problems regarding PAC operations

Over the past ten years, studies have analysed how the Thai PACs operate as well as their problems and obstacles. It has been found that the PAC lacks a clear role and responsibilities because it has no clearly specified authority in either the Constitution or the legislative regulations (Lertpaitune, 2003). Moreover, the authority to call government agencies or their representatives to be witnesses or submit documents is not clearly defined, thus making ambiguous the enforcement of their power. Furthermore, the PAC does not have the authority to penalise people who do not supply them with the required documentation or clarifications to questions. Consequently, this limits the PAC's sources of information to scrutinise government functions and decisions (Lertpaitune, 2003; Satpanroj, 2007; Suthatip, 2005).

The PAC lacks competent personnel; specifically, personnel with practical knowledge about public administration, budgetary systems and how to draft reports (Jitbun, 2012; Liisakul, 2007; Sangdetch, 2010). Added to this, there has been limited systematic interaction and coordination with the PAC members and government administration. Some sources of information are only uncovered through personal relationships of members and staff cross-checking the information and documents with other committees. This process can, however, be unreliable. Due to the lack of communication with the Auditor-General, the PAC cannot have complete oversight of issues raised in the Auditor-General's reports in a meaningful way and efficiently manage its workload (Wattana *et al.*, 2008).

The PAC often simply focuses on the current budget spending compared to previous expenditure. It does not consider 'value for money' issues and whether such expenditure complies with the Parliament's intention and the relevant legislation and regulations. The work of the PAC focuses mostly on what has already occurred and not new issues that should be monitored more closely (Tosaporn, 2003; Wattana *et al.*, 2008).

In terms of government response and following up on recommendations, the PAC's reports do not always result in a formal response from the government. There are also no follow-up procedures provided by the PAC to force the government to implement its recommendations or advice. Therefore, because the government does not often address the issues raised by the PAC, it calls the value of the PAC's reports into question. In the long term, this can harm the country's reputation for honesty and trust and the accountability of government operations and procedures (Lertpaitune, 2003; Suthatip, 2005; Tosaporn, 2003; Wattana *et al.*, 2008).

The intervention of the Executive is another problem. Indeed, the Executive can interfere with the operations of the PAC's operations (Suthatip, 2005; Tosaporn, 2003). There are also limitations regarding access to information. Currently, budget execution is done through the Government Fiscal Management Information System (GFMIS). Yet, the GFMIS does not apply to all government agencies, non-government organisations or public enterprises. The receipt of required information is thus limited. In addition, the PAC is not familiar with real-time information. Access to information about government budget expenditure cannot be gained online because this contravenes the Parliament's intentions and relevant rules and regulations (Wattana *et al.*, 2008).

The capacity of the PAC to operate effectively is further compromised by time and resources constraints. In effect, the PAC does not have access to data required to comprehensively monitor the government's budget and how or where it is spent (Lertpaitune, 2003; Wattana *et al.*, 2008). Furthermore, the PAC has no formal procedures or strategy for hearing witnesses. Secretarial staff are only informed at short notice when a hearing is to be conducted. Consequently, they cannot adequately prepare for the PAC's meetings and, therefore, are unable to provide members with enough information to monitor government functions (Jitbun, 2012; Liisakul, 2007; Sangdetch, 2010).

Comparison between PAC in Thailand and the 'ideal' PAC

Several publications have described the 'ideal' or successful PAC according to the following ten essential factors: 1) having proper staff and facility support systems (Jones and Jacobs, 2009; Pelizzo, 2011; Wehner, 2002); 2) non-partisan functioning of the PAC (Wehner, 2002); 3) implementing follow-up procedures on government action regarding committee recommendations (Jones and Jacobs, 2009; Pelizzo, 2011; Pelizzo and Kinyondo, 2014; Wehner, 2002); 4) maintaining a consistent relationship between the PAC and other committees and with other government departments, especially the Auditor-General (Jones and Jacobs, 2009; Pelizzo, 2011; Wehner, 2002); 5) making the PAC reports available to the general public (Wehner, 2002); 6) ensuring the PAC committees include both government and opposition members (Jones and Jacobs, 2009; Pelizzo and Kinyondo, 2014; Wehner, 2002; 7) including agenda items based primarily on the Auditor-General's report (Jones and Jacobs, 2009; Pelizzo and Kinyondo, 2014; Wehner, 2002; 8) having the power to investigate all past and present government expenditure (Jones and Jacobs, 2009); 9) assessing whether the government has obtained 'value for money' public spending (Pelizzo and Kinyondo, 2014; Wehner, 2002; and 10) establishing sub-committees that can manage or delegate a heavy workload.

It is evident from Table 15.1 comparing the PAC in Thailand with the ten factors of an 'ideal' PAC that the PAC in Thailand is far from 'ideal' in terms of functions and operations.

Table 15.1 Comparison between PAC in Thailand and ideal PAC

Ideal PAC	*PAC in Thailand*
1 Proper staff and facility support systems	No
2 Non-partisan functioning of the committee.	No
3 Follow-up procedures on government action regarding committee recommendations and questioning of witnesses.	No
4 Relationship between the PAC and other committees, and government departments such as the Auditor-General	No
5 Committee reports are freely available to the general public	Yes
6 The PAC committee comprises both government and opposition members	Yes
7 Agenda items are based primarily on the Auditor-General's report	No
8 Power to investigate all past and present government expenditure cases	Yes
9 Assess whether government has obtained 'value for money' in terms of public spending	No
10 Establish sub-committees to manage and delegate a substantial workload	Yes

Suggestions to improve the PAC

In this section, we suggest ways of improving the performance and effectiveness of the PAC. The following issues need to be closely considered to help PACs in Thailand improve their output.

First, it is necessary to provide the PAC with more staff and resources. It is better to have a small number of well-trained staff rather than many personnel who do not have the skills, knowledge or experience of PAC issues (Pelizzo and Kinyondo, 2014). Second, there is an urgent need to implement follow-up procedures on the government's responses to the PAC's recommendations. A formal response is needed to verify whether the government will act on its promises (Pelizzo and Kinyondo, 2014; Wehner, 2002). Setting up a proper and realistic time frame for responses to the PAC is also necessary (Pelizzo and Kinyondo, 2014). Third, it is critical to have a close working relationship with the Auditor-General, who can offer advice on the salient issues that the PAC needs to focus on (Wehner, 2002).

Moreover, the PAC's work should investigate government spending based on the 'value for money' principle and whether such expenditure reflects Parliament's intentions, legislation and regulations and whether they are accountable and transparent (Jones and Jacobs, 2009; Wehner, 2002). The chairperson of the PAC should be independent of all political parties so that scrutiny is not compromised by political or government interference (Wehner, 2002).

A report by Wattana *et al.* (2008) entitled *Strengthening the Capacity of the Legislature in the Budgetary Process* provides some suggestions for improving the PAC's effectiveness. The authors conducted their research using interviews and observations. Suggestions included: expanding the scope of authority of the PAC to control executive budget spending, pre-post and ex-post spending, and appointing a chairperson of the PAC to one of the committees to consider the current year's budget. The Thai Parliament should introduce regulations for penalties to be paid by government agencies and their representatives who do not provide the information required by the PAC. The PAC should also have the power to suspend government agencies' annual budgets when they continue to refuse to cooperate.

Wattana *et al.* (2008) also suggested development phases to improve the efficiency and effectiveness of the PAC as follows. In the initial phase, the strategy and operations should be planned. Then, the Board can use this as a framework to develop, operate, review and optimise their annual strategies. They also suggested developing and implementing processes and systems to support Committee Board meetings. Also, the PAC should continue to develop academic supporting units, such as library and information monitoring centres, to perform duties that support the Board's work around budget monitoring. Moreover, in this phase it would require providing academic support units, such as analysis and monitoring units of the Parliament, to perform duties that further support the work of the Board.

Suggestions for future research

The PAC has been studied in many countries including those of South East Asia. However, our knowledge concerning the PAC in Thailand is still very limited. This study's limitations are centred on its research method, solely based on an analysis of secondary data. This can be improved in future studies in several ways. First, in-depth primary source data about the PAC in Thailand can be collected, especially through a qualitative case study approach. A triangulated approach could be used where interview or survey data could be compared with data collected through observation and analysis of documents and archival materials. Second, a comparison could be made between the in-depth data concerning South East Asian countries that have similar cultures, historical traditions and economic systems in place. Third, due to an unstable political system in Thailand, a longitudinal study is suggested so that the changes in PAC operations over time can be observed and evaluated.

Note

1 BE means 'Buddhist Era', which refers to the Buddhist calendar used in South East Asia in Thailand, Cambodia, Laos, Burma and Sri Lanka.

References

Jitbun, W. (2012) *The improving of efficiency and effectiveness of the academic advice to the Public Accounts Committes of House Responsiveness*, Bankgok: Secretariat of the House of Responsiveness.

Jones, K. and Jacobs, K. (2009) 'Public Accounts Committees, New Public Management, and Institutionalism: A Case Study', *Politics & Policy*, 37(5): 1023–46.

Lertpaitune, N. S. S. (2003) *The Effectiveness of Thai Parliamentary*, Bangkok: King Prajadhipok's Institute.

Liisakul, P. (2007) *An improving of the efficiency of the PAC unit based on the sufficiency economy philosophy*, Bangkok: Thai Parliament.

Pelizzo, R. (2011) 'Public Accounts Committees in the Commonwealth: oversight, effectiveness, and governance', *Commonwealth & Comparative Politics*, 49(4): 528–46.

Pelizzo, R. and Kinyondo, A. (2014) 'Public Accounts Committees in Eastern and Southern Africa: A Comparative Analysis', *Politics & Policy*, 42(1), 77–102.

Sangdetch, A. (2010) *An improvement of the operation of the secretary unit of the PAC*, Bangkok: Thai Parliament.

Satpanroj, W. (2007) *The Development of the Committee of the Senate*, Bangkok: The Thailand Research Fund.

Suthatip, T. (2005) *The Role of Committee to the Government Policy*, Bangkok: King Prajadhipok's Institute.

Tosaporn, S. (2003) *The Development and Monitoring of Public Administration*, Bangkok: Thailand Research Fund.

Wattana, D., Patamasiriwat, D. and Saikaew, S. (2008) *Strengthening the Capacity of the Legislature in the Budgetary Process*, Bangkok: Secretariat of the Senate.

Wehner, J. (2002) 'Best Practices in Public Accounts Committees', contributing paper for the *Handbook for Public Accounts Committees*, Association of Public Accounts Committees, South Africa.

Part V

Public Accounts Committees in African and Caribbean nations

16 Evolution and effectiveness of the Kenyan Public Accounts Committee

Robert Ochoki Nyamori and Bosire Nyamori

Introduction

Recent studies have remarked on how African Parliaments are becoming more assertive institutions in holding the executive to account (e.g. Johnson, 2009; Nakamura and Johnson, 2003). Though the studies mention the development of parliamentary committees within this shift, they do not pay specific attention to how the individual committees have developed. Meanwhile, in other international contexts, great attention has recently been directed at Public Accounts Committees (PAC) as mechanisms through which the excesses of government can be checked and through which democracy can be nurtured (e.g. Wehner, 2003). This chapter seeks to complement this recent interest in legislative studies through an examination of how the Kenyan PAC has evolved during the shift from colonialism to independence, from the one-party dictatorship to multi-party democracy and from the old to the new Kenya Constitution Act 2010. The author argues that though the Kenyan Parliament generally and the PAC in particular is becoming more assertive, its ability to check the executive is limited by the effectiveness of the other institutions of government. The chapter therefore contests the thesis that stronger legislatures are a bulwark against the excesses of executive power (Fish, 2006).

The chapter is organised into five sections as follows. The second section describes how the PAC was formed and the rationalities advanced for its formation. The third section describes the legal and institutional framework for the PAC. The section discusses the powers and privileges of the PAC, its membership and operations and the relationship between the PAC and the Auditor-General. The fourth section describes the PAC following the formation of county governments. The fifth section evaluates the effectiveness of the PAC while the sixth concludes the chapter.

Context and evolution of the Kenyan PAC

The first Kenyan Parliament, the Legislative Council (LEGCO), was appointed by the colonial governor in 1906 (Barkan and Matiangi, 2009). The LEGCO established the first Kenyan Public Accounts Committee on Wednesday 9 June

1948 (Government of Kenya, 1948a) at the behest of the British Government, which required colonies to account for the revenues and grants they were receiving from the colonial government (Institute of Economic Affairs, 2009). The need for the PAC was outlined by the Finance Secretary, and mover of the motion, Mr Troughton, who argued that the Council members did not take enough 'interest in what happens to the money once it has been voted' (Government of Kenya, 1948a: 33). The PAC was therefore presented as a mechanism for awakening this interest.

This interest was expected to translate to probity in public finance. The seconder, Mr Rankine, argued that:

> the committee may well contribute greatly to the development of the country if it sees that wasteful expenditure is checked, and that every spending department knows that there is over its head a watchdog on that particular aspect.
>
> (Government of Kenya, 1948a: 35)

The PAC was to discharge this watchdog role through 'the examination of the accounts, showing the appropriation of the sums granted to meet the public expenditure, and of any such accounts laid before the Council as the committee may think fit' (Government of Kenya, 1948a: 32). This committee was expected to compare appropriations against expenditures and highlight any areas of overspending and waste. The raw material was the accounts of the government in a broad sense, but the reports of the Auditor-General in particular, as will be shown later.

The PAC was specifically assigned the task of ensuring economy and efficiency and establishment of sound accounting systems to ensure these objectives were met. The mover laid out wide expectations for the Public Accounts Committee:

> We rely on the committee, for example, to help us and to indicate how loss of cash may be avoided; to deal with cases such as where an officer may travel by air when his journey perfectly easily can be done more economically by train; where the establishment under any head is exceeded and so on. This committee will have a very responsible task, and it should report to this Council on the way in which the money has been expended.
>
> (Government of Kenya, 1948a: 33)

The purpose of the PAC was thus to examine government accounts so as to establish how the government had spent the money, and specifically to ascertain whether money had been spent for the purpose intended, within budget and whether spending had been economical. There was little attention to the effectiveness of government spending nor the wisdom of government policy. This purpose does not seem to have changed in spite of the various changes to forms of government in Kenya since then.

The PAC was promoted as the sole 'custodian and watchdog of all public funds' until 1974 (Institute of Economic Affairs, 2009: 28) when Parliament decided to amend the Standing Orders to split the PAC into two: the PAC and the Public Investments Committee (PIC).[1] The PAC retained its more reduced but significant role of scrutinising expenditure by government departments through examination of parliamentary appropriations and government expenditure (Government of Kenya, 2002: 56). Its role and focus remained intact.

The PIC on the other hand was assigned the role of watchdog for the government commercial sector. The 2002 Standing Orders enumerated the functions of the PIC more clearly compared to those of the PAC. These are:

1   To examine the reports and accounts of the public investments;
2   To examine the reports, if any, of the Auditor-General (Corporations) on the public investments; and
3   To examine, in the context of the autonomy and efficiency of the public investments, whether the affairs of the public investments are being managed in accordance with sound business principles and prudent commercial practice.

(Government of Kenya, 2002: 57–8).

The 2002 Standing Orders, however, limited the examination powers of the PIC. Specifically, the PIC was not to examine:

i   matters of major government policy as distinct from business or commercial functions of the public investments;
ii   matters of day-to-day administration; and
iii matters for the consideration of which machinery is established by any special statute under which a particular public investment is established.

(Government of Kenya, 2002: 57–8)

This limitation on the scope of the PACs seems to be common practice in Commonwealth countries.[2]

Evolution of the institutional and legal framework of the PAC

This section describes the shifts in the institutional and legal framework of the PAC following Kenya's governance transitions.

Powers and privileges of the PAC

The founders of the Kenyan PAC had great ambitions for the PAC and they sought to vest it with wide-ranging powers. These powers included:

1   Summoning any government officer as a witness;
2   Requiring to be provided with all information and documents it needed, unless such provision was not in the public interest;

3   Examining any such accounts, beyond the Colony's revenue and expenditure accounts, as the Council deems fit.

(Government of Kenya, 1948a)

Such was the desire to vest the PAC with effective powers that the seconder of the motion for the establishment of the PAC, Mr Rankine, called for a change to the Standing Rules and Orders to give the PAC 'wider powers than are allowed to a select committee under our present Standing Rules and Orders' (Government of Kenya, 1948a).[3]

The PAC therefore came to enjoy wide-ranging powers and privileges. The PAC conducts its business under parliamentary privilege (National Assembly Powers and Privileges Act, Cap 6). The PAC can travel anywhere to gather evidence.[4] It can call witnesses who enjoy the same privileges as in a court of law. The PAC can engage experts with the Speaker's approval (Government of Kenya, 2013, sec. 203). The deliberations of PAC members are privileged and enjoy immunity from prosecution (Institute of Economic Affairs, 2009).

In spite of these wide-ranging powers, the government was not obligated to respond to PAC recommendations within any set time. The government therefore tended to take its own sweet time responding to PAC queries, or ignored them altogether. There was no mechanism to track and ensure that PAC recommendations had been implemented (Institute of Economic Affairs, 2009).

The 2008 Standing Orders, however, sought to remedy this anomaly by requiring that the relevant minister report to the House within 60 days of the House resolution or adoption of a select committee report. The 2008 Standing Orders also specified that where a minister fails to comply with this order, he or she shall be deemed to be disorderly. Where a minister was deemed disorderly, he or she could be suspended from Parliament for not more than two days. What happens after the two days is, however, unclear.

The 2008 Standing Orders tightened the requirements around implementation of parliamentary committee recommendations by introducing the Committee on Implementation, whose function was to scrutinise whether and to what extent the resolutions of the Parliament and its committees have been implemented. This committee can recommend sanctions against any minister or Cabinet Secretary[5] for failure to implement such resolutions. The 2013 Standing Orders require the relevant portfolio Cabinet Secretary to report to the PAC. While we could not obtain evidence to assess the effectiveness of this committee, Hansard records (Government of Kenya, 2014) indicate that some legislators have been calling on this committee to impose tough penalties and sanctions on officers suspected of mismanaging public investments. This committee has been retained in the 2013 Standing Orders.

Membership of the PAC

The founders of the PAC were adamant that the membership of the PAC be made up of people with the competency and interest to discharge the functions of the PAC. Mr Troughton opined that for the committee to 'function properly', the members should be chosen because of their competency or willingness to learn government accounting instead of their party affiliation or race or whether they were an official or private member.

The desire to delink the PAC from politics was to obtain even in 1970 when the PAC sat without members of the opposition.[6] The Chairman of the PAC remarked then:

> Gentlemen, I would like to start by saying that although there are no members of the opposition on this Public Accounts Committee I am sure that with your assistance we will do the work we are supposed to do. As far as I am concerned, it is not a political matter we are concerned with, it is just to consider whether public funds have been well spent or not and whether the correct procedure has been followed.
>
> (Government of Kenya, 1970)

The Chairman viewed the role of the PAC as merely concerned with financial accountability, devoid of politics and therefore one which could not be affected by its lack of opposition members.

This view was to obtain throughout the one-party era. Thus even during the Kenyatta and Moi Governments, the PAC still contained Members of Parliament that could be interpreted as constituting an opposition within the one-party system. These included George Anyona, Lawrence Sifuna, Martin Shikuku, Mashengu wa Mwachofi and Koigi wa Wamwere, legislators who were to be nicknamed the 'Seven Bearded Sisters' not only for their characteristic beards but also their perceived Marxist leanings. It could therefore be argued that it is the composition of the PAC that distinguished it as an effective committee within this constrained political environment. In this kind of arrangement, decision-making was not expected – at least in theory – to reflect the partisan interests of the members; after all, there was only one party.

This arrangement was later to change in a number of ways. First, the 2008 Standing Orders specified that the composition of the PAC was to take into consideration the ethnic, geographical, cultural, political, social, economic and gender balance. This measure introduced equity concerns – instead of just competency or interest – into the composition of the PAC.

Second, ministers (now Cabinet Secretaries) were excluded from membership of the PAC. This is significant because the PAC is a watchdog over the executive, but if the executive is also a member of the PAC, then it is tantamount to expecting the PAC to watch over itself.

Third, there were moves to define the member contribution of the different parties to the PAC. This move raised the question of which party or parties should have a majority in the PAC. In theory, PACs might be expected to be more effective if the majority of members are from the opposition party, but in reality it could be that a government majority makes it easier for the recommendations of the PAC to be accepted by the government. This, however, is an area future researchers might want to examine.

The 2002 Standing Orders specified that the PAC was to be composed of not more than ten members nominated by the House Business Committee from the political parties in the Parliament in proportion to their elective strength (i.e. the number of seats held by each at the beginning of each session). This arrangement suggests that the party with the highest number of seats would have a majority membership in the PAC and would likely have a proportionate influence on the final decisions of the PAC.

The 2002 Standing Orders specified that the ruling party will not have a majority of more than two members, suggesting that it would still have a majority, albeit small. But the 2008 Standing Orders, recognising that the party in power cannot check itself, stipulated that the opposition parties have a majority of one (Section 187(3)), a clear departure. The new stipulation suggests that, at least in theory, the government could not run roughshod over the committee.

This 2008 amendment was, however, to be reversed in the last days of the last Parliament in circumstances which remain unclear. The last Parliament amended the Standing Orders on 6 May 2013 to state that 'In the Membership of the Public Accounts Committee, the majority party or coalition of parties shall have a majority of one' (Government of Kenya, 2014, Section 20(5)).

With this amendment, the last Parliament stripped the opposition of a majority in the PAC, effectively taking the legislature back to those days when the government had control of the PAC. It does seem that the adage that the more things change, the more they remain the same holds true in the case of the Kenyan Parliament. Thus even as recently as 2013, after the first general elections under Kenya's new Constitution, the membership of the PAC continues to be hotly contested with the ruling party claiming that it ought to have a majority of the membership (Ngirachu, 2013).

A development of the 2013 Standing Orders was a requirement that the PAC append a minority report to the majority report along with the minutes of a committee's proceedings. This provision was aimed at ensuring that dissenting voices are heard and not muzzled by the majority. This provision has, however, witnessed divisions along party lines, with the majority party denying the minority party the right to include their minority report. For example, the Coalition for Reform and Democracy (CORD) presented a petition to the Parliament calling for the disbandment of the Independent Boundaries and Electoral Commission (IEBC), claiming it did not competently handle the 2012 general elections which were won by the Jubilee coalition. This petition was heard by the House Justice and Legal Affairs Committee, which tabled a report to the Parliament rejecting the petition. The opposition CORD was refused the right to present a dissenting minority report, with claims by the Speaker that their concerns were captured by the House Justice and Legal Affairs Committee (Ayanga, 2014). This development seems to be a departure from the Standing Orders which provide for the inclusion of such a report, thus negating its potential to provide for dissenting views.

Chairman of the PAC

The role of the Chairman of the PAC is considered critical to the effectiveness of the committee. The ideal political party of the Chairman is, however, contested. Some argue that the Chairman should be a member of the opposition party while others argue that the Chairman should come from the party in power. Yet others argue that it is not so much the political party but the kind of person the Chairman is. The old Constitution (Section 56) empowered the Parliament to establish and regulate committees but did not spell out which party the Chairman should hail from or the powers and composition of these committees (Johnson, 2009). Perhaps this was deliberate because in a one-party state, as Kenya had become, it was not necessary to specify which party the chairman should come from or how many people should come from a non-existent opposition.

There was a change in the Standing Orders 2002, which specified that the Chairman should come from a party other than the ruling party. The 2002 Standing Orders reflected the fact that Kenya had become a multi-party democracy once again.

The 2008 Standing Orders were more far-reaching and probably reflect the more assertive nature of the Kenyan Parliament that has become the subject of recent interest (e.g. Johnson, 2009; Barkan and Matiangi, 2009). These Standing Orders specified that the Chairman shall be the leader of the official opposition. Where there was no official opposition, the Chairman was to be drawn from a party which is not in government.

The Chairman was to be elected by the members of the PAC. Where the Chairman was absent, his or her deputy was to take the chair. Where the designate was absent the members were to elect one of the members to be the Chairman. The Chairman remains a member of the official opposition party today.

Term of the PAC

The control of the parliamentary calendar has potential to affect the effectiveness of the PAC. Previously, this control was vested in the President, who could prorogue Parliament at will, thus impairing any ongoing investigations.

The 2008 Standing Orders, however, now stipulate that the PAC can continue its deliberations even if Parliament is prorogued or adjourned (160(3)). This stipulation gives PACs great powers because they can pursue an issue until it is exhausted without worrying about the parliamentary calendar. Previously, such issues lapsed with the parliamentary calendar. With recent legislative changes that vest control of the parliamentary calendar on the Parliament, this institution is now well placed to assert its independence from the executive.

Public access

This assertiveness is also coupled with the award of access to members of the public to committee proceedings. The 2002 Standing Orders did not mention public access to the proceedings of parliamentary committees. The 2008 Standing Orders expressly allowed members of the public to attend the deliberations of committees unless the committee decided to exclude them or where it was compiling the report (Section 180). The 2013 Standing Orders reiterate this provision. This provision improves the transparency of parliamentary committee deliberations.

Relationship between the PAC and Auditors-General

The relationship between the Auditor-General and the Parliament is important in the ability of the PAC to discharge its accountability role (e.g. Funnell and Cooper, 2012). The report of the Auditor-General is, after all, the key document that the PAC is expected to deliberate on. This relationship was established early on by the founders of the Kenyan PAC.

The LEGCO approved expenditure for the colony. Government expenditure was audited by the Director of Audit, who then submitted his or her report to the Director of Colonial Audit in London. The Director of Colonial Audit's report, which included the government's comments, was then tabled before the Council (Government of Kenya, 1948b).

The relationship between the Director of Audit and the LEGCO became recalibrated when the Finance Secretary recommended that the Director of Audit should be a servant of the Council, tabling his or her report before the Council with a copy of his report then going to the Director of Colonial Audit. The Public Accounts Committee was to then examine this report and 'take the strongest possible action in any cases which may seem to the committee to constitute irregularities or to constitute uneconomic expenditure' (Government of Kenya, 1948b: 33).

This line of direct reporting to the Parliament was, however, changed in later years. The Auditor-General came to be required to submit his/her report to the Minister of Finance, who then was required to table this report before the National Assembly. This arrangement made the relationship between the Auditor-General and the Parliament indirect, but it also provided that if the Minister of Finance failed to submit this report to the Parliament, then the Auditor-General was to submit the report to the Speaker of the National Assembly, who was then to table it before the Parliament (Government of Kenya, 2001).

The new Kenya Constitution Act 2010 restored this direct relationship between the Auditor-General and the Parliament. Section 228(7) requires audit reports to be submitted to Parliament or the relevant County Assembly.[7] This direct line of reporting is likely to remove delays to submission of reports to the Parliament. Previously, the Minister of Finance could sit on an Auditor-General's report that was considered critical of the government or possibly interfere with it.

The other notable change which has significant implications for the Auditor-General's independence and the effectiveness of the PAC is the manner of appointment. Previously, the Auditor-General was appointed by the President. This approach meant that the Auditor-General was amenable to executive control, though the Constitution provided that he or she could only be removed through a tribunal. The Kenya Constitution 2010, however, introduced important changes that improved the independence of this office. The role of the President is to nominate, and Parliament has a role of approving this nominee (Section 229). This approach is in line with practice in countries such as Australia.

The Kenya Constitution 2010 also established the Kenya National Audit Commission, whose role is to approve funding for the Auditor-General and remuneration of his or her staff. This body is chaired by the Auditor-General and is composed of the Chairmen of the PAC and PIC. This arrangement provides the Auditor-General with considerable independence over funding but also cements the relationship between the PAC and the Auditor-General. The Auditor-General is funded directly by the Parliament through a separate vote. The Executive cannot withhold funding in order to punish a recalcitrant Auditor-General (Funnell, 2003). The independence of the Auditor-General is under-scored by the Constitution Act 2010, which expressly provides that independent offices such as the Auditor-General 'are independent and not subject to direction or control by any person or authority' (Section 249(2)(b)).

Funding and resourcing PAC

It is not only the Auditor-General whose funding fortunes have improved, but also the Parliament. For many years, funding to the Parliament was controlled by the executive. The Parliament tended to be poorly resourced in many aspects including staffing, office space and library resources (Barkan and Matiangi, 2009). A development of the multi-party era is that the Parliament has been vested with greater powers to determine its remuneration and budget. The enact-ment of the Parliamentary Service Act 2000 has improved the resourcing and independence of the Parliament and its committees. The Act delinked the Parlia-ment from the executive, creating the Parliamentary Service Commission with power to appoint and decide remuneration. Since the ninth Parliament, each committee is supported by an assistant clerk to provide administrative support. It is now able to employ research and support staff for committees and provide more suitable office space and library resources for committee members to conduct research and investigations into government accounts (Barkan and Mat-iangi, 2009). The Parliament has also introduced a system of interns drawn from Kenyan universities and trained at SUNY University in New York who provide valuable administrative support (Barkan and Matiangi, 2009). This enhanced resourcing would be expected to improve the PAC's effectiveness.

Public Accounts Committees under county governments

Following the enactment of the Kenya Constitution Act (2010), the Government of Kenya enacted the County Governments Act No. 17 of 2012, which gave effect to a devolved system of government consisting of 47 counties and a strong national government. The counties are semi-autonomous governing units with their own parliaments called county assemblies. Members of the county assemblies are elected by residents of the respective County or nominated by their respective parties. County governments are headed by an elected executive governor who constitutes a cabinet to which he assigns various responsibilities.

Section 14 (1) (a) of the County Governments Act No. 17 of 2012 provides that a county assembly 'may make standing orders consistent with the Constitution and this Act regulating the procedure of the county assembly including, in particular, orders for the proper conduct of proceedings'. This subsection establishes 'orders' which are akin to the Standing Orders that govern procedures in the national Parliament. This section therefore opens the door for the establishment of county assembly Public Accounts Committees. Subsequently Section 14(1)(b) provides that 'subject to standing orders made under paragraph (a), (county assemblies) may establish committees in such manner and for such general or special purposes as it considers fit, and regulate the procedure of any committee so established'.

Since the County Governments Act No. 17 of 2012 gives leeway to counties to decide what committees to establish, there might be variability in the kind of Public Accounts Committees which each of the 47 counties have established. Our examination of Kisii County reveals that it has established a 'County Public Investments and Accounts Committee'. This committee, which consists of a chairperson and not more than four other members, was established to serve for a period of three years. The functions of the Kisii County Public Investment and Accounts Committee are listed as to:

> Examine accounts showing appropriations by the County Assembly to meet public expenditure; Examine reports, accounts and workings of the County public investments; Examine whether the affairs of the County Public investments are managed with sound financial or business principles.
>
> (Kisii County Government, 2015)

Examination of these functions suggests that they are similar to those performed by both the Public Accounts Committee and the Public Investments Committee at the national government. Mombasa County, just like Kisii County, has combined the PAC and PIC into a single committee. Nairobi City County, the biggest county in the country, on the other hand, has mirrored the national Parliament by establishing two related committees, the County Public Accounts Committee and the County Public Investments Committee (Nairobi City County Assembly website). The functions of these two committees are similar to those of the national Parliament.

The relationship between these County Public Accounts Committees and the Auditor General is not well defined, unlike in the case of the national government. The county governments are seemingly not required to establish their own offices of Auditor-General. Preparation of the accounts and the financial reports is vested in county accounting officers (key among whom is the County Treasurer) and then these reports are forwarded to the Auditor General. Section 163(4) of the Public Finance Act provides that:

(4) Not later than four months after the end of each financial year, the County Treasury shall –

(a) submit the financial statements and summaries referred to in subsection (1) to the Auditor-General; and

(b) deliver a copy to the National Treasury, Controller of Budget and the Commission on Revenue Allocation.

Since it is not clarified what reports the County Public Accounts Committees would rely on in their deliberations, it can only be inferred that these would include audited reports by the Auditor-General. Be that as it may, the institution of the Public Accounts Committees seems to be taking root in the newly established county governments though not all of them seem to have established PACs.

Effectiveness of the PAC

The role of PAC, as explained above, is to examine the accounts with a view to establishing whether the money appropriated by the Parliament has been spent as stipulated. The PIC on the other hand examines the accounts of state corporations to give an opinion as to whether these entities have been managed according to commercial principles. The raw material for the PAC and PIC are the accounts of the government, the Treasury Memorandum (which details what the government has done with the previous year's PAC and PIC recommendations) and the reports of the Auditor-General. This examination as explained involves summoning public officials and witnesses, travelling around the country to observe the subjects of interest and then compiling a report which is tabled before the Parliament. The report contains recommendations on what action should be taken where public resources have been misappropriated or weaknesses identified (Institute of Economic Affairs, 2009).

The above process has not dramatically changed since the PAC was formed in 1948 and, as noted above, the only notable change was the distribution of the PAC's responsibilities between the PAC and the PIC. But as we have seen there have been notable changes to the Standing Orders regarding the membership and operation of the PAC and actually to all the committees of the Parliament. Some of these changes have occurred in line with the shifts in governance within the country, especially the shift from a single-party to a multi-party form of government and to a new Constitution. We assess how effective the PAC and PIC have been in discharging this role.

There is no single framework of assessing PAC effectiveness, but the assessment of the Kenyan PAC conducted by the Parliamentary Centre (2012) provides a useful framework. This assessment was conducted using 11 items, namely existence of the PAC; chairing by a member from a party outside government; power to subpoena witnesses and documents; requirement for all public officials to appear before the PAC; openness of its sittings to the public; review of all Auditor-General's reports in a timely manner; right to initiate independent investigation on any matter of concern to the public; implementation of the

PAC's recommendations by the executive; existence of mechanisms for ensuring implementation of its recommendations; adequacy of resources; and freedom to collaborate with anti-corruption institutions. The assessment scored each of these attributes on a scale of 1 to 6, with 6 indicating strong agreement, and then developed a composite index.

The Parliamentary Centre (2012) assessment found that the Kenyan PAC scored 5.4/6 and had the highest marks among the Kenyan parliamentary oversight bodies on oversight of the budgetary process.[8] The assessment found that the Kenyan PAC was not chaired by a member from a party outside of government, but that it scored highly on all the remaining attributes.[9] A closer examination of these attributes, however, indicates that they are more of the conditions which if fulfilled will make the PAC effectively discharge its accountability and oversight functions.

The other source of assessment is the Public Expenditure and Financial Assessment Accountability (PEFA) Public Financial Management Performance Assessment Reports for 2006, 2009 and 2012. The summary of the Kenyan Government's performance on external and legislative oversight for these periods is presented in Table 16.1.

The 2006 PEFA reported average performance on scope of the audit and its adherence to auditing standards. It reveals that there has been no marked improvement in the scope and quality of audit since 2006 as indicated by the static score of C.

The 2006 PEFA explained that the Controller and Auditor-General's reports were late for submission to the Parliament in the last three years. The 2008 and 2012 scores indicate that there has been some improvement in the timeliness of submission, although more needed to be done to improve on this indicator.

Regarding follow-up of audit recommendations, the 2006 PEFA explained that there was little evidence of follow-up of the Auditor-General's recommendations by both the PAC and the Ministry of Finance. The PEFA observed that the same type of errors and mismanagement highlighted by the Controller and Auditor-General continued to be highlighted from year to year. This situation did not seem to have changed, as indicated by the static score on this dimension. The PEFA paints a picture of an underperforming PAC that contrasts with that painted by the Parliamentary Centre (2012). This difference might be

Table 16.1 Scope, nature and follow-up of external audit – score

	Indicator	2006	2008	2012
i	Scope/nature of audit performed (incl. adherence to auditing standards)	C	C	C
ii	Timeliness of submission of audit reports to the legislature	D	B	B
iii	Evidence of follow-up on audit recommendations	D	D	D

Source: Prepared by the authors based on Public Expenditure and Financial Assessment Accountability (PEFA) Final Reports 2006, 2009 and 2012).

explained by the fact that the latter's report is partially based on a self-assessment by Members of the Kenyan Parliament.

Our own analysis of Hansard and the PAC reports from 1948 to date reveals that the PAC has addressed a narrow range of issues around economy and legality. Some of the issues have included concern that issues raised by previous committees had not been resolved and kept on getting worse, that the government continued to spend in excess of parliamentary approvals, and that accounting officers were spending money beyond their budgets. There was a recurring concern that the government was not adequately accounting for imprest (e.g. Government of Kenya, 1988, 1989, 1990, 1991, 1992, 1993). The reports themselves seem quite uneventful. The PAC often decried that public officials 'were still not sensitive to the ever-rising public demand for transparency and accountability in the handling of public issues', causing audit queries (Government of Kenya, 1993: v). The fact that the PAC continued to unearth, condemn and make recommendations suggests that it is discharging its work. The fact that the identified ills seem to have been escalating over the years suggests that, at least tentatively, the PAC recommendations were not changing government behaviour.

This escalation in abuse and misuse of government resources culminated in major scandals starting from 1991. The first was the Goldenberg scandal[10] in which the country lost millions through fictitious exports of gold and jewellery. The 1992 PAC investigated the scandal but became deadlocked and could not issue any recommendations (Government of Kenya, 1992). The following year, the PAC took up the issue again: this time, it concluded that the extra 15 per cent export compensation had been approved by Parliament, though irregularly, and recommended that all parties meet their contractual obligations: Goldenberg to export the expected value of gold and jewellery and pay outstanding VAT and the government to pay Goldenberg's outstanding claims (Government of Kenya, 1993). These recommendations were, however, to prove misguided as the scale of the scandal unravelled, occasioning the formation of a Commission of Inquiry (Government of Kenya, 2005).

The PAC seems to have pursued subsequent scandals with a lot more vigour. The PAC is credited with bringing another scandal to light, that of Anglo-Leasing (Barkan and Matiangi, 2009).[11] The PAC investigated the scam by interviewing senior public officials and travelled to London to meet former PS John Githongo, who had exposed it and fled the country fearing for his life. The PAC recommended that certain measures be taken to strengthen weak controls and that officers found culpable be sacked and prosecuted. Three ministers subsequently resigned. These developments have been attributed to a timely report by the Auditor-General, strong action by the PAC, and an aggressive press (Barkan and Matiangi, 2009).

The PAC again demonstrated its mettle in 2008 when it emerged that the Minister of Finance, Mr Amos Kimunya, had directed the Central Bank to sell the Grand Regency Hotel[12] to some investors at a price which was considered to be too low, leading to a big loss for the government. The Parliament censured Mr Kimunya, compelling him to resign. The PAC has also been seeking a forensic audit, prosecution and recovery of public assets lost through the 1970s KenRen scandal, through which the country guaranteed a fertiliser factory that was never built (Odhiambo, 2012). The PAC and PIC also currently seem to be aggressively seeking to unearth the circumstances surrounding the award of the Standard Gauge Rail (SGR) contract to China Road and Bridge Construction (CRBC).[13] The fact that these committees are pursing this matter after the President asserted that the tender was legitimate and will go forward (Sambu, 2014; Kenyatta, 2014) demonstrates that the PIC and PAC have become more assertive. In previous years, they would probably have dropped the investigation for fear of retribution.

From this brief broad-brush survey, it can be concluded that the Kenyan PAC seems to have diligently carried out its mandate of examining government expenditure against budgets (Johnson, 2009). There is discernible improvement in the PAC, evidenced by a push by the PAC and the PIC (in addition to the other house committees) to scrutinise government projects before they take off, unlike previously where they conducted mostly post mortem examinations (e.g. Ngirachu, 2014). The PAC has appeared fearless in its questioning of some of the proposed government projects such as the SGR project. This push has, however, been viewed by some as an attempt to extract rents from the government, suggesting that current efforts to improve the legislature have some way to go (Ngirachu, 2014; Wanga, 2014). The Kenyan Parliament has been able to cause changes to the estimates and indeed has caused amendments to the Appropriations Bill 2012, a first in Kenya's legislative history (Parliamentary Centre, 2012). The recent legislative changes seem to have improved the capacity of the PAC to discharge its watchdog role, though whether that translates to eradicating ills like corruption depends on the active commitment of the other institutions of government. Since PACs have only recently been implemented in the county governments, their effectiveness in holding these governments accountable is yet to be determined.

Conclusion

This chapter has analysed the way Kenya's PAC has evolved following changes in the forms and systems of government in Kenya. The chapter indicates that the PAC changed its membership and operations to meet these governmental changes. Prior to independence and after independence, when the system of government was a multi-party one, the PAC seems to have been constituted with an eye towards who best could carry out the roles expected of them. During the one-party era, party affiliation was not an issue because there was only one party. But at the same time, the conditions of the time were such as to limit the capacity of the PAC. For example, the PAC, just like the rest of the Parliament, was poorly resourced, and there was no public access to its deliberations. Following the repeal of laws that criminalised multi-partyism, the membership of the PAC changed, as did its operations, to reflect the more democratic environment. However, the ruling party still maintained a grip on the membership until the late 2000s when the coalition government seems to have opened up the democratic space with greater control of this committee by the opposition.

The chapter also reveals that, since its formation, the PAC has tried to diligently discharge its duties of scrutinising government accounts, but that its effectiveness was hampered by a number of factors. First, the PAC's performance is tied to that of the Auditor-General (AG) because the PAC relies on the work of the AG. Since the AG's reports were often late, the PAC could not be expected to hold the executive to account in a timely manner (Barkan and Matiangi, 2009). Second, parliamentary committees were poorly resourced: they neither had professional staff nor offices from which they could work. Third, legislators were poorly paid, which made them captive to the advances of the executive (Barkan and Matiangi, 2009; Johnson, 2009). But, we think more significantly, the autocratic governments of Jomo Kenyatta and Daniel arap Moi made it dangerous for legislators to pursue issues of corruption and misuse of government assets vigorously.

Since the 2000s, however, the Parliament has become more assertive, thus enhancing the capacity of the PAC to discharge its watchdog responsibilities more effectively. This assertiveness has arisen from recent legislative changes accompanied by changes of form of government which seem to be restoring the PAC to its expected role. The office of the Auditor-General has been revamped. Barkan and Matiangi (2009) argue that the Auditor-General has been able to bring the government accounts to date, therefore enabling the PAC to deal with financial matters in a timely manner. The PAC's effectiveness has also improved thanks to strong chairmen and a sizeable number of committed members (Barkan and Matiangi, 2009). This improved assertiveness has, however, not been accompanied by improvement in the government's performance on corruption and misuse of government assets and office. The country seems to stumble from scandal to scandal, suggesting that there are serious problems with the way government manages its affairs, oblivious of PAC/PIC scrutiny. Whether this enhanced capacity leads to better management of government finances, including the eradication of corruption, will depend on the effectiveness of the other organs of government.

Notes

1 From this point on, PAC refers to both the PAC and the PIC.
2 A recent welcome development in public accountability in Kenya is the establishment of departmental committees. First provided for in Article 151 of the 1997 Standing Orders, these committees have been retained in all subsequent Standing Orders. These committees are mandated to examine the policy and operational matters of their relevant portfolios. Article 151(4)(e) of the 2002 Standing Orders assigns them the responsibility to 'investigate and inquire into all matters related to the assigned ministries and departments as they may deem necessary and as may be referred to them by the House'. Departmental committees counteract the limited examination powers conferred on PIC and PAC, which enhances the reach and potential influence of the Parliament in how the executive runs government. It also suggests that while PACs might be somewhat tied to *ex post* examination of government activities, departmental committees can scrutinise the Executive on a more timely basis and can potentially be more effective in influencing government action.
3 We cannot find any evidence to suggest, however, that the PAC was more powerful than other committees.

4 The PAC for example travelled to the UK in 2006 to gather evidence from Mr John Githongo on the Anglo-Leasing contracts.
5 Cabinet Secretary is the new term used for heads of portfolios who were formally known as Ministers. This change occurred after the new Constitution (Kenyan Constitution Act, 2010). But, unlike Ministers, Cabinet Secretaries are not elected or nominated Members of the Parliament.
6 The only opposition party, the Kenya People's Union, had been proscribed and its leaders detained.
7 County Assemblies are the Parliaments for the elected members of the County Governments. Following the new Constitution, Kenya became divided into 47 County Governments, each of which is governed by an elected governor and elected members (Members of the County Assembly) who deliberate the County's affairs in the County Assembly.
8 The African Parliamentary Index (API) is based on legislators' own assessment of Parliament's engagement with the budgetary process and the effectiveness of the Parliament in budgetary oversight. This assessment is then validated by civil society organisations.
9 There was no opposition in this year because Kenya had entered into a coalition arrangement.
10 Goldenberg International Ltd was granted 20 per cent compensation for the export of gold and jewellery. Later Parliament approved an additional 15 per cent, but concealed as an ex gratia payment. The expected gold or jewellery was not exported but the company was able to claim compensation.
11 In this scandal, contracts were awarded to fictitious companies for security-related contracts.
12 This hotel, which was bought with money from the Goldenberg scandal, was surrendered to the government in exchange for a promise not to prosecute Kamlesh Pattni, the owner.
13 The government awarded a tender to CRBC to build a standard-gauge railway from Mombasa. The PAC has raised questions regarding the transparency of the tendering and the cost of the tender. It is also raising questions about the identity of the company awarded the tender.

References

Ayaga, W. (2014) 'Double blow for CORD as push to remove IEBC fails, *Standard Digital*, 30 July, www.standardmedia.co.ke/?articleID=2000129983&story_title=double-blow-for-cord-as-push-to-remove-iebc-team-fails (accessed 31 August 2014).
Barkan, J. and Matiangi, F. (2009) 'Kenya's tortuous path to successful legislative development', in J. Barkan (ed.) *Legislative Power in Emerging African Democracies*, Boulder: Lynne Rienner Publishers, pp. 33–72.
Fish, M. S. (2006) 'Stronger legislatures: Stronger democracies', *Journal of Democracy*, 17(1): 5–20.
Funnell, W. (2003) 'Enduring fundamentals: Constitutional accountability and Auditors-General in the reluctant state', *Critical Perspectives on Accounting*, 14(1–2): 107–32.
Funnell, W., Cooper, K. and Lee, J. (2012) *Public Sector Accounting and Accountability in Australia*, second edition, Sydney: University of New South Wales Press.
Government of Kenya (1948a) *Hansard*, 9 June 1948, Government Printer, Nairobi.
Government of Kenya (1948b) *Hansard*, 24 June 1948, Government Printer, Nairobi.
Government of Kenya (1959) *Report of the Public Accounts Committee on the Colony's Accounts for the Year Ending 30th June*, Government Printer, Nairobi.

Government of Kenya (1960) *Report of the Public Accounts Committee on the Colony's Accounts for the Year Ending 30th June*, Government Printer, Nairobi.

Government of Kenya (1970) *Evidence on the Report of the Public Accounts Committee on the Government of Kenya Accounts for the Year Ended 30th June, 1970*, Government Printer, Nairobi.

Government of Kenya (1987) *Report of the Public Accounts Committee on the Government of Kenya Accounts for the Year 1986/1987*, Government Printer, Nairobi.

Government of Kenya (1988) *Report of the Public Accounts Committee on the Government of Kenya Accounts for the Year 1987/1988*, Government Printer, Nairobi.

Government of Kenya (1989) *Report of the Public Accounts Committee on the Government of Kenya Accounts for the Year 1988/1989*, Government Printer, Nairobi.

Government of Kenya (1990) *Report of the Public Accounts Committee on the Government of Kenya Accounts for the Year 1989/1990*, Government Printer, Nairobi.

Government of Kenya (1991) *Report of the Public Accounts Committee on the Government of Kenya Accounts for the Year 1990/1991*, Government Printer, Nairobi.

Government of Kenya (1992) *Report of the Public Accounts Committee on the Government of Kenya Accounts for the Year 1990/1991 and 1992/1993*, Government Printer, Nairobi.

Government of Kenya (1993) *Report of the Public Accounts Committee on the Government of Kenya Accounts for the Year 1992/1993*, Government Printer, Nairobi.

Government of Kenya (1997) *National Assembly Standing Orders*, Government Printer, Nairobi, Kenya.

Government of Kenya (2001) *The Constitution of Kenya*, Government Printer, Nairobi, Kenya.

Government of Kenya (2002) *National Assembly Standing Orders (Revised Edition 2002)*, Government Printer, Nairobi, Kenya.

Government of Kenya (2003) *The Public Audit Act 2003*, www.kenyalaw.org:8181/exist/rest//db/kenyalex/Kenya/Legislation/English/Amendment%20Acts/No.%2012%20of%202003.pdf (accessed 26 August 2014).

Government of Kenya (2005) *Report of the Judicial Commission of Inquiry into the Goldenberg Affair*, October 2005, Government Printer, Nairobi, Kenya.

Government of Kenya (2006) *Public Accounts Committee Report on Special Audit on Procurement of Passport Issuing Equipment by the Department of Immigration*, Office of the Vice-President and Ministry of Home Affairs, Government Printer, Nairobi.

Government of Kenya (2008) *National Assembly Standing Orders*, Government Printer, Nairobi.

Government of Kenya (2009) *Hansard*, 23 July, Government Printer, Nairobi.

Government of Kenya (2010) *The Constitution of Kenya*, 2010, Government Printer, Nairobi.

Government of Kenya (2012) *County Governments Act No. 17 of 2012*, http://kenyalaw.org/kl/index.php?id=3979 (accessed 17 February 2015).

Government of Kenya (2013) *National Assembly Standing Orders*, Government Printer, Nairobi, Kenya.

Government of Kenya (2014) *National Assembly Standing Orders*, Government Printer, Nairobi, Kenya.

Institute of Economic Affairs (2009) *The Parliamentary Budget Oversight in Kenya*, IEA Research Paper Series No. 19.

Johnson, J. (2009) 'Parliamentary Independence in Kenya and Uganda 1962–2008', unpublished PhD dissertation, University at Albany, State University of New York.

Kenyatta, U. (2014) 'Press Statement by His Excellency Hon. Uhuru Kenyatta, C.G.H, M.P., President and Commander-in-Chief of the Defence Forces of the Republic of Kenya on the Standard Gauge Railway, State House Nairobi on 28th January 2014', www.nation.co.ke/blob/view/-/2163828/data/674106/-/3edhxaz/-/uhuru-statement-railway.pdf (accessed 14 February 2014).

Kisii County Government (2015) 'County Assembly Committees – Functions, www.kisii.go.ke/index.php/county-assembly/house-committees/functions (accessed 16 February 2015).

Mombasa County Assembly (2015) 'Public Accounts and Investments', http://assembly.mombasa.go.ke/index.php/committees/select-commitees/item/public-accounts-and-investment (accessed 16 February 2015).

Nairobi City County Assembly (2015) 'Welcome to Nairobi City County Assembly', http://deveint.com/assembly/ (accessed 16 February 2015).

Nakamura, R. and Johnson, J. (2003), 'Rising legislative assertiveness in Uganda and Kenyan', paper prepared for delivery at the 19th International Political Science Association World Congress in Durban, South Africa, 29 June to 4 July.

Ngirachu, J. (2013) 'Cord in House boycott threat as bosses clash', *Daily Nation*, 6 May, www.nation.co.ke/news/politics/Cord-in-House-boycott-threat-as-bosses-clash/-/1064/1844216/-/seln35z/-/index.html (accessed 27 November 2014).

Ngirachu, J. (2014), 'House teams come under scrutiny as they assert their oversight function', *Daily Nation*, 27 July, www.nation.co.ke/news/politics/House-teams-come-under-scrutiny-oversight/-/1064/2399736/-/5qiuolz/-/index.html (accessed 31 August 2014).

Odhiambo, A. (2012) 'Parliament seeks audit in fertiliser factory scandal', *Business Daily*, 27 December, www.businessdailyafrica.com/Parliament-seeks-audit-in-fertiliser-factory-scandal/-/539546/1652644/-/13k83ow/-/index.html (accessed 27 November 2014).

Parliamentary Centre (Africa Programme) (2012) *The African Parliamentary Index (API) 2012: Summary Country Report*, Ottawa, Canada.

Public Expenditure and Financial Assessment Accountability (PEFA) (2006) *Final Report 2006*, www.pefa.org/en (accessed 3 February 2015).

Public Expenditure and Financial Assessment Accountability (PEFA) (2009) *Final Report 2009*, www.pefa.org/en (accessed 3 February 2015).

Public Expenditure and Financial Assessment Accountability (PEFA) (2012) *Final Report 2012*, www.pefa.org/en (accessed 3 February 2015).

Sambu, Z. (2014) 'Rail tender probe will not stop: MPs', *Daily Nation*, 29 January, www.nation.co.ke/business/Rail-tender-probe-will-not-stop--MPs/-/996/2165914/-/5sitei/-/index.html (accessed 27 November 2014).

Wanga, J. (2014) 'House committees under probe for graft', *Daily Nation*, 28 June, www.nation.co.ke/news/House-committees-under-probe-for-graft/-/1056/2365424/-/vgw4wiz/-/index.html (accessed 31 August 2014).

Wehner, J. (2003) 'Principles and patterns of financial scrutiny: Public Accounts Committees in the Commonwealth', *Commonwealth and Comparative Politics*, 41(3): 21–36.

17 Strengthening PACs in small Parliaments

Perspectives from the Caribbean[1]

Anthony Staddon

Introduction

This chapter provides an analysis of the forms, procedures, attributes and practices of parliamentary Public Accounts Committees (PACs) in Jamaica and Trinidad and Tobago. Both countries achieved independence in 1962 and celebrated their 50th anniversaries of independence in 2012; they are also symbolic of the wider Commonwealth Caribbean in the sense that they have made the transition to democracy successfully. Both countries have met Huntington's (1991) peaceful change of government criteria and witnessed at least two turnovers of government based on different political majorities. Both countries operate bicameral legislatures and are based on the Westminster model. In keeping with this tradition, both Jamaica and Trinidad and Tobago have PACs responsible for the non-partisan audit of public expenditure and control of the public purse.

Pelizzo (2011: 530) argues that the international community has become committed to legislative strengthening because of studies that have shown the benefit of efforts to strengthen legislative oversight capacity. One line of research has focused on the PAC as a specific oversight tool. This is reflected in the Caribbean as recent efforts to strengthen the oversight capacity of both legislatures have paid particular attention to the role and performance of the PAC, in particular through an examination of its structural and organisational features (Staddon, 2012; World Bank, 2013). This work is particularly important in the Caribbean as many of the PACs in the region have not met for some time (e.g. Dominica and St Kitts and Nevis). The challenges facing PACs have led to some discussion on possible alternatives to the PAC model within the region (for example at the 2012 ParlAmericas workshop in Antigua and Barbuda).

It is also relevant to analyse the particular issues facing PACs in small jurisdictions. Many writers (for example Alesina, 2003) have argued that the size of a state may have a profound effect on its institutional configuration, and outcomes and legislatures in small jurisdictions often have greater difficulties in the operation of the committee system simply because of the small number of members available to participate in the full range of committees (O'Brien, 2009).

The aim of this chapter is to examine the PACs in Jamaica and Trinidad and Tobago and highlight some of the critical issues discovered in recent efforts to strengthen the PACs in both countries. The first section examines the background and political context in both countries which have a critical external impact on a PAC's performance. The second section examines some of the critical internal characteristics of the PACs, including their powers and functions, relationship with the Auditor-General (AG) and composition and chairing. The next section examines the outputs of the PACs and the final section concludes.

Background and political context

Both Jamaica and Trinidad and Tobago are based on the Westminster system, with government being responsible and accountable to Parliament. However, Ghany (2013) argues a 'Westminster–Whitehall' description is more apt because of a unique bicameral system: a bill of rights in the constitution; the codification of Westminster constitutional conventions; and the entrenchment of constitutional articles.

Jamaica's Parliament consists of an elected House of Representatives and an appointed Senate (Upper House), as well as the Queen or her representative, as the ceremonial head, who appoints the Governor-General as her representative. The Governor-General nominates the 21 members of the Senate: 13 on the Prime Minister's advice and eight on the Leader of the Opposition's recommendation. As a result of universal adult suffrage, persons have the right to elect Members for a five-year term (subject to dissolution) in elections held in each of the country's 63 constituencies. The Constitution requires that the Prime Minister call a general election no later than five years after the first sitting of the previous Parliament.

Trinidad and Tobago's first Republican Constitution came into effect on 1 August 1976 (replacing the independent Constitution of 1962). The President is the head of state and the Prime Minister is the head of the government. The President is elected by an Electoral College consisting of all the members of the Senate and the House of Representatives assembled together (voting by secret ballot) and holds office for a term of five years. The President appoints the Prime Minister, who is a member of the House of Representatives and usually the leader of the political party which commands the support of the majority of Members of that House. The Prime Minister selects other Cabinet Members from Parliament. There are 34 Government Ministries and 14 municipal corporations. There are currently 42 Members in the House of Representatives and the appointed Senate (Upper House) consists of 16 Government Members who are appointed on the advice of the Prime Minister; six Opposition Senators appointed on the advice of the Leader of the Opposition and nine Independent Senators appointed by the President (the only function the President takes in his sole discretion without consultation).

Consideration of the wider political system is important as it enables better understanding of what the PAC and legislature more generally are *capable* of achieving in both countries. The operation of the Westminster system in smaller-sized English speaking Caribbean countries has been a challenge. One problem facing small societies is the limited number of human resources in Parliament, making it difficult to have sufficient numbers to establish an efficient and effective committee system. It is not surprising therefore that Trinidad and Tobago, which has a smaller Parliament than Jamaica in terms of members (reflective of its smaller population), also has fewer committees – ten compared to the 17 in Jamaica.

Undertaking appropriate oversight becomes even more problematic when the size of the Executive may be disproportionate to the size of the legislature and the latter has a dominant position not only in relation to the substantive business and proceedings of Parliament, but also in relation to the organisation and operation of Parliament. In Trinidad and Tobago the Cabinet consists of 33 persons (21 Members and 12 Senators) and there are a further five non-Cabinet Ministers (four Members and one Senator). There are only four Government backbenchers who have no executive responsibilities; three had previous executive responsibilities but were relieved of their ministerial duty following allegations of inappropriate behaviour, and one acts as the Deputy Speaker. A second issue in Trinidad and Tobago and Jamaica – and in the Caribbean generally – is the high degree of party discipline and the power and strength of political parties together with the expectation that MPs must give support to their political leaders. Therefore, it is not difficult to see how parliamentary scrutiny of the Executive is compromised by party loyalties. Wehner (2004) suggests that political party majorities and party cohesion are two key variables that shape the context in which Parliament exercises its budget oversight functions: this argument is pertinent to the application of oversight in Trinidad and Tobago and Jamaica.

A further issue is whether the job of a parliamentarian is expected to be a full-time activity, as this point will influence how committee-oriented a Parliament can become. Parliamentarians in Trinidad and Tobago who serve in the executive branch of government are considered to be holding full-time jobs. The same is not true for normal parliamentary service. Most other Members work in a profession in parallel to their parliamentary mandate and are essentially treated as part-time parliamentarians. This is reflected in the salaries and allowances (see Table 17.1) and the business of the House where the Senate sits on a Tuesday (afternoon/evening) and the House sits on a Friday (afternoon/evening). A Job Evaluation Exercise and Compensation Survey is to be carried out by the Salaries Review Commission of Trinidad and Tobago and this will consider the issue of the full-time demands on parliamentarians today.

Table 17.1 A comparison between Jamaica and Trinidad and Tobago

	Trinidad and Tobago	*Jamaica*
Population	1,227,505	2,868,380
Number of elected Members (Lower House)	41	63
Member per population	1: 29,939	1: 45,529
Number of Members in Upper House	31	21
Basic monthly salary (US$)	$2,750	$2,205
Number of committees	10	17

The PACs in Jamaica and Trinidad and Tobago

The PAC of Jamaica was established in May 1945 as a subcommittee of the Finance Committee before being formally established as a full committee in 1964. Today it operates as a bipartisan committee of the House of Representatives. Standing Order 68 names the PAC as a Sessional Select Committee; Standing Order 69 lists the matters under the purview of the committee as follows:

- the accounts showing the appropriation of the sums granted by the Parliament to meet public expenditure;
- such other accounts as may be referred to the Committee by the House or under any law;
- the report of the Auditor-General on any such accounts.

The Standing Order proceeds to state that all accounts and financial statements laid upon the Table of the House in respect to Statutory Boards, Public Corporations, and Public Companies in which the government holds majority shares are deemed to be automatically referred to the PAC for examination and report. The PAC also has restricted right of access to non-governmental or private sector organisations if public monies are obtained (agreements are made to enable scrutiny of the accounts related to those funds).

Section 119 of the Constitution of the Republic of Trinidad and Tobago provides the authority for the PAC. The PAC has the responsibility for examining the appropriation accounts of moneys granted by Parliament to meet the public expenditure of Trinidad and Tobago. It examines the audited accounts of government ministries and departments, paying close attention to the comments made by the AG which relate to financial management. Therefore both PACs have a similar mandate such as the unrestricted right to access government agencies within and outside the finance ministry, statutory authorities, government-owned corporations and local authorities. Both PACs can undertake self-initiated inquiries and do not consider budget estimates – again in keeping with normal practice elsewhere in the Commonwealth (although many smaller jurisdictions have combined *ex ante* and *ex post* activities, for example Solomon Islands and the Isle of Man.)

Unlike Jamaica, Trinidad and Tobago has a second audit committee, also provided for in the constitution, that examines the reports and accounts of the public undertakings and determines whether the affairs of these institutions are being managed in accordance with sound business principles and prudent commercial practices. The Public Accounts Enterprises Committee (PAEC) was established as a result of the increase in the number of State Enterprises covering a wide range of industrial and other economic activities since the early 1970s in an attempt to ensure Parliament maintains effective scrutiny over public sector projects. The practice of a second committee is fairly unusual within the Commonwealth and generally more prevalent in larger countries such as India and Sri Lanka.

An advantage that PACs possess over other committees is that they can draw upon the resources of the Audit Office. The audited reports of government ministries and departments and public sector enterprises by the AG form the basis of the scrutiny exercised by these committees. However, one issue is that the Audit Offices in both countries are not fully independent of government; for example, the AG in both countries has constitutional independence, although their staff do not and neither body fully complies with the standards of the International Organisation of Supreme Audit Institutions (INTOSAI). As with most other jurisdictions, the PACs have unrestricted access to examine their AG's report, but the lack of full independence can result in the Audit Office being helpless to withstand cuts to its budget and has the potential to result in a lack of confidence in audit reports.

The relationship between the AG and PAC can often appear functional and rather arm's length, particularly in Trinidad and Tobago. In both countries, the AG or his or her representatives generally attend PAC meetings; liaise with the PAC; and provide regular consultation on the ongoing business of the PAC as well as for specific inquiries/hearings. However, there is very little contact between the PAEC and AG in Trinidad and Tobago and there is only one entity under the PAEC's purview audited by the AG. While the AG is empowered to audit state-owned enterprises, these entities are normally audited by private audit firms because of the resource constraints on the AG; indeed the AG historically did not routinely receive a copy of the audit report of such bodies. The PAC has recently started asking entities to forward their accounts audited by private firms to the AG. However, this has not been standardised and there has been no commitment from the AG's office that these accounts would be reviewed.

Neither PAC has the right to be consulted in determining the Audit Office's annual budget and resources and the appointment and removal of the external independent auditor of the Audit Office. The Parliament of Trinidad and Tobago has sought meetings with the AG for discussion on supporting action to ensure the oversight of State Enterprises and the timely submission to Parliament of financial reports as well as general support of the operations of the PAC and PAEC through the provision of audit and budget review services. The AG in Trinidad and Tobago has publicly welcomed the proposal for an annual review of the performance of the office of the AG, with the budget and business plan of the AG being presented to the PAC. Two options that could be considered are the Bermudan model, where a separate Audit Committee examines the funding and requirements of the AG Office, and the Guyana PAC, which has a role in monitoring the AG's budget (ParlAmericas, 2012).

The vast majority of PAC work in both countries is in response to AG reports and the PAC's principal witnesses are the accounting officers, other heads of agencies and their support staff. In addition to having unrestricted access to examine public accounts and financial affairs, both PACs possess an unrestricted right to consider issues of efficiency and economy of programme implementation. Yet there appears to be a greater variety of audit attempted in Jamaica. According to the 2013 Annual Report, the Jamaican AG engages in compliance audits (to ascertain the extent to which the government bodies follow the rules, laws and regulations, policy and established codes); financial audit; activity-based audit (defined as an examination of an entity's core activity to ascertain whether the management has implemented a robust system of control to guarantee the achievement of its overarching objective or mandate); and special or performance audits (aimed at assessing if adequate planning had been done, proper management control systems instituted and whether the programmes and projects were achieving their intended objectives).

The movement towards wider forms of auditing has not progressed as far in Trinidad and Tobago. Stakeholders cite deficiencies within the legislative framework, in particular the existing Exchequer and Audit Act, where there is no clear mandate to conduct value for money (VFM) audits in state-controlled entities and audits in the parliamentary and public interest. The development of further VFM audits forms one of the pillars of the AG's strategic plan for 2012–15 and collaboration with the Inter-American Development Bank (IDB) and UK National Audit Office is designed to strengthen the capacity of the Audit Office by producing new Financial Audit and VFM manuals, as well as a functional Quality Assurance Unit to provide guidance across the AG's Department (AGD) and ensure compliance with new manuals and INTOSAI standards.

Audit backlog

The backlog of accounts has been a problem in both countries. In Trinidad and Tobago for example, the AG and the PAC are unable to cope with the volume of audit reports and no PAC has ever been able to accomplish the work constitutionally assigned to it. The PAC explains this deficiency by highlighting capacity constraints within the AG's Department, the late submission of accounts by entities and the sheer number of reports to be examined by the PAC. Even at a rate of one entity being examined per meeting and for a maximum of 20 meetings per annum, 78 entities would remain unexamined and would be carried over to the following year (Staddon, 2012).

There have been some modest improvements in recent years. Ministries generally comply with the due date of four months after the year-end and the AG has been able to report to Parliament on time every year since independence. However, there has been less progress in terms of wider entities. Efforts are being made for a regular and systematic review of the entities which fail to submit financial reports in accordance with the relevant statute. For example, at its meeting on 24 January 2012, the PAC met with the AG *in camera* and asked her for a list of these entities and to come up with any proposals/recommendations on how to deal with them. Part of the problem is the lack of incentive to compel entities to submit their financial reports on time. A fine of just TT$150 is the result of a contravention of the various reporting regulations, and it is also unclear whether appropriate procedures are in place for enforcing this provision and whether it is the Accounting Officer in the line ministry or the accounting officers in the statutory boards, municipalities and commissions who are accountable.

The PAC is now focusing on those entities that have not appeared before the committee in the last few years and post-2008 accounts. The PAC and PAEC have made some attempt to review the entities which fail to submit financial reports in accordance with the Exchequer and Audit Act by writing and asking for status updates from audited entities, and it will make practical sense to group financial statements even further to clear the backlog (such grouping should ignore election dates/changes of government). The PAEC is also in communication with the Investments Division of the Ministry of Finance to explore measures to address the difficulty of outstanding financial reports.

Increasing focus on special reports and VFM activities in Jamaica has impacted on the PAC's formal schedule of work for completing its annual report. However, the Committee has been able to eliminate the backlog. The 2009–10 report was tabled in January 2011 and the Committee began examination of the accounts at the end of January 2011. Yet the timeliness of audit reports remains an issue; the PAC's report on the examination of ministries/departments/agencies during the period April 2010 to March 2011 relate to the AG's Report for the Financial Year 2007/8. Given the existing and likely increasing pressures on both Committees, a more formal policy that details the regularity of meetings, notice of meetings, agenda structure and so forth could prove useful. Other options available are to meet more regularly; establish a subcommittee or subcommittees to examine particular entities; and invite other committees to use relevant audit reports in their inquiries.

Whatever approach is taken, each committee should develop a strategic and needs-based approach to their work. It is therefore encouraging that the PAEC in Trinidad and Tobago has recently approved a new work programme to allow that Committee to plan its work schedule for each session more effectively; identify trends across entities and sectors with the increased number of entities being examined; give a well-defined focus to inquiries; achieve a reduction in the number of times the Committee is required to meet with an entity in public; and allow interested persons and stakeholders to submit evidence. It is hoped that the PAEC's efforts to review and assess the way in which they actually discharge their work will be followed by the PAC in the near future.

Composition and chairing

Generally, developed committee systems have a small and permanent membership, but McGee (2002) argues that small PACs work less effectively than larger committees. Across the Commonwealth, the size of a PAC can vary considerably. The typical size of a PAC in the Commonwealth is 11 members, with the average within Canada nine and that in Caribbean, Australian and New Zealand Parliaments being six (McGee, 2002: 61; KPMG, 2006: 6; Stapenhurst and Kroon, 2010). This variation is also true of small jurisdictions: according to a survey of small country Parliaments carried out by the World Bank Institute (WBI), the size of the PAC varies from 14 members in Papua New Guinea and 12 members in Fiji to three members in Tuvalu and Kiribati (O'Brien, 2009).

The PAC in Jamaica has 13 members. In Trinidad and Tobago the Standing Orders stipulate that the PAC should be composed of not fewer than six, and not more than ten members, inclusive of the Chairman. In both jurisdictions, the size of the committee appears a little high for the size of the Parliament and according to the Commonwealth average. However, both PACs have a balanced and fairly stable membership proportionate to party membership in the House (therefore the government will have a majority on each committee). One difference is that the Trinidad and Tobago PAC includes members from the Senate.

Ministers are not normally appointed to the PAC although exceptions do occur across the Commonwealth in both large and small states. In Sri Lanka, for example, a senior minister chairs the committee. However, the WBI survey reveals that small states are more likely to have government members working on committee work because of the need for all members to play multiple roles. The small Canadian Province of Yukon, for example, has ministers serving on its PAC. In Jamaica, the Standing Orders prevent ministers or parliamentary secretaries from serving on the PAC, but the current PAC does include Ministers of State. In Trinidad and Tobago there are 12 representatives from the government on the two committees and there are currently six Ministers, four Ministers of State and two backbench Government Members. It is imperative for the PAC to be seen to exercise their responsibilities independently and objectively and this becomes difficult if members of the committee have executive responsibilities. One option is to restrict membership of the PAC to Ministers of State (the practice in Jamaica) and/or Parliamentary Secretaries. A second option would be to include lay members on the Committee, a practice used successfully in other small jurisdictions, such as Jersey and Guernsey.

The customary practice in Jamaica is for the PAC to be chaired by the Opposition Spokesman on Finance, who is formally nominated by the Leader of the Opposition. The Constitution of Trinidad and Tobago ensures that the Chairmen of the PAC and the PAEC are members of the Opposition. While it has long been thought important for senior Opposition figures to be associated with the PAC's work, recent research from Pelizzo (2011) on the effectiveness of PACs found no evidence that PACs chaired by an Opposition MP are more effective than PACs chaired by an MP affiliated to the governing party (although of course the presence of an Opposition chair may be of symbolic importance and ensure wider confidence). It is open to debate whether the presence of a high-profile chair from the Opposition (the Shadow Minister for Finance) and a front-bench Opposition MP in Trinidad and Tobago is helpful in ensuring the non-partisan ethos of the committees. Furthermore, as one of the regular problems facing the two countries is the backlog of accounts, it is possible that a PAC will be examining accounts from a previous administration, making the importance of an Opposition Chair less important.

PAC activity

McGee (2002: 72) argues that the level of activity is important as 'committees that meet on a frequent basis have a better opportunity of promoting consensual

Table 17.2 Total number of meetings held by Joint Select Committees (JSCs), PAC and PAEC in Trinidad and Tobago between June 2010 and August 2014

	JSC1	*JSC2*	*JSC3*	*PAC*	*PAEC*
First session	7	8	7	2	7
Second session	7	7	7	6	6
Third session	6	8	8	6	7
Fourth session to date	9	9	10	4	8
Total	29	32	32	18	28
Number of reports laid	9	15	14	4	4
Ministerial reports received	3	12	9	4	3
Draft reports pending	4	7	6	2	2

working practices than committees whose members come together infrequently'. According to the WBI survey, PACs in small jurisdictions meet on average 12 times per year (although there is significant variation). The PAC in Trinidad and Tobago meets about eight or nine times a year with the result that no more than ten or so reports are reviewed (out of about 100 a year) with a rapidly accumulating backlog of audit reports building up (PEFA, 2008). The activity of the PAC has slowed down since the 2008 report although the PAEC has been more active (see Table 17.2). While activity levels are increasing again, the number of meetings has lagged behind the three Joint Select Committees empowered to inquire and report to both Houses of Parliament in respect of the administration of government ministries; Municipal Corporations; Statutory Authorities; State Enterprises and Service Commissions.

In contrast, the PAC is one of the most active parliamentary committees in Jamaica: it meets every week when the House in session and, on average, has one to three inquiries in progress concurrently and averages about 18 meetings per session. This may be a reflection on the number of opposition MPs on the Committee.

Staffing, outputs and outcomes

The level of staffing resources available to a PAC is a factor often raised at international meetings and training events. There is considerable variation both across the Commonwealth and within regions. The WBI survey found that average large states had the equivalent of four full-time staff members compared with two full-time equivalent staff for the average small state. This does not appear to explain the lack of meetings in Trinidad and Tobago as, compared with many other Parliaments, the PAC and PAEC are fairly well resourced in this area. Four staff service the two committees – a clerk, an assistant clerk, a secretary and one in-house researcher (although it should be noted that these staff members have other responsibilities in Parliament). This can be compared with the Parliament of Jamaica, which has one full-time member of staff servicing the Committee. The work of the PAC in Trinidad and Tobago is also supported by a financial analyst on a needs basis.

Pelizzo (2011) demonstrates that the number of staff members serving the committee has a major impact on the PAC's ability to draft reports. This is perhaps best reflected in Jamaica, where PAC outputs are not commensurate with the number of meetings. For example, there was just one report produced between 2007 and 2010, and only two reports were released in 2010–11. Given the number of staff servicing the PAC in Trinidad and Tobago one might expect a higher number of reports than found in Jamaica. However, there has been very little output from the PAC/PAEC in recent years. This is, of course, partly explained by the lack of meetings. There are often difficulties in forming a quorum as members have to attend government or private business. Given the one-day-a-week attendance to parliamentary matters there is little incentive to attend a weekly PAC meeting. In addition, the quorum – five members, inclusive of the Chairman and at least one other Opposition member – for both the PAC and PAEC – does seem a little high for a committee of ten persons.

PAC outcomes

One explanation for the lack of output may simply be a lack of political will among the committee members themselves. When speaking to PAC committee members in both countries it is clear that many are disillusioned because of the difficulty in engaging the executive and Parliament for more effective follow-up of their recommendations. The feeling is that while the committees are generally respected, there is little serious follow-up. In Jamaica there is no requirement for responses from the government to be tabled in Parliament (although the AG conducts verification exercises to determine whether PAC recommendations have been implemented; in other cases, the Committee Clerk is directed to conduct follow-up action). The PAC has recommended that a special unit be established in the Ministry of Finance and Public Service with specific responsibility to monitor agencies and update the Financial Secretary on whether the Committee's recommendations have been implemented. It would then be the Financial Secretary's responsibility to take the appropriate action and provide progress reports to the PAC and the AG. A further option, subject to the availability of resources, is for the PAC to be equipped with a Research Officer to carry out this function as part of his or her duties.

No formal processes were in place to monitor and follow-up implementation of government responses to PAC/PAEC recommendations in Trinidad and Tobago: unlike the other 'watchdog Committees' no requirement existed for a 60-day response for PAC reports. After being adopted in the Houses, PAC recommendations were simply forwarded to Cabinet for implementation through the relevant portfolio Ministers. Although the committee could do some follow-up on its recommendations on an ad hoc basis, such work could not immediately be published because of a Standing Order limiting the premature publication of evidence. Therefore the PAC had to present a report to Parliament in order for this follow-up to be published. However, the revised Standing Orders of the House of Representatives, amended on 14 March 2014, which took effect from the commencement of the Fifth Session of the Tenth Parliament on 4 August 2014, have strengthened the requirements for an executive response to PAC reports in line with other scrutiny committees. Standing Order 110(6) states:

> The Minister responsible for the Ministry or body under review shall, not later than sixty (60) days after a report from a Standing Committee relating to the ministry or body has been laid upon the Table, present a paper to the House responding to any recommendations or comments contained in the report which are addressed to it.

This applies to PAC, PAEC and the three departmental Joint Select Committees (JSCs) as well as the other new committees that were established. The new provision for a Ministerial Response to be tabled will ensure that the initial information is immediately made public.

One notable feature of the Jamaican committee system is the use of a further committee to address the concern that Ministries, Departments and Agencies are not fulfilling their responsibilities and being held to account. The Public Administration and Appropriations Committee (PAAC) examines budgetary expenditure of government agencies to ensure that expenditure is in accordance with parliamentary approval; monitors expenditure as it occurs, keeping the Parliament informed of how the budget is being implemented; and enquires into the administration of the government to determine hindrances to efficiency and to make recommendations to the government for improvement of public administration. The PAAC also reviews the Estimates and Supplementary Estimates of Expenditure tabled in the House and presents a report to the Standing Finance Committee, a Committee of the Whole House, on the proposed levels of expenditure.

In terms of the PAAC's impact on the PAC, the PAAC's current Chairman is of the view that the work of the committee has reduced discrepancies identified by audits and oversight committees because problems have been identified far earlier in the budget cycle. This claim is worthy of further research, as a common criticism of many legislatures is the failure to draw upon the work of other stages of the budget cycle in audit findings/recommendations (and vice versa). The Parliament of Trinidad and Tobago does not currently have a similar committee studying budgetary estimates and supplementary estimates as well as the execution of the budget over the course of the budget year, preferring the use of a Standing Finance Committee, which sits as a Committee of the Whole House. However, the revised Standing Orders of the House of Representatives allow for the creation of a similar committee in Trinidad and Tobago. The Trinidad and Tobago PAAC will have the same powers as all other Joint Standing Committees: the power to send for persons, papers and records and the requirement for Ministers to submit a response to any reports produced. It will be chaired by the Speaker of the House of Representatives.

Conclusion

Recent efforts to strengthen the oversight capacity of the Parliaments of Jamaica and Trinidad and Tobago have paid particular attention to the role and performance of the PAC. Both PACs have struggled to be truly effective, partly because of problems faced by many small jurisdictions such as the small number of parliamentarians available to participate fully in the full range of committees. This is particularly a problem in the Westminster system as Ministers are drawn from the legislature, and the problem is exacerbated when the size of the Executive is disproportionate to the size of the legislature. The Trinidad and Tobago PAC in particular has not always met with sufficient frequency, which is a basic requirement for any effective committee.

One possible solution is to legislate to stipulate a maximum size of the Cabinet, as a smaller body will ensure a larger parliamentary component for the PAC and other oversight committees. This will also reduce demands on the public purse. Alternatively these savings could be reallocated to increase the salaries of backbench MPs or improve the Committee Service Allowance to ensure that parliamentary responsibilities are treated as a full-time activity. The reduction in the size of the Executive could also eliminate the need to include Government Ministers and Parliamentary Secretaries as members of the PAC (assisting the non-partisan objective of the PAC and general confidence in the audit process). Other options include appointing lay members to the PAC as they do in Jersey, Guernsey and Denmark.

The PACs in Trinidad and Tobago and Jamaica experience similar features to PACs in other countries in terms of mandate and composition. The introduction of a Public Accounts Enterprises Committee in Trinidad and Tobago is unusual compared with other small jurisdictions, but its efforts to ensure parliamentary oversight over public sector projects have been hindered by the limited oversight carried out by the AG. Jamaica has made greater progress in terms of attempts to introduce a wider variety of audit across the island, but there still remains great scepticism across parliamentarians in both countries at the speed of change and the capacity of the Office of the Auditor-General to achieve the required outputs and also deliver real outcomes. Part of the problem is the lack of a similar breakthrough to improve financial management from the ministries and other public bodies. A further issue is the need to strengthen the independence of the Audit Office, particularly in terms of staffing and financing.

The experience in Jamaica and Trinidad and Tobago appears to provide some support to Pelizzo's (2011) argument that PACs chaired by an Opposition MP are no more effective than MPs affiliated to the governing body. It is, of course, impossible to prove that a PAC chaired by a governing body would be more effective, but the practice of appointing high-profile Opposition spokespersons as chairs of the PAC is unlikely to assist the non-partisan audit of public expenditure. In some circumstances, the examination of old accounts may negate the need for an Opposition Chair in any case. Jamaica has made greater progress in clearing the backlog of audit reports, although the problem in Trinidad and

Tobago is now focused on the entities under the direction of line ministries than the ministries themselves. The PAEC's efforts to plan its work schedule more effectively are a necessary but not sufficient step to improve the submission of financial reports in accordance with the relevant statute. The legal framework will need to be strengthened, financial penalties increased, and the AG will need to demonstrate greater oversight over such entities. It is sensible for both PACs to prioritise those audited entities that have a history of poor compliance as well as those audits which involve a qualified audit opinion. The Committee should also have regard to whether an inquiry is considered to be in the public's interest and whether the activity being considered is significant in financial or other terms. A greater focus on remedying systemic issues of financial management rather than highlighting individual transgressions may also prove more productive.

The progress made by the PACs in Trinidad and Tobago and Jamaica in recent years suggests the outlook for both committees should be one of cautious optimism. Both PACs have capable staff support (although there may be a need to increase research support in Jamaica) and the committees are taking steps to meet more regularly and strengthen working practices, often in the face of an unhelpful external environment and difficult political context. Broader efforts to strengthen the legislature, particularly in Trinidad and Tobago, are also encouraging. The developing work of the PAAC in Jamaica in monitoring the implementation of the budget, and the establishment of a similar committee in Trinidad and Tobago is a further positive development; the relationship between the two committees is a suitable area for further research. The PAAC has the potential to flag up concerns that public funds are not being spent efficiently and/or in accordance with parliamentary decisions far earlier in the budget process, thereby assisting the work of the AG and PAC. Similarly the implementation of audit recommendations may prove to be a useful tool for the PAAC to use as part of their budget execution monitoring work.

It is essential for this progress to endure into the next Parliament (an election is due in Trinidad and Tobago in May 2015). Supporting, encouraging and training the relevant parliamentary staff will help to withstand the problems caused by normal electoral cycle and turnover of members. This chapter has identified some further steps that can be taken, such as strengthening the independence of the Audit Office, and greater consideration of the most appropriate chair of the committee. Yet it will become necessary to demonstrate greater outputs and outcomes from the work of the PAC. This will require greater emphasis on tracking corrective action, monitoring results and improvements in the administration of public policy and communicating with other stakeholders, including the public. This will require support from the wider Parliament and some cooperation from the Executive: the donor community could perhaps pressurise and support the PACs to increase the number of outputs (i.e. reports) and track their recommendations and at the same time exert some influence on the government to exercise a more responsive attitude on the part of ministries to the advice and recommendations of the PAC.

Note

1 The author acted as a parliamentary consultant in Trinidad and Tobago and Jamaica between 2010 and 2012. This article is based on his work in both countries and discussions with key stakeholders, and summarises some of the key conclusions from the output reports published following this work.

References

Alesina, A. (2003) 'The Size of Countries: Does It Matter?' *Journal of the European Economic Association*, 1(2–3): 301–16.

Ghany, H. (2013) 'The Commonwealth Caribbean: Legislatures and Democracy', in N. Baldwin (ed.) *Legislatures in Small States: A Comparative Study*, New York: Routledge.

Huntington, S. (1991) *The Third Wave: Democratization in the late Twentieth Century*, Norman: University of Oklahoma Press.

KPMG (2006) *The Parliamentary Public Accounts Committee: An Australian and New Zealand Perspective*, KPMG Australia.

McGee, D. (2002) *The Overseers: Public Accounts Committees and Public Spending*, London: Pluto Press

O'Brien, M. (2009) 'Public Accounts Committees in Small States', data paper, first Plenary Session, 29th Small Countries Conference, Arusha, Tanzania, 30 September and 1 October 2009.

ParlAmericas (2012) *Strengthening Parliamentary Oversight in the Caribbean*, Ottawa: International Secretariat of ParlAmericas.

PEFA (2008) *Republic of Trinidad and Tobago Public Financial Management Performance Assessment Report*, December 2008, Washington CD: PEFA.

Pelizzo, R. (2011) 'Public Accounts Committees in the Commonwealth: oversight, effectiveness and governance', *Commonwealth & Comparative Politics*, 49(4): 528–46.

Staddon, A. (2012) 'Activities on Strengthening Parliamentary Practices in Trinidad and Tobago: A Study on Parliamentary Scrutiny and Existing Parliamentary Practice', report commissioned by the European Union Delegation in Trinidad and Tobago available at www.ttparliament.org/documents/2181.pdf (accessed 27 November 2014).

Stapenhurst, R. and Kroon, C. (2010) 'PAC Profiles and Performance in Canada', *Canadian Study of Parliament Group*, January 2010.

Wehner, J. (2004). 'Back from the Sidelines? Redefining the Contribution of Legislatures to the Budget Cycle', World Bank Working Paper, Washington DC: World Bank.

World Bank (2013) 'Jamaica Parliamentary Oversight of Public Finances – An Institutional Review', Report No: ACS3596, Financial Management Unit, Operations Services Department, Caribbean Country Management Unit, Latin America and the Caribbean Region, Washington DC: World Bank.

Appendix
Review process and list of reviewers

This volume is a peer-reviewed collection of chapters. Each submitted chapter has been subject to the following review process: (a) it has been reviewed by the editor for its suitability for further referencing; and (b) its final acceptance for publication has been subject to double and triple peer review.

The editor would like to thank the following reviewers for their constructive comments and suggestions on the chapters included in this book:

Louise Bringselius, Lund University, Sweden
Rosemarie Douglas-Beckford, PAC Clerk, Jamaican Parliament, Caribbean
Bikram Chatterjee, Deakin University, Melbourne, Australia
David Gilchrist, Curtin University, Western Australia
Haslida Abu Hasan, University of Malaya, Malaysia
Zahirul Hoque, La Trobe University, Australia
Keiba Jacob, Procedural Clerk, Parliament of Trinidad and Tobago, Trinidad
Danielle Morin, HEC Montréal, Canada
Des Pearson, Former Auditor General, Victoria and Western Australia
Sarah Petit, Clerk of the UK PAC
Zakiah Saleh, University of Malaya, Malaysia
Anthony Staddon, University of Westminster, UK
Thiru Thiagarajah, La Trobe University, Australia
Marie-Soleil Trembley, École Nationale d'Administration Québec, Canada
Graeme Wines, Deakin University, Australia

Index

Page numbers in *italics* denote tables, those in **bold** denote figures.